COUNTY OF
KERRY

English Miles
0 1 2 3 4 5   10   15

Railways ——— Sta. Roads ——— Canals ———
Baronies thus IVERAGH
Parliamentary Divisions EAST KERRY ------

Revised by P. W. JOYCE. LLD; M.R.I.A.

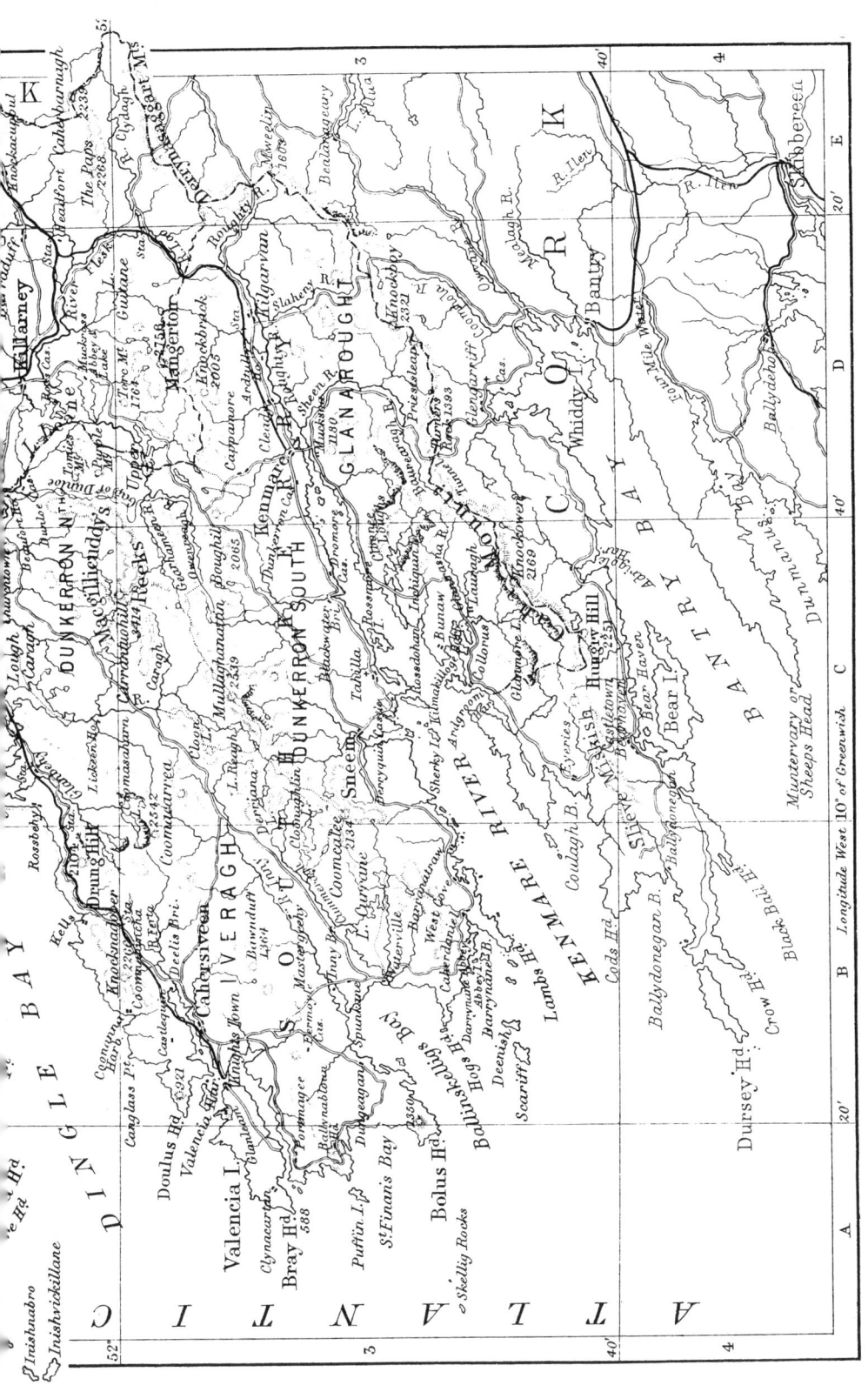

Families of Co. Kerry Ireland

From The Earliest Times To The 20th Century

Family Surnames
With Locations & Origins

Including Old Irish, English And Anglo-norman
Settlers And Settlements

O'LAUGHLIN

Published as a supplement and an addition to the original:
Book of Irish Families, great & small
Volume 2 of the set

The Complete Irish Family Library

Works below made possible by members of the IGF & OLochlainns Irish Family Journal. Membership starts at $49 per year for regular members, and $97 per year for gold members. Regular members receive the Journal 6 times yearly. Gold members 12 times yearly. Your membership is invited. Thank You.

Hardbound Works By the Same Author:
Complete Book For Tracing Your Irish Ancestors. $26. (0-940134-02-0)
The Complete Book of Irish Family Names. 1987. $15. (0-940134-41-1)
The Irish Book of Arms. 1988. $75. (0-940134-07-1)
Irish Settlers on the American Frontier. $34.50. 1985. (0940134-43-8)
The Book of Irish Families Great and Small. 1992. $28. (0-940134-08-X)
Master Book of Irish Surnames. $23.95. 1993. (0-940134-32-2)
Master Book of Irish Placenames. 1994. $23.95 (0-940134-33-0)

Other published works by the author:
Beginners Guide to Irish Family Research. ($12.95) 1990.
Journal of Irish Families. 1986 - present. monthly. (ISSN 1056-0378)
Ortelius Map of Ireland 1572. ($20) (ancient map reprint)

Rare Book Reprints Published: by the I.G.F.:
Keatings' 'History of Ireland' 3 volume set. $97. (0-940134-44-0)
The Poetry and Song of Ireland. O'Reilly. orig. pub. 1865. $45 (0-940-134-43-8)
Irish Names and Surnames by the Rev. Patrick Woulfe $39.95 (0-940134-40-3)
Tribes/Customs of Hy-Many. O'Donovan. (orig.1873) $104. (0-940134-39-X)
Tribes/Customs of Hy-Fiachrach. O'Donovan. (1874) $129. (0-940134-38-1)
Essays.. Kingdom of Munster. MacCarthy Mor. $30. 1994. (0-940134-29-2)

Published exclusively by and available from:
Irish Genealogical Foundation
Box 7575
Kansas City, Missouri 64116 U.S.A.

Write For Free Catalogue

© 1994 I.G.F. All Rights Reserved.

Volume II of the Book of Irish Families, great & small:

The Families of County Kerry, Ireland

Original First Edition

By

Michael C. O'Laughlin
president, I.G.F.
editor, *Irish Family Journal*
noted author & lecturer.

Over Three Thousand Entries
From the Archives of the
Irish Genealogical Foundation.

ISBN: 0-940134-36-5
© 1994 Irish Genealogical Foundation.
Box 7575, Kansas City, MO. 64116 U.S.A.
All Rights Reserved. Write For Free Catalogue

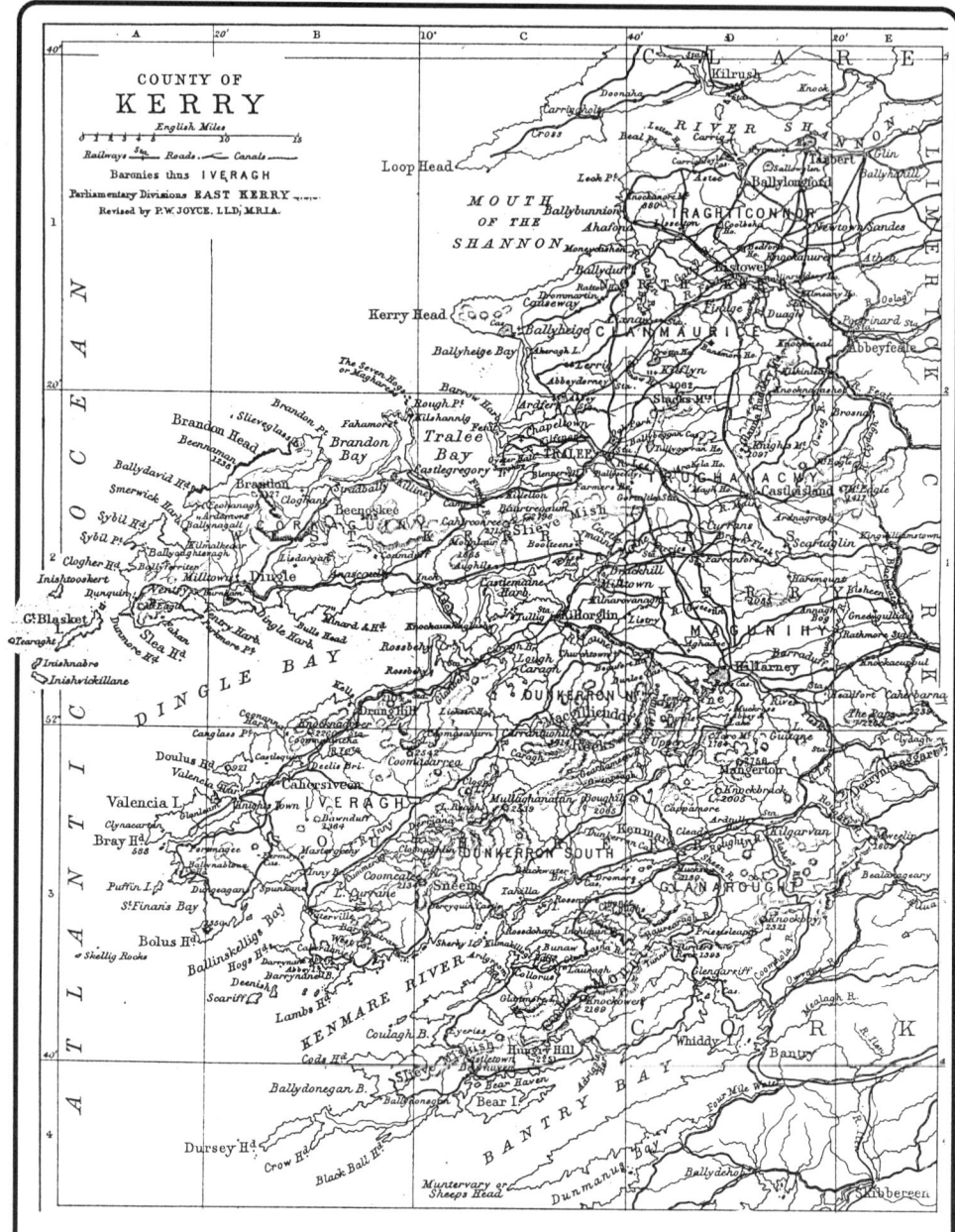

Map of Kerry from the 19th century. Note that spellings of place names can change, and that sometimes the place name is changed altogether.
(i.e. Queenstown, a port of departure in Cork, is now Cobh)
Map courtesy the *Master Atlas and Book of Irish Placenames. 1994. IGF.*

Families of County Kerry, Ireland
Volume II of the Book of Irish Families

Table Of Contents

Frontis
List of Books, ISBN data.................................. ii
Map of County Kerry, Ireland........................... iv

Ortelius Map of Kerry 1576............................. vi
Introduction by the Author............................. vii
Ancient Sketch of Kerry Castle........................ x
Invasion and settlement................................ xi

Some Settler Families................................... xiii
Denny Muster Roll xiv
Palatine Families.. xvi
Irish Forces, Settlement of Tralee.................... xvii
    Chart of Settlers before 1641............. " b
    Chart of Settlers after 1641................ " c
    Ancient sketch of Castle Maine........

Sources, Old Kerry Newspapers Listed............ xviii
1776 List of Papists.................................... xix
Ancient Families of Co. Kerry........................ xxi
Kerry Family History Sources........................ xxiii

Families of County Kerry, Ireland................... 1
  History and Locations as available.
  (Listed in Alphabetical order, disregarding the
  O', Mc, or Mac prefix before the name.)

Appendix... 157
Bibliography, suggested reading.................... 158
Families given in the Master Book of Surnames... 159
Co. Kerry Landowners List........................... 161
Extract From the Master Book of Irish Placenames... 167
Household list of some major Kerry families..... 173

Index of Surnames 219

Ortelius' Map of Ireland, 1576.
What was known of Co. Kerry by way of maps is represented in this extract from The Ortelius Map of Ireland, 1576. (reprinted 1992, I.G.F.). Note the Province of Munster (Mononia or Mounfter), and MacCarthy Mor (MacArte more) shown. To the extreme right is the Shannon river (past which is Co. Clare.)
Several families are noted such as MacGillicuddy (Mac Gylecod.), Fitzmaurice, O'Connor Kerry (O Comere kery), and O'Sullivan Mor (Ofwilevan more).
(Map reprint courtesy the Irish Family Journal)

Introduction

The arrival of the Eoganacht (Eugenian) families of MacCarthy, O'Sullivan and O'Donoghue in the 12th century marks a time of great transition in Co. Kerry. Cormac MacCarthy, in 1124, banished three ruling families of the area: O'Shea, O'Falvey and O'Connor. O'Shea and O'Falvey of the Corcu Duibne had ruled alternately as chiefs of the land, but fade away subsequently. O'Connor of the Ciarraighe, still controlled north Kerry upon the arrival of the English there. O'Moriarty of LochLein was also being dispossessed by O'Donaghue.

These banishments were not without bloodshed and reversals, (Cormac MacCarthy himself was banished to the monastery at Lismore for a time), but the Eoganacht families eventually prevailed. O'Moriarty, sponsored by O'Connor the King of Ireland, (this is not O'Connor Kerry), returned and caused some havoc on land and sea.

The Eoganachts were opposed by older families in Kerry and by O'Brien of Thomand (Co. Clare), who wanted to keep the power of the Eoganacht families in check. O'Connor Kerry was perhaps the most contentious - raising a fleet and establishing a base of power at Innisfallen, before being forced to flee with his fleet left behind on Loch Lein.

MacCarthy, with O'Donaghue and O'Sullivan, received support from O'Connor, king of Connaught and others. Culminating in the battle of Moin Mhor in 1151 in which O'Brien and allies were defeated, MacCarthy was firmly established as king of Desmond. O'Briens power was held in check from that time forward outside of the area of Thomand (Co. Clare and surrounds).

The MacCarthy is usually found with headquarters in Cork however, until the 13th century, when he was driven by the Anglo-Normans to refuge in Kerry.

The O'Donoghue movement into Kerry comes after battle in Cork with the O'Mahoneys (another Eoghanacht family). In the 12th century they established themselves in Killarney and surrounds, breaking the power of the resident O'Carroll and O'Cahill families. The Moriartys held on longer, but to no avail. The O'Connells were forced from Magunihy into Iveragh. The O'Donaghues, from the 13th to the end of the 16th century were most powerful.

The 16th century brings an abrupt end to the way of life established. The land of 'Onaght O'Donoghue' was lost due to the Desmond rebellion, and we find the Browne family assuming some of the remaining territory of O'Donoghue.

The O'Sullivans arrived near the end of the 12th century. Coming from Co. Tipperary, near the Suir, they established themselves in Kerry (Dunkerron South along the Kenmare River) and West Co. Cork. They were driven here by pressure from O'Brien of Thomand and/or the anglo-normans.

The Falveys and O'Sheas, anciently ruled the Corcu Duibne. One seat of power for the clan is given near Ballycarberry. The O'Falveys of the Dingle Peninsula were driven out by the anglo-normans. The O'Sheas had been chiefs of Iveragh, but were totally dispossessed of lands by the 17th century. Pettys survey shows no land owning O'Sheas in 17th century Kerry.

O'Cuilein or Collins of Connelo, Co. Limerick also settled in west Kerry due to pressure from O'Brien of Thomand.

©1994. IGF. Families of Co. Kerry, Ireland - Box 7575, K.C., MO. 64116

In The Year 1200

The picture of Irish families around the year 1200 must have been something like this. The year before, in 1199, Meiler Fitz Henry was granted the barony of Corkaguiney, and Eoganacht Locha Lein of which the O'Donaghues were just gaining control from Moriarty. The Irish chieftains would never have recognized such an edict. One wonders if they knew what was in store.

The O'Sullivans were settling along the Kenmare river, and the MacCarthys held Iveragh and most of Magunihy but were doing battle on many fronts. The Corcu Duibne of the Dingle Bay area, as represented by O'Falvey and O'Shea, begin to fade from power. Pressure from MacCarthy in Iveragh and the anglo-normans in Dingle brought down this ancient tribe from its prominent place.

The anglo-normans were pressuring in the North and in the East of Co. Kerry. Raids were made into north Kerry, including the Killarney area. Meiler Fitz-Henry built Dunloe Castle in 1207 on the old territory of Moriarty. Donal MacCarthy died in 1206, and the ensuing web of rivalries and alliances led to major battles by the year 1215. This left the door open for the posterity of Meiler to attack from Limerick. The English King John died in 1216 leaving room for more intrigue and assumption of power by Geoffrey de Marisco.

De Marisco and Thomas Fitz Anthony came to hold some sway in North Kerry. Meanwhile, the successors to de Cogan and Fitz Stephen prepared to enter Kerry from the East, having established a line of castles and supplies along the coastline, coming from Cork.

The Irish could do no fair battle with the archers, the cavalry, and the soldiers clad in armour. The Irish carried swords slings, and axes, but were generally an army on foot, with no armour and no archers to call upon. Thus, the invasion was not repelled.

Callan Glen

The battle at Callan Glen however, near Kilgarvin in 1261, was a historic battle that took place in Kerry. The Irish victory here kept the south of Co. Kerry and the West of Co. Cork out of the reach of English domination for three centuries. The river Maine came to be the dividing line between the foreigner and the old gaelic powers. Even castles to the south and the east of the Maine fell into the hands of the Irish. As early as the 14th century however, the Mac Carthy acknowledged the sovereignty of the Earl of Desmond and paid tribute.

The Spanish Armada

A well noted event, the shipwrecks of the Spanish Armada, occurred in 1588. Of the Spanish ships wrecked off the Irish coastline, 3 or 4 did so on the coast of Co. Kerry. Few made it to land. One crew surrendered, but had their throats cut, courtesy of Sir E. Denny. It is possible that there was one survivor - but no settlement of the Black Irish here as a result of the Armada shipwrecks!

In the 17th century the conquest of Ireland continued, culminating with the wholesale land confiscations during the Cromwellian times. The words ' To Hell or Connaught' gave the baronies of Burren and Inchiquin in Co. Clare and and Artagh in the north of Roscommon as the places of banishment for the Irish in Kerry. The order was largely ignored.

The first half of the 18th century brought on ruthless rule and penal laws. The gaelic powers were broken, and the English feudal system of former years was disappearing. Co. Kerry was now in the hands of English settlers who held the land, remained loyal to England, and were of the Protestant religion.

Accounts of penal days will be easy for the reader to obtain. There was great pressure for the old Irish to conform to the Protestant religion. In order to hold property, a good job etc., it was given that one be, or become Protestant. Economically it became a necessity for many. Hence, Catholic landowners like Falvey, O'Mahoney of Dromore and MacGillicuddy are found conforming to the official religion early in the 18th century, and retaining holdings.

Remnants of the gaelic family power of earlier days remained with MacCarthy Mor seated at Pallis, Killarney; the O'Sullivan Beare seated at Eyries and O'Sullivan Mor at Toomies; and the O'Donaghues at Glenflesk. One need also mention the figure of Donal O'Mahoney of Dromore, who created some havoc against the absentee landlords in Co. Kerry.

The late 1840's brought famine to Kerry as elsewhere, the cries of hungry children, death in the field, the glen, and in the street, sent Kerry men and women abroad as never before.

In the Penal times many Kerry wild geese went to France, Spain, and Austria. Kerry Emigrants from 1851 to 1911 numbered 234,716 - in just 60 years; most went to the U.S.A., New Zealand and Australia.

We pray this work will help all these wild geese find home in Kerry again.

Format

The spelling of names and places appear here as they were found originally written. Hence, at times Killaha and Killaher mean the same place, just as MacCarthy, McCartie and McCarthy refer to the same family.

We have left the old English spellings alone, leaving the reader to make educated judgments as to places and persons. Chronicled here are compiled works of earlier historians and researchers. Hence, within these pages, conflicting statements and claims will appear, sometimes side by side.

Just as we found that Smith reported incorrectly on the branches of the O'Donoghue family, there are surely other errors inadvertently passed on here that have not caught our eye.

Having not the facilities nor funding to see the truth in every instance, we report here what was given by others, in earlier times. We will publish additional research and opinions in the monthly *Journal of Irish Families*, should you have new material. In this way old errors can be corrected for all to see.

Those interested in further research should consult Smiths *History of Kerry*, the works of Jeremiah King including his *History of Kerry*, as well as early issues of the *Kerry Archaeological Magazine* and the data given in the bibliography of this work.

Some abbreviations found used:
m. = married   d. = died   b. = born
L. = Lord   unm. = unmarried
Co. = County   P.P. = parish priest.

Let the reader understand and uncover errors and misstatements made within these pages, it is the best I could do.
                                    -Michael C. O'Laughlin

©1994. IGF. Families of Co. Kerry, Ireland - Box 7575, K.C., MO. 64116

Old Sketch of The Castle of Carrigfoile in Kerry

x

The English invasion

According to Smith, upon the arrival of the English here, they found the O'Connors holding the north of the County - commemorated today in the lands of Iraghticonnor. The middle of the county was held by Moriarity. To the south the O'Sullivans held large tracts of land including 'O'Sullivans Country', today known as Dunkerron barony, where O'Sullivan was prince of the Irish. They held parts of Iveragh, as did the Crehans (or Macrehans), given to be a branch of the O'Sullivans.

Present as well, according to Smith, were the O'Donoghoes - later to be distinguished into two branches, incorrectly given as O'Donoghoe Mor and O'Donoghoe Ross. This mistake has been repeated in other works a result of the commentary by Smith! Mor and Ross refer to the same branch - it is actually O'Donoghoe Mor centered at Ross Castle and O'Donoghoe of the glen (an gleanna) centered at Killaha castle. The O'Donoghoe Mor line is long given as extinct. The Mahonys were also given on hand at that time.

A considerable part of Co. Kerry was a distinct county of its own prior to becoming incorporated in its latter day form. The older territory known as Desmond, consisted of the part of Kerry which is south of the River Mang, with the barony of Bear and Bantry in Co. Cork, which was a palatinate under the jurisdiction of the earls of Desmond. The ancient county of Desmond or south Munster, was even larger according to the grant of King Henry II to Robert Fitz-Stephen and Milo de Cogan, which is given at large in Smiths History of Cork. Its' limits were from the hill of St. Brandon, to the river Blackwater near Lismore, and it comprehended Co. Cork as well as Co. Kerry.

In 1172 Dermot MacCarthy, king of Cork and Desmond, swore fealty to Henry II.. His lands included all the tract of the country from Lismore to Brandon Hill in Kerry, with some part of Waterford. Desmond was divided into three districts - Clancare, which lay next to the sea, between Dingle and the Kenmare river; Bear, which lay between the Kenmare river and Bantry; and Iveragh, between Bantry and Baltimore.

But it was a necessity that the Norman knights be provided with estates, to stay in Ireland, and to subdue resistance. Often they would have to take by force, that which was 'bestowed' upon them by royalty. Dermot was gradually driven westward, and the MacCarthys in Cork, became as a result, located in in Kerry.

The MacCarties (MacCarthys') were the most eminent family of south Munster immediately prior to the invasions. Their best lands subdued by the English, they retired into south Kerry for security, due to its' inaccessibilities. MacCarthy was not long settled when he was imprisoned with great cruelty by his son, (according to Smith). He relied on the help of Raymond Le Grosse (or Crassus), an English adventurer then found at Limerick, to be rescued.

Le Grosse rescued Dermoid McCarthy by subduing McCarthys son and delivering him to his father. The son was beheaded soon after. MacCarthy then granted a considerable tract of land to Le Grosse, where his son Maurice settled. Soon the old territory of Lixnaw became Clan-Maurice, with the family adopting the surname of Fitz-Maurice (not using the Le Grosse name).

The English Settlement

The aforementioned event is given at the date of 1177, one of the earliest English settlements made in Ireland.

Giraldus Cambrensis finds the above Dermoid McCarthy, renting the lands of Milo de Cogan (Miles Cogan) & Robert Fitz-Stephen who held lands in Cork, at a nominal fee in 1179. But by 1185 he rose up, and with O'Brien of Thomand, wasted English settlements and besieged Cork. Fitz- Stephen was in Cork and in trouble until Raymond Le Grosse arrived from Waterford with archers and soldiers. The next year Dermoid Mac Carthy Mor was slain by Theobald Walter, (ancestor of the Butler family in Ireland), while meeting with other Irish chiefs at Cork.

Daniel Mac Carthy Mor ni Carra, so named for the river Carra, was the successor to Dermoid, making peace in 1196. There were great battles and bloodshed between the MacCarthys and the English from this time forward, particularly between the MacCarthys and the FitzGeralds, who came to hold their lands. In 1261 they 'completely defeated' the Fitzgeralds at Callan in Co. Kerry. Dissension among the followers of MacCarthy led to a reversal of fortune, but they always remained of note, retaining the title of MacCarthy Mor. Donald MacCarthy Mor was ennobled by Queen Elizabeth, becoming earl of Glencare in 1565, denoting lands between Dingle Bay and the Kenmare River. He surrendered his title to the Queen, and had it regranted to him in the English manner. (The surrender and regrant policy which transferred ultimate authority of appointment to the Queen).

As the great O'Neil rebelled in the north of Ireland, Mac Carthy pursued his example in the south assuming the title of King of Munster. They joined forces in 1568 but the MacCarthy was forced to submit before years end. The title of MacCathy Mor soon fell to Florence MacCarthy, son of Sir Donough MacCarthy Reagh of Carberry, Co. Cork. This title was confirmed on him by O'Neil the King of Ireland. Florence joined with O'Neil, who was created the Earl of Tyrone, and with the Earl of Desmond, in rebellion. 'He was grandfather to Randal Mac-Carty Mor, the father of Florence, the late MacCarty Mor, who by his wife Agnes, daughter to Edward Herbert of Mucruss, Esq; left a son, now a minor, and at school in England, who is heir and representative of this antient family'.(-per Smith)

Of the principal English families settling here from the time of Henry II to the end of Queen Elizabeth's reign is the family of Fitzmaurice, the posterity of Raymond Le Grosse; and the Fitzgerald branch, the earls of Desmond. The history of both families is found in the Peerage of Ireland by Lodge, where the posterity of Raymond, is in the history of the earls of Kerry, and the house of Desmond is in that of Kildare.

Maurice Fitz-Gerald, the first knight of Kerry, was the third son of John of Callan, ancestor to the Fitz-Geralds of Munster which John was slain at Callan by Mac Carties, with his son Maurice.

His eldest brother was Gibbon, ancestor to the white knights, otherwise called Clangibbon. The second brother was John, ancestor to the knights of Glin or of the valley in Co. Limerick. The 4th youngest brother to this Maurice was Thomas, progenitor to the diverse families of the Fitz-Geralds in this country and that of Limerick.

Settler Families

The main families who settled in Kerry under Queen Elizabeth were named undertakers, for they had to perform or undertake several conditions as set down by the queens articles. These undertakers were all given to be English gentlemen, sent to Ireland to plant and occupy some 574,000 acres of land in Cork, Kerry Waterford and Limerick. The names of these undertakers follow:

Sir William Herbert, knt. 13,276 acres.
Charles Herbert, Esq..3,768 acres
Sir Valentine Brown, knt. 6,560 acres.
Sir Edward Denny, knight. 6,000 acres.
Captain Jenkin Conway. 5,260 acres.
John Holly. 4422 acres.

John Champion, alias Chapman, (so called by Moryson and John Stone - neither of whose posterity remain in the male line here) 1434 acres. These lands passed to the Rt. Hon. John, earl of Orrery, purchased by the first earl of Cork, from Chapman and Stone.

The Herbert Family

The largest undertaker was Sir William Herbert of St. Julians, in the county of Monmouth. His daughter and sole heir, Mary, married Edward, lord Herbert of Cherburry, created lord Castle-Island in Co. Kerry. The first of the Herbert name who settled in Kerry, and whose posterity remained, was Thomas Herbert of Kilcow, Esq.. His father Matthew, son of Sir John Herbert, was one of the secretaries sent to the earl of Essex, to require his attendance at the treasurers house in 1601. His father was William, the eldest son of sir Mathew Herbert of Colebrook, lineally descended from the said sir Richard Herbert, brother to William, earl of Pembroke.

This given Thomas Herbert 'stood out until the last extremity, in defense of Montgomery Castle, when it was besieged by Oliver Cromwells forces.'.

The Brown Family

The first of the Brown family name here was Sir Valentine Browne of Crofts, C. of Lincoln, and of Hogesdon, C. of Middlesex, knt.., created auditor general of Ireland in 1555, d. on Feb. 8, 1567. His heir, sir Valentine Brown, in 1583 received orders with sir Henry Wallop, for surveying lands in Ireland. He sat for the County of Sligo in 1585, and returned to England, but returned to Ireland in 1588, the year of the Spanish invasion. He purchased large amounts of land in Kerry from the MacCarthy Mor (Donald, earl of Clancare), married Thomasin, sister to Sir Nicholas Bacon, knt, sometime keeper of the great seal in Ireland, having issue Sir T. Brown(e) of Hospital, Co. Limerick, and Sir Nicholas Browne of Molahaff, and Ross, Co. Kerry, Knt, immediate ancestor to the L. Kenmare.

The Denny Family

In the reign of Elizabeth, Sir Edward Denny, Knt., had 6,000 acres granted him, and Tralee castle, the seat of the earl of Desmond. The first of the family arrived in England with the conqueror from Normandy. Sir Edward was the 2nd son of sir Anthony Denny of Waltham Abbey in Hereford shire, Knt., keeper of the palace at Westminster.

Arthur Denny, Esq; son of Sir Edward, went at a young age into Ireland, and m. Elizabeth, dau. of sir Anthony Forest, by whom he had Sir Edward Denny, Knt., father of sir Arthur Denny, Knt., who had Edw. Denny, father to col. Edw. Denny, who had three sons; Arthur, Sir Thomas, and the Rev. Barry.

1598 Muster Roll

On April 10, 1598, we find the Muster roll of Sir Edward Denny's soldiers, mustered by Mr. Staughton at Denny Vale. It gives the following:

Mr. Arthur Denny, Gallor Page. Mr. Thomas Blennerhassett, entered for John Lewin, discharged. Mr. Anthony Randall, for Richard Smith, dead. John Russell, without sword, rapier. Wm. Adames, pike, horseman for Simon Rokes in England with Sir Edward Denny. Robert King for Robert Prise. James Stanley, pike, for Jerome Halsey. Robert Curtesse, without flask and touch box., for Thomas Ryder. John Hercules, musketeer, a good shot, a horseman for Hugh Baker, hurt at Dublin. John Harrowe, mason, ill shot, for John Spencer, gone to Dublin at Easter. Francis Christian, good shot, for Robert Campe. Thomas Boundes, pikeman for John Ashe. Christopher Barton, musket, gunpowder maker. John Phillips, halbert. Peter Kelly, halbert. Wm. Foundes, sick, bayly in Tralee. Wm. Fleete, sick, butcher, in Tralee. John Prince, without sword, flask, and touch box, for John Bright. Anthony Fitzwilliams, halbert, a horseman before. Donnell O'Sullivan, shot, for Wm. Taylor. Harry Smith, alias Warren, shot. James Fitz-John, a birding piece. Thos. Symons, for Wm. Farthing. John Boye, for Robt. Stringer. This muster roll was delivered by Thomas Blennerhassett.

We see not only names on this list, but that names are spelled any number of different ways. Hence Adames and Adams can be the same surname, as can Campe and Camp, Ashe and Ash, Symons and Simons, Prise and Price, Boye and Boy, Seghrue and Sugrue.

The Conway Family

Jenkin Conway was granted the seignory of Killorglin. He brought three brothers into Ireland, whom descended from sir Hugh, and sir Henry Conway in Wales, viz. Hugh, Edward, and William, who were undertakers for him. He married Mary, the daughter of sir Wm. Herbert, by whom he had an only son Jenkin and two daughters, Alice and Elizabeth. Jenkin the younger was the father of Edward who left two daughters as coheirs, viz. Alice and Avis Conway. The elder married Patrick Dowdal, of Kippagh, Co. Limerick, Esq., by whom he had issue John Dowdal, counselor at law. The younger daughter Avis married Robert Blennerhassett, Esq., grandson of Robert Blennerhasset who first came into Ireland, in which family the seignory of Killorglin (the manor of Castle Conway) remained when Smith wrote his History of Kerry.

Blennerhasset(t)

The first was Robert Blennerhasset, who with his aged father Thomas, came from Flimby in Cumberland as undertakers. Robert m. Elizabeth Conway, and from this union come all of the name of Blennerhasset in Kerry.

The Crosbie Family

The Crosbie family descended from a family of the name in Great Crosbie in Lacashire, settling in Kerry towards the end of Queen Elizabeth's reign. In the reign of King Henry VIII one of the name was prior of Trim in the County of Meath, with several church lands granted to him at the dissolution of religious houses. Two brothers of the name are given in Ireland at the end of Q. Elizabeth's reign, Patrick, and John who was the ancestor to the Crosbies of

Kerry. John was prebendary of Disert, and advanced to the episcopal sees of Ardfert and Aghadoe in 1600. He died, a bishop, in 1621, buried in the cathedral church at Ardfert. By his wife, daughter to O'Lalor, in Queens County, he had issue Sir Walter Crosbie, Bart., member of Parliament for Kerry in 1634, and David Crosbie, Esq; governor of the county in 1641 who withstood a long siege against the Irish in his fortress, Ballingary, near the Shannon. He then was governor of the old fort of Kinsale, but was obliged to surrender it to L. Broghil, who took possession of it for the parliament. John's brother Patrick, born in Queens County, had lands granted to him there for his service against the O'Moors and other septs. He was father to Sir Pierce Crosbie, Bart, who served as col. of an Irish regiment.

The Spring Family

The Spring family of Lavenham in Suffolk, settled in Kerry in Queen Elizabeth's reign. The first of the family here was captain Thomas Spring, who by his wife Annabella Browne, had two sons, Walter and Thomas & 5 daughters.

The Rice Family

The Rice family of Kerry descend from Stephen Rice of Dingle, Esq., who arrived here as an undertaker under Queen Elizabeth. He was representative for Kerry in the parliaments of King James I. He died on March 31, 1622. James Rice of Ballynruddel was his son & heir.

The Morrice Family

John Morrice of Northal in Essex, 30 miles from London, was the first to settle in Ireland. Francis Morrice, the eldest son, and his father came to Ireland 'having spent' their fortune in England. He came to Ireland during Queen Elizabeth's wars, along with his 3 brothers, John, Mathew and Luke, and leased lands in Iraghticonnor.

The Gun Family

The Gun family had settled in Kerry at least by the time of Charles I. William Gun of Liscahane castle is found in 1641, who had issue William Gun of Ratoo, Esq., and George Gun.

The Hussey Family & Others

The English family of Hussey settled early at Dingle in Co. Kerry according to the History of Kerry by Smith. Also given are the families of Trant, Ferriter, etc..in the barony of Corckaguiny where they had several lands and castles.

The Ponsonby Family

Ponsonby origins are from Picardy; settling in Cumberland with good estate, taking their name from the lordship of Ponsonby, that they owned. They also had conferred on them the office of Barber to the kings of England.

John Ponsonby, Esq., of Haugh-heal in Cumberland, was father of Simon, whose son Henry had by his wife Dorothy Sandys two sons, Sir John, and Henry, both of which settled in Ireland. In 1649 they are found attending O. Cromwell along with other officers. Sir John, eldest brother, was ancestor to the earl of Besborough; and Henry, the younger, had lands confirmed to him in 1666, becoming seated at Stacks-Town, and Crotto, in Co. Kerry and having issue 7 sons and 11 daughters, with 3 sons and 7 daughters living to maturity. His son Thomas succeeded at Crotto.

The Wren Family

After the wars of 1641 a branch of the Wren family settled in Kerry. They stem from captain Thomas Wren, an adventurer under Cromwell. He was descended from the Wrens of Sherborne

©1994. IGF. Families of Co. Kerry, Ireland - Box 7575, K.C., MO. 64116

House, Billey-hall and Binchester, in the bishopric of Durham, of Danish origin.

The Godfrey Family

The first Godfrey here was major John Godfrey; with estates granted him by King Charles II, for his service against the Irish in the wars of 1641. From him descends John Godfrey of Bushfield, Esq.

The Mullens Family

Col. Frederick Mullens settled at Burnham, near Dingle. Burnham (formerly Ballingolin) was so called from his place of origin in England. He had his lot in the north of Ireland, which he then exchanged for lands in Co. Kerry, and from him the family of Burnham are descended.

Acts of Settlement

In 1666 the following had estates granted to them under the acts of settlement, and their posterity remained settled in Co. Kerry; Captain Henry Ponsonby, Sir Arthur Denny, Knt., John Carrique, Esq, including the lands of Glandine and Magharies, 2,370 acres.; John Blennerhasset, Esq.

In 1667 Lancelot Sandes, Esq., who had parts of Ballymalus and Kilbonane in Magunihy barony. John Fitz-Gerald of Innishmore, Esq., commonly called the Knight of Kerry. Anthony Raymond, Esq.. Major John Godfrey Edward Rice, son of James Rice Fitz-James.

Forfeited Estates

In King James day the estates of Donough, earl of Clancarty, and of sir Patrick Trant were purchased by the hollow blade company of London. Another large estate of Patrick Trant was purchased by the Earl of Inchiquin. The Hollow Blade also purchased estates of Nicholas Skiddy and Thomas Skiddy, and that of Daniel Mac-Fineen Carthy with the lands of James Fitzmaurice.

Other forfeiting persons in Kerry were Edward Rice, whose lands were purchased by Edward Cosgrave of Dublin, and John Lyne whose lands were sold to Thomas Connor of Dublin.

Separately we find again a listing of Cromwellian settlers who were granted lands in 1667 in Kerry. These lands had been taken from Irish and Anglo-Norman landowners, who supported the King, Charles I. Sir William Petty surveyed the escheated lands and bought 50,000 acres in Dunkerron from the soldiers who were granted lands.

Among the names of the grantees were: Carterett, Compton, Ames, Welstead, Yeeden, Sands, Sankey, Raymond, Bigg, Barrow, Green, Brett, Sweetman, Owens, Ball, Richardson, Jones, Sterne, Covert, Hardier, Northcott, Hughes, Anglesey, Austin, Mercer, Power, Atkins, Reading, Coote, and Marshall among others.

Palatine Families

Of the Palatines at Arabella: Col. Hasset brought a colony of Palatines from Co. Limerick about 1746, and settled them near Tralee, said to have been brought to the Blennerhassett estate. In 1776, there were 16 families of small farmers. Each settler got a cow, a horse and 'everything they wanted for a year', besides having the land for half of its value. They introduced ploughing with a wheel plough, and planted potatoes in dril's. They brought in cars with wheels, as there were only sliding carts before. They arrived during Queen Anne's reign '(to stamp out Irish Catholicism)' at a cost of £24,000.

The Palatine's Daughter, was a popular Irish Ballad.

The Irish Forces

As settlements in Co. Kerry continued to strenghten in the 16th century, the Irish held considerable influence of their own until the devastating war of 1641-2.

Kerry's Army in 1568, and the power of the Desmonds at this date can be estimated from a document in the Lansdowne MSS., British Museum, entitled: 'A Discourse of the Power of the Irish Menne':

MacCartie (MacCarthy) Mor is called prince of that portion and will bring of his name and kind, xl horsemen, two battalions and two thousand kerne.

O'Sullivan is Lord of Bere and Bantry, and will be xvi horsemen, cc. kerne, and useth long gallies.

Mag Guyn (Mac Finneen) is Lord of Glonough, and will be cc. kerne.

O'Donoghue More is Lord of Lough Lene, and will be xvi horsemen and cc. kerne.

O'Donoghue Glanlish (Glenflesk) will be vi horsemen and cc. kerne.

MacGilgoddy (MacGillicuddy) is lord of his country and will be lxx kerne.

O'Conner Kerry will be xxiii horsemen and lxxvi kerne.

While Irish forces did not prove enough to permanently drive the invaders from Irish soil, many a valiant battle was fought and won. For centuries, entire sections of the county remained unconquered. This delay gave Co. Kerry a unique blend of old and new cultures. This helped bring the character of the Kerry people to what it is today.

My refuge is in Ireland or Virginia
- an old seventeenth century phrase

Settler Families in Tralee

Tralee was incorporated in 1612, and its charter named the first provost and burgesses as: Robert Blennerhassett, Arthur Denny, Edmond Roe, Humphrey Dethick, John Stiles, John Leeser, Edward Vaucleere, John Humpton, Francis Adams, Thomas Bramstone, Giles King, and John Curlestone.

Sir Edward Denny, Knt., Bart, came to Ireland in 1580 joining with Arthur, Lord Grey de Wilton, Sir Walter Raleigh, Fulke Greville, John Cheke, Edmond Spenser, John Zouche, etc.. in the subjugation of Munster.

In 1587 Denny received a grant of an estate, named 'Seignory of Dennyvale', extending from Castle Island to near Castle Gregory and Fenit, with the town and Castle of Tralee. Undertakers of the plantation of Munster received lands from the Earl of Desmond's forfeited estate in Kerry then, namely Sir William Herbert, Charles Herbert, Sir Valentine Browne, Capt. Jenkin Conway, John Chapman and John Holly.

These undertakers were bound to place on their estates only those of the 'British race and Blood'. In the patent of Charles I, re-granting the Denny estate. there was a proviso against any long term lease being given to any 'mere Irish, not of British race, blood, and surname.'

It is no surprise that many new tenants were younger sons of 'noble' British families. Younger sons in need of proving success may have gone to Ireland, or to America and Australia.

"My refuge is in Ireland or Virginia" is an old seventeenth century phrase coined by a dramatist, illustrating the fact. Those who did not do well, or that had no prospect of doing so, were in need of new endeavors. Some would do well,

---

©1994. IGF. Families of Co. Kerry, Ireland - Box 7575, K.C., MO. 64116

Settler Families
given on estates near Tralee, Co. Kerry

Adams	Curlew	Huddlestone	Sawyer
Arnes	Dashwood	Hynton	Shortcliffe
Arnold	Davis	Isham	Skipworth
Ashwood	Dethick, De Thick	Jackson	Spratt
Barham	Dew	Jeffcott	Spring
Barrett Bariod	Dutchman	Jones	Stiles, Styles
Barton, de Bartun	Dyer	Joy	Stoughton
Bayley, Bailey	Edalicke	Knight, Knightley	Street
Beckford	Exham	Lentall	Swift
Benson	Farding	Lynne Lyn	Thurston, Thryston
Bernard, Barnard	Fell	Mannering	Towell
Berry	Fleete	Martin	Trassy
Best	Fletcher	Mason	Trawdsome
Bordell	Forest	Meredith	Treddle
Boreham	Foulkes or Foundes	Morris	Tristam
Boyle	Fuller	Natt	Truman
Bramstone	Gabriel	Nihill	Turner
Brooke	Gibson	Norris, Norreys	Vauclier Voakley
Brookes Brooks	Giunings Giney	Page	Vynes, Vine
Buckford	Godolphin	Palmer	Ware
Cade	Gooding	Payne Paine	Warham
Callues	Gorham	Pendred	Warren
Cambridge	Gould, Gul	Pepys	Watkins
Carpenter	Grey	Periman, Perryman	Watts
Chapman	Groome	Philips, Phillips	Westcombe
Church	Hale	Preste	White
Chute	Hampton	Raleigh	
Cicill, Cecil	Harrison	Randal, Randall,	
Collier	Harrowe	Roe	
Collis	Hart Harte	Rookes	
Conway	Hicks	Rycroft	
Cooke	Hoar Hoare	Ryder	
Curbstone	Hooper	Ryeves, Ryeeves,	

Given as settling on estates near Tralee, mainly from the time of the coming of the Elizabethan undertakers to the rebellion of 1641. These family names may also have settled in Ireland subsequently. Some of these names were also adopted by old Irish families as the English form of their surnames.

Settler Families
given as settling in Co. Kerry subsequent to the 1641 rebellion

Bernard, Barnard	Amory	Chuse	Godfrey, Mac
Benson	Alton	Comyn	Meredith
Chute of Chute	Bradshaw	Covert	Payne Paine
Church	Brett, de Britt	Cranfield	Ponsonby
Gorham	Babington	Cary	Raymond
Jeffcott	Bateman	Cameron	Spring
Lynne Lyn	Boreman	Damer	Stiles, Styles
Stoughton	Collins, Coilens	Daniel	Ginnis Gennys
Vauclier Voakley	Corbet	Darby	

These family names may also have settled in Ireland at other times.

CASTLE MAGNE IN 1600, A.D.

Settler Families in Tralee

others failed miserably.

John Cicill, given to be of the 'great Lord Burghley's' family, of which Lady Mary Cecil married Edward Denny, Earl of Norwich. Edward Grey was the son of Lord John Grey, brother of the Duke of Suffolk. His sister was stepmother to Edward Denny, Earl of Norwich (nephew of Sir Edward, the "undertaker".). Daniel Grey of Tralee, in 1641, was probably his son, but his descendants disappear.

These tenants are further given to be sons of families connected by blood, marriage or friendship, with the "undertaker" or yeomen from the estates of his family or relations in England.

Hence we have many families noted as settling on estates around Tralee, from the coming of the Elizabethan 'undertakers' to the rebellion of 1641-2. A listing of these families is given on the chart following this page.

After the subjugation of Kerry by Cromwell, consequent upon the rebellion of 1641-42, many new names appear in the Tralee neighborhood. Some are likely new tenants brought from England to replace those exterminated by the rebellion. Others are Cromwellian officers and soldiers of the Commonwealth army, granted lands in lieu of arrears of pay, etc..

Oak Park and some other portions of the Denny Estate were forfeited for this purpose. But on the whole it escaped very well, owing probably to the fact that the Dennys had many influential relatives on the Cromwellian side, as the Lord Protector himself was connected with them. J. King said that accounted for the Cromwellians being shown favor subsequently by the Dennys.

Sources

''Births, Marriages and death records should be kept for reference in the district and not collected in Dublin for gunmen to make a bonfire.''

This quote from Jeremiah King, author of numerous works on Co. Kerry, was striking. He further stated that records and artifacts should be kept in local custody or sold to Americans for safe keeping! A drastic measure to endorse. So many records had been lost from the year 1200 onwards, after sending them to Dublin, and fires destroyed much even in local custody. Yet much remains.

When searching for records in Co. Kerry, there are many sources from which to draw. Perhaps a bit like a jigsaw puzzle, in total they represent a considerable body of information.

These records include: coroners' inquests, informations, recognizances, indictments, assize trials, presentments, maps, civil bill books, statutes, decrees, freeholders' lists, arms' licenses, forge register, spirit licenses, deputy governors, militia officers (an example of which is shown in this section), high constables' accounts, insolvents, convictions, magistrates, burgesses, freemen, court records, charters, by-laws, common seal, lists of provosts and town clerks and serjeants at mace and marshal; diocesan records, registers, visitation books, prospects, parishes, wills since 1606, administration grants, marriage licenses 1773, consistorial court 1677, presentation to parishes 1674, glebe houses 1678, terriers 1698, declarations 1742, benefice titles, curates' licenses, leases, parochial registries, liber niger

1616, visitation books 1615, 1692 onwards sometimes kept at Limerick register house (noted circa 1920's).

The county Library at Tralee is a vital source of information and direction. The Public Records office in Killarney (near the St. Columbanus Home), holds considerable records of Births, Marriages and Deaths in Kerry as well.

Newspapers

The best collection of newspapers concerning Co. Kerry, was housed at the British Museum. Those printed in Tralee follow: Chutes' Western Herald 1812-35; Kerry Evening Post 1813-1917; Tralee Mercury 1829-39 or later; Kerry Examiner 1840 - 56; Tralee Chronicle 1843-81; Raymond's Kerry Herald 1856; Kerry Star 1861-3; Weekly Chronicle 1873; Kerry Sentinel 1878-1917; Kerry Independent 1880-4; Kerry Weekly Reporter 1883-1925; Kerry News 1894-1917; Munster Life 1897; Killarney Echo 1899-1925; Kerry People No. 1121 in 1925; Kerryman -1925.

The Post 1774; Journal 1782; Chronicle 1783; Mercury 1793; Herald 1793; Dispatch 1807; were printed in Tralee but not deposited in the British Museum before 1812.

The foregoing list from written sources earlier in the century, will prove a good beginning reference point.

The Rev. H. L. Denny utilized the names of tenants from the Family Muniments, Grants, & Rental Books of the Denny family, also depositions connected with 1641, etc... For the places of origin of the various surnames in England he used Guppy's 'Homes of Family Names in Great Britain', Burke's 'General Armory', Herald's 'Visitations', and we have relied upon these as well.

1776 Papists List

An example of an untapped source, the following is a list of Papists swearing the new test oath of allegiance:

Barry, Edward, gent. Killarney.
Barry, John, Woolcomber, Killarney.
Brennan, Denis, farmer, Mount Eolus.
Byrne, Joseph, farmer-gardner, Killarney
Cahill, Jo., parish priest, Kilgobbin.
Carney, John, merchant, Killarney.
Coffe, Edmond, inn-keeper, Killarney.
Connell, Cornelius, M.D., Carhen.
Connell, Daniel, gent., Comego.
Connell, Daniel, gent., Farmars.
Connell, Maurice, gent. Daurinane.
Connell, Maurice, gent. Ballinaclaun.
Connell, Morgan, gent., Carhen.
Connell, Richard, gent., Comego.
Cooper, James, farmer, Droum.
Cronin, Daniel, Esq., Rhamore.
Cruden, Daniel, gent, Rhamore.
Curtais, Daniel, gent, Killarney.
Curtayne, James, gent, Annaghbeg.
Curtayne, John, gent. Killarney.
Curtayne, John, farmer, Annaghbeg.
Curtayne, Patrick, gent., Mastergeehy.
Curtayne, Thomas, gent., Ballycassen.
Daly, Anthony, friar, grdn. of Irelagh.
Duggan, Daniel, gent., Knocknaseed.
Duggan, Denis, jr., gent., Knocknaseed.
Duggan, Denis, Esq., Knockanane
Duggan, Henry, gent, Knocknaseed.
Duggan, John jr., gent, Knockeerverk.
Einey, Daniel, farmer, Maularcane.
Falvey, Michael, Esq., Killarney.
Gallway, Christ., merchant, Killarney.
Galwey, Thomas, Esq., Killanrey.
Griffin, Michael, gent, Rossanean.
Heily, Maurice, friar of Listoghken.
Hoare, John, merchant, Killarney.
Hoare, Maurice, gent. Killarney.
Huolahan, James, fmr. pastor Killarney.
Kifee, Denis, gent, Shinnagh.
Lawler, Hugh, M.D., Doctor, Killarney.

Lawler, Mar., Apothecary, Killarney.
Leary, Daniel, P.P. Droumtarrive.
Leary, Denis, farmer, Doonrine.
Lee, James, P.P., Ballymacelligott.
Linnegar, Richard, gent, Killarney.
MacCarthy, Florence, gent. Knocknagree
MacCarthy, Justin, Doctor, Killarney.
MacCrohan, Andrew, gent, Charen.
MacCrohan, Owen, gent, Portmagee.
MacDonagh, John, gent, Killarney.
MacEgan, Thomas, P.P., Kiltalogh.
MacSheehy, Ml., merchant, Killarney.
MacSwiney, Bryan, farmer, Mauliarcane
MacSweeney, Owen, frmr, Maulianane.
Madgett, John, pastor of Tralee.
Mahony, Daniel, condjutor, priest Tralee
Mahony, Daniel, gent, Cappanagraun.
Mahony, Denis, gent, Gurrane.
Mahony, Eug., gent. Castlefarm.
Mahony, Florence, gent. Cullinagh.
Mahony, James, P.P., Killeenane.
Mahony, James, Esq., Killarney.
Mahony, James, jr., gent., Killarney.
Mahony, John, Esq., Killarney.
Mahony, Kean, gent, Cappanagroun.
Mahony, Kean, gent., Clahanmacquin.
Mahony, Kean, gent., Cullinagh.
Morrogh, James, gent, Ards.
Moylan, F., chief clergy, dioc. Killarney
Moynihan, Arthur, gent., Stagmount.
Moynihan, Darby, farmer, Carrum.
Moynihan, Malaky, gent., Knockaliffan.
Moynihan, Thady, gent. Rhabeg.
Moynihan, Thady, farmer, New Bridge.
Murphy, Danell, Esq., Killarney.
Murphy, John, gent., Killarney.
Murphy, Martin, gent., Killarney.
O'Connell, Morgan, P.P., Killarney.
O'Leary, Darby, gent, Coome.
O'Leary, James, merchant, Killarney.
O'Rourke, Dermod, P.P. Listry.
O'Scanlan, Edmund, farmer, Fusah.
O'Sullivan, Jerry, P.P. Aglis.

O'Sullivan, Tim, P.P. Kenmare.
Plunkett, Thomas, priest. Killarney.
Purcell, Edmond, merchant, Killarney.
Riordan, Thomas, gent, Knock.
Segerson, Christ., gent., Cannuge.
Segerson, Christ., gent., Kinnard.
Segerson, Edward, gent., Comb.
Segerson, James, gent., Cahirbarnagh.
Segerson, John, gent., Caherbranagh.
Seghrue, James, gent., Fermoyle.
Shanaghan, Ter., P.P., Castleisland.
Shine, Thady, gent., Shinnagh.
Stack, John, P.P., Brosna.
Sullivan, Daniel, P.P., Knockany.
Sullivan, Jery, gent., Killaha.
Sullivan, Matthew, gent., Killarney.
Sullivan, Owen, priest, Rhamore
Sulivan, Thady, Nohavale.
Sweeney, Morgan, farmer, Foremore.

The gentlemen, clergymen and others, Papists, in this list, 'voluntarily came this day before me, one of his Majestys Justices of the Peace of the County of Kerry, and severally swore to and subscribed the new test oath. Given under my hand at Killarney, March the 7th, 1776. -(by) Henry King.'
James Crewly, P.P., Skull.
Jeremiah Driscoll, Curate of Skull.
Taken and sworn before me this 9th day of February, 1776 - (by) John Chetwood
Sworn before me this 19th May, 1776 - by Robert Blennerhassett.

(An example of one of the pieces of the jigsaw when searching for information on families in Co. Kerry. This test oath allegiance gives the name, location, and religious affiliation of each signer. Many such loose end documents exist to help in research. One wonders how much interest the American Revolution generated among these men in 1776 ?)

Ancient Families of Co. Kerry

Ciar raige : The Kingdom of Kerry, most likely meaning the kingship of the people of Ciar.

Ancient Peoples of the Kingdom of Kerry

√ **The Ciarraige** - originating near Tralee, these people settled the baronies of Iraghticonnor, Clanmaurice and Trughanacmy. By the 6th century they ruled north Kerry. Some give them as partially descended from the Picts. From the 8th to the 17th century they held power in north Kerry under the banner of O'Connor Kerry. Their last stronghold was in Iraghticonnor, centered near Ballylongford.

√ **The Corcu Duibne** (Corca Duibhne)- from the seed of Dovvinias, as found inscribed on ogam stones. A specially talented people. They are given as the builders of the great stone forts, and originators of the ogham script - the earliest form of Irish written language. Their center of power is given to be the Dingle Peninsula. Corkaguiney marks the name and the territory of this old family line, once led by O'Falvey and O'Shea. They apparently lived in peace for centuries, leaving little record of their history. They fade from view in the 12th century.

√ **Eoganacht Loch Lein**- A goidelic or gaelic sept, settling around the lakes of Killarney. They are the descendants of Mug or Eogan, hence being called Eoganacht or Eugenian. The Eoganacht families are numerous. In the 12th century MacCarthy, O'Sullivan and O'Donoghue create a major lasting impact in Kerry.

√ **The Alltraighe** - were rivals of the Ciarraige, centered on the cantred of Altry, roughly equivalent to the barony of Clanmaurice. The Ciarraighe forced them into Clare in the 8th century.

√ **The Ui Fearba and the Ui dTorna** were among other tributary peoples given in Kerry, remembered in in place names such as O'Dorney parish and Offerba, in Kerry. (Keating gives O'Leyne or Lane as chief of the Ui Ferba, see page xxii).

35. The O'AHERNS, O'RONAYNES, and O'HEYNES, were also old and respectable families in the county of Cork.

IAR-MUMHA.

36. The O'CONCOBHAIR, or O'Conors, kings of Kerry, are thus mentioned by O'Heerin in his topographical poem:

"Let us leave the warlike race of Conari,
Princes of Erna of golden shields,
We come to our friends the race of Fergus,
They are entitled to command our attention.

"The king of Kiarraide over the clans of Kiar,
O'Conor rules the land by right,
Chief of the plain of fertile fields,
From the sea shore to the Shannon of clear streams."

They took their name from Conchobhar or Conor, one of their ancient chiefs. The O'Conors Kerry were very powerful as kings and princes of Kerry. In the thirteenth century, the Fitzmaurices, earls of Kerry, got much of the possessions of the O'Conors, whose ancient principality was diminished to the territory called Oireacht Ui Chonchobhair, signifying the inheritance of O'Conor, now forming the barony of Iraghticonor. The O'Conors Kerry had several strong castles, the chief of which was that of Carrigafoyle, at the small island of Carrig, near the mouth of the Shannon, but after the Elizabethian and Cromwellian wars most of their estates were confiscated.

37. O'DONNCHADHA, or O'Donoghoes, given by O'Heerin as chiefs of Lough Lein, and also of Clan Selbhuidhe, and thus designated in his topography, together with the O'Carrolls:

"O'Donoghoe of Lough Lein
And of the Flesg, who is full powerful,
Rules over the Clan Selbaide,
They are men of happiness in Munster."

"O'Donoghoe of Lough Lein—
He is prince of that Eoganacht;
O'Carroll is there our kinsman,
Of pure and noble origin."

The O'Donoghoes were of the Eugenian race of Ibh Echach, the other great sept of which tribe took the name O'Mahony; and originally settled in that part of Desmond, now the county of Cork, where they possessed a large territory, extending from Iniskean to the borders of Bantry, and from thence northward to Ballyvurny and Macroom, comprising the district called Iveleary, (which is part of Carbery,) and also a great portion of Muskerry: but in the twelfth century, the O'Donoghoes were expelled from Cork by the Mac Carthys and O'Mahonys, and settled in Kerry, where they became proprietors of all the country about Loch Lein and Killarney. The O'Donoghoes continued powerful chiefs down to the reign of Elizabeth, when, in consequence of having joined the earls of Tyrone and Desmond, most of their estates were confiscated. The O'Donoghoes were divided into two great branches, namely, those of Loch Lein, and those of Glenflesk, the latter called O'Donoghoe More. The O'Donoghoes, lords of Loch Lein, had their chief castle at Ross Island, on one of the lakes of Killarney, the romantic ruins of which still remain.

38. O'DOMHNAILL, or O'Donnell, of the same race as the O'Donoghoes, is given by O'Heerin as a chief of Clan Shalvey, and mentioned as follows: *

"Clan Selbaide of the limpid streams,
Recorded as a well known land,
Belongs to O'Domnaill of the powerful hand,
Who took possession of the brown nut plain."

39. O'CATHAILL, or O'Cahill. A branch of the Kiarraide took this name from Cathal, one of its chiefs. The race is of the same blood as the O'Connors Kerry. The name is still numerous in the counties of Kerry and Cork.

40. The O'CARROLLS, princes of Loch Lein, are mentioned by O'Heerin, and also in the Annals of Inisfallen, in the eleventh and twelfth centuries.

41. O'FALBHI, or O'Falvey, given by O'Heerin as chief of Corca Duibhne, and of the territory from the Mang, westward to Fiontraigh or Ventry. *Corca Duihhne*, is now the barony of Corcaguiney, in the county of Kerry. The O'Falveys were powerful chiefs, and in ancient times held the rank of hereditary admirals of Desmond.

42. O'SEADHA, or O'Shea, is also given as a chief of Ibh Ratha or Iveragh.

43. O'CONGHAILL, or O'Connell, is given by O'Heerin, as chief of *Magh O g-Coinchinn*, now the barony of Magonihy, in Kerry. The three last mentioned chiefs are stated by O'Heerin, in his topography, to be of the race of Clan Conari, that is, the descendants of Conari II., monarch of Ireland, in the beginning of the third century, who was of the race of the Clanna Degadh, of Munster. They are thus designated by O'Heerin:

"After the battalions of Clar Broni,
Let us treat of the clans of Conari,
Fair Fenian heroes from Tulach-an-Trir (an ancient name of Tara,)
Rulers in Munster of the smooth streams.

"Three chiefs who possessed the lands,
Of Corca Dubni of the fine forces,
O'Falvey the warrior, and O'Shea,
The strengthening bond of the eastern parts.

"O'Connell of sharp swords
Rules over the shady fortress of Magonihy,
Like a stately tree in hazel woods,
Is the Munster leader of the cavalry forces.

"From Mang, westward, is the estate,
Possessed by O'Falvey as far as Ventry;
Without dispute an extensive land,
Was obtained by O'Shea, chief of Iveragh."

44. O'LAEGHAIN, O'Leyne, or Lane, chief of Ui Ferba; and O'Duibhduin, chief of Ui Flannain, districts in the county of Kerry, are thus mentioned by O'Heerin:—

"O'Laeghain, a warrior of fame,
We found him over Ui Ferba;
O'Cathnendaigh obtained the land,
Firmly settled under the high hills of Cualan.

"Ui Flannain an extensive land,
A verdant country of delightful streams,
O'Duivdin over this fertile soil,
Rules as its chief and protecting lord."

* These must not be confounded with the great O'Domhnaills or O'Donnells of Tirconnell.—ED.

Keatings *History of Ireland*, (IGF edition), giving O'Donoghue, O'Leyne or Lane, O'Cahill, O'Carroll, O'Connell, O'Shea and Falvey in County Kerry.

xxii

Family History Research

The following sources are given in the British Museum Library according to J. King, earlier in this century. Many will exist in Ireland as well. As follows:

1681, Kerry quit rent, Sir Wm. Petty; 1747, Ardfert const eccles; 1750, Killarney Lakes, Plinius Fertius; ditto, 1750; Jos. Atkinson, ditto, 1751, Rev. Rd. Barton; history of Kerry, 1756, Dr. Chas. Smith; letters from, 1767, Saml. Derrick; Killarney, 1772; John Leslie; 1774, Kerry history, Chas. Smith, new edtn.; Killarney, described, 1776; 1778. works of Hugh Kelly, B.L., Killarney; Killarney, by Danl. Rodk. O'Connor, Kerry, 1780; 1788, Prize of Venus, Robinson; 1790, Killarney; 1793, Denis MacCarthy's petition; 1793, history of Fitz Maurice of Kerry, by Bryan O'Connor, Kerry; 1806. Bibliotheca Lansdowniana, sale catalogue; 1808, Judge Robt. Day, charges to Grand Juries; 1812, Killarney, Pat O'Kelly, 1791; 1814, Annals of Innisfallen. by C. O'Conor, D.D.; 1815, O'Donoghue of Ross, poem by M. J. Sullivan; 1818, the Maid of Killarney, a tale; Killarney, G. N. Wright, 1822; 1822, Mucross Abbey, Catherine Luby; 1825, poems by Agnes Mahony, 1827, C. Otway, sketches; 1828, Killarney, Geo. N. Smith; 1828, Killarney, Charles Hoyle; 1829, Killarney Legends, T. C. Croker, 1831; 1830, Kerry recruit, ballad; 1834, Crown land report; 1834, Ballybunion caves, Wm. Ainsworth; 1837, A. B. Rowan, poems; 1838, Killarney, by Pedestrian; 1839, Killarney, tour to; Killarney, J. Windele, 1839; 1840, Christabel, Mary Downing, poems; 1843, Kerry Pastoral, M. O'Connor, 1719, see v. 1, pp. 12-5; 1844, Jacobite poetry, Edw. Walsh; 1844, O'Sullivan, poem by Visct. Massereene; 1845, Iveragh tales, by Mce. O'Connell; 1845, Kerry tour, by Lydia J. Fisher, 1846, Killarney, D. E. FitzPatrick; 1850, Kerry Eagle ballad; 1850, O'Donoghue's white horse. Panto, T. H. Lacy; 1850, MacCarthy More. drama, Saml. Lover; 1851, Sir Wm. Petty's Down Survey, ed. by T. A. Larcom; 1851, Wm. P. Mulchinock, poems, N.Y.; 1852, Tribes of Ireland, satire by A. O'Daly, ed. by J. O'Donovan; 1852. Tralee Provost, by Wm. Rowan; Killarney lake lore, 1853, A. B. Rowan; 1853, Killarney, by Wykehamist; 1854, Rev. Moore MacIntosh. sermons; 1854-6, Kerry Magazine; 1855, John D'Alton's Jacobite Army list; 1857, Killarney, Jas. Fraser, 1849; 1858, Killarney, N. J. Gannon; 1858, Killarney. Geo. W. Asplen; 1858, Conduct of T.C.D.; 1860, Caher Conri, John Windele; 1861, Rev. A. B. Rowan, memorial, 1800-61; 1862, Book of Lismore, ed. by Sir Jas. MacGregor; 1862, Killarney sketches, by Fitz-Erin, Rev. John F. Day; 1863, Darrynane poems, by Ellen Fitzsimon; 1863, Kerry, Religious. Movement; 1864, Irish Church history, ed. by Rev. Daniel MacCarthy, Bishop of Kerry; 1865, Irish family history, by R. F. Cronnelly; 1865, Killarney, by R. M. Ballyntyne; 1867, Object Teaching by Jas. N. MacElligott; 1868, Royal presents, by Col. Wm. Denny; 1868, Brandon pilgrimage, by Jas. J. Long; 1867, Killarney, John Hudson; 1867, the MacGillycuddy Papers, ed. by Wm. Brady; 1867, Florence MacCarthy Reagh, by D. MacCarthy Glas; 1871, Killarney. John Bradbury; 1871, Thomas Gallwey, poems; 1871, History of Kerry, M. F. Cusack; 1872, St. Brendan, life by Cardinal P. F. Moran; 1872, Killarney; 1872-4, Kerry Records, M. A. Hickson; 1872. Tralee antiquities, A. B. Rowan; 1875, Past Events, Morty MacElligott; 1875-6, life of Wm., 1st Marquis of Lansdowne, by Lord E. FitzMaurice; 1875, Killarney, Rev. W. J. Loftie; 1878, the Geraldines, by Rev. D. O'Daly, ed. by C. P. Meehan; 1878, Killarney, S. C. Hall; 1878, Killarney, by J. P. Atkinson; 1881, Lansdowne estate, by Lord Lansdowne; 1882, Battle of Ventry, K. Meyer; 1884, Ireland, 17th c., M. A. Hickson; 1887. Headley estate, Glenbeigh, Pierse Mahony, M.P.; 1887-93, Franciscan Annals on Kerry history, by Fr. Jarlath; 1888. Juverna, Geraldine tales. by H. D. Spratt; 1889, Two Chiefs of Dunboy, 1750, by J. A. Froude; 1889, poems, essays, Sir Edw. Denny; 1890, St. Brendan's life, ed. Whitley Stokes; 1890, Killarney, Fanny Fisher; 1892, O'Connell, Col. of Irish Brigade, by Mrs. M. A. O'Connell; 1893, O'Sullivans of Ardea, by T. C. Amory; 1893, Brendaniana, by Rev. Denis O'Donoghue; 1895-1900, Anglican Church, Rev. Edw. Denny; 1895, Sir Wm. Petty, by Baron FitzMaurice; 1895, Kerry lakes and fjords, G. S. W. Rly.; 1895, Kerry Fairies, by Jerh. Curtin; 1898, Henry O'Brien on the Round Towers; 1900, Egan O'Rahilly, poems, ed. by Rev. P. S. Dinneen; 1901, Killarney, by B. S. Woolf; 1902, Kingdom of Kerry, by M. P. Ryle; 1903, Irish Bibliography, a subject guide to Irish books, by J. King; 1903, Ireland under Elizabeth, by Philip O'Sullivan Bear, translated by M. J. Byrne; 1905, R. N. W. Mounted Police, Canada, by Capt. Cecil E. Denny; 1906, Rev. David Moriarty, Bishop of Kerry, sermons; 1907, Geo. Sigerson, bards of the Gael and the Gall; 1907, Kerry, by C. P. Crane; 1908, Father O'Flynn, by A. P. Graves; 1909, J. M. O'Sullivan, Old Criticism; 1911, Bligh Talbot Crosbie, poems; 1912, Killarney, Mary Gorges; articles on Kerry in Ency. Brit., Catholic Ency., R.S.A.I.J.L., R.I.A. trans., Ulster J.A., Arch Jl., Ord. Survey letters, Cork A Jl., Kerry A. Jl. in various periodicals, and in Irish and Kerry newspapers; and in this book, Leabar Catair Conroi, King's History of Kerry, 1905-24.

Foundation Aids

For those wishing to further research their Kerry family roots, the Irish Genealogical Foundation offers help with a variety of publications.

Americans need to research in America first, a point sometimes forgotten. Birth certificates and obituary columns sometimes yield the key to success.

The small, but very directly written *Beginners Guide to Irish Family Research* is for those just beginning the search. OLochlainns *Journal of Irish Families* is the Foundations monthly publication, which recieves timely information from all points.

It is through the Foundation and the Irish Family Journal that this work has been published. A sincere thank you goes out to all Foundation members once again, for your continued support.

There are also substantial collections of records in the National Library of Ireland in Dublin on the following families in Kerry: Knights of Kerry; McGillycuddy of the Reeks; O'Connell of Derryane Abbey; Rowan of Bayview, Tralee; Sandes of Greenville, Listowel; and Talbot-Crosbie of Ardfert Abbey.

The County Library at Tralee holds information on many Kerry families as well. (see also sources listed in Bibliography at the end of this work).

This work dedicated in memory of
Jim Donaghue
still working from the other side.

©1994. IGF. Families of Co. Kerry, Ireland - Box 7575, K.C., MO. 64116

Families of County Kerry, Ireland

Listed in alphabetical order.
Mc, Mac and O' names are alphabetized
by the first letter after the Mc, Mac or O'.
(i.e. O'Connell is sorted as Connell etc...)

Some random listings of names and
locations have been taken from the 1901
census or the works of J. King.

In Muckross Abbey this epitaph was carved on the tomb marked as holding the descendants of Mac Carthy Mor and O'Donoghue Mor (and O'Donoghue Glenflesk) pictured below:

"What more could Homer's most illustrious verse,
Or pompous Tully's stately prose rehearse,
Than what this monumental stone contains
In death's embrace, Mac Carthy Mor's remains.
Hence reader, learn the sad and certain fate
That waits on man spares not the good or great;
And while this venerable marble calls
Thy patriot tear, perhaps, that trickling falls;
And bids thy thoughts to other days return,
And with a spark of Erin's glory burn;
While to her fame most grateful tributes flow,
Oh! ere you turn, one warmer drop bestow!
If Erin's chiefs deserve thy generous tear,
Heir of their worth, O'Donoghue lies here."

Note: the above ground tomb shown displayed the O'Donoghue arms, carved into the vase visable here on the end of the tomb. The carving now much erased from time and exposure is not fully legible. MacCarthy was given as the tomb beneath the above ground casket shown

Adams

A settler family, given on estates near Tralee, from the coming of the Elizabethan undertakers to the rebellion of 1641. Descent: Herts, Essex, Devon, Cornwall, Berks, Wales, etc.. Victor Adams resided in Tralee in 1908.

Of Adams and Mac Adaim, J. King gives one Francis Adams in 1611 as among the first Burgess of the town of Tralee; Johanna of Dingle; Thos. of Kilfarnogue; Victor of Castle Street, Tralee and one Wm. who wrote poems on Killarney in 1870.

Ahern

The Ahern family, given as descended from O'Eactigeirn, the brother of Brian Boru, who was the chief of Hy Cearnaidh, near Mitchelstown, as given by J. King who found 61 householders of the name in Kerry in his day.

Ainsworth

W. Ainsworth was the author of the Geology of Ballybunion Cliffs, 1834.

Aldwell

The Aldwell family of Kenmare. John Aldwell of Co. Cork had a son Morgan whose son was Basil of Gorthagas, who had Richard, Morgan, Basil, John, Samuel, Rachel, Dorcas and Mary.

Aldworth Aylworth

Sir Richard Aldworth, taken from Aylworth in Berkshire, was provost marshall of Munster in 1613, and was granted lands at Newmarket, Co. Cork in 1621. There were 7 householders of the name in Kerry at the turn of the century.

Allen Allan Mac-Ailin

Given as Mac Allen, from the Campbell Clan of Erin and Scotia, with some 13 households of the name near the turn of the century in Kerry, when the spelling of Allen was predominant.

Nora MacAllen of Ballymullen and Mary MacAllen of Moneyflugh, are both given in Co. Kerry.

Mac Allister

Wm. MacAllister of Boherbee, Co. Kerry.

Allman

A family name of 15 households in Co. Kerry at the turn of the century, including: John D., John J., and Timothy of Rockfield, Johanna of Ardmeelode; Rev. Michael of Boulenshare; Thomas of Rathoneen; Kate of Barrow; Thomas of Knockenagh; Pat. of KeelaCloghane; Timothy of Curraheen; John and James of Curravough; and John and Daniel of Caheranne Road.

Alton

Given as the name of a settler family in Kerry, subsequent to the 1641-42 rebellion. Homeland: Of Derby.

In 1831 William Alton, M.D., lived in Tralee. Thomas and Joyce Alton are found of Tralee in 1779 and had two daughters.

Ambrose Ambros

Daniel of Trieneragh Annagh or Annaghten Ambrose, near Blennerville was granted to Sir. E. Denny in 1584. William Ambrose, vintner, was outlawed as a Jacobite in Dublin in 1689. Miss Ambrose was the Catholic belle of Dublin Castle; and Lord Chesterfield said she was the only dangerous Papist he had seen in Ireland.

Ames

The name of a Cromwellian settler granted lands in 1667 in Co. Kerry.

Amory

Given as the name of a settler family in Kerry, subsequent to the 1641-42 rebellion. Descent/ homeland:

Of Devon. Thomas Amory. The only son of Thomas Amory (one of the victualers of the navy in 1656 under Sir Dennis Gander), who married Elizabeth Fitzmaurice, dau. of the ninth Lord of Kerry. The latter Thomas was member for Dingle in the Parliament, and died in 1667, leaving an only son, a Commissioner, who was styled 'of Bunratty', and his daughter married Richard Hart, of Grange Br., Limerick.

In 1666 the first mentioned Thomas Amory was granted Ballyboneene, Knockenagh, Gloury, Culeard, Inshy Carvenknock, Shrone, Clounmeteene, Balahidoeig, Dramanny, Carrowmanagh and Carrowneightragh, mostly in Galey parish in Iraghticonnor.

T. C. Amory in 1893 wrote a history of John O'Sullivan, who fired the first shot in the American War of Independence. (See Kings 'History of the Sullivans in Kerry'.)

Anderson

(Given in Kings work as from Mac Aindrui) We find Andrew of Ardfert; Mary of Killowen; and Richard of Derryvorraig near the turn of the century.

Andrews

(Given in Kings work as from Mac Aindrui) We find one Cyril Andrews of Spunkane.

Anglesey

Arthur, Earl of Anglesey in 1686 was granted Inchy, Inch, in Corcaguiny, 1038 acres profitable and 624 acres unprofitable land.

Also given as the name of a Cromwellian settler granted lands in 1667 in Co. Kerry.

Angove

We find one William Angove of Spunkane, Co. Kerry.

Annesley

Edward Annesley was granted confiscated lands in 1653; Sir Francis Annesley, 1620, Secretary for Ireland, became Viscount Valentia in 1622 after Sir Henry Power died without issue; and subsequently made Baron Mountmorris.

Anthony

Louis Anthony of High Street, Killarney, Co. Kerry.

Appleyard

John Appleyard, in 1562 proposed to plant and inhabit at Baltimore for the fishing traffic, having a letter supporting such from Donyll M'Arti More to the Queen on June 30th.

Archer

Margt. and Timothy Archer of Cloonaneela, Co. Kerry.

Armstrong

Thomas Armstrong of Listowel and Margaret of Ballinskelligs.

Arnes

A settler family on estates near Tralee, from the coming of the Elizabethan undertakers to the rebellion of 1641. Originally from Cornwall.

Arnold

A settler family, given on estates near Tralee, from the coming of the Elizabethan undertakers to the rebellion of 1641. Descent / homeland: Herts, Essex, Devon, S. Wales. Thomas Arnold of Tralee was killed at Ballinskelligs in 1641.

Mac Arthur Arthur

Philip of Derrynacaheragh; Patrick of Henry Street.

Ashe (Ais Atasac Agas)
Some 49 Ashe families were in Kerry. Thomas Ashe, 1885 - 1917, was educated at Lispole school and at the De La Salle college in Waterford. He became school teacher at Kilduff, Co. Dublin, founded the Black Ravens Pipers' Club, came to the USA on behalf of the Gaelic League, and then was imprisoned shortly after the 1916 rising. He was buried at Glasnevin.

Ashwood
A settler family, given on estates near Tralee, from the coming of the Elizabethan undertakers to the rebellion of 1641.

Atkins
The name of a Cromwellian settler granted lands in 1667 in Co. Kerry.

Mac Auliffe
There were 45 MacAuliffe families given in Co. Kerry. In 1656 Mac Amhlaoibh of Duhallow was confiscated, and the lands of the clan were granted to Aldworth.

Austin
(Mac Aihistin) Daniel Austin of Annagap, Co. Kerry.

Also given as the name of a Cromwellian settler granted lands in 1667 in Co. Kerry.

Averill
John Averill was Protestant Bishop in 1770.

Avery
John Avery of Ballinskelligs, Kerry.

Aylward
James Aylward of Boherbee, Co. Kerry

Babbage
Alfred Babbage of Farranreagh, Kerry.

Babington
The name of a settler family in Kerry, subsequent to the 1641-42 rebellion. Descent/ homeland:
Of Notts. Cromwellian. Uriah Babington was a native of Cork, who had a son William who died, and 5 daughters who came to hold the lands of their father and uncles Pierce and William Babington, and carried it into the Sealy, Leslie, Meredith, Supple and Scott (of Cahircon) families.

Wm. Babington was the owner of Maglass which passed to his niece Alice, daughter of Uriah Babington. Pierce Babington of Dromartin died unmarried as did the aforementioned Wm. Babington. The three brothers, Uriah, William and Pierce Babington were all natives of Cork. As the only son of the first died unmarried, and the latter two died unmarried, this line died out in Kerry, but other branches may remain on in Co. Cork.

Bailey Baily Baille
(O'Bealaigh = large lipped? from Breasal bealach, or large lipped, was the second Christian king of Leinster or so interpreted by J. King). There were 14 householders named Bailey in Kerry, including James of Ballybrannagh, Denis and Robt. of Mweelinroe, Pat of Rathanny, Michael and Bridget of Mullen, John of the Mall, Jas. of John Street, Tim of Cloonbeg, Margaret of Oakview Tce., Thos. of Castlegregory, James of Gray's Lane, John of Tralee, John of Tonevane.

William G. Bailey lived at Tobermang in 1821.

Bainley
James Bainley of Ballyhorgan is found in 1821, but I have found no other trace of the name, which is not surprising as J. King stated that the name had died out in Kerry.

Baker Baicer
There were 16 Baker households in Co. Kerry, including Pat, Pat John, Pat Michael of Caherdorgan, Pat of Ballinana, Mary of Ballyheabought, William of Ballinlohig, Ellen of Spa road, Oliver of Fenit without, Michael of Derrymore West, Ellen of Gallerus, John of Goat Street, Thos. of Main Street, John of Burnham West, Pat of Ballinbooly, Albert of Spunkane, and Albert of Cappamore.

Baldwin
Timothy Baldwin of Rock Street, Tralee.

Ball
The Rev. Nicholas Ball in 1405 was appointed to Ardfert see, but eventually got Emly see instead. We find George Ball of Killorglin in 1821.

Also the name of a Cromwellian settler granted lands in 1667 in Co. Kerry.

Ballard
Richard Ballard of Pembroke Street in Tralee.

Bambury
Eight families of the name are recorded in Kings day, those of Mary, Michael and John of Tullahinnell; George and John of Ballyline; Thomas of Coolnagraigue; Michael of Ballymacassy; and Daniel of Cloonamon.

Bannion
John Bannion of Strand Street.

Barden O'Burdain
Robert Barden of Tralee and Alice his wife had a daughter Mary, baptized 17. 12. 1784. One Michael Burden is found in 1908 of Green Lane.

Barham
A settler family, given on estates near Tralee, from the coming of the Elizabethan undertakers to the rebellion of 1641. Homeland:
Kent, Suffolk. Arthur Barham was killed at Ballinskelligs in 1641.

Barkey
Michael Barkey of Ardnamweely.

Barnard
Thomas Barnard, Prot., bp., 1794.

Barnes
Barnes of Nelson Street in Tralee.

Barrett Bariod Baireid
Barrett was the name of an Anglo Norman Lord of Tirawley in 1440 with branches in Munster and 73 families of the name are given in J. Kings day.

Also given as a settler family, given on estates near Tralee, from the coming of the Elizabethan undertakers to the rebellion of 1641. Descent / homeland: Norfolk, Suffolk. Edward Barrett, yeoman, was shot during the siege of Tralee in 1641. There were several of the name in Tralee in 1908.

Barron
Patrick Barron of Ardoughter.

Barrow
The name of a Cromwellian settler granted lands in 1667 in Co. Kerry.

Barry, de Barra
The name of an Anglo-Norman family in Cork in 1208, Baron of Olethann, viscount of Buttevant, Earl of Barrymore. Some 84 families of the name are given by King. Among those, in 1776 Edw. and John resided at Killarney; in 1821 David and Garrett at Woodpark; in 1876 Col. Jas. owned 740 acres in Kerry and John of Caherciveen 1964 acres; Lt. Col. David died at Killarney in 1819, he was Major in the Irish Brigades.

Bartholomews
W. L. Barholomews of Ballybunion.

Bartlett
Charles Bartlett of Cromane Lower.

Bartley
The Rev. J. R. Bartley of Muing.

Barton, de Bartun
A settler family, given on estates near Tralee, from the coming of the Elizabethan undertakers to the rebellion of 1641. Descent / homeland: Devon.

16 families are given in Kings day, including Denis and Denis Thomas of Bushmount; Thos. of Knocknakilla, Daniel and John and Patrick of Ballyarkane, Patrick of Strand Street, Patrick and Denis of Gortaleen, Daniel of Clogherbrien; Daniel of Ballintarmon; Sara of Laghtacallow; Patrick of Ballinakilla; Thomas of Coolnaharigill, John of Droum, Thomas of Letter; R. Barton wrote on Loch Lene in 1751. Rev. Patrick Barton, P.P., Ardfert, 1924. Patrick Barton of Tralee in 1908.

Bass
Arthur Bass of Tralee, 1923, trading as Benson, Bass, and Slattery.

Bastable, de Bastabla
Four families are given in Co. Kerry by King, those of Thomas of Nohoval, Mary of Bawnluskoha, Johanna of Direen; Julia of Park Street; Arthur of Molahiff castle, 1770-80, had a daughter Eliza, who m. John Twiss of Ballyhanorough.

George of Ardcrone is found in 1750.

The Protestant settlers, the Herberts were buried in a tomb there, and also the Bastables in another. (The church of Currans, Ardcrone, Co. Kerry.)

Batchelor
William Batchelor of Tinnahally.

Bateman
A settler family in Kerry, subsequent to the 1641-42 rebellion. Descent/homeland: Of Norf., Suff., Essex. A Cromwellian family.

Rowland Bateman, first settler of his name in Kerry was a Cromwellian officer, custom collector at Tralee, and high sheriff in 1669. John Bateman, minister of Okenham, was first on a list of subscribers who sent money to support the quelling of the Irish rebellion of 1641-49. His son, John, also a Commissioner, is of the family of the name at Dromultin in North Kerry, and at Altavilla in Co. Limerick. In 1697 Rowland Bateman leased on favorable terms parts of his estate between Loghercannon and Strand-street, to James Yielding, and old people, thirty years ago, used to describe the handsome holdings that the Yieldings had there.

In the list of Grand Jurors for 1679 the name of 'Rowland Bateman de Traly' is given. The family may have moved to Oak Park when the lease was given to James Yielding.

In 1758 Col. Rowland Bateman, M.P., of Oak Park (Killeene 1 mile NE of Tralee), married Letitia Denny. In 1831 Wm. Bateman lived at Oak Park.

Oakpark (1846), was the Bateman residence since 1697. Collis Sandes lived there, in Tralee parish.

Lohercannon (1846), Tralee parish, was the Yielding residence since 1697, leased from Bateman of Oak Park.

Rowland Bateman, son of the Rev. Rowland of Kilcaragh, m. 1870 Eliz, dau. of Edward Day Stokes, and d. 1881, leaving issue a son Rowland, who married Marion Mac Adam of the U.S.A. In 1876 John Bateman of Dublin owned 2,406 acres in Kerry and Rowland of Tralee 1,259 acres.

Bayley, Bailey

A settler family on estates near Tralee, from the coming of the Elizabethan undertakers to the rebellion of 1641.

Jeffrey Bayley, merchant, was shot during the siege of Tralee in 1641. J., J. and T. Bailey are in Tralee in 1908.

Bean

James Bean of Ballyhemikan.

Bear

James Bear of Waterville.

Beasley Beaslai Beasly

Eight Beasley families are given in Kerry, including those of John of Scrahanfadda; James of Ballyrehan; Martin of Kilconly; Rev. James of Duagh d. 1924; Michael of Killehanny; James of Ballybunion; Anne of Charles Street; John of Carhoolbeg.

Beckford

A settler family on estates near Tralee, from the coming of the Elizabethan undertakers to the rebellion of 1641.

Begley, Begly

Some 37 families of the name were found in Co. Kerry.

Behan, O'Beacain, of Leix

Some 15 families of the name are given in Kerry, by King, and he gave the names of Behan and O'Beacain of Leix (Queens County), as one in the same.

Beirne, O'Beirne

Martin of Laccabane and Catherine of Main Street are listed in 'Co. Kerry, Past and Present' by J. King. This family is given as Beirne, or O'Beirne of Tir Briuin na Siuna in that source.

Bell

Five Bell families are given in Co. Kerry: Ellen of Knockaderry; Francis of Ballinagrown; Robert of Aunascaul; Rd. of Droumloughane; and Catherine of Pound Lane.

Benn

William Benn is given of Quay Street.

Benner

Of five Benner families given were John of Scrahane, James of Ballymullen, John of Castle Street in Tralee, Georgina of Dingle and Rowland of Croompanereekard.

Paul Benner, of Bally MacElligott, a Palatine, d. 1760 aged 78 leaving two sons Henry and John who married to sisters named Delmege. Henry had 3 sons, Adam, Samuel and Henry. Samuel had four sons; John, Robert, William and Arthur. He was postmaster and kept the Blennerhassett Arms Hotel in Tralee, being succeeded by his son Robert who had two sons, Samuel who was a solicitor in Dublin, and William who had four sons: Robert, John S., William G., and James Arthur. Of whom Robert m. Georgina Revington of Dingle; John S. was of the Blennerhassett arms in Tralee; William G. was the president of the Illinois Automobile Co. of Chicago; and John Henry d. 1910, aged 69 at Pongakawa, in New Zealand, leaving issue there.

One of the above lines had a brewery at Ballymullen in 1828. In 1798 on Nov. 28 it is given that Thomas and Eliza, twins of Mary and David Benner were baptized in Tralee and in 1792 Grace, dau. of Eliza and Thomas Benner, and in 1798 William, son of Anne and Samuel Benner. Also in 1798 Henry Benner of Bally MacElligott married Anne Stephens of Ballyseedy.

By 1828 Benner and Ferguson's Brewery at Ballymullen was for sale, and it is noted that by 1846 the temperance crusade had closed many such concerns.

In 1846 Arthur Blenner was an attorney in Tralee; Henry a coal merchant; Robert a Hotel Keeper; Thomas a deputy clerk of the peace; and Sarah, an ironmonger.

Bennett

Of families given in Kerry there was Kate of Inch, Thomas of the Square, William of Ardfert, John of Ballybunion, David of Killarney Road and Castlequin, and Bank and Main street, Thomas A. of Waterville, and Julia of Pound Lane.

Benson

A settler family, given on estates near Tralee, from the coming of the Elizabethan undertakers to the rebellion of 1641. Descent / homeland:

Of Essex, Cumb., Westmoreland. John Benson is found in Tralee in 1908.

Also given as the name of a settler family in Kerry, subsequent to the 1641-42 rebellion.

In 1772 Isaac, son of Enoch and Margaret was baptized in Tralee; and Mary, daughter of Francis and Honora was baptized on Dec. 17, 1787.

In more recent times we find John Benson of Castle Street in Tralee.

Bently

The Rev. Wm. Bently of Kilmanihan.

Bergin, O'Beirgin

Thomas Bergin of Ballyhar, and it was also noted that Denis J. Bergin published Christmas almanacs in Boston, U.S.A..

Bland of Derriquin Castle, Co. Kerry
From The Irish Book of Arms. (IGF) 1988.

Bernard, Barnard

A settler family on estates near Tralee, from the coming of the Elizabethan undertakers to the rebellion of 1641. Descent / homeland:

Bedford, Northants, Essex, Barnards in Norfolk. Bernards were related to Carews, Barretts, Darcys of Tolshun(_) D., and to Mildmays. Isaac Bernard is given in 1908. Faha, in Kilbonane parish, was the seat of Morrogh Bernard.

The Morrogh Bernard family of Fahagh was a joining of the Morrogh family of Cork with the Bernards of Ballynagare, Kerry, in 1816, by the marriage of Edward Morogh to Martha Bernard. Their son John took the name of Morrogh Bernard and died in 1866. His son was E. J. Bernard.

Also given as the name of a settler family in Kerry, subsequent to the 1641-42 rebellion.

Four families of the name in Kerry are given as those of Bertram Morrogh of Faha; Morrogh Edward of Killarney; Mary of Tooreenastooka; and Isaac of Moyderwell.

Bernard of Tralee

Epaphroditus Bernard is found holding lands of Sir Edward Denny in or near Tralee in the year 1639-'40. It is thought that this Bernard was one of a new group of tenants from Britain. In England the Bernard name is found in Northamptonshire and Essex. Those of the latter are connected to the Carews, the Mildmays, and the Darcys of Tolshunt Darcy, who were in turn related to or connected with the Denny family.

John, son of Joseph Bernard, gent., of Tralee is mentioned in a lease (of Garrane) by Edward Denny in 1726. John Bernard was a freeholder of those lands in 1744. John Bernard held those lands of Garrane in 1750, while at the age of 60. He also held a marble quarry

Bernard (cont'd.)

under a lease from Sir Thomas Denny, for the lives of himself, his son Richard aged 21 and his son John aged 19.

John Bernard of Ballynegar, Esq., is given in a list of resident Justices of the Peace of Co. Kerry in 1785. In 1816 Martha Bernard of Ballynegar, Co. Kerry, married Edward Morrogh of Co. Cork and had a son John who took the name of Morrogh-Bernard. Robert Bernard, perhaps son of John, was of Tralee Parish in 1787, who died around 1804, was married to Alicia Jeffcott. Of this line is William Bernard who died in 1828 and was buried at Tallaght, Co. Dublin. Others of this line are found in Dublin as well.

Berry

A settler family, given on estates near Tralee, from the coming of the Elizabethan undertakers to the rebellion of 1641. Descent / homeland:

Of Devon, Cornwall. (see also Barry)

Best

A settler family, given on estates near Tralee, from the coming of the Elizabethan undertakers to the rebellion of 1641. Descent / homeland:

Of Kent, Cornwall. Arthur Best lived in Tralee in 1622.

Bigg

The name of a Cromwellian settler granted lands in 1667 in Co. Kerry.

Binane

Pat Binane of Cloghanesheskeen.

Bingham

Chas. Bingham of Ballybunion and William Bingham of Boherbee.

Birmingham, Ferris

David of Bishops Lane, Co. Kerry.

Mac Birney

John MacBirney of Staughton's row is given in Co. Kerry.

Blacker

J. T. Blacker of Armagh owned 8159 acres in Kerry in 1876.

Blackwood

Sir Henry Blackwood in 1876 owned 1,940 acres in Kerry. Sir Francis Blackwood is given in 1906.

Blake, de Blaca

William Blake of Spunkane.

Bland

The Rev. James Bland of Sedburgh in Yorkshire, was chaplain to Lord Deputy Sidney in 1692 and m. Lucy, daughter of Sir Francis Brewster who was Lord Mayor of Dublin in 1674, he resided at Killarney in 1717, and was dean of Ardfert. He had two sons, Rev. Francis and Judge Nathaniel; his son Francis, his grandson James and his great-grandson Francis were vicars of Killarney.

The 1821 list gives James, J.F., Rev. Thomas, Francis, Nathaniel Bland of Killarney; Chris. and Jas. F. of Derryquin; and Arthur of St. Annes.

Three Bland families are given in more modern times, those of Ellen of Henn street in Killarney; James of Drimnabeg and Josephina of Drimnabeg.

Derriquin Castle, for generations the seat of the Bland family; passed to the property of Colonel Warden.

Blennerhassett of Ballyseedy
Extract From The Irish Book of Arms.

Blennerhassett

The manuscript pedigree of the family, 1580-1736, was owned by the Hurley family of Fenit, and it showed the intermarriages among the various Munster families of the day. It closed with the rhyme: 'Show me the country, place, or spot of the ground, Where the 'Hassetts or their allies are not found.'

This is the name of settler families on estates near Tralee, both before and after the rebellion of 1641. (Homeland: Cumberland, Norfolk, Herts.) Thomas Blennerhassett and his son Robert, of Flimby, Cumberland, settled in Kerry after the Geraldine confiscations. Sir Edward Denny granted in 1611-1628, lands about Tralee, namely Ballycham, Ballycarter, Killroan, Knockomane, Ballychamallick, Carrignafeely, Ballyshiddy (Ballyseedy etc), Ballymacthomas, ... Robert was M.P. for Tralee in 1613. His son, John, was High Sheriff, 1641. His son John was M.P. for Kerry in 1658. His son, John was M.P. for Tralee in 1709. His son, John, was High Sheriff in 1740. His cousin, William, was Sheriff in 1761. His son, John was M.P. in 1794. His brother Arthur was Sheriff in 1821. His son, Arthur, was Sheriff in 1821 (?). His second son, Charles, was Sheriff in 1858, and his son Arthur Blennerhassett.

In 1634 Robert Blennerhassett of Killorglin was M.P. for Tralee. In 1692 John Blennerhassett was was M.P. for Tralee and his son and grandson were also members. The Killorglin and Ballyseedy branches of the family were leading people in Co. Kerry, 1692-1792, with the Crosbies & Dennys.

Harman Blennerhassett became a republican in France and sold the Castle Conway estates to Lord Ventry, in 1798, when he settled in America. He was a friend of Thomas Addis Emmet in New York, being related through the Masons of Ballydowney, mother of Robert Emmett.

The seventh Baron Grey de Ruthyen and fourth Earl of Kent, m. Anne, dau. of John B'hassett. Thomas B'hassett witnessed the will of Henry Denny of Waltham, in 1573. Both of Henry Denny's wives were Greys. The town of Tralee was incorporated in 1612, and its charter named Robert Blennerhassett, as among the first provost and burgesses.

John B'hassett resided at Ballyseedy House in 1756 and that remained the family residence in 1846. Elm Grove was the seat of William Blennerhassett in 1756. (Ballyseedy parish).

Killorglin Castle and Manor reverted to the Fitzgeralds from the Knights Templars. It was then granted to Capt. Conway, and later bought by the Mullins from the B'hassetts. Florence MacCartie More had the castle burned around 1600, fearing that Sir Charles Wilmot would settle there. John H. B'hassett lived at Ardmoniel Cottage (1846) in 1821. (Killorglin parish).

Twenty families of the name are listed by King, including Arthur of Ballyseedy, Arthur and Thomas of Glanageenty, Wm. of Cragganoona, Thomas of Cullenymore, Wm. of Cullenybeg, Richard of Urrohogal, Jas. of Kilnanare, Geo. of Nelson St., Arthur of the Terrace, Cherry of Gortbrack, Arthur of Ballyard, Thos. of Skahanaugh, R. P. of Kells, Arthur of Tralee, Thos. W. and James and Arthur and Thomas of Gortatlea, and Thomas of Barakilla. Geo. and A. B'hassett in Tralee 1908.

Robert, M.P. for Tralee in 1634, was ancestor of the Blennerville and Kells branches of the family. Sir Rowland's son, Rowland, had a son Richard, whose son was Rowland Ponsonby, of Kells,

Blennerhassett
who was the Home Rule M.P. for Tralee in 1872. Some 14 families of the name are given as living in 1831 in the works of J. King, including those of Ballyseedy, Churchtown, Blennerville, Tralee, Killiny & Killorglin.

Bloomer
Thomas Bloomer of Dromore.

Blount
Ernest Blount of Spunkane.

Blundell
William Blundell of Church Street.

Blythe, de Blagd
Robert Blythe of Lr. Castle St., Tralee.

Boake
Francis Boake of Avenue, Killarney.

Boland, O'Beoilain
16 Boland families are given: John of Farranstack, Daniel of Lyre, Thomas of Listowel, John of Ballinleague, Mce. of Coumaleague, John, Lce., and Denis of Fahan, Patrick of Glenfahan, Michael and Ml. W. of Kilvickadowning, John of Vicarstown, John of Doorah, Mary of Fahamore, John of Holyground, John of Goat St.. O'Beoilain of Co. Clare is noted as one origin of the name.

Bolster
4 Bolster families in Kerry are given as John of Garryard; Elizabeth of Oakview; George of Oakview Terrace; and Richard of Rock Street.

Bolton, de Bolltun
Thomas Bolton of Ballyea is given.

Bona
James Bona of Waterville is given.

Bonguelimi
Margaret Bonguelimi of Moanmore, Co. Kerry.

Bonham
John Bonham of Strand Street is given.

Bonney
One John Bonney, of Causeway, was Inspector of Police in London, d. 1924.

Bordell
A settler family, on estates near Tralee, from the coming of the Elizabethan undertakers to the rebellion of 1641.

Boreham
A settler family, given on estates near Tralee, from the coming of the Elizabethan undertakers to the rebellion of 1641. Descent / homeland: Devon.

Boreman
Given as the name of a settler family in Kerry, subsequent to the 1641-42 rebellion.

Bothwick
Robert Bothwick of Burnham is given.

Bouldger, Bolger
Lieut. Bouldger, who died in Clohane in 1640, and was interred in Tralee parish church, leaving no known issue.

Bounce
John Bounce of Clounmackon, Kerry.

Boursin
Amadee Boursin of Nelson street, Tralee, dentist is given, d. 1924.

Bovenizer
Michl. of Carhoona, and Peter of Nelson St., Co. Kerry.

Bowen, de Botun
Robert Bowen of Gortagass; Robt. of Kenmare owned 835 acres in 1876.

Bower, Mac Cullagh
Five Bower families given in Co. Kerry, viz: Daniel Bower of Banna, Edw. of Green lane, Edw. of Chute's lane; Patrick of Cronin's lane; and John Bowers of Dromore.

Bowers and Mac Cullagh are given alongside Bower as a variant spellings.

Bowler, alias Fuller

Probably from Maurice Fitzmaurice le Faigheler, coroner of Kerry in reign of Edw. II. Taken not from fulling or bowlmaking, but from netting hawks or falcons, tassels fulle, rendered yearly as tribute to King John by John Fitz Nicholas Geraldin; compare Ferriter. There were 59 families of the Bowler name given in the works of King, amounting to a substantial population for a family name here.

Bowles

Capt. Henry Bowles of Mounthawk, son of Capt. Hy., and heir of Maj. Gen. Bowles, C. in Chief, Bombay, m. Eliz. Stokes.

Boyd

3 Boyd families are given in Kerry: Allan of Fair Hill, Catherine of Moyderwell, and Catherine of Quay St..

Boylan

Richard Boylan of Flemings lane is given in Co. Kerry. It is noted that O'Baoigeallain was chief of Oriel.

Boyle

Some of the name here are descended from the Irish Chiefs of Boylagh in Co. Donegal. Given with 38 families of the name in Kerry.

Also known as a settler family, given on estates near Tralee, from the coming of the Elizabethan undertakers to the rebellion of 1641. Descent / homeland: Of Kent. Probably related to the Earl of Cork. Some of the name are found in Tralee in 1908.

Richard Boyle, Earl of Cork purchased the barony of Corkaguiney in Kerry from the Undertakers and was a student at the Middle Temple in London, going to Ireland in 1588 with £27 and his rapier and dagger, in 1616 was Lord Boyle and in 1620 was Earl of Cork, in 1629 was Lord Justice of Ireland, and in 1631 Lord High Treasurer, he died in 1633, aged 77.

Brackleyer, De Brackleyer

In 1254 Walter De Brackleyer was king's officer in Kerry.

Bradford

Thomas of Ranaleen, and John of Ballybeg, Co. Kerry, are given.

Bradley, Bradly

12 Bradley families are given in Kerry, viz: Jerh. and Ml. and Jerh. of Tooreengarriv; Daniel of Ballinahulla; Tim and Pat of Carker; Thomas of Coom; Pat of Ballybeg; John of Clover's Lane, Pat of Nelson Street, William of Farranahow; Jas. and Julia Kinneigh; Mary of Dromid; Wm. of Laharn, Ellen of Baslickane, John of Ballymacelligot, Francis Bradley of Knockrour m. Mary, only daughter of Rd. Twiss of Killeentierna and first of the name in Kerry.

Bradshaw

Given as the name of a settler family in Kerry, subsequent to the 1641-42 rebellion. Descent/ homeland: Of Northants.

William Bradshaw of Sackville, Co. Kerry, agent for the Crosbie estate.

Brady

Four families of the name are given in Kerry, William of Pound Row, John of Moyeightragh, Mary of Moherbee, and Pat of Blennerville.

Bramstone

A settler family, given on estates near Tralee, from the coming of the Elizabethan undertakers to the rebellion of 1641. Descent / homeland: Of Essex.

The town of Tralee was incorporated in 1612, and its charter named Thomas Bramstone, as among the first provost and burgesses.

(Thomas and John Bramstone were burgesses of Tralee in 1611 according to the works of J. King.)

Brandon, Lord

Gheramine (1846), (in the parish of Killarney) was Lord Brandon's Cottage.

Brandon, Mac Breandain

Some 14 families are given in Kerry, including those of Mac Brandon, burgess, who had a castle in Tralee in 1588, and was killed in that war.

Brassill, Brassel

17 Brassill Families are given, viz; Thomas, John and Tim of Lislaughtin, Thomas of Coolnagraigue, John of Ballylongford, Denis of Fortwilliam, Pat and Mrs. Tim, and Pat of Tarmons, Matt of Pulleen, Michl. and Wm. of Rahealy, William of Gortnaminch, David of Aughrim, John of Beheens, Dan. of Kilelton, and Mary of Garrynagore.

An older form of the name was given to be O'Breasail.

Breen

A healthy contingent of 126 families are given in Kerry according to the works of King, who gives O'Braoin and Mac Braoin as earlier forms of the name.

Bremmer

Jas. Bremmer from Scotland was steward to the Knight of Kerry and tenant at Kilbeg in 1886.

John D. Bremmer of Kilbeg is given in more modern times.

Brennan

Maurice Brennan lived at Coolbane in Kilcredane parish in 1821. Some 85 families of the name are given in Co. Kerry according to J. King.

O'Brennan parish noted (1846).

Brett, de Britt

Given as the name of a settler family in Kerry, subsequent to the 1641-42 rebellion. Descent/ homeland: Of Northants, Sussex, Cornw., Devon, Kent. The name of a Cromwellian who had a grant of Ballybeggan in 1668.

Separately, Mary Brett or de Britt, of Cork, is given in Co. Kerry, in Kings, 'Co. Kerry, Past and Present'.

Brew

Thos. S. Brew of Littor, son of Wm. of Kilrush, d. 1911, aged 71.

O'Broder

Brewer
Michael and John Brewer of Callahaniska; and Johanna of Old Road are given in Co. Kerry.

Brewster
Ballymalis Castle of Kilbonane parish, a Ferris stronghold confiscated in 1677, was granted to Sir Francis Brewster, who gave it to Alexander Eagar.

One James Brewster of Strand Street is given in Co. Kerry. Brewsterfield was a baile in Killaha, granted to an undertaker by the name of Brewster.

Brick
31 Brick families are given in Kerry.

Mac Bride
John MacBride of Moyeightragh, Kerry.

Bridges
John Bridges of Doonard is given.

Brien, O'Brien, Bryan
A numerous name of Co. Kerry, and in all of Ireland, some 209 families of the name are given. Henry O'Brien (1808-1835), wrote on the Round Towers, and was buried in Hanwell. John B. O'Brien and his son, were colonels in the Austrian army. The spellings of Brien, O'Brien and O'Briain were given. Today of course, we may add many other spellings, of the most popular name, such as O'Brian and O'Bryan etc..

Broadhurst
Wm. Broadhurst of Spunkane is given.

Broder
There were 36 Broder families given in Co. Kerry. 'Broder.' is likely not the shortened form of Broderick, but we must assume they stem originally from the old Irish surname of Bruadar. It is interesting to note that Bruadar was anglicised into the English name of Broderick. If shortened back into Broder, it would more closely resemble the original gaelic.

Broderick, O'Bruadair
Some 25 Broderick families are given in Co. Kerry by King. It is given that families of O'Bruadair (Broder) are on record as adopting the surname of Broderick, in the English fashion. Hence, many O'Bruadair families are found today as Broderick.

Also given is the Broderick family name of the Viscount Midleton; Rev. Alan, b.1840 rector of Alverstoke 1901; George Charles son 7th Viscount who was warden of Merton College, Oxford, 1881; William, son 8th Viscount, secretary for War 1900.

Brooke
A settler family on estates near Tralee, from the coming of the Elizabethan undertakers to the rebellion of 1641. Descent / homeland: Essex. Robert Brooke of Carrignafeely was killed at Ballinskelligs in 1641.

Brookes Brooks
Brookes is the name of a settler family, on estates near Tralee, from the coming of the Elizabethan undertakers to the rebellion of 1641.

John Brooks of New street, Samuel of Coolclogher, Edward of Main street, and Robert of Spunkane, all of Co. Kerry.

No distinction is to be made between the spellings of Brooks and Brookes in modern times, as they represent the very same family in many instances.

Brosnan Brosnahan
A popular family name in Kerry, as evidenced by some 264 families given.

Brown Browne

The Anglo-Norman family of Brown or Broun were settled at Brown's castle in Killury, and at Camus in Limerick, from 1200 to 1584. Sir Reginald was sheriff, and Sir Gilbert guardian of Traly in the 13th c.. John Brown was warden of Awney in 1580. Thos. Browne in 1640 held Anye hospital and Ratow, Kiltome, Mynarue and Dingle lands. Joan,, dau. of Annabella Browne, m. Richard Boyle, 1st Earl of Cork, and was the foundation of his fortunes in Ireland.

Crioch Browne is marked on the Eliz. maps of Kerry. George Brown of Camus was a Count and Field Marshal of Russia, and died Governor of Riga in 1792. Ulysses and George Browne of Camas, brothers, were officers in the Austrian army, and Counts of the Holy Roman Empire in 1724. George in 1726 was created a Baron, Viscount, and Earl by the titular King James III. Ulysses died in 1731 leaving an only son, Ulysses May, b. 1705, Austrian field marshall in '753, and d. June 26, 1757, after the battle of Prague, from wounds received there.

Whittall Brown was a Cromwellian officer in Kerry, his son m. Anne Mullens of Burnham, and their son m. Mary Morris of Urly. Arthur Brown of Ventry m. 1770. Alice Hurly having issue two sons unmarried and they sold the family property to Lord Ventry.

The Browne family, Earls of Kenmare, descend through Valentine Charles Browne, 5th earl b. 1860. In 1583 Valentine Browne, Knt., of Crofts, in Lincolnshire, surveyed lands in Ireland becoming Auditor General, d. 1589.

The Browne landowners in Kerry in 1876 were Rev. Geo. of Nottingham, 1,477 acres; John of Geneva; J.P. of Crotta; T. B. of Tarbert; and the Earl of Kenmare with some 91,000 acres.

Brown (cont'd)

In 1620 Sir Valentine Browne had a re-grant of Cosmaigne and Onaght O'Donoghue and Downemarke and Ballycarberry manors, lands, castles, lakes and islands. The Kenmare estate included some 22,000 acres in Cork; 91,000 acres in Kerry and 4,000+ acres in Limerick.

Brown's Castle, was built in the 13th century by Sir Reginald Brown. (Killury parish)

Prospect Hall, in 1846 was residence of the Hon. T. Browne, brother of the Earl of Kenmare. (Aghadoe Parish).

Bruce, de Brus

Thos. Bruce of Droumquiana, Co. Kerry, is given.

Brunkar, Broncar

Sir Henry Brunkar in 1604-6, was granted part of the estates in Allagha of Mac Con O'Flavey in Annagh of Gerald, Earl of Desmond.

Bruton, de Briotun

Three Bruton families are given in Kerry, those of Edm. of Killurly; and Pat and John of Rhodes.

Bryant

John Bryant of Dromquinna is given.

Buckford

A settler family, given on estates near Tralee, from the coming of the Elizabethan undertakers to the rebellion of 1641. Descent / homeland: Essex.

Buckley, O'Buacalla

A numerous family in Co. Kerry, some 155 households of the name are given in Kings work.

Buey, O'Buadaig

Thomas Buey of Ballymullen is given.

Buggy, O'Bogaig

Michael Buggy of Clover's lane, Kerry.

Bull
The Rev. William Bull, dean of Cork, was Bishop of Ardfert in 1379, and not popular with the Geraldines.

Bunbury
The Protestant bishop of Ardfert in 1899 was bishop Bunbury.

Bunce
Four families of the name are found in Kerry, Mce. of Baurangoogeen; Pat of Leitrim; Mary of Dirtane; and Pat of Tarmons

Bunnion Bunyan
There were 28 Bunnion families given in Co. Kerry by King (coming from Buinnean of Baile an Bhuinneanaigh or Ballybunion 'of Ballybunion').

Bunworth
Chas. Bunworth of Knocknagoshel.

Burchill, Buirreil
Edward Burchill of Gortreagh.

Butcher of Co. Kerry
Extract From The Irish Book of Arms.
(IGF) 1988.

Burke Bourke de Burc
A fairly common name of Co. Kerry, as evidenced by the 76 families of the name there given in Kings work.

Richard Burke came to Ireland in 1228 as Justiciary. Redmond Bourke, d. 1798 at Derrine, whose son John d. 1826 in the French army. In 1793 John Bourke of Content Poline, Montego Bay, Jamaica, and had been an officer in Walsh's regt. in France in 1789. In 1876 Maj. Gen. Thos. Bourke owned 940 acres in Kerry. In 1604 Theobald Burke, Baron Bourgh of Castle Connell, was granted Kiltarsne, Carrubeg, and Gortkeanlier, lands of Fynan Mac Cormacke, Mac Carty of Twohilkenveara... Glinfleiske of Geffrey O'Donnoghue of Glinne...etc.. In 1612 Richard Fitzwilliam Burke was granted lands as well.

John Burke, a noted schoolmaster was born in Tralee in 1744, entered Sorbonne college in Paris in 1768, made the tour of Europe with the Crump Bland, returned to Tralee in 1777, set up a school there but the penal laws forced its closing, hence he became tutor to the O'Connell family of Iveragh, and later a Tutor in Tralee and a collector of hearth tax in Cork, where he died at Liscarroll in 1793.

Burkett
Six Burkett families are given in Kerry; Thos. of Castleshannon; Geo. of Killorglin; Chas. of Pembroke street; Hy. and John and Jas., of Dooaghs.

Burnham
Edward Burnham of Boherbee is given.

Burns, (O'Broin)

There were 36 families of the name given in Kings work and it was noted there-in that John Burns, a farmer of Coolanealig, was the strongest man of his time, performing great feats of strength which were 'still talked about' in the Abbeyfeale district.

Burscough

The surname of a Protestant Bishop of Ardfert in 1725.

Bustead

Isabella Busteed owned 704 acres of land in Kerry in 1876, and Mary 1,685 acres. Richard, son of John, b. 1783, died unmarried. Wm., son of John, b.1784. John, son of John, b. 1788. William m. Mary Hickson, having John Wm., M.D. of Castlegregory. Morgan, M.D., m. Ellen Hickson. John of Killarney, h.p. Lieut. of 16th Regt., m. Mary, dau. of Major Rd. Ellis of Youghal, in 1818.

John of Tralee, given in 1827; John, printer of Tralee, given in 1827; Geo. W. owned the Cavan Herald in 1824; Thos., newsagent, given in 1802; M. O'C., M.D. of Tralee, 1827.

Butcher

Samuel Butcher, a Protestant bishop of Meath, b. 1811, d. 1876, a native of Killarney, Professor of Divinity, and brother of Surgeon Butcher, m. Mary Leahy, having issue Samuel Henry b. 1850; John Geo., Lord Danesfort and four daughters, the eldest of whom became Lady Monteagle in 1875.

A full account of Henry Butcher (Samuel Henry Butcher) is given in the Kerry Archaeological Magazine, April, 1911. He was the eldest son of Samuel Butcher, Bishop of Meath and Mary Leahy, a member of the well known Kerry family.

Butler, de Buitileir

Edmond Butler was deputy of Ireland in 1307. The Marquis of Ireland was given as the chief of the name by J. King, and 17 Butler families were given in Kerry.

Captain Whitewell Butler, youngest son of Theobald Butler of Priestown, Co. Meath, was a naval and revenue officer in Iveragh in 1782. His son James died in 1863, his son James died in 1887, his son, James Edward, was high Sheriff in 1892.

In 1876 Arabella of Waterville owned 790 acres in Kerry and James 1,417 acres. T. O'Brien Butler, lost in the sinking of the Lusitania, was a musical composer, his opera 'Murgheis' was written in Iveragh. Michael Butler and his brother Joseph, owned the Castle Desmond Brewery in Tralee. Their father, Joseph was one of the proprietors of the Ballymullen brewery.

Butterly

Laurence of Listowel owned 1052 acres in 1876.

Bynane

Pat Bynane of Duagh is given.

Byrne, O'Broin

King gives the Byrne family as chiefs of Hy Kinsellagh and east Leinster in 1119, and gives 14 families of the name in his works.

Caball

Mary Ann Caball of Moyderwell, Kerry.

Mac Cabe

Michael MacCabe of Ballybunion, Denis of Murhur, and Wm. of Ahanagran, are given in Co. Kerry.

Cade
A settler family on estates near Tralee, from the coming of the Elizabethan undertakers to the rebellion of 1641. Originally of Essex. John Cade of Herts m. (circa 1590) a Jennings of Herts. John Cade of Tralee was killed at Ballinskelligs in 1641.

Cadgan, O'Ceadagain
Dennis Cadgan of Churchground is given.

Cadogan
Ellen Cadogan of Dunkerron is given.

Mac Cafferty
James MacCafferty, of the Wood, Co. Kerry.

Cagney
Edward Cagney of Inch is given.

Callinane, O'Callanain
John Callinane of Tullamore is given.

Callues
A settler family on estates near Tralee, from the coming of the Elizabethan undertakers to the rebellion of 1641. Originally of Kent, Somerset, Hants.

Calverly
Charles Calverly of Muckross is given.

Cambridge
A settler family on estates near Tralee, from the coming of the Elizabethan undertakers to the rebellion of 1641.

Cameron
Given as the name of a settler family in Co. Kerry, subsequent to the 1641-42 rebellion.

Campbell
Ellen Campbell of Ballymullen, Margt. of Francis street, and Wm. of Main St. are given.

Canlon
Edmond of Strand street is given.

Mac Cann
James MacCann of Kilnabrack, Co. Kerry.

Cannell
Ellen Cannell of Duagh is given.

Cantillon, Cantlon
Some give the Cantillon family in Kerry as the 'Cantelupes', who arrived in England with William the Conqueror in 1066. In the 12th century we find some of the name in Kerry, alongside the Fitz Henry, Fitz Maurice and de Hore. They are given as settled in Ballyheigue, between the mouth of the Shannon and Tralee Bay. Here it is given that one Tadhg de Cantelupe, or de Cantillon built the castle of Baile Thaidhg.

We also find that De Cantlon's Castle, was built in the 13th century by Maurice Cantillon, according to the works of J. King. (Killury parish).

Ballyheigue Castle fell into the hands of the Crosbies after the Williamite confiscations, but the Cantillons remained fairly numerous at Ballyheigue, Causeway, Ardfert and Lixnaw at the start of the 20th century. The Cantillon graveyard on an island at Ballyheigue was known as the temple or graveyard under the waves, for erosion gave way and the sea now washes over the burial place of the old lords of Ballyheigue.

Some 18 families of the name are given by King, including Richard, Sheriff in 1299; James of Ballyheige and Belview, b. 1650 was a captain in 1690 and went to France; his grandson Anthony in 1839 was granted a French barony as Baron of Ballyheigue; Richard of Ballyheigue was the father of political economy in his noted essay and was a wealthy banker in Paris, but was murdered in London in 1734.

Burke's Heraldic Visitations, page 51, gives a Cantillon pedigree, and some of the family is found in O'Connells 'Last Colonel of the Irish Brigades'.

Variant spellings of de Cantelowe and de Cantelupe are given as equivalents of Cantillon and Cantlon on occasion.

Cantwell, de Canntual

John Cantwell of Coolnaharrigil.

Canty

Some 11 Canty families are given in Co. Kerry, and some are given to have originally come from the name of Cantillon being shortened to Canty.

Carew, de Carrun

A Norman invader from Wales, in 1213 Carew built stone castles in Ardtully, Dun na Mbare, Dunkerron, on Kenmare river, and at Cappanacushy; after the Norman defeat at Callan in 1261, three castles were captured and held by Mac Carthy Mor and the O'Sullivans until 1661. (Dunkerron Castle belonged to O'Sullivan Mor.)

William de Carew or Fitzgerald was the eldest son of Gerald Fitz Walter Nesta the daughter of Rhys, prince of south Wales, and was heir to her castle and lands of Karin of Carew. He also built Ballymarter, Macroom, and Lixnaw Castles. His brother Maurice Fitz Gerald built the castles of Dunloh, Killorglin, Callanaferey, Castle Cois Maing, Molahiffe, Clounmellane and Fieries. This William Fitz Gerald de Carew, left issue Griffin or Griffith; William; Raymond le Gros, ancestor of the Fitz Maurices; and Odo, who had a son William de Carew of Mulresford in Devon granted to his gr-grandfather by Henry I. (See the life of Sir Peter Carew by Sir John Mac Lean). Griffin had lands in Carlow, held by his sons Gilbert, Matthew and Raymond. Gilbert had a daughter Clarice, who had a son John Fitz John.

The name is also found settling in Kerry, subsequent to the 1641 rebellion, and is found near Killarney, 1656-70. Sir Arthur Denny was guardian to Honora Carew in 1670.

Ardtully Castle, in Kilgarvan parish was dismantled in Cromwells war, but was built by Carew in 1215. It was the residence of Mac Tyneen Mac Carthy.

Lixnaw Castle, built by Carew in 1215, was taken by Sir Charles Wilmot in 1600.

Carey, O'Ciarda

A fairly numerous name in Co. Kerry, some 59 families of the name are given by King. Other surnames given as variant spellings of Carey were Carew Fitz Gerald, Carhoo, Ua Ciardha, Cairach.

Carish

Joseph Carish of Tarbert Island, Kerry.

Carmody

A numerous family of Co. Kerry, some 75 families are given by King.

Carney

O'Cearnaig of Cashel was keeper of St. Patricks Crozier and a tomb in the cathedral there. Nine Carney families are given in Co. Kerry by King; Michael of Dromcunning; Tom of Milltown; Thos of Ballyrobert; Jerh. of Clogher, Denis of Ballinbrannig, John of Farran, John and John of Ballinclemesig, Thos. of Ballinahoulart, and John of Killarney, 1776.

Carpenter

A settler family, given on estates near Tralee, from the coming of the Elizabethan undertakers to the rebellion of 1641.

Carr, O'Carra

There were 10 Carr families given.

O'Connor Kerry
Extract From The Irish Book of Arms.

Carrick Carrique Carrig

Glandine castle was built before 1611 and it likely marks the spot of Camp castle on which the Carriques, Carrigs or Carricks, built an undertaker's bawn or dwelling house. John Carrick resided at Glandine castle down to 1731. It was well in ruins by 1854.

Cloghers was the seat of William Carrique in 1756. (Clogherbrien parish).

William Carrique was a surveyor of lands forfeited in 1649; and was granted some lands in Kerry; In 1666 John Carricke was granted Glandayne castle and lands. Curraduffe, Knockglasse..etc. (In 1679 William Carricke, son of John had an abatement of £3 rent). John Carrique of Glandine had a son, William Carrique Ponsonby who had a large estate in 1762, John resided at Glandine until 1731. William Carrique resided at Cloghers, near Tralee, and John in 1779.

Many of the Carrique family were buried in Kilgobban churchyard, but the inscriptions on the tombs were no longer visible earlier in this century.

Hy. Carrick and Hy. Carrick, both of Daly's lane and John Carrick of Ballymullen are given in Co. Kerry.

John and Pat Carrig of Doon, Pat Carrig of Carhoonakennelly, John Carrig of Ballylongford, and James Carrig of Gurteenavallig are given.

O' Carroll

O'Carroll, ancient prince of Lough Lein is cited by O'Heerin, as well as being found in the Annals of Innisfallen, in the 11th and 12th centuries.

Very numerous in Co. Kerry as well as in other parts of Ireland, some 133 families are given in Kerry by King.

Carson

Elizabeth Carson of Coolmagort.

Carter, MacArtuir

Some 9 families of the name are given in the works of J. King, including Wm. of Castle Conway; Lieut. of Arthur Carter of Kilbonane and Listry, in 1668 willed to be buried at Kilbonane parish church, his houses and gardens of Listry to his wife, Eliz., his son Arthur and his daughter Frances; his lands and money due as a 1649 officer for his services done in the wars of Ireland, were left to his wife and children.

Carterett

The name of a Cromwellian settler granted lands in 1667 in Co. Kerry.

O'Connell of Lakeview & Ballybeggan
Extract From The Irish Book of Arms. (IGF) 1988.

MacCarthy
From The Irish Book of Arms. (IGF) 1988.

Mc Carthy

Eleven septs of the illustrious McCarthy family in Kerry are given in Kings *History of Co. Kerry*, thus;
(1) Sliocht Owen Mor of Coshmaing
(2) Sliocht Cormac of Dunguile
(3) Sliocht Fyneen Duff of Ardeanaght
(4) Sliocht Clan Donnell Finn
(5) Sliocht n Inghean Riddery
(6) Sliocht Donnell Brick
(7) Sliocht Nedeen
(8) Sliocht Clan Teige Kittagh
(9) Sliocht Clan Dermond
(10) Sliocht Clan Donnell Roe
(11) Sliocht MacFyneen

Sept of Clan Donnell Finn

In the direct line this sept was given to be extinct. They descended from Donal Fionn, 4th son of Cormac Fionn MacCarthy Mor, Prince of Desmond (b. 1170, d. 1242.) They held lands under MacCarthy Mor, in the baronies of Iveragh and Magonihy.

To settle conflicting claims at the death of Donall MacCarthy Mor, Earl of Clancare, in 1596, the lands of the family were enumerated by Reports of surveyors, as given in *Kings* work. By the year 1803 it appears these lands had fallen away, with final parcels passing to Morgan O'Connell of Carhan.. One of these townlands, Lissballymihill is found under several spellings, including that of Lisnamohill, which may cause some confusion to those involved in research.

The family is given as extinct with the passing of Madame Evelina MacCarthy who left home at an early age spending most of her life on the continent, returning a few years before her death on July 11, 1902 at the Presentation Convent in Caherciveen. One of her Uncles emigrated at an early age to the West Indies, to meet an unknown fate.

Mc Carthy

It is interesting to note that this family was locally known as the Mac Carthys 'na Buillagh', it was not known if that label applied to the whole sept or not.

Sliocht Fyneen Duff of Ardcanaght

In the civil parish of Kilgarrylander, north of the river Maine, near its mouth, there are two ploughlands called the townland of Ardcanaght. These paid chiefry to the Earls of Desmond, but nothing to Mac Carthy Mor. This seems to indicate that the Sliocht Fyneen Duff were planters in West Kerry, or that some arrangement existed for the settlement of a Mac Carthy sept in Geraldine territory.

They also held five plough lands in Magunihy, called Knocknahornaght, or Barleymount, in the civil parish or tuath of Aglish, near MacCarthy Mor's headquarters at Pallis on the Laune side. (Also mentioned is that 'to this day may be seen the old forts of the septs of MacCarthy, O'Sullivan and O'Donoghue, set in a ring around the chief's residence at Pallis-Mhim-Carthaigh in the civil parish or tuath of Aghadoe.)

In 1597 part of the lands of Fynen Duff McCormacke were granted to Trinity College. In 1641 the remaining possessions of the sept held by John Mac Fyneen Carthy of Ardcanaghty were confiscated by the Cromwellians. The lands under the protection of Trinity College in 1597 continued in the possession of the MacCarthys until the death of Justin MacCarthy, who m. Mary Mahoney, dau. of Denis Mahoney of Dromore, her will dated 1764. Justin's two sons, Florence and Daniel were 'left out of the lease'. The College however, paid Florence a yearly pension until his death.

Mc Carthy

In 1600 the chief of the sept is given as Finghin or Florence MacCarthy, whose son John was living in 1641, and whose son was Dermod or Jeremiah.

Of these families are given Florence b. 1734 & Justin b. 1762. Dermod McCarthy b. 1796 who m. Ellen Counihan, resided at Castledrum, but moved to Coolnacalliagh in Killeentierna (Currans) parish. He died there in 1879 and was buried at Keel. They left issue Justin, John, Florence, Edmond, Jeremiah, Mary and Ellen.

Jeremiah McCarthy, of Coolnacalle, eldest son of Justin, was b. in 1841. He m. Ann Nagle in 1865 and had John Justin MacCarthy of Courthall, Dunboyne, Co. Meath; Justin, of Rathcoole, Banteer, Cork; and George, Garrett, James, Jeremiah, Mary and Sheila.

King gives with documentation the 'present' (@1908) direct chief of this branch of the name (Fyneen Duff), as Jeremiah MacCarthy of Coolnacalliagh in Killeentierna (Currans) parish. Several junior branches of the name were given as living in Kerry at that time.

Jeremiah MacCarthy b. 1836, also given as son of a Jeremiah MacCarthy, was a medical doctor residing in Kensington, London, NW.

Some information on this branch was credited to S.T. MacCarthy, Esq., JP, Mainisidir, Srutgreine, and through him, Dr. Jeremiah MacCarthy of London.

Pallis-m/M-Carthaigh was the castle of McCarthy Mor, captured in 1519 by the Earl of Kildare. It was the McCarthy Mor's chief residence. Castle Lough and Ballycarbery castle were two more of his manors.(Aghadoe Parish)

Sir James O'Connell purchased Ballycarbery in 1857. His ancestors had lived there in 1641.

Mc Carthy

The lands of this sept in 1597 are given in Magunihy and Iveragh baronies. Dunguile (Dungeel) in Killorglin district, included Dounguile, Lismacfinin, Corbally, Ballyberane, Dromen, Anglont, Dromanahin, Doneh and Kilmore. These lands were bounded by the Laune and Sliocht Murry (Ferris), and the Geraldines seemed to have given the lower reaches of the Laune and Maine to the Knights of St. John at Killorglin. On the coast of Dingle Bay their neighbors were the Clan Donnell Finn on the east, O'Sullivan Mor and N'Inghean Riddery to the south, and Sliocht Donnell Brick with Mac Crehan to the west. Valentia Island was divided among the Sliocht Cormac of Dunguile, Donnell Brick and the Earl of Glencar, or MacCarthy Mor.

By 1641 the Lord of Kerry held some of their Laune territory and other of their former holdings.

Some controversy was stirred up by the appearance of the articles and genealogy of the Sugrena sept of MacCarthy. Several letters of dispute etc.. are included in Kings original work, including conversations on Ahert vs. Sugrena being the center of power for the family.

More extensive information can be found in the Kerry Archaeological Magazine, circa 1914 onwards.

Misc. Notes.

Muckross (1846), at one time served as the seat of H. A. Herbert. Charles MacCarthy in 1770 left the estates to his mothers family, the Herberts, but the O'Donoghue of the Glen recovered by law the Caragh property.

Srugreana Abbey was the home of S. Trant MacCarthy, J.P. as given in Kings History of Co. Kerry.

Castle Fieries was one of the 3 castles

Mc Carthy

held by the Sliocht Owen Mor Mac-Carthys of Cosh Maing (Fieries and Currow parishes). The Kenmare estate included Cosh Maing and Eoghanacht O'Donoghue, 129 plowlands.

Ardtully Castle, in Kilgarvan parish was dismantled in Cromwells war, but was built by Carew in 1215. It was the residence of Mac Tyneen Mac Carthy.

Mc Carthy of Sugrena or the Sliocht Cormac of Dunguil. *King* gives a detailed line of descent from Muireadach who d. in 1092. Directly from this line springs Samuel m. 1806, who had two sons, Daniel and William. The elder son Daniel m. in 1841 and was father of Samuel Trant McCarthy, then of Sugrena Abbey, Cahirciveen, Co. Kerry.

As one would expect the McCarthy family is a most numerous one in Co. Kerry. There were 604 MacCarthy householders given by J. King.

Extensive research on the MacCarthy family is found in the Kerry Archaeological Magazine, notably for the years 1912 - 1916, with several major articles on the same appearing in those years, and likely subsequently.

*(Please see *Historical Essays on the Kingdom of Munster*, 1994, IGF, by MacCarthy Mor. Munster history, and the MacCarthy line of descent, are given here in a new light.)

Cary

Given as the name of a settler family in Co. Kerry, subsequent to the 1641-42 rebellion. Originally of Essex. J, E, D, and W. Carey, are in Tralee in 1908.

Casey, O'Catasaig

Given anciently as of Muintir Casey in Devenish in 1411; chief of Saithne and tuath Luighne in 1086, with a very numerous count of 218 families of the name in Co. Kerry according to King.

Mac Cauley
Edward MacCauley of Ballyheigue and John MacCauley of Ballygrenan, Co. Kerry.

Cavan
Mary Cavan of Carhoonoe, Dan of Ballyeigh, Michael of Ardfertoughter, and Michael of Tubridmore are given.

Cavanagh
John of Tieraclea, Edm. of Ahanagran and James of Coarabeg are given.

Caxon
John S. Caxon of Killarney in 1821.

Cecil
John Cecil of Tralee given in 1622.

Ceilor
Henry Ceilor of Clashatlea (Clashbatlea?) given.

Chambers, (Seambar)
Edgar of Waterville; John Chambers gent., of Ballingown in 1673. A will was on record in the Public Records Office.

Champ
Augustine Champ of Montanagay.

Champion
Frederick Champion of Burnham; in 1584, Jan. 8, Ormond wrote: 'The ward at Castlemaigne discharged by one Champion'; and Cornelius Champion was granted in 1586 the Ferriter or Blasket islands, afterwards purchased by Sir Richard Boyle.

Chandley
John and Thomas Chandley of Dooncaha.

Chant
Henry of Boherbee, Co. Kerry.

Chapman
A settler family on estates near Tralee, from the coming of the Elizabethan undertakers to the rebellion of 1641. Originally of Devon, Cornwall. Related to Gilberts, Predeux.

William Chapman of Barry's Lane is given in Kerry, by J. King.

Chesters
Stephen Chesters of Moyderwell.

Chestnut
Harry Chestnut, fourth son of Rvv. Wm. of the Presbytn. church of Tralee, died in 1914.

Cheston
Thomas Cheston was constable of Castlemayne in 1584, and claimed £1,000 head money on the death of the Earl of Desmond.

Chrisholm
Mary of New street, Killarney.

Christian
John of Dungoel and John of Reen.

Christison
James of Spunkane.

Church
A settler family on estates near Tralee, from the coming of the Elizabethan undertakers to the rebellion of 1641. Originally given to be from Essex. Connected with the Daniels, Gorings and Cades families.

Also given as the name of a settler family in Co. Kerry, subsequent to the 1641-42 rebellion, originally of Berks, Essex, Northants.

Listed separately we find James and John and Hanora Church were of Dromkeen in Killury. Thomas was of Caherslee in Tralee. John Church of Gurtenard in 1823. In 1826 John Church was a land agent for 30,000 acres in Kerry, and a magistrate for 28 years.

Chuse
Given as the name of a settler family in Kerry, subsequent to the 1641-42 rebellion.

Chute of Chute Hall
A settler family on estates near Tralee, from the coming of the Elizabethan undertakers to the rebellion of 1641 and subsequently others of the name are given to have settled in Kerry as well. Originally of Kent, Hants, Somerset.

Chute Hall (1846) was acquired by marriage from the Mac Elligotts in 1630 by Daniel Chute. Richd. Chute lived here in 1756. (Tralee parish.)

George Chute came to Kerry during the Geraldine confiscations. His son Daniel, by marriage with a daughter of MacElligot, acquired Tulligaron or Chute Hall in 1630. His son was Richard, whose son was Eusebius, whose son was Richard, whose son Francis was Sheriff in 1757. His son Richard was Sheriff in 1786. His son Francis married in 1810, and his son was Richard, whose son Francis was Sheriff in 1865. His son was Richard.

D. Chute is found in Tralee in 1908. Some 19 Chute families are given by J. King in 1831, including those of Tralee, Caherciveen, Ballyheigue, Chutehall, Springhill, & Ballyheigue Castle.

Cicill, Cecil
A settler family, on estates near Tralee, from the coming of the Elizabethan undertakers to the rebellion of 1641. Originally of Herts (Cecil). John Cecil lived in Tralee in 1622.

Clancy
James of Tarbert Island, Dr. John of Listowel, Bridget of Ballybunion, Joseph of Castlegregory. John MacClancy was chief brehon to the Earl of Desmond in 1578. Mac Clancy was also recorded as chief of Dartry.

Clandenan
Arthur Clandenan of Aughrim.

Clapman
William Clapman of Kilfarnogue.

Claridge
Alfred Claridge of Emlagh west.

Clarke, O'Cleirig
Pat of Coolcorcoran, John of Rusheen, Thomas of Murreigh. The will of John of Killarney in 1719, was in the Public Records Office.

Clayton, de Cleatun
In 1806 Capt. Clayton, of the Sea Fencibles, was buried in Garfinny.

Cleary, O'Cleirig
There were 11 Cleary families in Kerry. Ua Cleirigh was given as chief of Ui Fiachrach Aidhne in 964.

Clegg
George Clegg of New Street.

Clenesha
Robert of Cloghane.

Clifford, O'Clumain
The Clifford family is one of the more numerous of Co. Kerry, with J. King giving some 224 families of the name in that county.

Clifton
John Clifton of Duckett's Lane and John of Clover's lane are given.

Mac Clintock
Thomas MacClintock of Ballyheige, Co. Kerry.

Clohulle, de Clohulle
Geoffrey de Clohulle, of Offerbe, in 1284 was granted forever the wreck of the sea on his land.

Clotherty
Bridget Clotherty of Gortcreen.

Mac Clure
Given in Co. Kerry were Anthony of Poulnamuck, Robt. and Robt. of Denny street, Robt. of Kenmare, tomb in Tralee churchyard was marked Anthony MacClure, 1817.

Mac Cluskey
John MacCluskey of Connors lane, and Geo. of Chapel street, given in Kerry.

Coakley
Some 22 Coakley families are given in Co. Kerry.

Cock
Annie Cock of New street, Killarney.

Coffey, Coffie
Listed under O'Cobhthaigh of Nenagh. There are 150 families of the name given in Kerry, making Coffey one of the more numerous names of the county. John Coffey was bishop of Kerry in 1889. Shane Coffey of 1701 had a son Dermod, whose son Edmond, had a son Edmond who d. in 1841 and had a son Edward.

Coghlan, Mac Coclain
Given in descent as from the chief of Delvin in Kings Co., 1217-1620; there are 13 families of the name given in Co. Kerry.

Cohey
Michael Cohey of Ballyarkane.

Coke
Capt. Coke of the 69th Regt. married Miss Talbot Crosbie.

Colclough
John Colclough of Coolclogher.

Coleman Colman Colmain
Michael Coleman of Rock Lane, Walter of Walterville, John of Coolnagoppogue.

Coll
Mary Coll of Rock Street.

Collier
A settler family, given on estates near Tralee, from the coming of the Elizabethan undertakers to the rebellion of 1641. Joseph Collier of Ballyvelly, yeoman, was shot during the siege of Tralee in 1641. Anne Collier of John street is given in Co. Kerry as well.

Colligan (O'Colgan)
John Colligan of Boherbee.

Collingwood
Francis Collingwood of Strand Street.

Collins, Coilens
A popular name in Co. Kerry, some 136 Collins families are given there by J. King, who gave the name as from O'Coileain, of the 'Ui Conaill of the battalion of Munster..a great tribe, with whom it is not usual to contend..are the battle trooped host of the O'Coilens; from Connilloe in Limerick: compare O'Connell: chief lower Connells and Ara and Claonglas; Hy Cuileann'.

Also given as the name of a settler family in Kerry, subsequent to the 1641-42 rebellion. Descent/homeland:
Of Berks, Cornw., Devon.

Cahircullane or Collins Castle, was an ancient oblong enclosure in the parish of Kildrum.

Collis-Sandes of Oak Park, Co. Kerry
Extract From The Irish Book of Arms.
(IGF) 1988.

Collis

A settler family on estates near Tralee, before and after the rebellion of 1641. Descent / homeland: Of Herts.

Mary Fitzgerald, dau. of Maurice, Knight of Kerry by Elizabeth Crosbie, and 14th in descent from the Princess Elizabeth Plantagenet, dau. of Edward I, married first Robert Collis who was son of Wm. Collis of Lisodigue, Co. Kerry. She had John, who married his cousin.

In 1831 eight of the name are given as; John of Barrow, Edward of Spa, John of Taullaght, Thos. of Barrow, William of Fortwilliam, Samuel of Spa, John of Barrow, and Edw. of Dingle.

Fort William (1846) was the residence of W. Collis, (Killahan Parish).

Of Tieraclea

Collis of Tieraclea - William Collis, an officer in Cromwell's army, had a son, John, whose son was William of Lisodege, Kerry in 1685. His fifth son was Robert, whose fourth son Stephen was born in 1794, and had a son Stephen Edward of Tieraclea, Tarbert, Co. Kerry who d. in 1912, aged 80. (230)

The Collis family wills in the Public Record Office show: Robert, tide surveyor, Dingle, 1763; Anne, widow 1762; Edward of Barrow 1762; Eliz. of Barrow, widow, 1785; John of Bannagn, 1728; Rev. Thomas of Monaree, 1766, was vicar of Dingle since 1731; Thomas of Tralee, 1790; Rev. Wm. of Tralee, 1772. In 1801 Capt. Geo. Collis died, Mrs. G.B. Collis d. 1822, Mrs. Avice Collis d. 1781.

Baptisms on record; Ellen 1774, Eliner 1772, Sarah 1775, Catherine 1778, Samuel 1783, Eliz. 1884, children of Eliz. and Thomas Collis; Mary 1774, Arabella 1778, of Anne and Robert Collis. Stephen Edward Collis of Tieracles, owned 3,598 acres in Kerry in 1876 and d. 1912, aged 80, leaving his personal estate to his widow, and his son, Stephen Edward. In 1807 Margaret, dau. of Edward Collis of Lismore, m. Francis Twiss of Castle Island. W. J. F. Collis of Tieraclea, d. 1915, aged 74, at Natal; his brother was Major Gen. in the Indian Army.

Collum

Arthur of Waterville. Captain Robert Collum, in 1600 (?), was granted the lands and monastery of Muckross, consisting of 4 acres, two orchards and one garden, he also had a grant of Innisfallen monastery.

Colohan

Margaret Colohan of Listowel, Joseph of Tieraclea.

Coltsmann

The Coltsmanns were a Northumbrian family of Danish extraction, John Coltsmann of Manchester Square, London, purchased lands in Kerry, and 'built Glenflesk castle at Droumhumper in 1818'.

Flesk Castle (1846) (also cited as Glenflesk castle by King) was the seat of D. Coltsman in 1824. It sits on the site of two forts and was formerly Droumhumper. Illustrations may be found in Neales Views of Seats, 1824.

Mac Coluim

Rionan Mac Coluim was a Gaelic language pioneer since 1898.

Columb

Sir John C. R. of Dromquinna; son of Gen. Geo. T., who m. 1819 Mary King, have issue Col. Geo., Inspr. Genl. Wellington, Vice Admiral. Philip H., Sir John C.R., Eliz, Mary, Harriett; Sir John, b. 1838 m. 1866, Emily Palmer, having issue Rupert, Laura and Gwendoline.

Colvin

Laura of Ballyheige, Co. Kerry.

Comerford
Geo. Comerford; h.p. lieut, 57th Foot, 1821 Killarney.

Commane O'Comain Comyn
Batt and Tim of Strand Street. Wm. of Francis Street, Edw. and Magt. of Rock Street, Thos. of Knockanush, John of Clogherbrien, John of Castle Gregory.

Commane, O'Comain, Comyn, Cummins, and Hurley were all given as variant spellings.

Compton
The name of a Cromwellian settler granted lands in 1667 in Co. Kerry.

Comyn
Given as the name of a settler family in Kerry, subsequent to the 1641-42 rebellion. Descent/ homeland:

Of Essex. Mrs. Joan Commyns lived in Tralee in 1665. B., W., E., and T., Commane are in Tralee in 1908.

Mac Conarchy
Donald MacConarchy was bishop of West Munster, d. 1193.

Condon, Condun
Mary Condon of Inch, Robt. and Pat and Robt. of Ardoughter, John of Cloghane, Denis of Castletown, John of Knocknacaska, Henry of Strand-street, Bidget (Bridget?) of Farranreagh

Conneff
John Conneff of Ranaloug, Co. Kerry.

Mac Connell
Robert MacConnell of Mangerton view, and David of Edward street are given in Co. Kerry.

O' Connell.
O'Heerin gives O'Connell as chief of Magh o gCainchinn, or the Barony of Magonihy in Kerry. They are said to be a branch of the O'Connells of Hy Conaill Gawra, now the baronies of Upper and Lower Conello in Co. Limerick. Burke's 'History of the Commoners' mentions several of the family in Kerry. They are found earlier styled as 'lords of Bally Carberry' in the barony of Iveragh. Altogether some 376 households of the name are given in Co. Kerry in the works of King, many are given to be of O'Conghailes of Maguhiny; the Hy Congill Gabra in 869 owned the Connello baronies in Limerick; the Kinel Connell are the O'Donnells of Tyrconnel or Donegal; the O'Connell and Harrington and Collins and O'Donovan clans were given to be expelled from Limerick, beyond Mangerton in 1178 by Donald Mor O'Brien of Thomand, and many of these settled in Kerry.

O'Connell of Derrynane Abbey
This family is given to have come from Connells, Limerick, to Iveragh, and in 1641 were ordered to transplant to Clare. Jeffrey O'Connell, of Ballycarberry, was Sheriff of Kerry and died in 1635. His son, Maurice, was transplanted. The second son, Daniel, married Alice Segerson of Ballinskelligs Abbey, having John and Maurice. Maurice died in 1715, and his grandson, Richard was captain in the legion of Maillebois, Holland. John O'Connell of Ahabore and Derrynane, joined the Stuart regiment of his cousin, Col. Mce. O'Connell, and was at Derry, Boyne, Aughrim, and Limerick. He married Elizabeth Conway of Clahane, and died in 1741, leaving three sons, Daniel, Maurice, and Jeffrey. Daniel married Mary O'Donoghue Dhuv of Anwys, and

O' Connell

had 22 children. His second son Maurice, succeeded and married Mary Cantillon of Limerick. He died in 1825 and was succeeded by his nephew, 'The Liberator', Daniel O'Connell.

The celebrated politician, Daniel O'Connell was born at Carhen, 6th August, 1775, and m. Mary O'Connell of Tralee in 1802, having Maurice, Morgan, John, Daniel, Ellen, Catherine, Elizabeth. Maurice married Frances Scott, of Cahircon, Co. Clare, in 1832, having Daniel, John, Fanny, Mary. Daniel O'Connell of Derrynane was born in 1860, married Isabelle Lawlor of Greenagh, having issue Isabella, Margaret, Frances, Kathleen, Eileen. This Daniel was in the British Navy 1850-'3, and Sheriff of Kerry in 1860.

Derrynane (1846) was the residence of Daniel O'Connell. Donal Mor built a 'Fair new house' at Darrynane in 1745. (See Mrs. M.J. O'Connell's life of Count O'Connell.)

Grena, in 1839, was the seat of John O'Connell, in 1864 of D. Shiell.. Sir James O'Connell settled at Lake View in 1821, and died in 1872. (Aghadoe Parish).

Sir James O'Connell purchased Ballycarbery in 1857. His ancestors had lived there in 1641.

Connelly, Connolly

More anciently of Magunihy, of the Corco-Duibne Degad, and tuath sen Eran. Twelve families of the name are given: Pat of Ardoughter; Mary of Doonard; John of the Wood; Geo. of Fenit; Tom and John of Edward Street; Mary of Kenmare; Pat of Drombane; Dan of Letterdunane; Michael of Baureauragh; Pat of Mucksna; and Michael of Shelburne Street.

O' Connor, Conner, Connor

A most numerous family of the county of Kerry with a remarkable 1371 families given. The true Kerry O'Connors are given to be of the clan Conaire, who came from the south of Munster, from whence they had been expelled in ancient times. King states that the O'Connors of Connaught, Sligo and Corcomroe are branches of the same stock, of the Clan Conaire.

Ten septs of the O'Connor Kerry clan were confiscated in 1653, viz.: Carrigafoile, Tarbert, Knockanore, Lisselton, Ballyline, Nohoval, Rahinane, Annah, Beal, Ahavallen. Coirbri was the ancient seat.

In the works of O'Heerin we find the O'Connor family given as Kings or princes in Co. Kerry, descended from Con, an eleventh century chief and further from Ciar another illustrious ancestor, forming the roughly name of ConCiar or Conair which became O'Connor. Modern scholars find that the family name is actually taken from Conchobhar, another family chieftain.

Mention of the family can often be found in the Annals of Innisfallen and in the Annals of the Four Masters.

O'Connor-Kerry resided at Carrig-a-Foile Castle, their chief stronghold found by the mouth of the Shannon and the island of Carrig. The Elizabethan and Cromwellian wars led to the loss of most of the family lands. The castle was given by T.C.D. in 1666. It was captured by Sir William Pelham in 1580. (Aghavallen Parish). At that time the castle was fortified with some 19 Spaniards and fifty Irish, with an Italian Engineer on board for good measure. Pelham, none the less, took the castle on Palm Sunday, putting 50 defenders to the sword and executing six in the camp.

The illustrious John O'Connor, Lord of

O' Connor, Conner, Connor

Kerry and Iracht, due to his support of the Catholic party and efforts to promote the same, was brought to Tralee, and then half-hanged and beheaded in 1652.

A Canadian wrote to J. King in search of the genealogy of John O'Connor of Kerry, who married Mary O'Mara, both of Milltown. He was land steward for the Herberts of Muckross, and died about 1822. One of his ancestors married one of the Landers of Keel.

Castleshannon in 1760 was the seat of the Rev. Thomas Connor. (Killury parish).

Conroy, Conroi

Ballyconry, MacConroi's baile, is a town and a parish in Iraghticonnor composed of the townlands of Ahascra, Ballyconry, Gortagurrane, Mweevoo, Mweevuck and Toohana. The clan Conaire gave monarchs to Ireland and kings to West Munster and Scotic Kings to Alban and Britain. (K)

Conroi, or Cu Ri Mac Daire was king of West Munster in A.D. 1, and Temair Eran on Cathair Conroi was his residence as chief of the Ernans or tuath sen Eran. Catair Conroi, Dun Cearmna at Kinsale, and Dun Sovarki in Antrim were the three old buildings of Erin.

Richard Conroy of Bridge Street, Michael of Boherbee, and Rev. Charles of Sneem are given.

The surname of MacConroi, (clan Conaire), is also said to have been translated into the surname of King, and there were 49 King families given in Co. Kerry as well.

Conway

A settler family on estates near Tralee, from the coming of the Elizabethan undertakers to the rebellion of 1641. As given in the works of J. King, the family was originally from Wales. Sir John Conway of Bodrythian, had an eldest, second and a younger son, Robert. This younger son Robert, LL.D., Master in Chancery, came to Ireland in 1570, and died there in 1602. He m. Mary, dau. of Symon Purdon, of Taullaght, by whom he had a son, Christopher, and a dau. Christina, who m. Mark, eldest son of Henry Usher, Esq. Robert was buried in St. Patricks Cathedral.

Also given are Christopher (his son), who had a son James Conway who died July 6, 1620. He was exiled by Cromwell, but returned to Kerry where he married his cousin, Miss Roe.

Sir John Ayr Conway, of Bodrythan, had an eldest son, Edward. This elder son had two sons, both of whom came to Ireland. They were Lord Conway (1625) and Sir Fulke Conway. Lord Conway had a son and his branch became extinct in the male line with his grandsons death, that grandson leaving his estates away from the family.

Sir Fulke Conway was governor of Carrick-fergus, and a Privy Councillor. He died during his brothers lifetime and left his estate to his brother, Lord Conway. (see will in Record Office, Dublin - J. King)

Sir John Ayr Conways second son's family carried on the Welsh estates after his death, which finally fell away.

1st Jenkins Conway m. Mary Herbert, settled at Killorglin, was the younger son of Sir John Ayr Conway. He came to Ireland in 1583. He had one son, Jenkin, who had a son Edward who m. Katherine Rvoes. The male line went

Conway

extinct and the estates went to Dowdales and Colthursts, who married the heiresses.

1st Jenkin Conway had two daughters, Alice who m. Ed. Roe of Clahane, and Eliz. who m. Robert Blennerhassett. They were the great grandparents of 'Black Jack' (died 1737).

Thus it appears all these 3 branches of Conways of the 16th and 17th centuries were closely related, and that Capt. James Conway, of Clahane, was the grandson of the first arrival, Robert Conway, LL. D., who came over 1570. (- A.M. Rowan per J. King)

The Kerry Archaeological Magazine, July 1920 issue, has a full article and pedigree of the Conway family. They give the first of the family to arrive in Ireland as Jenkin Conway of Killorglin, one of the Munster undertakers, who in the reign of Elizabeth, came over with Sir William Herbert, Sir Edward Denny, and Robert Denny to plant forfeited estates of the Earl of Desmond. He obtained Killorglin, to be called Castle Conway, and Innisfallen etc.. . He was accompanied by his three brothers, Hugh, Edward, and William Conway. It would appear that this account is well documented, and must be considered more accurate than other accounts.

The family is well represented in the French-Irish brigades between the end of the 17th and end of the 18th century.

Killorglin Castle and Manor reverted to the Fitzgeralds from the Knights Templars. It was then granted to Capt. Conway, and later bought by the Mullins family from Blennerhassett.

34 families of the name are given.

Conyers

E. Fitzgerald Conyers is given as clerk at Knockane in 1831.

Conyn, O'Coinin

Roger O'Connyn in 1623 possessed St. Johns Lane tenement, a garden and one acre of land in Traly, granted to the Commandery of Awney, of the Knights' Hospitallers of St. John. Brown of Awney owned the property which passed to Lord Cork on his marriage with Joan Apsley, dau. of Annabel Brown. Roger O'Connyn surrendered his deed to Lord Cork for a lease of the property, paying rent to the agent, Thomas Joye of Listrim. The O'Conyns fostered the White Knights at Kilmallock.

Conyn, O'Coinin, O'Connyn, Counihan are given as variant spellings.

Cooke (also Mac Daboe)

A settler family, given on estates near Tralee, from the coming of the Elizabethan undertakers to the rebellion of 1641.

Debora Cooke lived in Tralee in 1622.

Skehaneirin (1771) was the residence of the Cooke family in Listowel parish.

Seven families of the name are given in the works of J. King; Thomas and Hy. of Togherbane; Hy. and Nic. and Hy. of Kilcooly; Mary of Garryantanavalla; Thomas of Gortnaskeha. Debora of Tralee is given in 1622. Bridget Cooke of Skehaneririn, in Listowel, m. 1771 George, son of Oliver Stokes. She was great granddaughter of Sir. Robt. Fitz Maurice of Ballykealy castle.

Cooney

Gerald Cooney of Glenlaharn and Pat Cooney of Loughanes are given.

Cooper

There were 18 Cooper families given in Co. Kerry by King. One of his footnotes gives that on July 4, 1768, Mary Cooper and 4 other young women died in bed in Giles Cooper's house, near Killarney. In 1776, James Cooper lived at Droum, and Giles in 1821.

Coote

Chidley Coote was, in 1666, granted holdings in Co. Kerry.

Also given as the name of a Cromwellian settler granted lands in 1667 in Co. Kerry. These two listings may actually be one in the same, or may be two separate grants of land.

Corbet

Given as the name of a settler family in Kerry, subsequent to the 1641-42 rebellion. Originally given of Norf., Glouc.. Tim Corbet of Lisheen and Kate Corbett of Gneeveguilla are given in Co. Kerry by King.

Corcoran, O'Corcain

Given as descended from the chief of Muinter Corcrain, Killenaule, Tipperary, until the year 1200, several of the name are given in Kings work.

Corkerry, O'Corcra

There were 23 Corkerry families in Kerry.

Mac Cormac, Mac Cormaic

Several of the name are given in Kerry, including John of Ahane, Sam of Ballinruddra, Alex or Tarbert, Mary and John of Tiduff, Robert of Gortnaskeha; and Catherine Mac Cormac who m. Lord Thomas Fitz Gerald who died at Rouen in 1420.

Mac Cormaic and MacCormack were also given as variant spellings by King. Today, we can add McCormack, McCormick and MacCormick, etc.. due to the great variety of spellings that time and immigration have given us.

Cornwall

Ewin Cornwall of Ballinskelligs.

Corridan, Corradain

Some 40 families of the name are given in Co. Kerry.

Corrigan, O'Corragain

Pat Corrigan of Hewson's Lane.

Cosgrove

James of Emlagh and Norah of Boherbee are given.

Costelloe.

The Anglo Norman Lord of Slieve Lugha and the plain, in Costello barony, Mayo; there are 99 families of the name given in Kerry.

Costigan, Mac Osticin

John Costigan of Aunascaul.

Cotter, Mac Oitir.

There are 38 Cotter families given, including William Cotter of Midleton in Cork, forfeited in 1641; and Edmond of Carrigtwohill in 1641, was ancestor of Sir James of Rockforest near Mallow.

Coulthurst

Danesport (1846), was the residence of Capt. Coulthurst (in Killarney parish).

Counihan Cunningham

Sean O'Coinneagain was a celebrated Munster poet in Jacobite times. There were 9 families in Kerry called Cunningham or Cuinneagain, and 38 families of the name spelled as Counihan given in Kings work.

Anciently the O'Conaing resided at the Pallas of Aos Greine. The rectory of Kill Conygayn, and the rectory and vicarage of Killenchan, were near St. Munchins in Limerick. The Conyn or O'Coinin, of Tralee and Kilmallock, fostered the White Knights in later days.

Courtayne Castle (1846) in Killarney parish, came to be known as 'The Hall', and was the residence of the Counihan family. It was built before 1829. In 1831 lived Francis Curtayne, h.p. 8th Hussars, Killarney. also John, Jeremiah M.D. Killarney, H.D. of Courteen Hall, and William Curtayne.

O'Cuanacain and O'Connaghain were given as older forms of the name.

County Canty Cantillon
Pat of Benmore and Pat of Knockavahig are given.

Cournane, O'Curnain
Some 77 Cournane families are given in Kerry.

Courtney, (O'Curnain)
Some 48 Courtney families are given in Co. Kerry.

Cousins, Cuisin
Thos. Cousins of Kenmare, Robt. of Henry-street, and Richard of Caherciveen are given.

Covert
Given as the name of a settler family in Kerry, subsequent to the 1641-42 rebellion. Originally of Sussex. This family was related to the Gorings. The first settler was a Cromwellian settler granted lands in 1667 in Co. Kerry.

Mac Cowen, Mac Comdain
Given in Co. Kerry were Wm. and Wm. of Clounalour, Robt of Cloghers, Mary of Barrow, Edwing of Nelson street, R.A. of Denny street, Thos. of Tralee in 1831. Robt. and Sons, Ltd., were merchants in Tralee.

Cox, Mac an Coilib
Some 10 Cox families are given in Co. Kerry: Pat of Shinnagh; Robt and Pat and Wm. of Ballyline; Mary of Coolnagraigue; Robt. and Wm. of Asdee; Dan and Diana of Lohercannon; Wm. of John street.

Coxon
Flesk Priory (1846) was the seat of the Coxon family. Michael Coxon of Killarney is given in 1793.

Mac Coy, Mac Aoda
Ml. MacCoy of Clountuhrid, Kerry.

Coyle
Jas. of Dayplace; Pat of Gortalinny; A. J. Coyle of Tralee, in 1913 went to South Africa.

Mac Crah
Cappanacoss Castle was built by Carew in 1215. It was the residence of the MacCrah, or senior, branch of the O'Sullivan clan. (see MacRae, Macray)

Cranfield
Given as the name of a settler family in Kerry, subsequent to the 1641-42 rebellion. Descent/ homeland: Of Essex., Beds. Robert Cranfield (1743). The last of the name was Sexton of Tralee. Edward son of Thomas Cranfield was born 1703.

Thomas Cranfield, in 1705, had a house on the east side of the market cross in Tralee; his son, Edward was born in 1703. Robert lived in 1743. The last of the name was given as the sexton of Tralee.

Cranitch
John Cranitch of Moyeightragh.

Crawford
Robt. Crawford of Denny street.

Creagh, Craobac, Nihell
Creagh is given of Tradree in Clare; Emma of Ardnameweely is given and in 1876 Francis and John of Tarmons owned 394 acres in Kerry, and Wm. of Mallow 829. In 1821 Francis lived at Dromin. In 1802, Francis of Ballybunion m. Margt. Moriarty. In 1831 lived Monchton Cary, John, O'Brien, and Monckton at Tarmons. John Creagh was a burgess of Kilmallock in 1628; Wm. was a merchant of Limerick in 1626; Sir Ml. served in 1690; Capt. James was in the Irish brigade at Fontenoy; Dominick was ancestor of John of Dromartin in Co. Kerry.

Ballybunion House was the Creagh family seat in 1770. (Killehenny parish) Creagh, Craobac, Nihell, and O'Neill were given as a variant spelling group by King.

Crean, O'Creain
Some 29 Crean families are given in Kerry. O'Creain and O'Croideain were given as older or variant spellings.

Creed, O'Croidain.
Some 10 Creed families are given in Kerry.

Creegan, O'Criagain
Martin Creegan of Caheranne road is given.
Edward Cregan of Chapelquarter; John of Lacca east; Jerh. of Carhoonakinealy; Ml. of Tieraclea are given in Kerry.

Mac Crehan
Litter Castle in Caher parish, belonged to the Mac Crehan family, an offshoot of the O'Sullivan Mor clan. The MacGillycuddys branched off the same stem.

Cremin, Cremins, Crimmins
Some 65 Cremin(s) families are given in Co. Kerry.

Critchley
Edward Critchley of Kenmare is given in Kerry.

Mac Crohan, Crehan
There were 28 MacCrohan families given in Co. Kerry.
The Mac Crehan castle at Letter was owned by Cnogher Mac Croghon in 1656 and Rynard by John Oge Creghon, Mac Crehan, alias O'Sullivan, of 1605; and Nicholas Browne says Mac Crohan was the third branch of the O'Sullivans. Mac Crehan earned distinction in Spain. In 1754, Daniel Mac Crohan of Nantes wrote about Connell O'Connell at Caen. Andrew of Charen and Owen of Portmagee are given in 1776.
Dan Crohan of Cumeenole and John Crohan of Dunquin glebe are given in Co. Kerry as well.

Croke of Tralee
Mr. Croke married Miss Plummer, and kept a general store where the Kerry Post was printed later on. Miss Plummer was from Killury. Their son, the Rev. James Croke died in San Francisco. Mary, their eldest daughter was born at Tralee in 1819, and died at age 86 at Bathurst in Australia.

Croker
Thomas Crofton Croker, in 1839, edited the book entitled 'Legends of the Lakes of Killarney'.

Cronin, O'Croinin
Some 261 householders of the name are given in Kings work in Co. Kerry. The O'Cronain family, according to Cathan O'Duinin in 1320, descend from Oilium Ollum, Eoghan Mor, Oiliol, Lewy, Cork, etc...down unto Cronan, whence O'Cronain or Cronin.
The will of Daniel Cronin of Knockagree, is date 1756; and his nephew Daniel of the Park, near Killarney, died in 1786, leaving his estate to his sisters grandson Daniel Duggan of Duhallow, who took the name Cronin, and m. Mary Lombard, having Daniel, James and John of whom Daniel m. in 1814 Christina Coltsmann, of Glenflesk Castle.
The Park (1846) was the seat of D. Cronin in 1824.
Daniel Cronin, of Park, Killarney, in 1814 married the heiress of John Coltsmann of Glenflesk. His son Daniel, was Sheriff in 1847. His son Daniel John Cronin Coltsmann was born in 1855, and was Sheriff in 1899.

Crosberry
Peter Crosberry of Tieraclea.

Crosbie, Crosby

Ardfert Abbey was the mansion of the Crosbie family since 1636, and was burned by Col. Fitzmaurice in 1653. It was modernized by the first Lord Brandon in 1720. Tubrid, in 1756 was the seat of Lancelot Crosbie. (Ardfert Parish).

Ballingarry Castle was built in 1641 by Col. D. Crosbie, but was taken by the Irish army. (Ballyheige Parish). Crosbie of Ballyheigue is given as a branch of the Crosbies of Ardfert and Queen's County. Thomas of Ballyheigue was M.P. for Kerry in 1709. His son James was Sheriff in 1751. His son was James, Sheriff in in 1792. His son was Pierce, Sheriff in 1815. His son was James, Sheriff in 1862. His second son James Dayrolles Crosbie, was born in 1865.

Castle Lough in Killarney Parish was demolished by Ludlow. A younger branch of the MacCarthys resided there, by patent of James II in 1684. It was sold to Col. Wm. Crosbie. Dennis Shyne Lawlor resided here in 1863.

Nine families of the name are given in Co. Kerry. In 1876 several remained owners of land there. Mr. John Crosbie was appointed Protestant Bishop of Ardfert, and died in 1621. He had a numerous family of whom Sir Walter and Colonel David left issue. Of this line are a sheriff, a baron and an earl of the name in the 17th and 18th centuries. Col. David Crosbie, the second son of Bishop John, was ancestor of several branches of the family including those of Ballyheigue. Patrick Crosbie, the elder brother of bishop John, was granted lands in Ballyfin in Queen's County and in Tarbert in Kerry.

In 1607, Patrick Crosbie was granted the lands of Tarbert, and taking with him from Queen's County most of the Moores, Kellys, Lalors, Dorans, Dowlins and Clandeboys, who agreed to pay rents fixed by the bishop of Kerry.

Crosbie wills in the public record office included those of: David 1658; Sir Pierce 1663; Sir Thomas 1695; David 1717; Thomas 1731; William Mce. 1762; Margt. 1765; Pierre 1767; Lancelot, 1781; Francis 1807; Rev. Mce. 1809. Sir Piers Crosby was compelled to sell his lands at Abbeydorney, Aulane, Killahin and Ballybroman, to Col. David Crosbie of Ballingarry and Ardfert in 1639.

Crossan

The Crossans were bards to the O'Moore chiefs and had custody of the book of Cluain Eidhneach, Clonenagh, in Leix.

Crowe

John Crowe of Ballybrack, Jane of New street, Jerh. of Ballymacassy, and Lizzie of Kilnabrack are given.

Crowley

Some 73 families of the Crowley name are given in Co. Kerry. More anciently the O'Crowley was chief of Kilshallow, west of Bandon, in Cork.

Crumpe of Barleymount

In Aglish parish, 1756, Barleymount was the residence of Mr. Crump and it is given then that Dorcas Crumpe m. Henry Blennerhassett. In 1784, Daniel Crumpe had a lease of Coolroel Crumpe of Barleymount sold his property to his cousin, Lord Ventry. In 1831, J. L. Crumpe, M.D., resided in Tralee; his son, Doctor Francis Crumpe, was L.R.C.S. in 1818 and died in 1877 leaving an annuity to his nephew, John L. Crumpe who died in 1913, the estate passing to the Protestant church of Tralee.

Mac Cuill, Quill
Mac Cuill, chief of the tuatha De Danann, a.m. 3471-500.

Culclough, Colclough
John Culclough of Longfield, Co. Kerry

Culhane
There were 10 families in Kerry of the name of Culhane.

Mac Cullen, Cullen
Magt. of Ballyseedy, Rev. J.J. of Balloonagh monastery, Rev. James E. Cullen of Buncurrig, rector of Ballyheigue in 1914. Pat MacCullen of Coad, Co. Kerry.

Cullinane
Of the chiefs of Orrery, hereditary physician of Munster; chief of Conailli in 998; Cormac Mac Cullinan, chief and bishop of Munster in 905. Twenty-two families of the name are given in Kerry.

Culloty
Some 30 families of the name are given in Kerry.

Cullum, Mac Coluim
John of Guranebane, Co. Kerry.

Cully, O'Colla
John of Lackabane, Co. Kerry.

Cummane
James of Ballincloher, Co. Kerry.

Cunningham, see Counihan
Several of the name are given including John Francis Cunningham, D.D., Bishop of Concordia in Texas, who became a Bishop in 1898, and was born at Irramore, who died at the age of 77.

Curbstone
A settler family, given on estates near Tralee, from the coming of the Elizabethan undertakers to the rebellion of 1641.

Curlestone
The town of Tralee was incorporated in 1612, and its charter named John Curlestone among the first provost and burgesses.

Curlew
A settler family on estates near Tralee, from the coming of the Elizabethan undertakers to the rebellion of 1641.

Curran, Currane, O'Corrain
Some 148 families of the name are given in Co. Kerry by King, making the Curran family a numerous one here. Currans parish in the barony of Trughanaicme of the the clann Conaire, in the year 1300 was called 'Curinys', which is similar to the local name of 'Currens'. Curreeny, cuirinidhe, means little moors according to King who gave that the Anglo-Norman family of Fitzgerald built a castle at Curreens between 1215 and 1260. By 1299 Gilbert Brun held the knights fee at Curryngs, at which time it was said 'it now lies waste among the Irish'.

Currans Castle, in ruins, was built by Maurice Fitzgerald, and was the residence of George Herbert in 1756. (Currans Parish) Currans fair was given as being held on May 6 in Kings work. The Catholic church at Currans was built in 1829 by the Rev. David O'Dwyer. Father Roche, who lived at Currans, died there in 1791. After 1583 it was given that the church of Currans was in ruins, and that the Catholics gathered there and recited the rosary, hence the name Ardcrone, meaning 'rosary height'. The Protestant settlers, the Herberts were buried in a tomb there, and also the Bastables in another. (The church of Currans, Ardcrone, Co. Kerry.)

Curry, O'Corra
Pat of Bawnbee, John of Milltown in 1821, Frances who died 1835 married Francis Twiss of Knockacarrin.

Curtayne

Courtayne Castle (1846) in Killarney parish, came to be known as 'The Hall', and was the residence of the Counihan family. It was built before 1829. In 1831 lived Francis Curtayne, h.p. 8th Hussars, Killarney. also John, Jeremiah M.D. Killarney, H.D. of Courteen Hall, and William Curtayne.

Several of the name are given, including J. D. Curtayne of Belleville who owned 1,165 acres in Kerry.

Curtin, Mac Cuirtin

Given by King as shown, listing Mac Cuirtin, ollav of Thomond in 1400; taken from the word 'cruitin', a poet or bard; O'Curathain, O'Cruitin, O'Cuarthain.

Some 64 families of the name are given in Kerry. Of these, Jeremiah Curtin, in 1895, compiled the tales of the Fairies of South West Munster. J. Curtin, of Molahiffe, in 1876, owned some 619 acres of land in Kerry.

Curtis, de Cuirteis

Richard of Ballinskelligs; Rev. Wm., Ballynacourty, 1831; Dan of Killarney, 1776.

Cusack

Pat of Mac Enery's Lane. Mary F. Cusack, the nun of Kenmare, authoress, wrote several books, including 'Story of My Life' in 1901.

Mac Cushion, Mac Oisin

Anie Mac Cushion of Tieraclea, Co. Kerry.

Cussen, Cuisin

Given were Edmond of Finuge, Pat of Ballybunion, John of Ballyhorgan, Richard of Knockercreveen.

Mac Cutcheon

Given in Co. Kerry was the Rev. Geo. MacCutcheon of Kenmare, in 1901.

Cuthbertson

Robert of Listowel, Co. Kerry.

Dackham

Thomas Dackham, of the Mall, is given by King.

Dagg

James of Listymurragh, William of Dingle, and William of John Street are given.

Dalton, de Aliton

Sir Walters de Aliton is found as an Anglo-Norman Governor of Meath in Ireland in 1172. Some 32 families of the name were given.

Daly, Daily, Daley, O'Dalaig

Said to have come from dalaighe, dawlee, a lawyer or advocate pleader in the law court from the bar. A very numerous family in Co. Kerry, some 220 families of the name are given there. The O'Dalys are given to have been a bardic family which gave chief poets to Ireland from the 12th to the 15th centuries.

They settled in Noghubhal Ui Dalaigh in 1320. In 1403 Nemerus O'Dalyd was canon of Ardfert. Daniel O'Daly, 1595-1662, was a Dominican Friar known as Dominic of the rosary who was a native of Kerry. He spent some time abroad subsequent to his entering the Dominican convent at Tralee, and is buried at Coimbra. He wrote the history of the Geraldines, and founded many convents and colleges and was Ambassador for Portugal in France.

Dalziel

Archibald Dalziel of Derryquin, and Robert Dalziel of Main street, Co. Kerry

Damer

Given as the name of a settler family in Co. Kerry, subsequent to the 1641-42 rebellion. Descent/homeland: Of Dorset.

Danaher, O'Duineacair
Only 7 families of the name were given in Kerry: Stephen of Ahane, Michael of Castleview, Dan and Joe and Johanna of Killarida, Pat of Ballygologue, and Pat of Lacca.

Daniel
Given as the name of a settler family in Co. Kerry, subsequent to the 1641-42 rebellion. Descent/ homeland:
Of Norf., Essex.
James Daniel of Listowel is given in the works of J. King.

Darby
Given as the name of a settler family in Co. Kerry, subsequent to the 1641-42 rebellion. Descent/ homeland: Of Essex.

Darcy, Dairsig
Nicholas Darcy of Ballybunion and William Darcy of Dingle are given.

Darley
Henry Darley of Dublin, in 1876, owned 663 acres in Kerry.

Darrack, Mac Darac
Catherine Darrack of Tralee, 1797.

Dashwood
A settler family on estates near Tralee, from the coming of the Elizabethan undertakers to the rebellion of 1641. Descent / homeland:
Of Norfolk, Kent. Hugo Dashwood, shoemaker, was shot at the siege of Tralee castle in 1641 and William Dashwood was also killed.

Daughton, Datun
Michael of Kiltean, John of Banemore, Edm. of Leamprehane and Edm. of Ballinageragh.

Davidson, Mac Daibid
Thomas of Reen, Co. Kerry.

Davies, Daibis, Mac Daibid
Only 7 families of the name are given in Kerry, viz; Ml. of Ballincloher; Keo. of Farranreagh; Wm. of Waterville; Wm. and John of Ballyrehan; Rev. Thomas of Listowel; Jos. of Dirtane; Wm. of Day Place; and Robert of Lackeen.

Davis
A settler family on estates near Tralee, from the coming of the Elizabethan undertakers to the rebellion of 1641. Descent / homeland: Of Wales.
W. A. Davies is in Tralee in 1908.
Sir John Davis, 1613, was granted escheated lands in Kerry.

Dawson, Mac Daibid
Thomas of James street, and James of Balloonagh.

Dawton, Datun
Dan of Montanagay, Co. Kerry.

Crosbie of Ballyheigue, Co. Kerry
Extract From The Irish Book of Arms.
(IGF) 1988.

Day

A settler family on estates near Tralee, both before and after the rebellion of 1641. Descent / homeland:

Of Essex, Herts, Norf., Cambs, Kent. In 1583, Rev. James Day was curate of Waltham Abbey. Thomas Day lived in Tralee in 1622. Lucy Fitzgerald, dau. of Maurice, Knight of Kerry, m. the Rev. John Day, whose descendants are given by J. King. This line is also given (Sir Edward Denny) to be eight in descent through the O'Briens, from the rebel Earl whose chief castle and Kerry estates were granted to their gallant ancestor.

Mrs. Hamilton Jones of Moneyglass House, Antrim, the Day Stokes family, and the family of Thomas Franks, Esq. of Dublin, the Mahonys of Dromore Castle, Mrs. S. M. Hussey, of Edenburn, dau. of John Hickson, Esq, formerly of the Grove, Dingle, John Godfrey Hickson of the Privy Council Office, London, one of the children of James Hickson, Esq., formerly of Lansdowne Lodge, Kenmare, all descend from the Rev. John Day and his wife, Lucy, dau. of Maurice, Knight of Kerry, and therefore inherit the blood of English, French and Spanish royalty.

Thos. Day died in Tralee in 1908. Rev. Edward Day, LL.D., died in 1808, aged 69. Rev. Edw. Day of Beaufort died in 1808.

In 1831 we find 6 families of the name including Robert of Loughlinstown House, John S. of Kilgobbin, Richard, Robert G. of Tralee, Thomas of Tralee, Edward of Kilgobbin.

Beaufort House (1846) was on the site of Short Castle, the home of Rev. Fitzgerald Day in 1864. (Knockane parish). Reenellen (1846) was the home of Rev. Mr. Day; later a De Lap seat.

Some 13 Day families of the name are given in Kerry. Rev. James Day was curate of Waltham Abbey in 1583. Thomas Day of Tralee is given in 1622. Thos. Day, warden of Short castle in Tralee, 1642, was son of Lieut. Day, who served in Kerry in the Elizabethan army, and was ancestor of Day of the Manor and Kilballylahive. More notes are found in Kings work.

One family settling subsequent to 1641 was given to be from Dorset. Some of the name were Cromwellian settlers, and some later settlers are found @ 1745.

De Clahull

Geoffrey de Clohuile, in 1285 was sheriff of Kerry. The De Clahull tower at Barrow guarded the port of Fenit.

De Courcy, Coursey

John De Courcy in 1291 held the king 'in capite' in Kerry. De Courcy, Lord Kingsale, is premier baron of Ireland. In 1876 William De Courcy of Tarbert owned 312 acres in Kerry. In 1821 Justin De Courcy lived at Ballylongford and Maurice De Courcy at Molahiffe.

One John Courcy of Kilgarvan is given in 1776.

Thomas MacRichard Coursey of Ballincluhere, in 1603, was attainted, forfeited Killahan, and other lands which were then granted to John Newton and later to Wm. Taaffe.

De Moleyns

Col. Fredk. Wm. Mullins, of Burnham in England, purchased lands in Kerry in 1666 and settled at Ballingoleen or Burnham near Dingle; he was M.P. for Dingle in 1695, d. 1712. His son Fredk. d. 1695 leaving a son William

Dea, O'Dea

Of Dysart O'Dea in Co. Clare as listed by King. John Dea of Tarbert island, and Ellen Dea of Killarney are given.

Deady, O'Deadig
10 families of the name are given including those of Lisnakealwee, Ballynahow, Ballinknockane, Ardamore, Clounmelane, Anagap, Lisanearla, Balliniry and Tawlaght.

Deane, O'Deagain
In 1876 Jas. Deane owned 1,753 acres in Kerry. In 1799, Sir Robert Titson Deane was a grand juror in Kerry; he married the daughter of John Fitzmaurice, nephew of the Earl of Kerry.

Dease
James Arthur Dease of Westmeath, cousin to Lord Kenmare, in the Kerry election of 1872 opposed the winning Home Rule candidate, Blennerhassett.

Dee, O'Dea, O'Deagaid
Some 29 Dee families are given by King, quite apart from the families of 'Day', and separately listed from 'O'Dea' as well. He gives the dee as the magicians or 'folk of power'. The Deagads or Ernans were a powerful military force in ancient times.

Deegan Deegin O'Duibginn
Pat of Ahanagran; Charles Deegin of Waterville.

Deen
16 families of the name are given in Kerry.

Deenihan
16 families of the name given in Kerry including those of Dooncaha, Kilmurly, Cloghane, Dromurrin, Ahima, Urlee, Ballymacassy, Carrigane, Ballybunion, Doon and Banllincloher.

Del, O'Del
John O'Del of Dromin, is given by King, under the heading of the family name of Del.

Delaney
Given by King as O'Dubslaine of tuath an Toraidh in Cos. Kilkenny and Queen's. 26 families are then given in Co. Kerry. The Delaneys are noted as coming to Kerry with the Crosbies in 1607.

DeLap, O'Lapain
Several DeLap are given including those of Reenellen, Strabane, Gurranebane, Knightstown, Farranreagh. In 1735 Rev. Samuel Delap was of Rawn, Co. Down, and in 1735 Mrs. Agnes Delap was of Dublin.

Reenellen (1846) was the residence of Rev. Mr. Day; now De Lap seat. (per J. King)

Deloughry, O'Duibluacra
Mary of Ardagh, Co. Kerry.

Dempsey, O'Diomasaig
Given as of Clan Maliere; Charles of Carrigeen; John and John of Derra, Co. Kerry.

Dennehy, O'Duineacda
Some 65 families of the name are given in Kerry. Mary Dennehy of Killarney owned 1574 acres in Kerry.

Dennis
M.C. Dennis of Baltinglass in 1876 had over 3,000 acres of land in Kerry.

Denny of Tralee

J. King gives the first of this ancient family arriving in England, of Norman origins. Sir William Denny, Lord Justice of Ireland under Henry III, fought with Sir John Fitzgerald (builder of the Castle and Abbey of Tralee), against the MacCarthys at Callan in 1260. Several Dennys' were distinguished in England.

Sir Edward Denny, Knight Banneret, M.P., Gentlemen of Queen Elizabeth's Privy Chamber, Governor of Kerry, and Desmond, etc., received a grant of the town and Castle of Tralee, became the founder of the Irish Denny family.

The town of Tralee was incorporated in 1612, and its charter named Arthur Denny among the first provost and burgesses. Sir Arthur Denny of Tralee Castle (eldest son of Sir Edward and Hon. Ruth) was b. 1629. When 12 years of age the rebellion of 1641-2 broke out in Ireland, he became known as one of 'those gallant gentlemen, styled as '49 officers, who were deprived of their commissions by Cromwell for their royalist sentiments. He apparently returned to Ireland around 1650, when the county had been reduced by Ludlow, Waller, Le Hunte and Sadlier. Sir Arthur restored his dismantled castle of Tralee, and was High Sheriff of Kerry in 1656, and came to command one of the two troops of horse then raised in Kerry. In 1670 he held his Kerry estate as well as 559 acres in Meath and Galway, some or all granted him at the Restoration, as a reward for his loyal services as a '49 officer. He d. in 1673 and was buried with his first wife in Tralee Church.

By his first wife he had; Col. Edward Denny of Tralee Castle; Arthur, b. at Castle Lyons, Co. Cork b.1660, d. prior to 1671. Extensive genealogical information is given in *J. Kings* work.

Wm. Denny was born at Prospect Hall in 1744 and Thomas Denny in 1746.(Aghadoe Parish).

Liscahane Castle was held by Stack against the Geraldines in 1600. Before 1599 the place belonged to Daniel Gray, an English Colonist under Sir Edward Denny. In 1641 it appears that the Gun family settled there, while Gray likely moved on to Tralee for better security. A new stone house erected by Gray is described by King. (Ardfert Parish)

Tralee Castle was taken by the Irish Army in 1641, and again in 1691. This Geraldine fort was granted to Sir Edward Denny, in 1587, and his grandson, Sir Edward Denny, restored the Great Castle and came to live in it on Dec. 22, 1627.

The Rev. H. L. L. Denny, M.A., London, was given as having a collection of Denny portraits and family records in Kings day.

A more extensive account of the Denny family of Tralee is found in the Kerry Archaeological Magazine, which runs in several issues, including October 1914, vol. 3, #13. Several of the family are noted entombed in the Abbey Church of Waltham, in Essex. One inscription (1599 A.D.) reads:

" Learn, curious reader, ere you pass,
what once was Sir Edward Dennye was,
A courtier in the Chamber,
A soldier in the field,
Whose tongue could never flatter,
Whose heart could never yielde"

Mac Dermott, Mac Diarmada

Jerh. and Con of Canguilla, and Anthony of Park, 1914, are given in Co. Kerry. The Mac Dermotts were chiefs of Moylurg and clann Mulrony in ancient times.

Desmond
Two families of the name were given in Kerry, Dan of Bawnluskaha and Richard of Tarbert Island.

Dethick, De Thick, Dettrick
A settler family, given on estates near Tralee, from the coming of the Elizabethan undertakers to the rebellion of 1641. Descent / homeland:

Of Norfolk. Humphrey Dethick was one of the first twelve burgesses of Tralee in 1611. William Dethick of Killballyahiff in Killiney deposed to his losses in the war of 1641.

Devane O'Dubain O'Duben
Given as a family of Corca Duibne; with 57 households of the name in Kerry.

Devaney, Devany
Peter Devaney of Ballymullen is given.

Devereaux
John of Ballinrudders is given.

Devine, O'Dobailein
Pat Devine had the Crosbie Arms Hotel in Tralee.

Devlin
Johanna Devlin of Market Place.

Dew
A settler family on estates near Tralee, from the coming of the Elizabethan undertakers to the rebellion of 1641. Descent / homeland: Kent, Berks, Herts.

Digby
Cecil Digby of Carhoolbeg is given, and one Digby was a Protestant bishop of Ardfert in 1673.

Diggin, O'Duibginn
Some 51 Diggin families are given in Kerry.

Dignan
Tom of Ballyheogue is given in Kerry.

Dillane, O'Duilleain
From Queens county in 1608 were families of the name who were transplanted to Co. Kerry with Patrick Crosbie and the Moores, Kellys, Lalors, Dorans, Clandeboys. There were 58 Dillane families recorded by King.

Dillane, O'Duilleain, O'Dowlin, and Dolin were given as variant spellings.

Dillon, O'Duilleain
The Dillon family was on of the families transplanted from Queen's County (Leix) in 1608, with 31 Dillon families recorded by King.

Robert le Dillon, the Sacsanach, came with the Anglo-Norman invaders; James Dillon was Earl of Roscommon in 1622. Bernard Dillon, the jockey, won the Derby on Lemberg, and married Marie Lloyd, the music hall favorite.

Dillane and Dillon were given separate listings by King, although he recognized that they could be different spellings of the same name. Dillon, O'Duilleain, O'Dowlin, Dolin, and Dillane were all listed together under Dillon.

Dineen, O'Duinin
Some 53 families of the name are given in Kerry. Several noted poets are found historically, including Rev. Padraig Ua Duinnin who wrote an epic poem on freedom in 1916, and compiling an Irish dictionary and editing the 'Irish poets and text books.'

Dobbs, Dob
James of Ballymullen, Co. Kerry.

Dodd, O'Dubda, Doda
There were 11 families of the name as given in Co. Kerry. In 1876 W. H. Dodd owned 1,000 acres in Kerry.

Doherty, Docartaig

Doherty is given as chief of Ardmire and Inishowen in Donegal. 46 families of the name are given in Kerry. Doherty, Docartaig, and Ua Dochartaigh were all given together. Many more variant spellings of the name are found today, such as Dogherty, Doughertie etc.. (see the Master Book of Irish Surnames for more complete listing.)

Mac Donagh

Ml. of Inch, Kate of Doory, Francis of High street and Lissyvigeen, all in Kerry

Mac Donald, Domnaill

Ml. of Demesne, Co. Kerry.

Donegan, O'Donnagain

Given to be of the clan na Deagad, chief of Muscry of the three plains, now Orrery barony in Cork; in 1597 owned Carrow ni Donegan, Kilmanneh, and Knocknegourgal, in Kilmanagh parish in Bere; they owned between Kenmare and Bantry on the coast. Six families of the name were given in Kerry by King: David and Michael and John of Cleanderry, Pat and John of Dromkeen, and Dan of Knockane are given.

Mac Donnell, Mac Domnaill

Some 47 Mac Donnell families are given in Co. Kerry. The family served as chiefs of Innsi Gall 1083, and high constable of Ulster in 1365.

O' Donnell, O'Domnaill.

O'Domhnaill, now given as O'Donnell, descend from the same line as the O'Donoghues, and are found as Chiefs of 'Clan Shalvey of the limpid streams, Recorded as a well-known land, Belongs to O'Donnell of the powerful hand, Who took possession of the brown nut plain', as recorded by O'Heerin.

Some 119 families of the name are given in Kerry, making (O')Donnell a fairly numerous surname of that county.

Donnelly, O'Donngaile

Chief of Muscraighe tire in Ormond; 41 Donnelly families given in Kerry.

Mac Donogh of Duhallow

Andrew of Killarney, 1821; John of Killarney, 1776; John, a surgeon is given in 1775; are given in Co. Kerry.

O'Donoghue of the Glens
Extract From The Irish Book of Arms.
(IGF) 1988.

Killaha Castle

Donoghue

Chiefs of this proud family are named in the old Annals of the 10th - 13th centuries. The Lough Lein branch was given extinct, as chiefs of the clan were not elected after Geraldine confiscations, and the abolition of clanship.

In 1013 is recorded the battle between the Ui-Eathach, that is the families of O'Mahoney and O'Donahue of South Munster. Ui-Eathach was the tribe name of both families. At the reign of Brian Boru and the Battle of Clontarf, Irish tribes began assuming family names.

Both of these families distinguished themselves at the Battle of Clontarf, where Cian (Kean), son of Maelmhuaidh (Molloy), the direct ancestor of the O'Mahoneys, commanded that family, and Domhnall (Donnell or Daniel), son of Dubh-da-bhoireann (Duv-Davoran), the direct ancestor of the O'Donahues commanded them.

The O'Donoughues, forced from Cork by the O'Mahoneys in the twelfth century, settled in Kerry on the lands of Killarney and Loch Lein. (Eoganacht chiefs of Lough Lein.) In 1107 MacCarthy Mor gave the land of Moriarty of loch Lein to O'Donoghue Mor. The family split into two distinct branches, those of Lough Lein (Ross Castle) being the O'Donoghue Mor, and those of Glenflesk seated at Killaha Castle. In 1158 O'Donoghue Mor rebuilt the church at Aghadoe. Jerpoint Abbey was founded in 1180 by Donogh O'Donoghue.

Prominent to the time of Elizabeth, they allied themselves with the Earls of Tyrone and Desmond, losing their estates, with the O'Donoghue Mor line becoming extinct. Many accounts and legends of the O'Donoghues can be found, including those in 'Windele's Notices of Cork and Killarney'.

O' Donoghue

The O'Donoghue Mor lived at Ross Castle in Loch Lein until 1560, and his pedigree is traced from Corc, king of Munster. Ross Castle, the O'Donoghue Mor stronghold, was in 1652 surrendered to Ludlow. The Browne (Kenmare) family resided at Ross castle in 1588. In 1756 it was used as a military garrison, probably since 1652.

The O'Donoghues of Loch Lein and of the Flesk, ruled over clan Sealbuidhe. O'Donoghue of Loch Lein was chief of that land which extended from the Roughty to the Loch Lein, and to Lios Ui Conchobhair, and contained 45 ploughlands, while the O'Donoghue of the glens had 20 ploughlands. Ballydonohoe, baile Ui Doncada, is given in Galey, according to J. King.

In 1613 Valentine Browne of Molahiffe, got a grant of the O'Donoghue Mor lands, forfeited by Rory O'Donoghue during the Geraldine confiscations.

Of the Glenflesk branch of the family "Jeffrey of Killaher," (Killaha) attainted in 1603, restored in 1609, left a son Teige of Glenflesk, 1628 whose son Geoffrey of Killaher d. 1655; his son Daniel 1700, had Geffrey, whose son Daniel d. 1800 whose son Charles had a son Charles whose son Charles had a son Daniel, 1833-89, whose son Geofrey b. 1859, had Geoffrey b. 1896.

Donoch or Donnchu d. 1057, gave the clan name to the O'Donoghues.

The O'Donoghues of Droumcarbin, or Anwys, lived near Brewsterfield.

Col. D. O. O'Donoghue, a native of Kerry, served in the army at Potomac, and died at Portland, Maine, aged 64.

Anciently of the Ua Donnchadha of Cashel in Cork, O'Donoghue had a very numerous 363 families recorded in Kerry by King.

O' Donoghue

Eoghanacht Cashel is in the plain of Cian, O'Donoghue is its lineal inheritor; its name in other days was Feimhin, extending to the border of the brown nut plain. In 1014 Dungal O'Donoghue was King of Cashel, his successor Magrath died in 1043, and Donchadh in 1057.

In the 14th century Geffrey O'Donoghue of the Glynn was chief. His son, Rory, 1420, who left a son Daniel. His uncle Teige, whose son was Jeffrey of Killher, attainted 1603, restored 1609, whose son was Teige of Glenflesk, living in 1628, whose son was Geffrey of Killaher d. 1655, whose son was Daniel, d. 1800 whose son was Charles, b. 1777, whose son was Charles, whose son was Daniel, b.1833 whose son was Geffrey, b. 1859.

In 1712, John Florence O'Donoghue of Glanfleska, second son of Owen, was created Marquess of Cleinchamps and La Ronce. Conor O'Donoghue, elder brother of the 1st Marquess, ancestor of the O'Donoghues of Belgium, Lords of Geldorp and Niel, naturalized July 27, 1716. The Wills of: Geffry O'Donoghue of Glenflesk 1678; Dan 1804; and Pat 1808 of Killarney; were in the public record office.

Egan O'Rahilly praised Killaha Castle, the house of Geoffrey O'Donoghue of the glen, and spoke of Finneen of the Glen in 1714 as the only bush of refuge left to the bards of Conn. In 1679 Geoffrey of the Glen wrote poems in Irish. In 1612 Francis Blundell was granted Killaha. Muckross (1846), at one time served as the seat of H. A. Herbert, Charles MacCarthy in 1770 left the estates to his mothers family, the Herberts, but the O'Donoghue of the Glen recovered by law the Caragh property.

O' Donoghue

The O'Donaghues came most anciently from Co. Cork, and are given as being driven from Cork into the area of Loch Lein and surrounding areas near Killarney. The family split into two branches, the O'Donaghues of Loch Lein under the O'Donaghue Mor, and the O'Donaghues of Glenflesk who became centered at Killaha castle. Smith, in his History of Co. Kerry, centuries ago mistakenly called the Glenflesk branch the O'Donaghue Mor, an error which has been picked up by several later writers.

Killaha Castle was the fortified castle or tower house of the O'Donaghues of the Glen, (Glenflesk, Co. Kerry). It was erected in the latter half of the 15th century to guard the pass in its route. It stands on an eminence at the mountains base, near the north-west extremity of the valley, the river Flesk winding at some distance beneath. A slender square tower of considerable elevation - perhaps five stories - was remaining a century ago, and it remains nearly in the same state today (1994).

The southeast angle, which contained the circular stone staircase, fell a few years prior to 1846, but its proprietor in that year, Mr. John McCarthy, with a good taste highly creditable to him, caused the rubbish to be cleared away and the place opened up.

A Forgotten Tomb

In the course of the clean up, a gaurd-chamber standing beside the entrance was explored; and beneath the floor were discovered portions of a massive coffin with some human bones. The mantelpieces, of which there where four, were of elaborate workmanship. The accompanying outworks and defenses of this old castle have crumbled away in the lapse of ages. Beside it, in the early part of the 20th century was the

O' Donoghue

modern mansion of Mr. McCarthy. Today (1994) it is the residence of Glenflesk pastor, Fr. Mulvehill, who is now guardian and historian to the cite. (above information is confirmed in the Kerry Archaeological Magazine from the year 1913.)

As it was told to me, the castle was slighted by a cannon, from a hillside some distance away, and evidence of its exact location and entrenchment remains to this day, and that location can be easily seen from the castle itself.

Many legends remain of the hospitality within the walls of Killaha castle, which was given to be one of the last strongholds of the Irish in the area, even after the ruin of the castle proper. Legends of the piper and harpist to the O'Donoghue of Glenflesk survive in old writings today. Every May Day the Donoghue is said to rise from the depths on a white stallion, appearing in his old grandeur.

Local historian, the late Dennis Spillane told me that the crooked knife, wielded by the O'Donoghue was given to have been a symbol of his authority, and the man carrying that symbol had had not to repeat a request twice. Upon questioning Mr. Spillane, he felt the knife would have been similar to a bowie knife in appearance, but no record of its exact shape has yet been found. Even after the castle was taken, the area was not judged safe, or subdued by the invaders. As late as 1679, Geoffrey O'Donoghue of Glenflesk is found as a noted poet who composed in Gaelic, and one of the 'Four Poets of Muckross Abbey'.

Killaha is said to have stood for 'Church of St. Agatha', whose feast is held on February 5 of each year. The ivy clad ruins of the roofless ancient

O' Donoghue

church of Killaha are only a short distance down the hill from Killaha Castle, to the side of the modern day cemetery. Many old tombs and graves are to be found there-in, and many markers have been lost to time there, as several slabs are found worn slick, with no decipherable writings left on them.

Coomacullen Mountain

The authors Donaghue line stems from Coomacullen Mountain nearby, where 13 yrs. ago, near the top of the mountain after the road had run out, a Gaelic speaking resident of the house, gave the Donaghue family as residing in that house 3 or 4 generations ago. This was done in my presence, with local historian Mr. Spillane speaking on my behalf. Just below that house on the mountain but out of sight, was a house resided in by two brothers, which others may have mistakenly identified in the past, but that is not the correct house. On my last visit, it was said that no native Gaelic speaker remained on that side of Coomacullen Mountain. There are in the old land records, Kealiher or Kelliher families on Coomacullen Mountain as well. It was Mary Kealiher (or Kelliher), and Cornelius Donaghue of Coomacullen mountain who gave rise to my mothers family who arrived in America circa 1854. - so attested by Michael C. O'Laughlin, June 14, 1994.

Variant spellings of the name are numerous today, including Donahue, Donaghue, Donahoo, Dunahoo, etc..

See also: The O'Donoghue Book, published by the Irish Genealogical Foundation, Box 7575, Kansas City, MO. 64116.

Donovan, O'Donnabain

The O'Donovans of Clan Cashel get the name from Donamhan, who was expelled from Limerick County in 977 by Brian Boru, and settled in Carberry in Co. Cork among the O'Mahoney's. In 1178 Donat O'Brien routed the O'Donovans and O'Connells out of Limerick County and beyond Mangerton.

Some 40 families of the name are given, including that of Hugh Donovan, of the School-house, Tralee, in 1806, who was a classical teacher who trained youths prior to entering Dublin University.

Doody, O'Dubda

Some 32 Doody families are given by King, who relates the family to O'Dowd, Dowda etc..chief of the Hy Fiachrach. Detailed information on that family is found in the 'Tribes and Customs of the Hy Fiachrach' by John O'Donovan, published complete by the I.G.F., Box 7575, Kansas City, MO. 64116.

Doohig, O'Dubtaig

John of Ballyganneen, Co. Kerry.

Doolan O'Dubhlainn Dowlin

The Dowlins of Queens County were among the families transplanted to Kerry in 1608. Dowlin has been interchanged with Doolan on more than one occasion. King gives the Doolan families of Joseph of Headfort; John of Buddaghauns; Joseph of Church Street; and Denis of Glanmore in Kerry.

Dooley, O'Dublavic

Given as of Feara Tullach as given by King. James and Tom of Moyderwell are given in Co. Kerry.

Dooling O'Dublainn Dowling

Some 36 families of the Dooling name are given by King, and it is there-in related that the Dowlins were transplanted from Co. Leix (Queens County) in 1608, noting the obvious interchanging of the Dowling and Dooling surnames.

Doona

Some 16 families of the name are given in Kerry.

Door

Ellen Door of Farranreagh is given.

Doran, O'Deorain

Some 12 families of the name are given in Kerry, and it is noted that Doran was one of the transplanted septs of Queens County, settling in Kerry in 1608.

William Doran, who was transplanted from Leix or Queens Co. in 1608, (and settled in Drienafoyle, Blackwater and Kenmare), his son Edmond (m. Matilda, dau. of Denis Mac Carthy of Slahana house and his wife, Jane Fitz Maurice) having Morogh, having William, having James of Bridge House, Blackwater; having Myles, having David of Templenoe House, having Alfred d.1890. David Doran was born in 1841, and was in the public life of Kerry for 40 years or more.

The Doran arms given by J. King were: Per pale sa and ar. a boar pass, counterchanged, on a chief az, three mullets of the second; the crest is Out of a ducal coronet or a lion's head proper.

Dore, O'Dogair

Some 11 Dore families are given.

Dorgan, O'Dorcain

John Dorgan of Gortnaleaha; Tom of Minard; John of Cloghaneanode; and Michael of Coolroe are given in Kerry.

O' Dorney Parish
O'Dorney parish is given in volume 3 of Kings History of Ireland. (see bibl.)

Dorohy
Michael Dorohy of Derreenaclaurig is given.

Douglas
Hy. of Kilfarnogue, M.V, of Armagh is given.

O' Dowd, O'Dubda
Some 56 families of the name are given in Kerry. O'Dowd was anciently chief of Hy Fiachrach. (see Tribes and Customs of the Hy Fiachrach by O'Donovan).

Dowdall
Capt. Dowdall, ward of Dingle in 1584, with 100 English soldiers. Given were Patrick of Cappa in Limerick who m. Avice Conway of Killorglin who had a son and four daughters. In 1854 Sir James was chief justice and in 1624 Sir John lived at Kilfenny in Limerick.

Dower, O'Dogair
Maurice Dower of Derk is given.

Dowling, O'Dublainn
Some 46 families of the name of Dowling are given in Kerry by J. King. The Dowlings are another of the families who came from Leix, or Queens County, in 1608. Batt Dowling 1823-63 wrote poems for the nation; he edited the San Francisco Monitor in 1858 and died in that city, he was born in Listowel then taken to Canada, returned to Limerick and then went to farming in California. His brother William settled in San Francisco, and wrote poems for the papers there. Batt Dowling, 1844-1912 was born in Kerry, went to Fort Wayne and moved to New Haven, Indiana, where he was a hardware merchant, he served from 1861, in 20th Ohio Vol. Regt, through the civil war.

Dowman
Wm. of Main Street, Co. Kerry.

Downes, O'Dubain
Robt. of Lisnakealwee, John of Teer, Robt. of Castle Gregory, Wm. of Driminamore, Jas. of Garryrooth; John, son of Jas., sergt. R. Munster F., d. 1913, at Maymyo in Burma.

Downey, O'Dunadaig
Some 26 families of the name are given including those of Brosna, Knockbrack, Tooreenascarthy, Kilsarcon, Ballyduff, Tarbert Island and Gleesk.

Downing O'Duinin O'Dinan
O'Duinin, was chief of Uaithne, Owneybeg barony in Limerick. Some 57 families of the Downing name are given in Kerry. Several of the name are found as solicitors in Kerry.

Doyle O'Dubhghuill O'Doyle
A family of Co. Clare in 1317 at the battle of Abbey according to the Annals of Innisfallen, and 124 families of the Doyle name are found in Kerry by King.

Drake
Frank Drake of Cloghane is given. John Drake was a mysterious hermit who lived among the ruins of Muckross friary about 1750; he used the refectory and lived on fish and fruit and potatoes.

Drew
Capt. Francis Drew of the English army in 1598 left issue John of Meanus in Kerry, and Barry of Ballyduff in Waterford. Rev. Browning Drew, of Castle Maine in 1849, had a son who was Lieut., in the 75th Regt.. Among lands held by the family were Meanus and Listry.

Driscoll, O'Driscoil

Given as O'Driscoll of Corca Laighe; some 74 families of the name are given in Kerry. Of the families given the following used the 'O' prefix: Alex and Pat and Alex of Farranreagh; Tim of Feighmane; and Pat and Nora and Kate of Main Street.

In 1442 O'Driscoll was chief of Corca Laighe in west Carbery in Cork, of the clan Conaire. In Cape Clear Island is a Franciscan friary built by Daniel O'Driscoll in 1450, and here is Dunamore Castle. Other castles of the O'Driscoll's were at Loch Hyne, Castle haven, Castle Ardagh, Dunasnad, Dunalong, Whitehall, Inisherkin island and Baltimore. The genealogy of O'Driscoll from Lugach Mac Con is given by J. King.

Drum, O'Droma

John and John Drum of Cordal and James of Knockanelig, Co. Kerry.

Drummond, O'Droma

Edward of Abbey street; Robert of London owned 29,780 acres in Kerry in 1876.

Drury, O'Druaid

Michael of Ballyheigue and James of Glenderry are given in Co. Kerry.

Ducey

Julia Ducey of Boherbee, in Co. Kerry.

Duckett

Maria Duckett lived at Mangerton view in Kerry. William Duckett, 1768-1841, b. Killarney, d. Paris, was an United Irishman with published poems in Paris in 1829.

Dudgeon

John Dudgeon of Farranreagh, Kerry.

Dudley

Philip Dudley of Mucksna, Co. Kerry.

Duffesy

Maurice Duffesy of Annascaul, Co. Kerry.

Duffield

Henry Duffield of Spunkane, Co. Kerry.

Duggan, Dugan, O'Dubagain

Some 32 families are given in Kerry. Ua Dubhagain was ollav of Hy Many in 1372. O'Dubhagan, chief of Fermoy, through Mogh Ruith. In 1776 lived Dan and Denis and Hy. of Knocknaseed, Denis of Knockanane, John of Knockeerverk. In 1821 lived Dan of Mount Henry.

Duhig, O'Dubtaig

Jas. of Ardfert and Mary and Michael of Castle Gregory are given.

Duke

Rev. J. A. Duke of Edward Street, Tralee, Co. Kerry.

Dumas

Capt. James 1716; Henry of Cloghereen in 1759; Thomas of Tralee in 1827; in 1817 a duel was fought in Killarney between Dumas and Lawlor.

Dunford

John Dunford of Aughrim, John of Glenalappa, Pat of Gortureen, and John of Trieneragh are given in Kerry.

Dunlea Dunleavy Dunlevy

An amazing group of theoretically interchanged names in one way or another is listed by J. King as shown below. Some 10 families of the name Dunlea are given, including those of Bohereens, Inchinveema, Knockaderry, Dromulton, Ardshanavooly, The Great Blasket Island, Kenmare and Kilmore.

Dunlea, Dunleavy, Dunlevy, Dunsleibhe, O'Dunshleibhe, Mac Dunshleibhe, Delap, Dunlop and Livingstone were all given together by J. King.

Dunlop

Andrew Dunlop of Main Street is given.

Dunne, O'Duinn

Ua Duinn was chief of Breagh and Hy Regan. Some 39 families are given in Kerry by King.

Dutchman

A settler family, given on estates near Tralee, from the coming of the Elizabethan undertakers to the rebellion of 1641.

Dwyer, O'Dubuidir

Some 57 families of the name are given in Kerry, and it is noted that Ua Dubhuidhir was chief of Kilnamanagh in Tipperary.

Dyche

Chas. and Sam Dyche of Well lane are given in Co. Kerry.

Dyer

A settler family, given on estates near Tralee, from the coming of the Elizabethan undertakers to the rebellion of 1641. Descent / homeland:
Of Herts, Suffolk, Devon, Cornwall.

Eadie

Robert of Ballymalis, Co. Kerry.

Eagar, Agar, Egar

An extensive account of the Eagar family and the genealogy of four branches thereof is found in the works of J. King on Co. Kerry. He credits Miss O. Eagar, of Bedford, Listowel, for information given at that time. He also notes the work of J.F. Eagar that was completed many years earlier.

The spellings of the name in Ireland at that time (1908) were given as Eagar, Eagars, Eager, Eagers, Egar and Agar. The family is given in Kerry for 'the past 250 years', said to descend from the Saxon Alcher, Ealcher, or Aucher, who was first Earl of Kent (836-'65 A.D.). King gave 20 families of the name.

There was a Walter Fitz Auger at the time of the Norman conquest of England. During King James time Thomas Fitz Aunger was lord of the manor in Losenham in Kent. Henry Fitz Aucher of Kent was with Edward I at the siege of Carlaverock. In 1309-24 Henry Fitz Aucher (Auger) had 75 summons as as Alcherus, Aucherus, and Augerus. In later times the name was rendered Augar, Ager, Eber, Agar. The Norman Achard in like way has changed into Acard, Agard, Echard, and Eachard.

In 1502 we find record of John Egyr in Dublin, in 1532 the widow of Harry Agar, Esq. was buried at Canterbury. In 1541 Francis Eagar held the benefice of Trim, in Ireland. David Eager is found as one of the 1649 officers, and in 1738 we find Jhn Eger of Surrey, changing the spelling of his name to Eager.

About 1784 Charles Agar, then Archbishop of Cashel, came to Kerry and held a meeting of the clan, at that time it was urged that the spelling of Agar be used, according to J. King.

Bedford, in Galey parish, was noted as a residence of the Eagar family.

Eagar, Agar, Egar

The armorial bearings registered in Dublin Castle were: Azure, a lion rampant, or, armed and langued. Gules, gorged with an antique Irish crown of the last; a chief ermine. Crest: On a wreath of the colours, a demi-lion azure, gorged with an antique Irish crown, and charged on the shoulder with a mullet, or.
Motto: Facta non Verba.

Major Robert Eagar, of the army of Charles I., resided in Queen's Co., and married a Miss Hamilton. He left issue, two sons, Alexander and Charles. Charles, second son, was the ancestor of the Agars of Kilkenny.

Alexander Eagar, the eldest son, sold the Queen's County property derived from his father, and he had settled in Kerry at the Restoration in 1667. He was the first of the family to settle in Kerry.

A 'Genealogical History of the Eagar family', by F. J. Eagar, was published in Dublin, 1861; and a reprint of 'The Eagar Family', Co. Kerry, by Frederick John Eagar, Dublin 1880, are sources for further research.

Ballymalis Castle of Kilbonane parish was a Ferris stronghold confiscated in 1677, and granted to Sir Francis Brewster, who gave it to Alexander Eagar. Minard (1846) was the seat of Captain Eagar. In 1876 Rev. Eager owned 1,003 acres in Kerry.

Earls of Kerry

Lixnaw Court was a later residence of the (titular) Earls of Kerry.

Eaton

John Eaton of Martramane; in 1666 Symon Eaton was granted Ballenruddrie and Illanamin, in Clanmorris, 489 acres.

Edalicke

A settler family on estates near Tralee, from the coming of the Elizabethan undertakers to the rebellion of 1641.
John Edalicke lived in Tralee in 1622.

Edgeworth

Some 11 families of the name are given in Kerry, including those of Castleview, Carrigane, Glanawillan, Littor, Bromore, Croughweensha, Knockaclare and Skahanagh. In 1615 Francis Edgeworth was granted Ballyvoilan, Kilshannen, Killmanhen, Knocknemenagh, Tulleleige, and lepers house near Killaha.

Edwards

James of Tieraclea; Bridget of Kilaspicktarvin; John of Tonaknock; Michael of Rock street; John of Francis street; and John of Castle street are given in Kerry.

Egan, Mac Aodagain

Some 57 families of the name are given by King in Co. Kerry. Ua h Aedhagain was chief of Dartry and Hy Neillain. Mac Egan of Kings County was brehon to the MacCarthy Mor at Cashel.

Egelton

Bridget Egelton of Old Bridge street is found in Co. Kerry.

Mac Elligott

Some 103 Mac Elligott families are given in Co. Kerry. Anciently the family lands were between Listowel and Tralee and Castleisland, and the castles of Carrignafeela, and Arabella and Bernagrillagh were held by them in Ballymacelligott. The family arms are given by King as azure, a tower triple towered, argent; the crest a falcon rising, wings expanded and endorsed proper; the motto: Si Deus Quis contra.

Mary Mac Elligott in 1297 was the wife of Maurice Fitz Maurice and she had as her marriage dowry the lands of Galey, O'Brennan and Cloghanmackin. In 1584 Ulick Mac Thomas Eligot of Carrignefeilge held Bally Mac Elligott and Tullygarron, which were granted to Sir T. Roper in 1613. In 1588, Morris Mac Eligott held Ballygrillaghe Castle. In 1597, the lands of Thomas Mac Elligott in Galey and of John Mac Thomas, were granted to Edmond Barrett and Wm. O'Ronan and George Isham and Thomas Fitz Maurice, the Baron of Lixnaw. In 1619 John Mac Elligott, son of Thomas and nephew of Maurice, inherited the family estate in Bally Mac Elligott and Ballyseedy parishes; he was the son in law of Bishop Crosbie and sold Tulligarron to Daniel Chute in 1630, when the latter married his daughter, Johanna.

In 1653 Edmond of Galey and Mce. of Bally Mac Elligott were forfeiting proprietors. Edmond Mac Gerald Mac Elligott of Ballydonohuein Galey was pardoned in 1594, and from him was descended Edmond of Ballylongford b.1749, whose tomb is at Lislaghtin Abbey; his daughter Mary 1785-1871, M. Ryan of Kilrush; his dau. Margaret b. 1800, married D'Arcy of New York. His son Michael 1776-95, d.s.p.; his son Gerald b.1792, m. Ellen O'Connor

Mac Elligott

of Listowel, having Gerald, b.1828, m. Eliz. Adams of Listowel, having Gerald d.1885; Edw. d.1871; John m E. Cussen and dsp.1896.

In 1688 Col. Roger Mac Elligott of Bally Mac Elligott raised a foot regiment which served in England, and was M.P. for Ardfert in 1689; he surrendered Cork city as Governor in 1689, fought at the Battle of the Boyne, was a prisoner in the Tower of London until 1697; was exchanged to France and took command of the regiment de Clancarty of the Irish Brigade. His son, Capt. Charles, won the Cross of St. Louis at Fontenoy in 1745. J. King reported that Dr. Maurice G. Mac Elligott was researching Austria and Europe for individuals of the name and listed several of the family members found, in his work. Several of the name are found in the Austrian Army, including Baron MacElligott who was born at Tralee in 1752, entering that army in 1770 and was buried at Saint Jakob's Church in Brunn.

This is another old family of Co. Kerry, from whom the parish of BallymacElligot is said to be named. One account gives the name of MacElligot to actually be a form of McLeod. Lodge's Peerage says that in the 13th century that a Fitzmaurice was married to the daughter of Sir John McLeod of Galway, and that others of this family of McLeod settled in Co. Kerry. The name of McLeod was changed to MacElligot, thus giving the MacElligot family a pedigree from the noted Scots clan McLeod. Of the reliability of this I do not know. Others have said MacElligot is a truncated from of MacGillicutty, (i.e. Mac Gillicut = Mac Elligott).

Ballingrilough Castle belonged to the MacElligotts. (BallyMacElligott

Mac Elligott

Parish). Carrignafeela, the stone fort of the poets, was another MacElligott castle, where Arthur Denny died in 1619. As Tralee was in ruins, the Dennys used this castle as the manor house in 1588. It was afterwards the home of Wm. Ryeves and Alice Spring. Mr. Verdon lived here in 1756. Arabella was a third castle of the MacElligotts.

Chute Hall (1846) was acquired by marriage from the Mac Elligotts in 1630 by Daniel Chute. Richd. Chute lived here in 1756.

Elliott

In 1876 Alex of Tarbert owned 35 acres in Kerry, and Mary of Listowel owned 557 acres. David Elliott lived at Dingle in 1756. Alexander Elliott, of Dowhill in Limerick, m. Ellen Granville, leaving issue a son, ancestor of the owner of Tanavalla, near Listowel.

Ellis

Pat of Leitrim. Pat of Rossdohan, Thomas Ellis M.P. d. 1330, was master in Chancery who purchased Kilconlea, and his father, Mayor Ellis, had previously bought the Abbeyfeale estate from Mr. Meredith of Dicksgrove.

Mac Ellistum, Mac Alustruim

Several families of the name are given in Co. Kerry including: Norah of Gortshanavally, Richard of Ballydwyer; Tom of Ahane; Rd. of Ardoughter; Ml. of Ballyline; Margt. of Ballybunion; John and James of Benmore; Margt. of Rock-street; Thomas, T.D., Castle Mac Ellistrum in Tralee, after the family was attainted in 1579-1604, was held by Chris. Walsh in 1641.

Elrington

Bishop of Limerick in 1820.

Emmet

Of Robert Emmet, his mother was a Miss Mason of Ballydowney, near Killarney in Co. Kerry.

Endean

Herbert Endean of Waterville in Kerry.

Mac Endoo, Mac Conduib

The Rev. Robt. MacEndoo of Green lane, Co. Kerry, is given.

Mac Enery, Mac Ennery

David and Edm. of Hight-street; Tom of Knoppogue; Hy. of Slieveawaddra; John and Mary and Mary of Tubberatooreen; John of Cromane; Wm. Of Rock street; John of Staughton's row; Hy. of Strand-street; Pat of Spa Road, are all given in Co. Kerry.

Listed separately was the Rev. John Gerald Mac Ennery, Rev. of Ardfert 1786-1861, educated at Killarney, ordained 1810, went to Sorbonne in Paris, was administrator of Killarney, parish priest of Tralee 1822-54, Dean of Ardfert, retired in 1854, reserving only £50 a year as pension.

English

Some 12 families of the name are found in Kerry, including those of Gullane, Cloghanebane, Deereenavarig, Asdee, Ballinskelligs, Canuig, Boola, Collorus and Kinard.

Enright, Mac Ionnractaig

Some 127 families of the name are given in Co. Kerry, making the Enright population here very numerous.

Entivistle

P. Entivistle of Spunkane is given by J. King in Co. Kerry.

Erraught, Airachdan

Thos. Erraught of Mweenalaa, James of Ballyegan, and Terrence of Rathass are given in Kerry.

Evans

Some 29 families of the name are given in Co. Kerry. Rev. Wm. Raymond Evans, successor of Anne Raymond of 1871, owned 443 acres at Moybella in 1914.

Eveleigh
Richard Eveleigh of Cromane is given in Kerry; John Eveleigh was Dean of Ross in Cork in 1661.

Everatt
John Everatt of of Boherbee is given.

Mac Evoy
James of New street; Denis of Aughrim; Denis of Ahanagran; Francis of Ballinskelligs, are given in Kerry.

Exham
A settler family on estates near Tralee, from the coming of the Elizabethan undertakers to the rebellion of 1641. Descent / homeland: Of Devon.

Eyles
William Eyles of Avenue is given.

Fagan
Chevalier Fagan had a brother, John of Kiltallagh who married Mary Hickson of Tralee, having issue 8 sons, 5 of whom served in India.

Fahy
Jas. of Rae street; John of Courthouse Rd; Pat of Ballinskelligs; Rev. John of Waterville.

Fairfield
Chas. Fairfield, Major, d. 1853, m. Arabella Rowan, having Digby, Arthur, Charles, Edward, and Arabella. (See Ulick Kerin's poem on Fairfield).

Falhan, O'Failbe
John Falhan of Tarbert Island is given in Kerry.

Falvey (O'Failbhe)
Though comparatively little is found on the family here in latter days, anciently the Falvey family ruled as powerful chiefs and came to hold the rank of hereditary admirals of Desmond. O'Heerin finds them as chiefs of Corca Duibhne (barony of Corcaguiney), and of the lands running from Mang westward to Fiontraigh (Ventry). O'Brien also records the family in relationship to Corca Duibhne and finds them as lords of Ibhearatha (barony of Iveragh), in Co. Kerry.

Before the Normans came to Munster the O'Shea's and O'Falvey's were principal families in Kerry.

In 1045, the two Falveys, the future kings of Corcu Dubne, were slain by the Eoganacht Caisil. In 1092 Ua Seaghdha (O'Shea) ruled as lord of Corca Dhuibhne. In 1103 Ua Failbhe (Falvey), was tanist of Corca Dhuibhne. In 1158 Ua Failbhe was lord of Corca Duibhne, and Ui Seaghdha was lord of Ivereagh. Dunmore was given as the great fort of the Corca Duibhne clans of O'Falvey, O'Shea and O'Conghaile.

The O'Falvey's, although a broken clan by 1653 after the coming of Cromwell, still remained landowners near Caherciveen and Ballinskelligs, and one branch is given by J. King represented by the Morrogh-Bernards of Faha. The O'Shea's do not appear at all in the 1653 landowners list.

In 1656 the forfeiting proprietors included Donnogh of Iveragh, Dermott of Ardgill, Teig and Donough of Allagae. In 1656 Dermot of Kilkeeveragh had 115 retainers, and Hugh of Faha was also ordered to transplant. In 1711 Darby of Faha died, his wife was Gobnett Galway, his tomb is at Aglish, his son, John had a son Hugh, who had a son John d.s.p. 1807.

Falvey (O'Failbhe)

Failbe Fion, a naval commander, defeated the Danes and rescued Ceallacan of Cashel. In 1103, O'Falvey, tanist of Corcaguiny, and O'Muiray, chief of Ciarraige, fell in the battle of Mag Cabha in Co. Down. In 1158 O'Falvey was slain by the by the O'Sheas of Ivereagh. In 1302 Dermot O Falvey served in Scotland and was allowed to use English laws during his life, but that grant was repealed. In 1617 Aliv. O'Falvey was confidential man to Florence MacCarthy in the Tower of London. In 1757 Counselor Hugh Falvey bought lands fro Catholics in the penal times. Jerry Falvey, son of counsellor Hugh Falvey, went to France in 1773, he was an officer in the Irish Brigade and returned to Faha in 1783.

Some 41 Falvey families are given in Co. Kerry by J. King.

Farding

A settler family on estates near Tralee, from the coming of the Elizabethan undertakers to the rebellion of 1641. Descent / homeland: Of Cornwall ?

Mac Farland

Robt. MacFarland of Ardnamweely, Co. Kerry.

Farmer, Mac an Scoloige

Richard of Montanagay; Richard of Ballyconnel; John of Killeen, Honora of Rock Street, Wm. of Dean's Lane, Robt. and Wm. of Canal new road, are given in Co. Kerry.

Farrell, O'Feargail

O'Farrell of Annaly in Longford is given by King in his works, along with 18 families of the name in Kerry.

Farressy, O'Fearguis

Michael Farressy of Tieraclea, Kerry.

Fay, O'Feic

Tom Fay of Ballymullen and Peter Fay of Coramore are given.

Fealy, O'Fidgeallaig

Some 17 families of the name are given in Kerry. Ua Fitcheallaigh was given as the old clan name of the Fealy family by J. King.

Feeney

Tom Feeney of Inch in Co. Kerry.

Fell

A settler family on estates near Tralee, from the coming of the Elizabethan undertakers to the rebellion of 1641. Descent / homeland: Of Cumberland.

Michael Fell of Ballybane, Co. Kerry.

Fenaghty Finaghty

Ua Finnactaig (O'Fionnacta or Fenaghty) of Cruaghan, chief of clann Murcada is cited by King, along with 11 families of Fenaghty in Kerry.

Fenix

Mary and Ellen Fenix of Dromkeen are given in Co. Kerry.

Fennell

Pat of Tarmons; Wm. of Shanaway; David of Leitrim; David and David of Leanamore are given in Co. Kerry.

Fenton, Fintan, Fiontain

Some 33 families of the name are given in Co. Kerry. In 1606 grant was made to Sir Geoffrey Fenton, Knt., of the wardship of Valentine Browne, son of Sir Nich. Browne, of Malahaff, in Co. Kerry.

The Castle of the Island of Kerry was built in 1226 by Geoffrey de Marisco, and taken by Sir Ralph Ufford in 1345 from the Geraldines. The lands were delivered to Walerond Fenton after the death of Wm. Mareschall, Earl of Pembroke. (Castleisland parish).

Fenton, Fintan, Fiontain, O'Fiontain, and O'Fiannacta were all listed together.

Ferris, Farris

Some 27 families of the name are given in Kerry by J. King. In 1613 Edward Southworth was granted lands of Daniel Mac Fearriss at Bealahamalis in Kilbonane, Ballymacpriorie in Killorglin, Bunglassie in Glanbehy, and Ceapinghucosy in Templenoe. In 1653 further confiscation and transplantation occurred against Murrough Mac Owen Ferris of Ballymalis, John Ferris of Dunkerron, and John Ferris of Ballymacprior.

In 1656 Sir Francis Brewster held the confiscated lands of Turlough MacOwen Ferris and leased Ballymalis castle and Culleenymore to Alex. Eagar, and they passed later to Col. Stokes. In 1799 Eugene Ferris was a tenant to the Eager family at Culleenybeg in Kilbonane. In 1796 Edward Ferris was an ensign in Col. Conways Irish brigade.

Ballymalis Castle between Killarney and Killorglin, of Kilbonane parish was a Ferris stronghold confiscated in 1677, and granted to Sir Francis Brewster, who gave it to Alexander Eagar.

This castle appears to be a 15th century building. On the projection at the W. angle can be seen the Fleur de Lys cut in the supporting limestone corbels. The castle stands on a rising ground on the bank of the Launne, and was a frontier fort between the Geraldine and MacCarthy lands. The Ferris family still reside in the district, and their burial tomb bears the coat of arms. For a pre-Christian history of Dun Ferris see the history of Liselton parish.

Ferriter

King gives us 16 families of the name in his work, including those of Balloughtra and Caherquin. In 1290, Martin, the Ferreter, paid 1 mark for trespass to the sheriff of Kerry. Pierce Ferriter, poet and soldier, was executed in Killarney by the English soldiers in 1652; he was a great Catholic bard and harper, he owned the Blasquet or Ferriter's islands and Ferriter's castle in Dunquin, under the Geraldines.

Dominick and Edmund Ferriter also followed the Stuart cause, and Maurice and Peter were attainted.

Castle Sybil, in Dunurlin parish was built by Widow Sybilla Ferriter. Some maps show it as Castle Sibbell.

Ballyferriter, Ferriter's baile, in Dunnurlin is given as the home of the poet and soldier Pierce Ferriter, who was executed in Killarney in 1652, here was found a stone circle, a cromleach, and a holy well.

Mac Fheorais, (see Ferris)

Field, O'Fitceallaig

Mary Field of Scartlea, Co. Kerry.

Figgis

Thomas Figgis of Tullahinnell is given in Co. Kerry.

Finaghty, O'Fionnacta

Simon of Rathmore; Margaret and John of Ballincota and John of Kildurrihy of Co. Kerry.

Finch

Simon Finch, lt. col., 1666, was granted Gortlicky and Commenacullane in in Magunnihy barony.

Mac Fineen

See MacCarthy. See Sullivan.

Finn, O'Finn

Some 24 Finn families are given in Co. Kerry, according to the works King.

Mac Finneen

Some give the Mac Finneen family to descend from a branch of the Mac Carthys, others say they were a branch of the O'Sullivans.

Finnegan, O'Fionnagain

King gives 22 Finnegan families in Kerry.

Finnerty, O'Fionnacta

Michael of Ballyegan; Michael of Lacca; Jerh. of Banemore; Jas. of Wilgulbin; Con of Curraghlea; Pat and John of Ferritersquarter are all given in Co. Kerry.

Finucane, Finnucane

Some 25 Finucane families are given in Kerry.

Fisher, O'Bradain

John Fisher of Pound lane; Fanny E. Fisher in 1890 wrote poems of Killarney. In 1611 Sir Edward Fisher was granted Barrow, Crotto, etc..lands of the Earl of Desmond, and of Mce. and Philip Stacke, attainted.

Fisher, O'Bradain, and Mac an Iascaire were listed together, the latter being older Irish forms of the name.

Fitz Anthony

Thomas Fitz Anthony in 1215 was granted the lands of Decies and Desmond, and they passed in 1259 to his daughter Margery, and to her husband John Fitz Thomas Fitz Gerald, thus laying the foundation of the Geraldine palatinate until 1583.

Fitz Erin

Rev. John F. Day Fitz Erin, wrote Killarney sketches in 1862.

Fitz Gibbon

Fitz Gibbon is given as descended originally from Gilbert Fitz Gerald, the White Knight of Mitchelstown, son of John Fitz Thomas lord of Decies and Desmond in 1260. Nine families of the name are given in Kerry by J. King: James of Hewson's Lane; John of Gortnaskeha; Gerald of Tieraclea; Wm. of Pound lane; John of Brogue lane; John of Boherbee; David of Strand street; Edw. of Chute's lane; and John of Ardtully.

Fitz Simon Fitz Symon(s)

Ellen O'Connell Fitz Simon wrote 'Darrynane' in 1832 and other poems.

Fitzell

Some 21 families of the name are given by J. King including those of Carhoonakilla, Glencullane, Gurteenavallig, Meelcon, Ballymacandrew, Togherbane, Trieneragh, Lislaughten, Kilcogan, Commons, Ballinascreena, Ballymullen and Knockawaddra. Demonsthenes Fitzell was resident in the last entry.

FitzGerald
Extract From The Irish Book of Arms.
(IGF) 1988.

Fitzgerald

The Fitz Geralds, or Geraldines, are given as a branch of the Gerardini of Florence and Elsa in Italy. Otho Geraldino came to England with William of Normandy, the Conqueror. Otho had a son Waltero, who had a son Gerald whose son Maurice came to Ireland in 1169 with the Norman invasions, and had Gerald, ancestor of the Duke of Leinster, and Thomas, ancestor of the Earls of Desmond and Kerry families. There were 16 earls of Desmond, of whom the first was created in 1329.

Soon these Geraldines are given as having become more Irish than the 'Irish tribes'. In 1244 the English King granted to John FitzThomas a charter of 'free chase and warren in Okonyl, Muskry, Kerry, Yonacht, and Orathat, that is, in West Cork, West Limerick and Kerry; and in 1259 he was granted Decies and Desmond when his wife's father Thomas FitzAnthony died; in 1261 he and his son were killed in battle against the Irish at Callan, near Kenmare. Of this line was Gerald, killed in 1583, when 500,000 acres of his land were confiscated by English Undertakers.

Jas. Fitz Gerald 17th earl of Desmond died unmarried in the Tower of London in 1601. The earl of Desmond had the power to create barons and hereditary knights, and had royal jurisdiction. The Earl of Desmond held his court at Castle Island without interruption until 1576.

Thomas Fitzgerald, Baron of the Island of Kerry (son of John FitzThomas, lord of Decies and Desmond in 1260) was ancestor of the sliochts Shane of Ardnagragh, Maurice Duffe and Edmund of Corkaguiney.

Kilmurry Castle was taken from the Fitzgeralds by Col. Phaire in 1650. Cala na Feirse, Callanfersey Castle, was built by Maurice Fitzgerald.

Killorglin Castle and Manor reverted to the Fitzgeralds from the Knights Templars. It was then granted to Capt. Conway, and later bought by the Mullins family from the B'hassetts. Florence MacCartie More caused the castle to be burned around 1600, fearing Sir Charles Wilmot would settle there.

Castlemaine fortress was the pass into Kerry in Geraldine times. It was frequently besieged between 1571 and 1652. It was built by Maurice Fitzgerald in 1240, with Dunloe and Killorglin.(Kiltallagh parish).

Dunloe Castle was bombarded by Ireton. D. Mahony resided there in 1864. It was one of O'Sullivan Mor's forts, but was built by Maurice Fitzgerald. It was usually in charge of the Sugrue O'Sullivans. Dunkerron was O'Sullivan Mor's chief seats.

Molahiffe Castle and Clonmellane Castle were built by Maurice Fitzgerald.

The inquisition into the estates of the Geraldines in Munster was taken in 1584. Morris and Edmond Fitz Gerald, the sons of Edmund Fitz John, forfeited Behinagh, and Glandyne in 1641.

It is no surprise to find a numerous 376 Fitzgerald families in Co. Kerry, as listed by J. King.

Fitzimmons

John Fitzimmons of Derryquin is given. It is just as likely that the name would be found today as Fitzsimmons...

FitzJohn

Morris and Edmond Fitz Gerald, the sons of Edmund Fitz John, forfeited Behinagh, Glandyne and other lands in 1641.

Fitzmaurice

In 1172 Dermot MacCarthy, king of Cork and Desmond, swore fealty to Henry II. It remained however a necessity that the Norman knights had to be provided with estates to stay in Ireland, and to subdue further resistance. They would sometimes have to take by force, that which was 'bestowed' upon them by official policy. Dermot was gradually driven westward, and the MacCarthys, who had been originally in Cork, became from these circumstances located in in Kerry.

Dermot's son, Cormac, rebelling against his father, called in Raymond le Gros to assist him in subduing the rebels. Raymond succeeded, and eventually beheaded Cormac! In return, Dermot MacCarthy bestowed on him considerable lands at Lixnaw, where the Norman noble settled his son, Maurice, and thus was founded the famous family of Fitzmaurice, while the district of land obtained the name of Clanmaurice.

Of the Fitzmaurice-Landsdowne family. The houses of Fitzgerald, Fitzmaurice, Windsor and Carew had a common ancestor in Walter Fitz-Otho, Castellan of Windsor, whose eldest son was William, who came to Ireland with Strongbow in 1171. His youngest son Griffin Fitz-William had a son Reimund Fitz-Griffin, whose son was Maurice Fitz-Thomas, 1st Lord of Kerry and Lixnaw, who founded the Grey Franciscan Friary of Ardfert in 1253. In the thirteenth century it is given that the Fitzmaurices, Earls of Kerry, assumed many territories of the O'Connors.

100,000 acres were granted to the barons of Kerry by the Henry II; the map of the estate in 1697 gives 72,000+ acres of which 1,093 were in Trughenacmy and the remainder in Clanmaurice and Iraghticonnor.

In 1876, the Landsdowne estate, in Dunkerron, contained 94,983 acres. In 1612 Thomas Fitz Maurice, baron of Lixnaw, was granted the lands of his father. The ancient seat was at Lixnaw, up to which the tide flowed. The Petty estate in South Kerry passed into the Fitz Maurice hands by marriage to the daughter of Sir Wm. Petty. The Petty arms and surname were assumed by John, son of Thomas.

Ardfert Castle, built in 1312 by Nicholas Fitz-Maurice was taken in 1600 by Sir Charles Wilmot. It was rebuilt in 1637 by Patrick, Lord Kerry. It was demolished in 1641 by the Irish Army. (Ardfert Parish).

Ballykealy Castle in Kilnanare parish was an old residence of the Fitzmaurices. Ballykealy Castle and Ballymacaquim Castle, on the plain of North Kerry, between Lixnaw and Ardfert were noted 'favorite residences' of the Fitmaurices.

Listowel Castle was captured in 1600 by Sir Charles Wilmot who put the entire garrison to the sword. This Fitz Maurice castle and manor was purchased from the Earls of Kerry by the father of the first Earl of Listowel.

Some 55 families of the name are given in Kerry by J. King.

Fitzpatrick, Fitz Patrick

It was given by J. King that Brien, Baron of Upper Ossory, in 1541, used the name Fitz Patrick. There are 20 families of the name in Kerry as given.

Flahavin Flahavin Flavin

Nine families of the name are found in Kerry: John and Michael Flahavin of Doon; James and James of Aughrim; Michael of Astee; John of Ahanagran; John of Ballylongford; Michael of Kilgarvan; and Martin of Coolaclarig.

Flahavin Flahavin and O'Flaiteamain were all listed together.

Flaherty

106 Flaherty families are given in Kerry by J. King. The family being fairly numerous in Ireland, it is not suprising to find it common in Kerry, but relatively little mention of the family is made by the author cited.

Flahive, Flaitim

Some 35 Flahive families are recorded in Kerry by J. King.

Flanagan, O'Flannagain

Given under the heading of Clann Cathaol in the work of J. King, Flanagan households included those of: Tom of Cloghane; Mary of Rea; Jerh. of Ballyeagh; Michael of Ballinclemesig; and James of Cahirdown.

Flannery, O'Flannabra

Pat Flannery of Strand road and Mary Flannery of Fair Green, in Co. Kerry.

O'Flannabra and O'Flanngaile were given as possible older forms of the name.

Flavin

King gave just 13 families of the name in Co. Kerry, including that of J. of Tawlaght and Rock-street who was M.P. for many years.

Fleete

A settler family on estates near Tralee, from the coming of the Elizabethan undertakers to the rebellion of 1641. Descent / homeland: Of Kent.

Fleming Flemyng Flyming

A sizable family of Co. Kerry, with some 97 families given by J. King.

Fleming, lord Slane, is given in 1726. John le Fleming in 1298 was a juror at the Manor de Insula, Castleisland. John Flemyng in 1398 was vicar of Cacybresleayn. Rev. David Fleming, O.F.M., b. 1851 at Ballycasheen, d. 1915 at Forest Gate, and was vicar-general.

Fletcher

A settler family on estates near Tralee, from the coming of the Elizabethan undertakers to the rebellion of 1641.

Florette

Susan Florette of Bishop's, Co. Kerry.

Flower

Harry Flower of Ballyheigue is given.

Flynn, Flinn, O'Floin

Anciently the Flynn family has been given from Carbery Musc and Conary II, the ard ri in A.D. 158, of the clan Conaire, chief of Muscraide O Flynn and Mitaine. A numerous surname in Kerry, some 131 families are given.

Fogarty, O'Fogartaig

Given of the territory of south Eile; some 21 families of the name are given in Co. Kerry.

Foley

One of the most numerous names in all of Co. Kerry, some 369 families are listed by J. King.

Anglont House, Killorglin parish, was the residence of the Foley family in the past. Connelly O'Neill lived there in 1821.

Jeramiah Foley of Killorglin wrote Gaelic books; rev. Daniel Foley 1815-74 compiled an English-Irish dictionary. In 1876 James Foley of Killorglin owned 1603 acres in Kerry and E. H. Foley of Ballyard 1604 acres.

Foran, O'Fuartain

Some 32 families of the name are given in Co. Kerry.

Forde, O'Fuartain

John Forde of Knockbrack; Wm. of Knockdarrive; Jerh. of Cummeenavrick; Denis of Ardnamweely; Edm. of Foil; Tim of Knoppogue; and James of Lackeen are given.

Forest

A settler family on estates near Tralee, from the coming of the Elizabethan undertakers to the rebellion of 1641. Descent / homeland: Of Hunts.

Timothy Forest is found in Cromane lower, Co. Kerry.

Fornan

Margaret Fornan of Minish is given.

Fosberry

George Fosberry of Blennerville, owned 1437 acres in Kerry in 1876.

Foulkes or Foundes

A settler family on estates near Tralee, from the coming of the Elizabethan undertakers to the rebellion of 1641. Descent / homeland: Devon, Wales.

Fox, O'Sionnaig

John Fox of Ratoo, Co. Kerry.

Foy, O'Fiaie

Hugh Foy of Knockawinna, Co. Kerry.

Francis, Proinseis

Robert and Honoria Francis of Lahaserough; Tom of Knockglossmore; Jas. and John and Jas. of Shanakyle.

Frawley, O'Freagaile

Jas. Frawley of Rackett lane, Kerry.

Frazer, Friseal, Frizelle

Sam Frazer of Derryquin is given. Askive, in the parish of Kilcrohane, was the home of Henry Stokes, C.E.; then home to S. Fraser, C.E., in the days of J. King. Reverts to owner of Derriquin Estate upon lease expiration.

Frazer, Friseal, Frizelle, and Frasier were all given as variant spellings.

Freeman, O'Saoraide

Michael Freeman of Caherbreagh; Pat and Jane of Blennerville; Pat of Nelson street; and Thos. of Tralee in 1714.

French, de Freins

Fred French of Lahard; Ellen French of New street; Sam French of Mangerton view.

Frewan, Friuin

Jerh. Frewan of Nelson street.

Friend

Capt. John Friend in 1666 was granted Cloumsey, Kearnekerry, Arde and Rattoo.

Frizelle, Friseal, Frazer

Robert Frizelle of Flemby is given.

Fry

The Rev. Charles Fry of Ballybunion.

Fuller of Glashnacree, Co. Kerry
From The Irish Book of Arms. (IGF) 1988.

Fuller

The Fuller family of Kerry, and formerly also of Co. Cork, likely came from Halstead, in Kent, the one branch deriving from Richard of St. Finn Barrie, whose will was proved in England in 1635. There he mentioned his third son John, and stated "if he ever comes over again", a phrase which points to Ireland.

John Fuller is mentioned in the Desmond Survey of 1583 a.d., as holding the town lands of Bowlerstown (Ballybowler) and lands in Ballybeg, Garfinny parish. He mortgaged Bowlerstown to Stephen Rice in 1610. It was stated that he received lands as a 'knights service', and he apparently also is on record as being pardoned in 1603, being then given located at Rahinane. His son was Maurice.

Richard Fuller of St. Finn Barrie, in his will proved in 1642, gives his wife Mary, 2 daughters and 3 sons, John, Richard and Ezekiel, one of whom was father of William Fuller, of Donoughmore and Donoughbeg, leased from Laurence, Lord Barrymore, in 1696.

Much genealogical material is to be found in Kings History of Kerry on this family. The line of George, who was Mayor of Cork in 1734, and several are found as treasurer/ sheriffs of Cork. There it was stated that Franklin Fuller of of Glashnacree said that the Rev. Father Michael Fuller and others of the name in Co. Kerry were all of the same original stock, though having become Roman Catholic, the links have been lost. He was able to trace back the Rev. Fuller to Stephen Fuller of Glenoe, Kilfeighney aged 60 in 1821 (census). One of the line is also given in Australia. Lands were owned in Cork, Kerry and Limerick in Ireland.

The Hibernian Chronicle of Cork on Sept. 13, 1770 gives an account of William Fullers cattle as among several others being damaged on the lands of Maligmore, Murrigh, Cooles and Killurly, in the barony of Ivereagh. There may be a connection to Sleevanmillig in Prior parish and this Fullers lands.

Also found listed as a settler family name, given on estates near Tralee, from the coming of the Elizabethan undertakers to the rebellion of 1641, originally of Essex. Of the Church Historians family. Related to the Ropers. Edw. Fuller lived in Tralee in 1622. In 1833 we find Thomas H. of Kenmare, Edward of Kenmare, Blennerhassett Fuller of Kenmare. John of Tralee in 1908, and Jas. F. Fuller of Glashnacree in 1908.

Beechmount (1846) was formerly the property of Capt. Edward Fuller, grandfather of James Franklin Fuller of Glashnacree. Glashnacree in the parish of Kilcrohane, was the residence of James Franklin Fuller as well.

William Fuller, (the brother of Thomas Fuller, treasurer of Cork), had the reputation of depopulating a large tract of land, and substituting cattle on grazing ranches. He married a daughter of William Harnet of Ballyhenry.

Some Royal, Noble, and Gentle Descents of the Kerry branch of the Fuller family, by James F. Fuller, was published in 1880. There is also a fairly complete account of this old Munster family in 'Burke's Landed Gentry.'.

Some 15 families of the name were noted in Co. Kerry by J. King.

Fullerton

Sir James Fullerton, 1603-1607, was granted church property at Rattoo, Lisselton, Galie, Aghavallin, Disert, Listowel, Murher, Knockanure, Kilnaghtin, Killeheny and Ballyconnery.

Fyfe, O'Fiaca
Thomas Fyfe of Spunkane is given.

Gabriel
A settler family, given on estates near Tralee, from the coming of the Elizabethan undertakers to the rebellion of 1641.

Gaffney, O'Gamna
John Gaffney of Mary street is given in Kerry.

Gage
Viscount Gage of Castleisland in Co. Kerry, and of Castlebar in Co. Mayo. (see also the peerage of Ireland.)

Mac Gailey, Mac Amalgada
Frank MacGailey of Quill Street in Co. Kerry.

Gaine, O'Geibinn
Some 13 Gaine families were given in Kerry by King.

Gallagher, O'Gallcobair
Cited was the Gallagher family of Donegal; for in 1666 Thos. Gallagher was granted Drumbegg and Shrone in Galey. Mary of Tieraclea, Catherine of Farranwilliam, John of Rock street and John of Caheranne road are given in Co. Kerry.

Gallen, O'Galain
Mrs. K. Gallen of Dromurrin is given.

Gallivan Galvin O'Gealbain
Some 171 Gallivan families are given in Co. Kerry by J. King.

Gallwey, de Gaillide
Thomas Gallwey in 1871 wrote 'Lays of Killarney'; Major Gallwey, R.M. for Abbeyfeale, d. 1864 and was buried at Templeglantine; Catherine, widow of Thomas of Killarney, d. 1914 aged 93; Sir Henry was governor of Gambia in 1876; M. Gallwey of Dingle owned 605 acres in Kerry and Edw. of Queens Co., 1,571. In 1796 Thomas was agent for Lord Kenmare at Killarney; Sir Jeffrey Gallway forfeited lands at Dunkerron in 1656; Jeffrey at Kinsale had a son Wm., the recorder of Kinsale, d. 1637. In 1776 Chris & Thomas resided at Killarney; in 1828 Chris was agent to Lord Kenmare; in 1821 John resided at Farmhill, and Stephen at Killarney. General Sir Thomas Gallwey, 1821-1906, was the eldest son of Major Gallwey, R.I.C. was born at Killarney, and was Governor of Bermuda; his son Henry was b. 1859.

David and Michael Gallwey of Gortshanavough and Stephen of Glandahalin are given in Kerry by J. King.

Gandsey
James Gandsey, 1769-1857, the famous 'blind piper' of Killarney, often written about, whose portrait was in the National Library in Dublin. An attack of smallpox caused his blindness. He was buried at Aghadoe.

Gannon, O'Gionnain
Edward Gannon of Tralee is given and N. J. Gannon in 1858 wrote the 'O'Donoghue of the Lakes'.

Gannon, O'Gionnain, and Mag Fionnain were all listed together.

Garvey, O'Gairbit
Some 44 Garvey families are given in Kerry by J. King.

Gavan
Mary Gavan of Barrow, Co. Kerry.

Gavey
Mary Gavey of Nelson street is given.

Gaynor, Gainor
Some 12 families of the name are given in Co. Kerry, including those of Tiduff, Glenderry, Ballinclemesig, Dreenagh, and Glandahalin.

Geany, O'Feibeannaig
John and Pat Geany of Rathmore; Johanna and Mary of Lackbroder; David of Knockaneacoolteen; and Jas. of Ballahantouragh are given in Kerry.

Geary, O'Gadra
Francis and Edward Geary of Tralee and Henry of Lounaghan are given in Kerry.

Mac Gee, Magee
Given in Co. Kerry were Ellen of Barry's lane; and Captain Magee, who m. Bridget Crosbie, d. in Lisbon Dominican Convent, having issue Geo. and Theobald, who conformed in 1725; Theobald in 1745 left Portmagee, Reencaragh, etc..to his nephew David Lauder, and Ballmore to Eliza Hussey's son.

Geehan Geahan O'Gaoitin
Batt and John Geehan of Meanus; Jerh. and Margaret and Jerh. and John Geehan of Dooaghs are given.

Gentleman of Ballyhorgan
Henry Gentleman of Knoppogue; Robert of Ballyhorgan; Hanora of Fahavane; Francis of Glandahalin; Geo. of Lixnaw had a son Francis, whose son Robt. b. 1787, had Goodman, whose son Robt. George Goodman Gentleman 1846-1913, had G. 1879, A. 1887, R. 1890, S., E.

Geraldine Fortress
Clonmellane Castle in Kilnanare parish was a Geraldine fortress.

Geran, O'Gearain
Some 16 families of the name are given in Co. Kerry, including those of Rockfield; Maulyarkane; Gortaree; Ballymacquin; Glandahalin; Ballyhadigue; Derrindaff; Clashmeloon; Tiershanaghan; Ballyheige; Strand road; Cromane; John street; Greenview tce.; Cooleanig; and Dunloe.

Mac Gibbon
Margaret Mac Gibbon of Carrig Island.

Gibson, Mac Gib, O'Gibealla
A settler family on estates near Tralee, from the coming of the Elizabethan undertakers to the rebellion of 1641. Descent / homeland:
Of Essex, Kent, Norfolk.
Tom Gibson of Listowel; Geo. of Caherciveen; and William of Spunkane are given in Kerry.

Gilbert, Gilbeart
Margaret and Garrett and Hy. of Ballynagare; Mce. of Loughanes; Pat of Ardcanaght are given and Gilbert in 1225 was bishop of Ardfert.

Giles, O'Glaisne
Robt. of Rossnacarteenmore; Marshall of main street; Mary of Gransha; Johnof Tonreigh; and John of Milltown are given in Kerry.

Mac Gill
Several of the name are given in Co. Kerry by J. King, including Darby Magill of Churchtown who married in 1767 Catherine Mahoney of Dromore.

Gill MacGiolla MacanGoill
John of Gortagass; John of Victoria Terrace; Tom of Lounaghan; Wm. of Cappanacush; Tom and Pat of Tullig.

Mac Gillycuddy

Mac Giolla Mocuda O'Sullivan is given by J. King as the fuller and more ancient form of the family name of MacGillycuddy, which today appears under many spellings. Some 80 families of the name are given in Co. Kerry, including The MacGillycuddy of Bauncluain.

The MacGillycuddy Papers were edited by Wm. Brady in 1867. The succession of the 18 chieftains from Domhnal Mor O'Sullivan have been Gilla Mochuda, Dunlaing, Gilla Mochuda Caech, Conchobar, Giolla Mochuda, Conchobar, Donnchadh, Domhnall Geraltach, Conchobar, Donogh, Cornelius, Dennis, Denis, Cornelius, Richard, Richard, Richard.

Denis Donogh McGillycuddy b. 1852 m. 1881 Gertrude Laura Miller, Ringwood, New Jersey, U.S.A..

MacGillycuddy's Reeks in Knockane parish, form a group of the highest mountains in the country, exceeding 3,400 ft..

The MacGillycuddy family held large tracts of land in the barony of Dunkerron, and note the place name of MacGillicuddy's Reeks in Kerry. Smith gives Mac Gilly Cuddy's Castle as standing two miles west of Dunlow, standing to the north of the mountains called Mac Gilly Cuddy's reeks.

Whitefield (1846) was the residence of MacGillicuddy. The old name was Banecluone. A full account of the MacGillicuddy sept of the O'Sullivan's was compiled by Dr. W. M. Brady in 1867. (Knockane parish). Castle Cor was the old fort of the MacGillicuddy O'Sullivans in the Knockane parish.

Litter Castle in Caher parish, belonged to the Mac Crehan family, an offshoot of the O'Sullivan Mor clan as were the MacGillycuddys.

Mac Gillycuddy Gillacoddy

Gilla-Mochuda, the eldest son of Domhnall Mor, or Daniel, the great O'Sullivan of Carrig Finvoy, in Carbury, Co. Cork, is the man from whom the name Mac Gilla Mochuda or Mac Gillacuddy is derived.

In a MS. History of Kerry in the Royal Irish Acadamy, written about 1750, it was stated that 'most of this family till Cromwells time still call themselves O'Sullivans, but the head of the family was still called MacGillacoddy. But since that time most of them call themselves McGilsacoddys, but such as go abroad, as did the Rev. Dr. Florence O'Sullivan, one time President of the Irish College at Louvain'.

The estates of the McGillycuddy sept in Kerry anciently were given to be vast, and the confiscated lands of Donald or Donough McDermott O'Sullivan, otherwise called McGillycuddy, was of considerable size as well.

Denis McGillycuddy in 1716, recovered by lease from the Crosbies, some land left to him in his grandfathers will. In 1718 he became a Protestant and in 1724 went to Guelderland to look after property his brother Cornelius gave him in 1723.

Richard McGillycuddy of Banecluone, or Whitefield, succeeded to the family estates in 1826, upon which he expanded and improved. He was high sheriff in 1824. He was succeeded by his eldest son by his second wife, Richard Patrick, who was born July 15, 1850, given as the present 'The McGillycuddy of the Reeks' in the Kerry Archaeological Magazine, October, 1915. Extensive material on the family is contained in that work.

Gilmour, Mac Giolla Muire

William Gilmour of Flesk is given.

Mac Ginley
Bernard Mac Ginley of Listowel, Co. Kerry.

Mac Ginn
Hugh Mac Ginn of Quay Street, is given in Co. Kerry.

Ginnaw, Mac Cineait
Michael and William of Knockanebrack are given in Kerry.

Mac Gillycuddy
Extract From The Irish Book of Arms. (IGF) 1988.

Gentleman of Ballyhorgan & Mountcoal
From The Irish Book of Arms. (IGF) 1988.

Ginnis Gennys Gynes

The Ginnis family name first appears in Tralee in 1677. The Hearth Money Rolls of 1667 give no one of the name at that time - so the first is thought to have arrived here at least by 1677. Under favor of the Denny family, they came to enjoy considerable leasehold property down to the 18th century when the male line appears to cease. This family was of the 'British race, blood and sirname', taking the place of those exterminated in the rebellion.

John Gennis, tenant of the Denny's in Tralee in 1677 is given to be of the same family as John Gennys, tenant of Lady Denny's father at Launceston at the end of the 16th century. The names John and William are most common in the Tralee family, and also common in the Cornish family. Variant spellings of the name in Kerry are given as Ginnis, Gennis, Guinies, Guinis, Guinness.

Abraham Ginnis is found in 1725 and living in 1728; and d. before 1750.

Arthur Ginnis of Tralee, b. 1670 had John Ginnis, proprietor of the 'King's Arms' Tralee, b. 1710, leaving by Mary his wife a son: John Ginnis of Tralee and Thurles, Co. Tipperary, alive in 1778. Another son was William Ginnis of Tralee and of Cork, b. 1716.

Some reasons are given for believing the Guinnesses of Kildare and Dublin (then represented by Lord Ardilaun and Viscount Iveagh) may have come of the same stock as the Gennyses of Launceston, and the Ginnises of Tralee. There existed an old and persistent tradition that the family came from Cornwall in the Cromwellian period. This was ignored by Sir Bernard Burke and Sir Samuel Ferguson when making the researches which resulted in their producing evidence, (later 'discredited'),

Ginnis Gennys Gynes
showing descent from MacGennises of Iveagh.

The first known ancestor of the Guinnesses was Richard Guinness of Celbridge, Co. Kildare. He was in the early 18th century, in the service of Dr. Price, Archbishop of Cashel, whose niece was wife of Rev. Bartholomew Vigors, Dean of Leighlin. The Vigors came from Launceston, where they were neighbors and kinsfolk of the Gennyses. Another Vigors was chaplain in Munster, in the end of the reign of Charles I., to Lord Broghill, uncle of Lady Ellen Denny of Tralee, and brother of the Countess of Kildare. These are possible links between Launceston, Tralee and Kildare at a period when many new settlers came to Ireland.

Mention is also made of Gynes or Ginnis families settling in Co. Kerry, subsequent to the 1641-42 rebellion. This was the Gynes family of Essex, related to the Carews and Bradshaws. Variant spellings given include Gennis, Genys, Ginnis, Genys of Devon, Cornw. Giney, Genney of Norf., and Gynes.

Also listed separately we find One John Ginnis of Tralee is found 1677-80. Abraham Ginnis in 1725 held a Denny tenement in Tralee, and had a son John. Arthur Ginnis, b. 1670, was quartermaster in Kerry Dragoons 1728-29, grand juror in 1721: left a son John who was owner of the Kings Arms public house in Tralee, and had a son John of Tralee and Thurles. Wm. Ginnis, owner of the Kings Arms in Tralee, d. 1727, had a dau. Isabella, b. 1692, m. Rev. Wm. Cameron having issue.

Girvan, O'Garbain
Wm. of Market street is given in Kerry.

Giunings Giney Ginney
A settler family on estates near Tralee, from the coming of the Elizabethan undertakers to the rebellion of 1641. Descent / homeland: Giney of Norfolk; or Ginney of Norf. and Suff.; or Jennings of Devon and Cornwall; or Jenynges of Suff and Devon.

Giunings Giney Ginney Jennings and Jenynges were given variant spellings.

Glandore, Earl of
Wm. Crosbie, Earl of Glandore, m. Lady Theo Blythe.

Glavin, O'Glaimin, O'Glavin
John Glavin of Lissyvigeen, Mary Glavin of Glanawillan, Mary of Muckenagh, Edm. of Lackamore, Edm. of Knocknacauska, Tom of Curravough, and John of Boherbee are given in Kerry.

Gleasure, Glazier, Gleasur
Adam and Henry and Rogt. of Tullig; George of Listowel and John of Annagh are given in Kerry.

Gleeson Gleason O'Gleasain
Some 35 Gleeson families are given in Kerry by J. King. O'Glaisin is given as ancient chief of Hy Mac Caile, later called Imokilly barony, in Co. Cork.

Glissane, O'Glasain
Some 15 families are given in Kerry under the spelling of Glissane according to J. King. He also relates the name to Gleeson, as some Glissane families have interchanged the spelling with Gleeson.

Gloster
Several of the name are found in Co. Kerry, although not given as numerous here. They included those of Clounmalane; Gortdromerillagh; Longfield; Boolacullane; Garryrooth; Strand road; Burnham; Ballydavid; Murreigh; Gallerus; and Kilcooly.

Glover
Geo. Glover of Ranalough and Wm. & Wm. of Moyderwell are given in Kerry.

Mac Glynn
John MacGlynn of Cragg, John of Coolavanny, Hanorah of Rock Street, and Wm. of Curragraigue in Co. Kerry.

Glynn, Mag Floinn
Andrew Glynn of Killarney is given in 1821.

Goddard
Given as the name of a family settling in Co. Kerry, subsequent to the 1641-42 rebellion. Descent/ Homeland:
Of Bucks, Norf., Suff. Cromwellian. Edward Goddard of Glenlough, is given in Kerry.

Godding
Charles Godding of Fenit Co. Kerry.

Godfrey, Mac Gotraid
Given as the name of a family settling in Co. Kerry, subsequent to the 1641-42 rebellion. Descent/ Homeland:
Of Beds., Camb., Herts. The first settler of the name m. Eliz. Davies, of Wale(?). In 1831 we find John Godfrey of Kilcoleman Abbey, J.P.; William Godfrey clerk at Kenmare and Edward Godfrey of Kenmare. Thomas Godfrey is found at Tralee in 1908.

Kilcolman Abbey (1846) was the residence of Sir W. D. Godfrey. Thomas Spring resided in 1588 at Kilcolman, granted to him at the dissolution of the churches.

Smith finds, on both sides of the Mang river, level tracts of swampy grounds, which on the south side belonged to Mr. Godfrey, being in good repair.

Col. John Godfrey of Romney in Kent was granted 4,980 acres in Kerry in 1653, and had Wm. of Bushfield, whose son John 1712, had John , who had Sir Wm., who had Sir John 1763-1841 who had Sir Wm. 1797-1873, who had Sir John 1828-1900, who had Sir Wm. b. 1857 of Kilcolman abbey. 10 families of the name are given in Kerry by King.

Godley
There were 7 families of the name given, including: John and James of Dromatoor, Tom of Ballylongane; Michael of Cloghane; Pierse of Ballyronan; Pierce of Drombeg; and David of Boheroe.

Godolphin
A settler family on estates near Tralee, from the coming of the Elizabethan undertakers to the rebellion of 1641. Descent / homeland: Of Cornwall.
Related to the Carews, Edgcumbes, Walsinghams. John Godolphin of Tralee, shoemaker, was killed at Ballinskelligs in 1641.

Godson
John Godson of New street and Chas. Godson of Bridewell lane in Co. Kerry.

Goff, Mac Eotac
John Goff of Mucksna Co. Kerry.

Gofton
Francis Gofton was granted part of the estate of the late abbey of Ratowe in 1608.

Goggin (de Cogan)
There were 21 families of the name given by King, as residing in Co. Kerry.

Golden Goulding O'Foillide
There were 20 families of the Golden name in Kerry according to J. King. This included Michael of Clonprohus, Tom of Ballinabloun, Tom of Glenareagh, Michael of Killanbuoinia, Michael of Old road, Dan and Johanna of Main street, John of Church lane, Catherine of Gleneragh, John and Michael of Gowlanes, Kate and Jas. of Cloghanelinaghan, Wm. of Mountluke, Pat of Emlagh, Tim and Pat of Dooneen, John of Killurly, and Michael of Knockaneyouloo.

Mac Goldrick
Kate MacGoldrick of Gneeveguilla, Co. Kerry.

Goode
Francis Goode of Nelson street is given in Co. Kerry.

Gooding
A settler family on estates near Tralee, from the coming of the Elizabethan undertakers to the rebellion of 1641.

John Gooding, yeoman, was shot at the siege of Tralee in 1641.

Goodlake
T. J. Goodlake of Curraghleha is given in Kerry.

Goodman
Given as the name of a family settling in Co. Kerry, subsequent to the 1641-42 rebellion. Descent/ Homeland:

Of Beds., Cornw.. In 1831 we find John Goodman, clerk at Dingle, along with Thomas, Henry and George Goodman all of Dingle.

Tom Goodman of Ballymeentrant is given in Co. Kerry.

Goodwin, O'Goidin
Singleton Goodwin is given in Ballyroe; Francis of Fahamore, Robt. and Jos. of Kilshanig, and John of Island, all of Co. Kerry.

Goold, Gould
James Goold of Cronin's lake in Co. Kerry.

Gordon
Michael and Michael of Tieraclea are given in Co. Kerry, and Home Gordon son of 11th Bart., married Edith Leeson Marshall in 1897.

Gorham
A settler family, given on estates near Tralee, from the coming of the Elizabethan undertakers to the rebellion of 1641. Descent / homeland:

Of Herts, Huntes. In 1831 we find George, Richard, Edward and James Gorham, all of O'Brennan or Tralee.

Also given as the name of a family settling in Co. Kerry, both prior and subsequent to the 1641-42 rebellion.

James Gorham of Kylebeg; James of O'Brennan in 1735. Gorhams Hotel was in Killarney in 1828.

Gorman
There were 27 families of the name of Gorman in Kerry according to J. King.

Goss
Alfred Goss of Droumatour, Co. Kerry.

Mac Gough
Terence MacGough of High street, Jas. of Ballyoughtragh, Batt of Main street, and Thos. of Bridge street are given in Co. Kerry.

Gould, Gul
A settler family, given on estates near Tralee, from the coming of the Elizabethan undertakers to the rebellion of 1641. Descent / homeland:

Of Devon, Wales. John Gould resided in Tralee in 1622. Jas. Gould is in Tralee in 1908.

Michael Gould of Green lane, John of Main street, Pat of Strand road and James of Tralee, Co. Kerry.

Goulding, O'Goillide
Dennis and Michael and John of Coolbane; John of Carhoona; John and Bridget of Kealid; Maurice of Tulligbeg, and Denis of Killorglin, Co. Kerry.

Gouran
Tim Gouran of Knocknacroy; and Pat of Meenscovane are given in Co. Kerry.

Mac Govern
John Mac Govern of Ballymullen, Co. Kerry.

Grace, Gras
Thomas Grace of Ardfert, Co. Kerry.

Grady, O'Grada
Ua Grada is given as chief of Kinel Dunghaile in lower Tullagh barony in Co. Clare in 1311. Some 59 families of the name are given in Kerry by J. King.

Graham, O'Greacain
John of College street; Tom of Dykegate lane; John and Pat of the Mall; James and Michael of Emlagh; Dan of Gray's lane; and George of Spunkane are given in Co. Kerry.

Granfield
There were 17 families of the name given in Co. Kerry by King.

Granger, Grainseir
T. M. Granger of Tieraclea, Co. Kerry.

Grant
Thomas Grant of Rock Street, given in Co. Kerry.

Granville
Tom Granville of Listowel; Ml. of Faha; Jas. of Ballygologue; and Robert of Islandganniv are given in Kerry.

Mac Grath
As given by J. King, the sliocht Mac Crah O'Sullivan was the senior branch, at Ceapa na coise castle. Several families of the name are given in Co. Kerry. Magrath, the ollav in poetry of Leth Mogha, died in 1343.

Graves, O'Griobtain
Five families of the name are given in Kerry by King, including: Tom of Strand street; Jas. and Arthur and C.J. and A. W. of Farranreagh; John in 1719 was sheriff of Limerick and had Rev. Jas. who had Rev. Thos., who had John, who had Rev. Chas. bishop of Limerick; who had J.C., A.P., A., C. L., R. W., and H.C., and Caroline, a literary family of poets and authors.

Gray, Mac Giolla Riabaig
Liscahane Castle was held by Stack against the Geraldines in 1600. Before 1599 the place belonged to Daniel Gray, an English Colonist under Sir Edward Denny. In 1641 it appears that the Gun family settled there, while Gray likely moved on to Tralee for better security. A new stone house erected by Gray is described by King. (Ardfert Parish). John Gray of Church street, Co. Kerry.

Greany, O'Grainne
Thirty-six families of the Greany name are listed in Co. Kerry by J. King.

Green, O h Uaitne
Seven families of the name are given in Kerry, including: Johanna of Gurrane; Jas. of Ahane, Wm. of Tawlaght; John of Nelson street; Harry of Farranreagh; Jas. of Dawros; and Michael of Derrylough are given in Co. Kerry as well as 'Green of Liscahane' in 1641 and John Green of Dingle in 1821.

Also found in one instance as the name of a Cromwellian settler granted lands in 1667 in Co. Kerry.

Mac Gregor
Joseph MacGregor of Ballymullen, Co. Kerry, is given.

Gregory
Kilner Gregory of Lixnaw in 1741, was master of the horse to the Earl of Kerry.

Mac Grevy, Mac Riabaig.
Tom Mac Grevy of Tarbert, Co. Kerry.

Grey
A settler family on estates near Tralee, from the coming of the Elizabethan undertakers to the rebellion of 1641. Ed Grey, son of Lord John Grey of Essex, settled in Co. Kerry, found in Tralee in 1600. Others of the name found at a later date are given to be his sons. Dean Grey lived in Tralee in 1637; he was also rector of Clogherbrien and Annagh. John Grey is in Tralee in 1908.

Grice
The Grice family had been settled in Limerick since the the 17th century. In the Book of Surveys and Distributions of counties Limerick and Tipperary, preserved in the record tower according to J. King, Richard Grice is given as the owner of the lands of Gortgariffe, and Gortyknockane, within the the liberties of Kilmallock, part of the forfeited estates of 'Sir Maurice Hurly Irish Papist', and in the parish of Elphin, the same Richard Grice obtained the lands of Rathnewbrittagh, forfeited by "Randal Hurley, Irish Papist'. Thomas Ponsonby, commissioner in Kerry, married Susanna, daughter of Samuel Grice, of Ballgahan, Co. Limerick.

Griffin O'Griffin O'Greefa
The Griffin family was found to be quite numerous by J. King who lists some 353 families of the Griffin name in Co. Kerry. It was also given that O'Grifin, O'Griobtha, O'Greefa, and O'Criomhthainn were all variations of the same name.

Murtagh Griffin, clerk of the common pleas in Dublin in 1700 purchased lands near Killarney, and by his will in 1712 directed that his lands be sold for his Catholic heirs who could not legally inherit same; (see Egan O'Reilly's poem on Murtagh).

In 1776 Michael Griffin lived at Rossanean. In 1828, the Abbe Griffin was chaplain to the late Hon. Catherine Browne, Countess De Durford Civerac. Muiris O'Griobtha wrote a poem on Owen Rua O'Sullivan, a copy was to be found in the British Museum, addl. 27,946. Henry Griffin of Molahife, (brother of Lce. Griffin, M.D., and Cannon Griffin), m. Frances Stokes and had: Alice, David, Mary and Henry.

Griffiths, O'Griobta
Hy. Griffiths of Farranreagh is given in Co. Kerry.

Grinson
M. B. Grinson of James street is given in Kerry.

Grogan, O'Gruagain
Margt. and Mary of Beale; Tom of Listowel; Margt. of Moyderwell; and Geo. of Farranfore are given in Co. Kerry by J. King.

Groome
A settler family on estates near Tralee, from the coming of the Elizabethan undertakers to the rebellion of 1641. Descent / homeland: Of Norfolk.

Grover
William Grover of Boherbee is given in Kerry.

Groves

Geo. and Tom of Ballydwyer; John of Gortagullane, Con and Con of Loughnacappagh; Mary of Cloghermore; John and Tom of Rusheen; John of Ballindooganig, c. Blenner Groves of the lime kilns at Bally Mac Elligot.

Grummell, Gromail

Mce. of Murreigh; Michael of Currane; John and John of Caherscullibeen, all of these are given in Co. Kerry.

Guaine

Maurice Guaine of Triereragh, in Co. Kerry.

Guare

Mce. of Trieneragh; Pat of Foildarrig; and John of Knockavallig are given in Co. Kerry.

Guerin, O'Gearain

There were some 27 families of the name given by King in Co. Kerry.

Guihan, O'Gaoitin, Guiheen

Given in Kerry were: Pat of Strand Rd.; Ml. of Balintlea; Jahn of Ballineanig; John and Pat and Michael and Pat and Michael of Great Blasket Island; Michael of Ballinahow; Tom of Claddanure; Ml. of Kenmare, Julia of Rossmore Island and Michael of Lehud.

Guihan, O'Gaoitin, Guiheen and Guihean were given spellings.

Guinaw, O'Guinide, Geany

Several families of the name of Guinaw are given in the History of Kerry by J. King. Guinaw, O'Guinide, Geany and Guinea given as spellings.

Guinell

Delia Guinell 'of Princes quay' is given in Kerry.

Mac Guire

Several of the name are given in Co. Kerry, including wm. of Kilsarcon, Margt. of Carrigafreaghane, John of Listowel, Ml. and Wm. of Ardfert, Mary of Staughton's row, John of Brogue lane, John of Poulawaddra, Ellen of Grey's lane, Tom of Strand street, Gerald of Green lane, Francis of Inchinclough, and Frank of Farranreagh.

Ballycarbery Castle

Gun, Gunn, Mac Giolladuinn

Liscahane Castle was held by Stack against the Geraldines in 1600. Before 1599 the place belonged to Daniel Gray, an English Colonist under Sir Edward Denny. In 1641 it appears that the Gun family settled there, while Gray likely moved on to Tralee for better security.

Ratoo Castle was taken in 1600 by Sir Charles Wilmot. In 1756 it was the seat of Townshend Gun..

Ploverhill (1846) in Tralee parish was the home of B. Wm. Gun in 1821. (220)

Given as the name of a family settling in Co. Kerry, subsequent to the 1641-42 rebellion. Descent/ Homeland: Of Norf.

William Gun of Lislahane, 1641, had a son William of Rattoo, 1699, whose son was William, whose son was Townsend, whose son was William 1765, whose son was Townsend, 1803, whose second son was Wilson 1809, whose second son was Henry Allen, 1842, whose son was William Townsend Jackson Gun of Rattoo, sheriff in 1902.

Given as the name of a family settling in Co. Kerry, subsequent to the 1641-42 rebellion. Descent/ Homeland:

Wm. Gun of Lislahane, 1641, had a son Wm. of Rattoo, 1699, whose son was Wm., whose son was Townsend, whose son was William, 1765, whose son was Townsend, 1803, whose second son was Wilson, 1809, whose second son was Henry Allen, 1842, whose son is William Townsend Jackson Gun of Rattoo, sheriff, 1902.

In 1831 we find William Townsend Gun of Rattoo, George Barry Gun of Plover Hill, Wilson Gun of Plover Hill, and George Gun h p 52nd Regt. (k231)

Wm. of Rattoo; John and David of Lyre; and Hanoria of Duagh, Co. Kerry.

Gunning

The Rev. Benignus, OFM, of Moyeightragh, is given in Co. Kerry.

Gurnett

John Gurnett of Ballyrobert; Michael of Brogue lane; Tom of John's street; Ml. of Dingle had Tom, Ml., Wm., and John, and they went to the U.S.A. in 1864, the brothers serving in the army.

Habbert, Habbart, Hoibeard

Pat and James and Pat and John of Shantalliv; Mce. of Barrow; James of Knockanish; Pat of Strand street; and James of Brogue lane, in Co. Kerry.

Hackett, Mac Haiceid

Martin Hacket of Firies; Pat of Tullaghua; Catherine of Lixnaw; Tom of Trippul; Pat of Cloghaneleesh, and Rev. E. A. of Cloghane are given in Kerry.

Hale

A settler family on estates near Tralee, from the coming of the Elizabethan undertakers to the rebellion of 1641. Descent / homeland: Of Essex, Herts. John Hale lived in Tralee in 1622.

Hall, de Hal

Given as the name of a family settling in Co. Kerry, subsequent to the 1641-42 rebellion. Descent/ Homeland: Of Northumb.

David Hall of Shelbourne street; and a Mrs. S. C. Hall, 1878, is given as having written a guide book.

Hallett

Fred Hallett of Boherbee and Harold Hallett of Glanleam are given in Kerry.

Halley, O h Ailee

Wm. Halley of New Street is given.

Hallidan, Halliden

Julia Hallidan of Faha, Co. Kerry.

Hallinan

Hy. Hallinan of Tonevane, and Wm. of Blennerville are given in Co. Kerry.

Hallissey Hallisey Hallissy

Some 26 families of the name are listed by King in Co. Kerry. Hallissey Hallisey Hallissy and O h Ailgeasa, were given as spellings.

O' Halloran

The Kerry family of the name descend from the importers of wine, lords of Clan Fergail, a district in which Galway town is found. They held a castle at Barna, close to the sea, 3 miles west of Galway. The Norman De Burgos in the 13th century expelled them, hence they moved into West Connaught, erecting the castle of O'Hery in Gnomore. According to The Wars of Thomond (1309), there was another branch of the O'Hallorans in Thomond, of the Dalcassions in Munster, that family held Faith-ua- Halluran in Tulla, Co. Clare.

The arms of Clan Fergail were given by King as: Gules a horse passant ar. saddled and bridled ppr. on a chief of the second three mullets az.. Crest: A lizard or. Motto: Clan Fergail Abu.

The O'Hallorans came to Kerry from Clare about the year 1600, settling near Lixnaw, and the children attended the private school of the Earl of Kerry where several languages were taught. One of the boys was a great linguist, being the only one in the area able to translate documents from a noted shipwreck off the Kerry coast. This was Thomas O'Halloran who lived about 1650. One of his sons, John, had issue William, John, Thomas, James, Robert, & Ellen.

The family burial vault at Kilfeighney, lands at Banemore house, and several Clerics of the name in France and Spain, were noted. Dr. John O'Halloran held Banemore, Pallas, Colnaleen, Grogeen, Killocrim, Lisculane & Ballingar. Maurice O'Halloran lived at Banemore House in Kilfeighny parish, in 1821.

Among the Hallorans listed were: Sylvester Halloran, the historian, had Genl. Sir Joseph, 1763-1843, who had Thomas, 1797-1870, and William, 1806 - 85. Thomas Halloran of Lixnaw in 1650 had a son John, who had Wm, John, Thomas, Jas, Robert and Ellen. Wm. born 1740, son of Thomas, had John, d. 1840, who had John, Jas., Roger, Mce., and Margt.. Rev. Jas. d. 1881, was P.P. of Tuagh; he was son of Wm., son of Thomas; his brother Simon, m. Anne Quilter having Wm., Jas., John, Mary, Susan, Hanora, of whom Rev. Wm. was ordained in 1874, Mary m. D. O'Sullivan of Firies, having Dr. Wm. and Lizzie, a nun who died 1909. Rev. John d. 1829, was P.P. of Lixnaw; his brother Tom of Banemore had Lieut. Mce., Dr. Tom, Jas., of Coolnaleen, and John of Killocrim, who had Tom, who had Dr. John of Ballyhorgan.

Variant spellings given by King were Halloran, Hallaran, Hallorin, Halloron, Holloran, O'Halloran, O'Hallaran, O'Halleran and O'Halleron. There were 41 Halloran and 46 O'Halloran families given in Co. Kerry by J. King. This is noteworthy, for few names had the O' prefix more often than not, at that time.

Halpin, Mac Alpin

Some 12 families of the name are listed by J. King, including those of Coolatoosane, Ballymacandrew, Lybes, Kilcaramore, Doon, Lacca, Gortaclohane, Finuge, Ballygloogue, Littor, and Cloonamon.

Hamilton, O'Hamailltin

Michael Hamilton of Maulagullane; James of Ardsheelanen and Lloyd of Main street are given in Co. Kerry.

Hammond

Arthur Hammond of Emlagh is given in Kerry.

Hampton
A settler family, given on estates near Tralee, from the coming of the Elizabethan undertakers to the rebellion of 1641. Descent / homeland:
Of Abingdon, Berks, Bucks, Midx.

Hamptson
John Hamptson of Cuhig, Co. Kerry.

Hanafin Hannafin
There were 59 Hanafin families, anciently given as Oh Ainfeain, listed by J. King, all in Co. Kerry.

Hancock
Robert Hancock, solicitor, was agent to the Denny estate, Tralee, d.1913.

Hand
Peter Hand of the Mall; Mag Laitim. Given in Co. Kerry.

Haniford
Edward Haniford of Farranreagh, Co. Kerry.

Hanley, O h Ainlige
William Hanley of Langford street; Robert of Henry street; and Pat of Main street, all of Co. Kerry. There were 43 families of the name listed by J. King, all in Co. Kerry.

Hannon, O h Annain
There were 18 families of the name given in Co. Kerry.

Hanover
Wm. Hanover of Killarney road, Co. Kerry.

Hanrahan, O h Anracain
There were 33 Hanrahan families given in Co. Kerry. The Rev. Daniel Hanrahan at Lislaghtan was killed April 6, 1580, by English soldiers.
O'Hanrahan is also recorded as chief of Corcaree in West Meath.

Hansard
Joseph Hansard of Killarney is given.

Hanswell
Ellen Hanswell of Ballyheigue, Co. Kerry, is given.

Hara
Ellen and James and Pat and James and John and Pat of Dreenagh, Co. Kerry.

Harbourne
Wm. Harbourne of Farrantooreen, Co. Kerry, is given.

Hardier
The name of a Cromwellian settler granted lands in 1667 in Co. Kerry.

Harding
In 1611 Rd. Harding was granted Ballinskelligs priory, Killaha Abbey, Tralee Friary and sundry church lands confiscated. Thomas of Ballyduhig, and Philip of Knockane are given in Co. Kerry according to King.

Hardy
Hy. Hardy of Tullygarron and Horatia Hardy of Farranreagh given in Kerry.

Hare
William Hare, the 1st Earl of Listowel, 1822, in 1800 became Baron Ennismore, and died in 1837. William, his grandson, became Earl, and died in 1856. His son was Sir William Hare, K.P., 3rd Earl of Listowel and he had issue.
Ennismore House (1846) gives the title of Baron and Viscount to the family of Hare, Earls of Listowel. J.F. Hewson lived at Ennismore in 1821. (Dysert (N.) parish.) See Peerage for details of the junior branches. Six of the name are given in the works of Jeremiah King.

Hargrave
A. Hargrave, M.D.; of Denny Street in Tralee, Co. Kerry, is given.

Harley
James Harley of Dromkeen, Co. Kerry.

Harman
Jno. Harman, Lacharne, m. Susannah Beversham. His son, Beversham Harman, m. Margaret Palmer, 4th dau. of the Rev. Thomas Palmer of Kenmare d.1702, leaving Thomas, Daniel, George, John and Catherine. Tom had Geo., who had Capt. Robt, who had Dr. Geo., Robt., Thos., Dr. Emanuel, Isabella, and Catherine.

Some 13 families of the name are given by King.

Harms
James Harms of Ballinskelligs, Co. Kerry.

Harnett, Hartnett
William fuller had the reputation of depopulating a large tract of land, and substituting cattle on grazing ranches. He married a daughter of William Harnet of Ballyhenry. (see Hartnett, per J. King)

Harold
Tom Harold of Maglass, Ellen Harold of Knickananlig, and Ellen Harold of Castleisland, are all given in Co. Kerry. In 1828 Rd. Harold of Maglass, died.

Harraghton (O h Arractain)
In 1580 Harraghton held the castle of Garranieraughton, Garran, in the parish of Tralee.

Harran
Hannah Harran of High Street is given in Co. Kerry.

Harrington, O h Arractain.
Some 90 Harrington families are listed by King in Co. Kerry. Tim and Ned Harrington were M.P.'s and leaders in the Land League movement, and Dan d.1915 aged 73, he was owner of the Kerry Sentinel.

Harris, Mac Hannraoi
Some 27 Harris families are listed by J. King.

Harrison
A settler family on estates near Tralee, from the coming of the Elizabethan undertakers to the rebellion of 1641. Homeland: Of Essex, Norf., Kent.

Harrowe
A settler family on estates near Tralee, from the coming of the Elizabethan undertakers to the rebellion of 1641.

Hart Harte
A settler family, given on estates near Tralee, from the coming of the Elizabethan undertakers to the rebellion of 1641. Descent / homeland: Of Norf., Suff., Cambs.

The Mahoney and Hart families lived at Batterfield in Kilnanare parish in the 18th century.

Mahoney Harte of Ballyard is the only person of this surname spelling, listed by J. King in Co. Kerry.

Hartigan, O h Artagain
John Hartigan of Ballinvarrig and Ellen of Killahane are given in Co. Kerry.

Hartley, O h Artgaile
Colonel Arthur Hartley of Drimnamore, Co. Kerry is given.

Hartnett, Harnett
Some 55 Hartnett families are given in Co. Kerry. One of these, Francis Hartnett, son of William of Kilcreen, d.1913, aged 67, leaving £10,000 to relatives.

Hartney
Tom and Pat Hartney of Tullamore, John of Gortnaskehy, Pat of Doon, and Edm. of Teer, all in Co. Kerry.

Hartop
Florence Hartop of Tullaha, Co. Kerry.

Harty
There were 26 Harty families listed by King in Co. Kerry. The Rev. Malachy Harty wrote a history of Holy Cross Abbey in 1640.

Harvey
Listed in Co. Kerry by J. King were Wm. of Kilfarnogue, Wm. of Emlagh, and Tom of Spunkane, Co. Kerry.

Hassett
Presumed to be a shortened form of Blennerhassett at least in some cases, 10 families of the name are listed by King. It is possible that family researchers will find 'Hassett' relations spelling their name as Blennerhassett at times.

Hastings
John Hastings of Ardnamweely, Co. Kerry, is given.

Hatheron
Alan Hatheron, was bishop of Ardfert in 1347.

Hattery
James Hattery, 'of the Rock', is given by King in Co. Kerry.

Hawkin
A rare name in Kerry, one Sam Hawkin of Ardfert is given.

Hawney
Eliza Hawney of Ballybunion, Harry of Castle street, and Wm. of Pound lane are all given in Co. Kerry.

Hayden
P. J. Hayden of Tralee, Co. Kerry.

Hayes
The Hayes family is found fairly numerous in Co. Kerry, and some 75 families are listed by King.

Hayslip
Rd. of Rock street, given in Co. Kerry.

Haywood
Herbert Haywood of Main Street, is given in Co. Kerry.

Headley
Chas. Mark Allanson Winn (Headley), Lord; of Aghadoe house, 4th Baron; created 1797; see Peerage; owned 12,769 acres in Kerry in 1876, d.1913; s. by his cousin Rowland George Allanson Winn, b. 1856, m.1899 Theresa Johnson, having issue.

Heafey
Thos. Heafey of Croughcroneen.

Healy, O h Eilide
One of the most numerous family names of Co. Kerry, some 222 families of the name are listed by J. King in his 'History of Co. Kerry'.

Heanne, O h Eanna
Pat Heanne of Gortatlea, Co. Kerry.

Heaphy, O h Eamtaig
Thos. Heaphy of Ballymacassy, Co. Kerry, is given.

Heard
Sam Heard of Rossdohan, Co. Kerry.

Heardinman
Fred Heardinman of Farranreagh, Co. Kerry, is given by King. This spelling appears so strange at first glance it leads to speculation as having come from a more familiar name such as Hardiman.

Hearnden
Wm. Hearnden of Farranreagh, Co. Kerry, is given.

Heffernan, O h Ifearnain
Some 39 Heffernan families are listed in Co. Kerry.

Hegarty
There were some 32 Hegarty families listed in Co. Kerry. Some family members also report the name being shortened simply to Hegart.

Hehir
Hehir was abbot of Innisfallen, he d.1197.

Helliwell
Guy Helliwell of Bawnboy, Co. Kerry.

Hempenstall
Robt. Hempenstall of the Rock, in Co. Kerry, is given.

Henchy (also Hinchy)
Rd. Henchy of Ahanagran, Co. Kerry.

Hendericken
Ml. Hendericken is given of Hogan's lane, in Co. Kerry.

Henderson
Wm. Henderson of Beheenagh is given.

Henigan Hennigan
Mary Henigan of Listowel, and Pat and Wm. of Skehenerin, all given in Kerry.

Hennessy
Some 40 families of the name are listed in Co. Kerry. It is noted that Ua h Aenghusa was chief of clann Colgain in King's County. One Wm. M. Hennessy, 1829-1889, of Castle Gregory, was a writer and author.

Henry
John Henry of Moyeightragh, James Henry of Curraghdarig, and Henrietta Henry of Glounagillagh, all in Kerry.

Heraghty
Rd. Heraghty of Dykegate Lane, Co. Kerry, is given.

Herbert (Harbord)
Sir William Herbert (Harbord) is given arriving at Castle Island on April 26, 1587, with a seignory of 12,000 acres. Mr. Charles Harbord, his kinsman, lived at a castle of the Currans, and had a seignory of 4,000 acres or more, additional. Lord Herbert of Chirbury married Sir Wm. Herberts only daughter and heir. At one time the manor of Mt. Eagle Loyal was granted to Lord Herbert and other planters. Giles Herbert was the son of Charles of Currens.

Thos. Herbert of Kilcow came from Wales is 1656, having Edward of Muckross 1684, who had Thos., who had Henry, who had Chas., who had Henry, who had Henry, who had Henry b.1867 of Muckross.

The Protestant settlers, the Herberts, were buried in a tomb near Ardcrone, and also the Bastables in another. (The church of Currans, Ardcrone, Co. Kerry.) In 1756 Kilcow, Coill-Cuaigh, was the home of Edward Herbert of Muckross. (Dysert (E.) parish).

Thomas Herbert of Kilcuagh came to Ireland under the patronage of Lord Herbert of of Cherbury and Castleisland in 1656. His son, Edward of Muckross, 1684, whose son was Thomas, whose son was Henry Arthur, whose son was Charles John, 1814, whose son was Henry Arthur, who was M.P. and Chief Secretary for Ireland 1857-'58. His son, Henry Arthur, was born 1840, whose son was Henry Arthur Edw. Keane Herbert, born 1867.

Muckross (1846), at one time served as the seat of H. A. Herbert. Charles MacCarthy in 1770 left the estates to his mothers family, the Herberts, but the O'Donoghue of the Glen recovered by law the Caragh property.

Torc Cottage (1846) was the residence of Capt. Sir Thomas Herbert.

Herbert of Muckross, Co. Kerry
From The Irish Book of Arms. (IGF) 1988.

Cahirnane (1846) was the seat of H. Herbert. It was sold by the MacCarthys to Col. Maurice Hussey in 1684.

Justin MacCarthy great grandson of Lady Ellen, married the daughter of Col. Mce. Hussey of Kerries and Cahirnane.

Dinis Cottage (1846), Tuosist parish, was Herbert's seat.

O' Herlihy

The O'Herlihy's were wardens of the church of St. Gobnata, of Barneach, of Ballyvourney, and of her beehive. A numerous family of Co. Kerry, some 65 families of the name are given there.

Hetreed

Agnes Hetreed of New street is given in Co. Kerry.

Hewson

Given in Co. Kerry were the following: John Hewson of Tubrid, John of Killarney, Lionel of Derreenfinlehid, Geo. of Askeaton had a son John who m. Margt., dau. of the Knight of Kerry, in 1737, and settled at Ennismore, having Rev. Francis, and Mce. of Finuge who had Rev. Mce. d.1847, having Mce. Falkiner, John, Wm., Robt., Francis, Jos., Dan, Helena and Sara.

J.F. Hewson lived at Ennismore in 1821. (Dysert (N.) parish.)

Hickey, Hickie

Some 72 Hickey families are given in Co. Kerry, making this family a fairly numerous one here. (The alternate spelling of Hickie was also given in the works of J. King.)

The Hickie or O'Hicky family of Kilelton, Ballylongford, descend from Eochy Baldearg, of the race of Cormac Cas, ancient king of Munster. James Hickie of Tulla, Co. Clare, was confiscated in 1652, and his son William settled in Kilelton. His son William, in 1682, by marriage came into possession of some of O'Connor Kerry's lands. His son was William, 1720, whose son was Michael, 1767, whose son was William 1791, whose son was William 1829, whose son was William Creaghe, 1853, whose son was Col. William Scott Hickie of Kilelton, born 1854, m.1887 Constance Knight of Devonshire, having Constance Knight of Devonshire, having Constance Hickie of Kilelton. (see also Hickey)

Killelton was the seat of the Hickie family in Aghavallen Parish.

Hickman

John Hickman of Mac Cowen's Lane, is given in Co. Kerry.

Hicks

A settler family, given on estates near Tralee, from the coming of the Elizabethan undertakers to the rebellion of 1641. Descent / homeland: Of Cornw., Norf.

STAIGUE FORT.

Hickson

Some 10 Hickson families are given in Kings work, including R.A. Rev. Chris Hickson of Cambridge, rector of Disert and Kilconly in 1613, his son Chris was transplanted, and his second son Thomas of Gowlane in Stradbally had John of Fermoyle in 1712, his second son Chris, 1745 had Robert 1770, having James who had Robert 1831, whose sons were James and Robert and George A. E. of Fermoyle, b.1854, m. 1884 L. Mahony Harte, having R.C. 1884 and G. L. O H 1887. Mary Agnes Hickson in 1872 wrote Kerry Records, and in 1884 on Ireland in the 17th century, besides many articles in the Kerry Evening Post.

Hickson of Fermoyle

The Rev. Chris. Hickson, of Cambridge, was rector of Disert and Kilconly in 1613. His son, Chris, a rebel and papist, was transplanted to Connaught, but returned to Kerry. His second son, Thomas, of Gowlane, Stradbally, had a son John, 1712 of Fermoyle. His second son Chris., 1745, had a son Robert, 1770, whose son was James, whose son was Robert, 1831, whose sons were James, Paterson, Robert and George. Paterson succeeded, and then his brother George Archibald Erskine Hickson, of Fermoyle, b. 1854.

Hifle

Rose Hifle of Castle Street, Wm. of Prince's Quay, and Sam of Cloonbeg are all given in Co. Kerry.

Higgins, O h Uiginn

Some 29 Higgins families are given in Co. Kerry.

Hill

Several families of the name are listed by King in Co. Kerry, and the personal names of Tom, and especially William, predominate in those listings.

Hillee

Pat Hillee of Lerrig, Co. Kerry.

Hilliard

Given as the name of a family settling in Co. Kerry, subsequent to the 1641-42 rebellion. Descent/ Homeland:

William Hilliard m. Barbara Mason; leaving Robt., whose son was William Hilliard of Cahirslee. In 1831 lived William of Tralee, George of Tralee, John of Spa, William, Jun. of Tralee, Alexander of Blennervile and H. Hillard.

R. and W. Hilliard are given in Tralee in 1908.

Some 19 families of the name are found in Co. Kerry, including Chris. of Baltigarron 1739. Chris. 1784 had Chris. and Wm. and Harriett, James of Ballyhorgan 1791. Lieut. James of Killocrim 1819. Hy. and Wm. and Geo. of Tralee 1821. Sam of Billerough, John of Tubrid in 1821.

Hingey

John Hingey of Lacca, Co. Kerry.

Hipwell

Charles Hipwell of Garryruth, Co. Kerry is given.

Histon

John Histon of Tarbert island, and Tim of Dromin are both given in Kerry.

Hitchcock

Richard Hitchcock 1824-56, born at Annagh, worked at Corca Duibne antiquities for Dr. Rowan, Dr. Graves & Dr. J. Graves, and wrote for the Kerry Magazine 1854-56, over the initial H.

Hickson of Fermoyle, Co. Kerry
From The Irish Book of Arms. (IGF) 1988.

Hoar Hoare

Gregory and Wm. le Hore in 1298 were jurors at the manor de Insula, Castleisland. Also spelled as Hoare, Hoar, le Hore, de Hor, etc..

Hoar is given as the name of a settler family, given on estates near Tralee, from the coming of the Elizabethan undertakers to the rebellion of 1641. One family is given originally of Cornw. Richard Hore of New Manor, husbandman, was killed at Ballinskelligs in 1641. Richard Hore lived at Killarney in 1831. Thos. and Maurice Hoare are in Tralee in 1908.

Some 22 Hoare families of the name are listed in Co. Kerry and Pat was a common personal name.

Hobbins

Tom Hobbins of Coolroe and Tom Hobbins of Caherciveen, Co. Kerry.

Hoffman

Frank Hoffman of Cloghermore, Wm. of Gortagullane, Jas. of Cloonbeg, George of Anagap, and John of Lisardboola are given in Co. Kerry.

Hogan

There were some 40 Hogan families listed by King in Co. Kerry.

Holbrow

Wm. Holbrow of Derryconnery, Co. Kerry, is given.

Holland

Dan Holland of Farranfore and Dan Holland of Curraheen, given in Kerry.

Holly

Some 11 families of the name of Holly are given in the works of King, in Co. Kerry.

Holt

Alfred Holt of Spunkane, Co. Kerry.

Holyoake

Joseph Holyoake of Listowel, Co. Kerry, is given.

Hooks

Mary Hooks of Main Street, is given in Kerry by J. King.

Hooper

A settler family, given on estates near Tralee, from the coming of the Elizabethan undertakers to the rebellion of 1641. Homeland: Of Cornw.

Hopgood

Albert Hopgood of Ballinskelligs, Co. Kerry, is given.

Horan

Some 74 families are given in Co. Kerry.

Horgan

Some 142 families of the Horgan name were given in Co. Kerry by J. King. One of the more numerous families of Kerry.

Horwick

Pat Horwick of Dooncaha, Co. Kerry.

Houlihan

Some 70 Houlihan families are given in Co. Kerry. Rev Thadeus Houlihan of Muckross died in 1626.

Hourighan

Tom Hourighan of Mangerton view, Co. Kerry.

Howard, Ivers

Some 16 Howard families are given in Co. Kerry.

Howatson

Archibald Howatson of Spunkane, Co. Kerry.

Howe

John Howe of Caherciveen, Co. Kerry.

Hubbort

Michael Hubbort of Killagh, Co. Kerry.

Huddlestone

A settler family on estates near Tralee, from the coming of the Elizabethan undertakers to the rebellion of 1641. Descent / homeland: Of Cambs, Essex. Cumbs. Henry Huddlestone of the Grange, in the parish of Ratass, was sworn to association with the Irish army in 1641, at the siege of Tralee.

Hudson

Rd. and Wm. of Kilbaha and Edward of Strand Street are given in Co. Kerry. Edward owned 440 acres in Kilbaha.

Huggard

Some 21 Huggard families are given in Co. Kerry.

Robert Huggard in 1674 was Captain in Dublin. In 1821 lived Stephen and John and John in Killarney, Tom and James of Tralee, and Martin of Clohane.

Marvell Eagar, wife of Steven Huggard of Milltown d.1828, issue of 5 children, Ann Huggard of Kilburn, Milltown, d.1913, a. 90. Dr. Wm. Huggard, M.D., 1875, d. at Davos, 1911, was son of Wm. the son of Martin of Clahane, and was b. 1851; his uncle Richard was a solicitor in Tralee.

Mac Hugh

Pat Mac Hugh of Tralee, Co. Kerry.

Hughes

Richard Hughes of Spunkane and Wm. of Quay, Co. Kerry.

Also given as the name of a Cromwellian settler granted lands in 1667 in Co. Kerry.

Huihir

Huihir was Archdeacon of Innisfallen, d.1197.

Humphreys

Wm. of Garryooth, and Edw. of Cloonbeg, Co. Kerry.

Humpton, Hampton

The town of Tralee was incorporated in 1612, and its charter named John Humpton, as among the first provost and burgesses.

Hunt

Some 11 families of the name are given in Co. Kerry.

Hunter

Mary Hunter of Mangerton view, Co. Kerry.

Hurley Hurly

There were some 51 Hurley families given in Kerry by J. King. On Dec. 10. 1583, Dr. Hurley, the Archbishop of Cashel, is given as beyond any form of intimidation by torture. In 1584 he was recommended to be executed, (see State Papers Calendar).

Sir Thomas O'Hurley, of Knocklong, in Limerick, had a son John, whose son Col. John, had Chas., who had Donough, who m. Anne Blennerhasset, having Chas., who had John who had John of Fenit. Donough had Chas., who had John, who had Robert, who had John b.1862, m.1891, having R.W., b. 1892.

Denis Hurly of Knocklong, m. Anne Blennerhassett, 1701, and had a son Thomas who was succeeded by his brother Charles, whose son was Thomas, who was succeeded by his bro. John, Clerk of the Crown of Kerry. The latter's son was Rev. Robert of Killiney, who was succeeded by his brother John of Glenduffe, 1814. His son was Robert, 1845, was father of John Conway Hurly of Glenduffe, born 1862.

Fenit House, in Fenit parish, was the home of John C. Hurly. Fenit Castle was taken by the English in 1600.

Hurrell

J. Hurrell of Ballymullen, Co. Kerry.

Hussey

Some 51 Hussey families are given in Co. Kerry according to J. King.

Hugh de Hoese came to Ireland with the Normans in 1180. The Hussey family of Edenburn, in BallyMacElligott Parish, is given as the Norman family that came to Meath at the time of the invasions, and subsequently settling in Co. Kerry. Edm., son of Sir John of Galtrim, was constable of Carberry in 1382. The Husseys held Dingle and other castles in Corca Duibne for the Earl of Desmond, and were confiscated with him in 1583, and again in 1653, at Ballinahowe, Castle Gregory, Maherabeg, and Farranlatiffe. Dingle Castle, Dingle parish, was held by the Hussey family for the Earls of Desmond. When the town was given a charter in 1585 it was given to the burgesses.

The Four Masters give Dingle as Daingean Ui Chuis, and some writers connect it with the Hussey family. In 1613 and 1616 Michael Hussey was M.P. for Dingle, and in 1688 another Hussey was a member. (The Norman De La Huse or Housaye appeared to have been corrupted into De La Cousa according to the works J. King.)

In the 1587 inquisition at Dingle mention is made of one Thomas Hussey of Ballinacourty, and his son Mce. of Glangortennarran and Farrenedell and Coumduffe; of John of Ballynacourty and Gorteenaffrin and Rathkoyn; of Jas. of Dingle; of Thos. and his son Mce.; of John of Dingle tholsel: Thos. was vicar of Killiney in 1613, and Meyler had lands at Tralee and Castle Gregory, which were confiscated from his son Walter of Minard in 1650. Castle Gregory was taken from the knight of Kerry by Sir Charles Wilmot in 1602. (Killiney parish). Minard Castle, built by the Knight of Kerry, was blown up in 1650 by Cols. Le Hunt and Sadler. Its' defender Walter Hussey of Castlegregory was killed.

In 1602 Hussey the scholar was in Ballingarry fort, and Maelbrighe O'Headhusa desired to go in 1605 from Douai to Louvain to study divinity, and Father Bonaventure O'Hosey was author of a gaelic catechism. In 1616 Thomas Hussey and Sir. Rd. Boyle agreed about Corca Duibne lands of Pepys, Dowdall and Champion. In 1653 Edm. Hussey of Kinard and Nicholas of Ballingown were transplanted with 84 persons.

In 1794, Thos. of Dingle had Walter, Rice, Stephen. Col. Mce. died at Cahirnane in 1714, and was buried in Killegus or Killegy, his dau. Cahterine m. Justin MacCarthy, and her sister m. Capt. Edm. Ferriter of Ballyoughtragh. Oliver Hussey, of Rath, m. Katherine, dau. of Walter Hussey of Minard in 1650, having Walter d.1728, having Edw. and Mce.. Mce. had John, who had Peter, d.1835, having Sam, m. 1853 Julia Hickson, having John, Mce., Mary, Charlotte, Eileen, Florence, Julia, Mce, M. Mabel Meux having Mce. and John. John m. Gledys Buckley, having Hubert, b.1892, and Eileen, Sam died 1913 at 89 at Aghadoe House, and wrote his Reminiscences of an Irish Land Agent in 1904. He gave evidence before the Parnell Commission in 1888.

Cahirnane (1846) was the seat of H. Herbert. It was sold by the MacCarthys to Col. Maurice Hussey in 1684. Justin MacCarthy great grandson of Lady Ellen, married the daughter of Col. Mce. Hussey of Kerries and Cahirnane.

Walter Hussey of the Pale was nominated by Mountjoy for the sheriffship of Kerry, having lands in Meath and Kerry. The Husseys are found forfeiting lands in Corcaguiny in

Hussey

Elizabeths reign however. The Carew manuscripts show Edward Hussey of Ballinahowe in the rebellion. After the wars of 1641 the family forfeited lands at Ballinahowe, Castlegregory, Maherabeg, Farranlatiffe, etc... Nine Husseys forfeited in Meath, and two in Kildare. The principal representative of the family in Kerry, around 1908, was given to be at Aghadoe House, Killarney.

Hubert Hussey had lands near Dingle in 1610. His son, Nicholas, had a son Meiler, whose son was Nicholas, 1625, whose brother was Walter of Castlegregory, whose son was Nicholas, whose lands were confiscated. His cousin Oliver of Rha, had a son Walter, 1728, whose second son was Maurice, whose son was John, whose son was Peter, 1804, whose fifth son was Samuel Murray Hussey living in 1908, whose son was John Edward, whose son was Hubert Murray, b. 1898.

Hutchinson

John Hutchinson of New-street, Sam of Mangerton View, Fred of Moorstown and Tom of Farranreagh, in Co. Kerry.

Hyde

The Rev. Arthur Hyde of Cork was vicar of Killarney in 1899, he m. 1787 Sara French of Innfield in Roscommon, having 13 children, and M. Miss Piersey of Youghal having 3 children; he died 1833.

In 1821 in Killarney resided Rev. Arthur Hyde, George of R.N., Ben of R.N., Fred, John (M.D.) his son, Rev. Arthur was vicar of Mohill, 1816-1863. Fred m. Eliz. Bland of Derriquin. Dr. Douglas Hyde is of this family.

Volume three of J. Kings word gives Hollywood, the former residence of Fredk. Hyde, Esq., as reverting to purchaser of Derriquin Estate on the death of his eldest son Capt. Arthur Hyde, then residing in America.

Hynes

Pat Hynes of Tieraclea and Wm. of Ballyard, Co. Kerry.

Hynton

A settler family on estates near Tralee, from the coming of the Elizabethan undertakers to the rebellion of 1641. Descent / homeland: Of Essex.

Mac Inerney

Mary Mac Inerney of Tralee, Kerry.

Mac Intosh, Mackintosh

Catherine Mac Intosh of Kilmurry, Alex of New Street, Rev. Archibald of Tralee 1828. Rev. Moore, sermons 1854. Kilmurry house was built in 1843 by Rev. A. Mac Intosh. J. King lists Mac Intosh and Mackintosh as the same name.

Ireton

Dunloe Castle was bombarded by Ireton. D. Mahony resided there in 1864. It was one of O'Sullivan Mor's forts, but was built by Maurice Fitzgerald. It was usually in charge of the Sugrue O'Sullivans. (Knockane parish)

Hurly of Bridge House, Co. Kerry Extract From The Irish Book of Arms. (IGF) 1988.

Irwin
Ellen Irwin of Ardnamweely, John of Bawnluskaha, Jas. of Tonevane, and Wm. and Thos. of Ballymacthomas are all given of Co. Kerry.

Isham
A settler family on estates near Tralee, from the coming of the Elizabethan undertakers to the rebellion of 1641. Descent / homeland: Of Kent, Northants.

Ivers, Howard
Edw. of Oakview Terrace and James of New street are given in Co. Kerry. King lists Howard as a form of Ivers.

Jackson
Jackson is given as the name of a settler family, given on estates near Tralee, from the coming of the Elizabethan undertakers to the rebellion of 1641.
John Jackson of Farranreagh, Co. Kerry

Jakeman
Henry Jakeman of Spunkane is given.

James, Seamus
Tom and Pat and Wm. James of Ballylongane, Tom of Bridewell lane, and Rd. of Farranreagh, Co. Kerry.

Jameson
Robert Jameson of Tarmons, Kerry.

Jeffcott
A settler family, given on estates near Tralee, from the coming of the Elizabethan undertakers to the rebellion of 1641. Descent / homeland: Of Northants, Warwick. Joseph is found in Tralee in 1908. One Joseph Jeffcott of Tralee died in 1806. In 1683, John Jeffcott was parish clerk (Prot.) in Tralee and Ratass. In 1758 John Jeffcott was parish clerk in Kiltalla. In 1737 two of the name were jurymen in Silver ship case. Sir Wm. Jeffcott was (R.C.) pastor of Colgan, Ont.

Sir Wm. Jeffcott of Tralee, 1800-55, was an Australian judge. Surgeon Wm. Jeffcott, son of Wm., b. 1760, had John of Castletown in the Isle of Man, b. 1813, who had John of Esquimalt and 5 daughters.

Given as the name of a family settling in Co. Kerry, both prior and subsequent to the 1641-42 rebellion. Descent/ Homeland: Of Northumb.

Jeffers, Mac Seafraid
Francis Jeffers of Caheranne road, Jeffers Institute, Tralee school.

Jeffreys
Admiral Edmund F. Jeffreys, Lickeen, Caragh Lake, Co. Kerry.

Jennings
Dan Jennings of Moanmore, Co. Kerry.

Jerm
Robert Jerm of Farranreagh, Co. Kerry.

Jess
Jane Jess of Prince's Quay, Co. Kerry.

Johnson
Some 19 Johnson families are given in Co. Kerry. Sam Johnson of Dingle is found in the year of 1612. MacSeain and MacEoin are given as variant forms.

Johnston, Johnstone
Some 12 Johnstone families are found in Kerry.

Jones, Mac Seoin

A settler family, given on estates near Tralee, from the coming of the Elizabethan undertakers to the rebellion of 1641. Descent / homeland:

Of Wales. Henry Jones, merchant, was shot at siege of Tralee in 1641. In 1831 lived Frederick (Col.) Jones in Tralee, William Jones, R.N., and later Michael Jones of Tralee is found in 1908.

A total of 35 Jones families are given in Co. Kerry, as listed by J. King.

Jordan

John Jordan of Countra, Co. Kerry.

Joy, Mac Sheehy

Joy is given as a name of a settler family, given on estates near Tralee, from the coming of the Elizabethan undertakers to the rebellion of 1641. Descent / homeland: Of Essex.

Michael and Timothy are given in Tralee in 1908.

Some 53 Joy families are given in Co. Kerry, some of which may descend from Irish origins, the name having been translated into the English form as Joy.

Joyce

Johanna Joyce of Pallas, and Hanoria Joyce of Tullig, both in Co. Kerry.

Julian

Several families of the name are given by J. King. Chris. Julian of Tullamore and Maryborough was agent to Lord Kerry. James Julian of 'Listowhill' is found in 1711, and a James is again found in Listowel in 1726. Chris. is given in Listowel in 1749. Sam of Crotta is given in 1849.

Tullamore House (1846) was the home of Chris Julian in 1821. (Listowel parish)

Kavanagh, Cavanagh

Some 41 families of the 'Kavanagh' spelling are given in Co. Kerry. Today, of course, many spellings of this same family name will be found; some as Cavanagh, others as Kavanaugh etc...

Mac Kay

John MacKay of Pallas, Co. Kerry.

Keane O'Cein O'Cain

One of the more numerous families found in Co. Kerry, some 180 are given by J. King. In his work King specifically states that the name stems from the forms given above, and not from O'Catain. Specific research is needed for family members to make a genealogical connection for much confusion and interchanging exists between names like Keane, Cain, Cahan.

E. T. Keane of Listowel, Co. Kerry, was editor of the "Kilkenny People".

Variant spellings given were: Keane, O'Cein, O'Cain, Y Cayn.

Kearney, Kearny, Carney

Some 36 Kearney families are given in Co. Kerry. Visitors to Kerry will note that the famous 'Kate Kearneys' cottage marks the tourist entrance for the Gap of Dunloe tours. See the ballad by Lady Morgan, and guide books on the lakes of Killarney for more information on that.

Spellings given were: Kearney, Kearny, O'Cearnaig, O'Ceitearnaig.

Keasit

Joseph Keasit of Emlagh, Co. Kerry.

Keating, de Keting

Some 73 Keating families are given by King in Co. Kerry. He as well lists 'de Keting, Geraldin, Fitzgerald' in the heading for the name. As far back as the year 1302 we find a James de Keting in Co. Kerry.

Keay, Kay
Jessie Keay of Dromin and Dan Kay of Ballinvounig are given in Co. Kerry. Keay and Kay, though separate spellings, are listed under the same heading in the works of J. King - thus tying the two forms together, at least in the above two listings.

Kedihan
Wm. Kedihan of Lissodigue, Co. Kerry.

Mac Kee
Tim Mac Kee of Rahanane, Co. Kerry.

Keeffe, O'Keefe
Some 84 Keeffe families are given in Co. Kerry, making it a fairly numerous name here, and Keeffe is given as the preferred spelling of the name in earlier days. Family researchers will note different spellings of the same name today. King gives the name as coming from the line of O'Caoimh, chief of Feara Muighe.

Keely
Catherine Keely of Scartaglin, Co. Kerry is given.

Kelliher, Kealiher, Keliher
One of the more numerous families of Co. Kerry, some 165 families are given here. In older records the name is presumably found spelled as Mac Ceileachair and Ykeleachair and O'Ceileacair, though neither the O nor Mac prefix is found often today.

The Book of Dun Cow, in R.I.A., was compiled by Moelmhuiri Mac Ceileachair in 1100. The Rev. Robt. Kelliher of Ballinana, d. at Hamilton, Ontario, aged 102. John Ykeleachair was vicar of Mogoflahyn in 1403.

Kelly
Some 185 Kelly families are given in Co. Kerry, making it a numerous name here, as well as throughout Ireland as a whole. Hugh Kelly, 1739-77, wrote plays and poems.

Kelter
Thos. Kelter of Gallowsfield, Kerry.

Mac Kemmie
Wm. MacKemmie of Waterville, Co. Kerry.

Kenmare, Lady
Glena Cottage was built by Lady Kenmare. (in the Parish of Killarney).

Mac Kenna, Kenna
There are some 87 Mac Kenna families given in Co. Kerry, and J. King noted the Mac Cionaoda of Triucha in Monaghan where 'in the green woods of Truagh Red Hugh O'Donnell was safe from his foes.'

Maurice MacKenna of Lispole, d. 1903 at the age of 103. Jas. Kenna of Laharan, and Dan and Dan Kenna of Cromane are given in Co. Kerry. The name is presumably taken here from Mac Kenna, of Triucha in Monaghan, according to J. King.

Kennedy
Some 166 Kennedy families are given in Co. Kerry, making this families one of the more numerous in Co. Kerry.

Kennelly, Kinnealy
There were 78 Kennelly families given in Co. Kerry. O'Kenealy was given as a chief of Eoganacht Grian Guara in Coshma, Limerick.

Kennington
Pat of Mastergeeha, Jos. of Knockawaddra, and John of Aunascaul are given in Co. Kerry.

Kenny Kenney
There were 33 Kenny families given in Co. Kerry.

Keogh Keough
Pat of Inch, Tim of Bishop's Lane, Denis of Lauragh, and Tom of Caherdaniel are given in Co. Kerry.

Kerin
Some 48 Kerin families are given in Co. Kerry. It is noted that Ulick Kerin was a Gaelic poet and classical teacher at Cordal. O'Caithreannaigh had the land under the battle peaks of Cualann in Kerry and Ciarraighe Locha na nairneadh in Mayo, Fiacha Mac Cethearnach Ua Ceirin being chief in 1155.

Kerrigan
Peter Kerrigan of Ardfert, Co. Kerry is given. Today the spellings of Carrigan and Kerrigan, etc..are interchangeable.

Kerrisk, O'Ceirise, Healy
Some 20 Kerrisk families are given in Co. Kerry, and it is noted that the surname of Healy was sometimes used for the same family. Spellings given were; Kerrisk, O'Ceirise, Healy, Mac Fiarais

Mac Kessy
John Mac Kessy of Moyderwell, Co. Kerry.

Kevane, O'Caomain
Some 18 Kevane families are given in Kerry.

Mac Kibbon, Mac Giobuin
John Mac Kibbon of Carrig Island, Co. Kerry.

Kidd
Catherine Kidd of Ballyheigue, Co. Kerry.

Kiely, O'Cadla
Some 14 Kiely families were given in Co. Kerry by J. King. Doubtless many descendants will be found spelling the name as Kelly, and its variants, due to the similarity in sound and spelling of the more populous name of Kelly.

Killian, O'Killian
Killian is given as the harper to Mac Carthy Mor.

King, Mac Conroi
There were 49 King families given in Co. Kerry, and those of the old gaelic families of the name may descend from Mac Conroi. Others will be found settling in Ireland over time. The Ernans, the Ernai of Loc Lein in A.M. 3579, gave monarchs to Erin in Eidersgol in A. M. 3965, Conaire More A.D. 60, and Conaire II, in A.D. 165. The race of Conary of battles, the princes of Erna of the golden shields, were kings of Munster of the smooth flowing streams, when Conroi held sway in Temair Erin on Catair Conroi. The arms of the tuath sen Eran, the clan Conaire, were; azure, three crowns or of the Kings of Munster, and that remained the arms of Munster into modern times.

According to King, the clan Conaire gave monarchs to Erin and kings to Munster and Connaught, and Scotic kings to Alban and Britain, e.g. King George V is 60th in descent from Conary II, the ard ri Erin who died in A.D. 165 through Cairbre Riada.

The town of Tralee was incorporated in 1612, and its charter named Giles King as among the first provost and burgesses. Spellings given were: King, Mac Conroi, Clan Conaire

Kingston
Richard Kingston of Derryreag, Co. Kerry.

Kirby
There are 52 families given in Co. Kerry of the Kirby name.

Kirwan
Martin Kirwan of Garryruth, Co. Kerry.

Kissane
There were 72 Kissane families given in Co. Kerry, making the Kissane family a fairly numerous one there.

Kitchener
Lord Kitchener was born in north Kerry, and his father, Col. Kitchener, resided at Gunsboro.

Klincke
Robert Klincke of Fenit without, Co. Kerry.

Knight, Knightley
A settler family on estates near Tralee, from the coming of the Elizabethan undertakers to the rebellion of 1641. Descent / homeland:
Elinor Knight lived in Tralee in 1622. Wm. Knightley is in Tralee in 1908.
Sam Knight of Chapel Quarter and Ernest Knight of Spunkane, Co. Kerry.

Knight of Kerry
The Grove (1846) was formerly the residence of the Knight of Kerry. (Dingle parish),
Ballinruddery (1846) was a seat of the Knight of Kerry, which extended into Duagh parish and also into Finuge.
Glanleam (1846), in Valencia parish, was the seat of the Knight of Kerry. Rahinane Castle belonged to the Knight of Kerry. For legends, see Jeremiah Curtin's 'Tales of the Fairies' 1895.

Knightly
There were 15 families of the Knightly name given in Co. Kerry.

Lacy, Lacey, de Lacy
Six families of the Lacy name are given, those of Jas. Lacy of Breahig, Bridget of Ballahantouragh, Pat of Coolnadead, Tom of Bawnluskaha, Edm. of Asdee, and Pat of Daly's Lane.
In 1205 Hugh de Lacy was granted all the lands of Ulster whereof the King belted him Earl, to hold in fee, rendering the services of one knight fee for every cantred, and saving to the King the episcopal investitures.
The Lacys of Rathcahill are buried in teampull Gleantain and Field Marshal Lacy of Austria was a nephew of Count Brown. Count Peter Lacy of Russia died in 1751. Spellings given include: Lacy, Lacey, de Lacy, O'Laiteasa.

Ladden
Michael Ladden of Farna and Bryan of Ballygamboon, Co. Kerry.

Laid, Laide, Leade, O'Laidin
Some 9 families of the name are given in Kerry; John of Gortatlea, John of Killegane, John of Dromatour, Pat of Ballinageragh, Pat and Martin of Ardoughter, Wm. of the Rock, Pat of Rock Street, and Pat of Tralee. The spellings above were all given in J. Kings work.

Lake
John Lake of Farrantooreen, Co. Kerry.

Lally, O'Maolalaid
Eliza Lally of Waterville, Co. Kerry. The name is often assumed to be a shortened form of the surname of Mulally or O'Mulally.

Lamb, O'Luain
John Lamb of Ballymullen and Garryruth and Tralee, Margt. of Ballyvelly, and John of Callinaferey are given in Kerry.

Lambert
Nora Lambert of Ardnamweely is given in Kerry.

Lander, De Laundre, Landers

Castle Linder of Kilgarrylander parish, must have been the castle owned by the Lander family, who held sway in Keelgarrylander, (the wood, or church, of Lander). Maurice Lander of Killarney was among the transplanted in 1650. Ewenny Priory near Dunraven Castle in Wales was founded in 1141 by Maurice De Laundre. (Kilgarrylander parish).

There were 23 Landers families given in Kerry, said to come from the older name of Laundre at least in some cases. In 1285 Wm. and Adam Laundre paid the sheriff 24s. on Oct. 20.

Landon

Samuel Landon of Tullahinnell, Co. Kerry.

Lane

Ralph Lane, High Sheriff of Kerry in 1585, was 'very anxious to' be granted the house and lands of Castle Island in Kerry.

Rafe Lane, in 1584, petitioned the Queen for a place and lands in Co. Kerry after the Geraldine confiscations, but he went to Virginia. (J. King, County Kerry Past and Present).

The two individuals given above may well be one in the same, although perhaps taken from two different sources.

Langan, O'Longain

John Langan of Tullamore, Peter of Kilpadogue, and Pat of Duagh are all given in Co. Kerry.

Langford

There were 13 Langford families given in Co. Kerry. In 1782 John Langford of Castle Conway is of note, and his will was in the Public Record Office. In 1818, Rev. Francis was vicar of Kilmoe, and Kilcornan in Limerick; he m. the daughter of Rev. Walter Stewart. He died in 1842 leaving George of Adare in 1861, Rev. Francis, Rev. John, Charlotte m. John Limerick, Agnes m. John O'Callaghan. Wm. Godfrey Langford of Annadale is noted in 1831.

Larkin

There were 18 Larkin families given in Co. Kerry.

Larmer

Hanoria Larmer of Ballymacassy, Co. Kerry.

Latchford

Rd. and Frank and Rd. and John and Francis Latchford were all of the town of Tralee in Co. Kerry. One Wm. Latchford was of Murreigh, and Pat Latchford of Ranaleen, Co. Kerry are given as well. Note the operation of Latchford, Ltd., of Tralee.

Latimer

John Latimer of Ballymullen, Co. Kerry.

Lauder

Major Lauder is of record in 1913.

Lavery

Dan Lavery of Abanagran, John of of Tieraclea, Arthur of Larha, Pat of Garryantannavally, Pat of Ballyline and Rd. of Farna, are all given in Co. Kerry.

Lavin

Ellen Lavin of Abbey-street, is given in Co. Kerry.

Laweless, Lawless

Stephen Laweless, canon of Ardfert, Co. Kerry, in 1343.

Lawlee

John Lawlee of Shrone, Co. Kerry.

Lawlor, Lalours

In 1609, some 87 Laulors or Lawlors were transplanted from Queen's County to Tarbert, Co. Kerry with Patrick Crosbie, and 102 Moores, 39 Kellys, 13 Dorans, 43 Clandeboys, and 5 Dowlins.

In 1807 Ellen, dau. of Martin Lawlor of Killarney, m. Denis Shyne, having Denis Shyne Lawlor of Castlelough, b.1808, poet, author of pilgrimages in Pyrenees in 1870, m. 1814 Isabella Hudleston of Sawston Hall in Cambridge, having Isabella who m.1861 Daniel O'Connell of Darrynane.

There were 58 Lawlor families given in Co. Kerry.

James Lawlor lived at Cahirdean in Kilcredane parish in 1821.

Castle Lough in Killarney Parish was demolished by Ludlow. A younger branch of the MacCarthys resided there, by patent of James II in 1684. It was sold to Col. Wm. Crosbie. Dennis Shyne Lawlor resided here in 1863. Jas. Lawlor, M.D. of Killarney, purchased Castle Lough.

Le hunt

Minard Castle, built by the Knight of Kerry, was blown up in 1650 by Cols. Le Hunt and Sadler. Its' defender Walter Hussey of Castlegregory was killed.

Leade

Richard Leade of Garrynagore, Co. Kerry.

Leader

John Leader of Knocknageeha and Hy. Leader of Spunkane, Co. Kerry.

Leahy of Southill, Co. Kerry
From The Irish Book of Arms. (IGF) 1988.

Leahy

The Leahy family of Southhill was a branch of the O'Brien family, having lands at Abbeyfeale from the 13th to 17th century. John Leahy, 1770, had a son John, 1810, who was Q.C. and Limerick Judge of Sessions. His son was John White Leahy of Southhill, Sheriff of Kerry, 1877. South Hill (1846), in Killarney parish, has been referred to as the residence of the 'White Leahy' family.

Some 101 Leahy families are given in Co. Kerry.

Leake

Given as the name of a family settling in Co. Kerry, subsequent to the 1641-42 rebellion. Descent/ Homeland:

Of Yorks. In 1831 lived Barry D. and John Leake of Tralee.

Mac Lean, Mac Giolla Eain

Sarah Mac Lean of the Mall, and Anne Mac Lean of Blennerville, Co. Kerry.

Carrig-A-Phuca Castle

Leane, Lane, Leen, O'Leyne

Given by King as descended from O'Laoghain, chief of Ui Fearba, cantred, some 116 Leane families are given in Co. Kerry. O'Laoghain's cantred of Ui Fearba comprised Ballyheige, Fenit, Barrow, Clogherbrien, Leath, Killury, west of Ui Flanannain cantred and south of Araghticonnor. After the Anglo-Norman invasion in 1172 the FitzGeralds and Cantillons and Brownes seized the lands of O'Laoghain and built the stone castles of the district.

In 1653 Teigue O'Leyne of Ballymullen had 170 tenants. Dr. Teigue Leyne d. 1723, Dr. Jeremy Leyne, 1759, M. Eliz. O'Connell of Kilkeeveragh, had a son Dr. Mce. Leyne, m.1786 Agnes Mac Gillicuddy, having a son, Dr. Jerh. Leyne, d. 1872, and Capt Leyne of Waterloo, and R. M. for Clare m. a sister of Baron O'Connor and d.1864 having issue.

In 1908 Rev. W. Leen of Ballyheigue and Iowa wrote poems on Ratoo and other Kerry scenes. Spellings given include: Leane, Lane, Leen, O'Leyne, O'Laoghain.

Leary

One of the more numerous families given in Co. Kerry, some 301 families were recorded in Kerry. The O'Leary was chief of Uibh Leaghaire or Iveleary or Hy Laoghaire, in Muskerry, between Macroom and Inchageela. Capt Diarmuid O'Leary of Kilmeen in 1696 was the subject of a poem by E. O'Rahilly; and the dirge of Arthur O'Leary in 1773 was made by his wife, Eileen Dhuv O'Connell. Arthur O'Leary, 1834-1919, b. in Tralee, was professor of piano-forte at R. Acadamy of Music in London. Rev. C.F. O'Leary of Missouri in the U.S.A. was born at Ballinclogher. Sara O'Leary died at Maglass in 1806, aged 120.

Ledman

Wm. Ledman of Maglass, Co. Kerry is noted in 1831.

Ledmon

Thos. Ledmon lived at Ballyhorgan in 1821 (Finuge parish).

Lee, O'Laidig

John and Wm. Lee of Feohanagh, David of Canal new road, Wm. of Gortamullen, and Michael of Tinnies are all given in Co. Kerry.

Leech

Mary Leech of Spunkane, Co. Kerry.

Leeser

The town of Tralee was incorporated in 1612, and its charter named John Leeser, as among the first provost and burgesses.

Leeson

Given under the heading of Leeson-Marshall of Callinafercy is given:

Robert Leeson (b. 1796) was second son of Earl Milltown and married Elizabeth Marshall of Ballymacadam, whose son was Richard Leeson Marshall (d. 1873), whose son was Markham Richard.

Tristam-Marshall came to Kerry in Wilmot's expedition in 1602 and married Mary Fitzgerald of Ballymacadam.

Lehane

King gives the surname of Lehane as coming from O'Liatain of Hy Listhain or Castle Lyons in Co. Cork. 10 families of the name were given in Co. Kerry; Con of Tooreencahill, Con of Leitrim, Flor of Blennerville, Jas. of Droumatouk, Catherine of Ownagarry, Con of Redtrench, Pat of Curraglass, Ml. and Ml. of Coolknoohill, and Con of Kilfadamore.

Mac Leish

David Mac Leish of Rae Street, Co. Kerry.

Lenihan
There were 42 families of the name listed by King, who also gave; Ua Lenachain of Clodagh and Suir in Waterford, expelled by Purcell and De Grandison in 1200.

Lennane, O'Leannain
Several families are given in Kerry, including those of Ballydonaghue, Letter, Derra, Tieraclea, Gortacrossane, Lacca, Knockenagh, Coolkeragh, Kilomerhoe and Ballyhearney.

Lentall
A settler family, given on estates near Tralee, from the coming of the Elizabethan undertakers to the rebellion of 1641. Descent / homeland: Of Essex, Abingdon, Berks. Robert Lenthal of Tralee was killed at Ballinskelligs, 1641.

Mac Leod, Mac Leoid
Angus Mac Leod of Droumyrourke, Co. Kerry.

Leonard
Mce. and Teresa of Killarney; Wm. of Bawnluskaha; Edm. of Knockenagh; John and Ml. of Lacca; John of Ballymacegogue; John of the Mall; Wm. of Carhoobeg. Maurice was land agent to Lord Kenmare.

Leslie
There were 17 Leslie families given in Kerry. Note that in 1773 John Leslie wrote on Killarney. In 1790 Rev. Richd. Leslie was of Aghadoe, and in 1821 Pierse Leslie was of Tarbert in Kerry.

The Leslie family of Tarbert came from England in 1633. James Leslie settled in Kerry, and had a son, James, Bishop of Limerick. His son was created bart., 1678, Sir Edward Leslie, of Tarbert House, succeeded by his cousin-german, Robert, whose son Robert, was born 1792, and who was succeeded by a son Robert. One Capt. Robert of Tarbert is given as died at 90. Ahanna (1846) was the seat of P. Leslie.

Letters
Patrick Letters, M.D., of Laharan, Co. Kerry.

Leventhal
S. Leventhal of Boherbee, Co. Kerry.

Levison
John Levison of Church street, in Co. Kerry.

Lewis
Laurance Lewis of Killahan, Co. Kerry.

O' Leyne, O'Layne
A well known Kerry family, there is given a note in Mrs. A. J. O'Connell's book about "a century and a half of Dr. Laynes of Tralee." The first was Dr. Teigue O'Leyne, who died about 1723. Next came Dr. Jeremy, who m. Elizabeth O'Connell. Their son was Dr. Maurice Leyne, a very clever physician and highly educated man, who was for fifty years the physician and friend of the principal families. He was a welcome guest at all the best houses, due in part to his conversational skills. He died in 1823, succeeded by his son, Dr. Jeremiah, the last of them, who died in 1872.

Keatings History (IGF edition), gives O'Leyne or Lane, as chief of the Ui Ferba, an old sept in Co. Kerry. O'Leyne is given as 'a warrior of fame..over Ui Ferba' by O'Heerin. Spellings included O'Leyne, O'Layne, Leyne, and Layne.

Lick Castle
Dismantled by Lord Kerry in 1600. (Kilconly parish)

Liddane, O'Loideain
John and Mce. of Buddaghauns, Co. Kerry.

Lindesay, Lindsay
Crawford Lindesay of Magh., Co. Kerry.

Lindon
Geo. Lindon of Clogherclemin.

Lisack or Gilliesaght
The Rev. Daniel Lisack in 1621, archdeacon of Ardfert and vicar of Kilcummin in the diocese of Aghadoe, united for this turn only and in the King's gift pleno jure.

Lloyd
Maud Lloyd of Ardroe, Co. Kerry.

Locke Lock
Fred Locke of Boherbee and Rd. of Canal new road, both in Co. Kerry.

Logue
Thomas Logue of Cloghane, Co. Kerry.

Lombard
Rd. and James Lombard of Doolaigue, Co. Kerry. One John Lombard was sheriff and Mayor of Cork, 1355-80.

Long
Some 46 Long families are given in Co. Kerry, and the Irish origins for the name are given as coming from O'Longaig, according to King. It is of passing note that Jas. Long of Dingle, was editor of the 'Tralee Chronicle', 'Kerry Vindicator' and 'Clonmel Nationalist'.

Looney
There were some 40 'Looney' families given in Co. Kerry.

Lord
Wm. Lord of Ballinorig, Co. Kerry is given. King gives the name as stemming from O'Tigearnaig.

Lordan
Jerh. Lordan of Faha, Co. Kerry. King gives the name as coming from O'Lordain.

Mac Loughlin, Mac Loclainn
Over 10 families of the name are given in Co. Kerry, and it was given that Lochlonn, chief of Aileach, 179th ard ri, destroyed Kincora in 1088, the O'Neills defeated the Mac Loughlins in 1241 at Caimirge, and became chiefs of cinel Eoghain.

Loughlin, O'Loclainn
Bridget Loughlin of Chute's Lane, and Denis of Brogue-Lane are both given in Co. Kerry. It is also of note that Dr. Wm. F. N. O'Loughlin was drowned in the Titanic in 1912. In 1666 Capt. Richard (Mac?)Laughlin in 1666 had a grant of 713 acres.

Loughnane, O'Lactnain
Some 22 Loughnane families are given in Co. Kerry.

Lovett
There were some 24 Lovett families given in Co. Kerry.

Lowden
Annie Lowden of Boherbee, Co. Kerry.

Lowe, Mac Lugada
Sarah Lowe of Sillahertane, Co. Kerry.

Luby, O'Lubaig
Catherine Luby, in 1822 wrote the 'Spirit of the Lakes of Killarney', Muckross Abbey.

Lucey, Lucy, O'Luasaig
There were some 42 Lucey families given in Co. Kerry. According to King, Lucey, Lucy, Lucid, Luiseid and O'Luasaig are simply variations in writing of the same name.

Lucid, O'Luasaig
There were some 21 Lucid families in Co. Kerry. According to King, Lucey, Lucy, Lucid, Luiseid and O'Luasaig are simply variations in writing of the same name. (see Lucey)

Lumsden
Madeline Lumsden of Denny Street, Co. Kerry.

Lunham
Annie Lunham of Strand Street, Co. Kerry is given. Robert of Tralee, whose children were Mrs. Agnes Benner, and Robert Lunham of Chicago, who d. 1913, aged 56.

Lunny, Lunney
Jas. Lunny of Listowel is given.

Lupton
Wm. Lupton of Ballinskellings, Co. Kerry.

Lyden
Colman Lyden of James Street, Co. Kerry.

Lynch
One of the most numerous families of Co. Kerry, some 288 families are given there. It is given that Lynch,(i.e. O'Linchy, O'Loingsigh, Ua Loingsigh) (longseach = a mariner), 'was chief of Uaithne thire, inhabit the wood in front of the foreigners or Danes of Limerick at Castle Connell, chiefs of cinel Bacat, lord of Dal Araidhe'.

In 1402 Cornelius Oloynsig was vicar of Limerick; and in 1411 Alan Olonsigh was a canon of Killagh de Belloloco. In 1821 lived Jeffrey and John Lynch at Dromin, Garrett at Killarney, John at Tralee. Diarmuid Lynch and Finian Lynch were prominent Irish scholars.

Lyndon
Thomas Lyndon of Kilpadogue, Co. Kerry.

Lyne, O'Laigin
A fairly numerous family of Co. Kerry, some 110 Lyne households were given there.

Lynne Lyn O'Loinn
King gives Geo. of Crotta, John of Montanagay, Bridget of Cloonsillagh, and Sam of Nelson Street in Co. Kerry. Wm. Lyn is noted as grocer of London in 1400; Rd. of Bassingbourne in 1571.

Also given as a settler family, given on estates near Tralee, from the coming of the Elizabethan undertakers to the rebellion of 1641. The family name is also found settling in Kerry subsequent to the rebellion of 1641-41. Descent / homeland: Of Northants, Norfolk. Related to the Cromwell family. Martha Lyn (m.1641?), was the wife of John B'hassett, son of Robert of Ballycarty in 1641. William Lyn lived in Tralee in 1624. Francis Lynne is found in Tralee in 1665. Saml. Lynn of Tralee in 1908.

Lyons
The Lyons surname accounted for some 64 families in Co. Kerry, and as given by J. King the Irish of the name descend from O'Liathan of Hy Lehan (now Barrymore in Co. Cork). Tom Lyons of Castle street in Tralee d. 1917, aged 77; Rev. John C. Lyons, O.P., of Tralee, d.1914, a.60.

Macintosh
Kilmurry House was built in 1843 by the Rev. A. Macintosh, the Protestant incumbent of the parish. (Ballincuslane parish)

Mackassy Macassy
Rd. Mackassy of Kilcock, Co. Kerry and John Macassy of Glounaphuca, Co. Kerry. The spellings of Mackassy and Macassy are given by J. King under the same heading, the spelling of Mac Kessy, is given separately, listing John Mac Kessy of Moyderwell, Co. Kerry.

Mackey, Mac Aoda
Robt. Mackey of Farranreagh and Bernard Mackey of Spunkane, Co. Kerry.

Madden

The will of Ambrose Madden of Lacken, Co. Kerry, 1700, was recorded in the Public Records Office. Also given in Kerry were Ml. of Listowel, Nicholas of Leanamore, Dan of Curraghdarrig, Tom and John of Kilgarvan, Tom of Knockenagh, John of Market Place, Tim of Dykegate lane, Tom of Kenmare and the Rev. Joseph Madden of Dromhall.

Madget, Madgett

Given as the name of a family settling in Co. Kerry, subsequent to the 1641-42 rebellion. Homeland/ descent: Of Devon.
Nicholas Madgett, b. 1799, was a French-Irish official known to Wolfe Tone. Another Madgett was an officer in the Spanish or American navy, and was some connection with the Daltons of North Kerry..

Nicholas Madgett, D.D. 1752, Nov. 10, of the College of St. Barbara in Paris, 'to be Bishop of Killaloe; 1753, Feb. 8, exchanged to Ardfert with Wm. O'Meara; he built a residence in a narrow lane off Strand street in Tralee, and occupied it until his death in 1774, when he was buried at Ardfert in the same tomb as Bishops Moriarty 1737, and O'Sullivan d. 1739; he was born in Ballynorig in Kilmoiley, with eight sisters who married locally, with issue, and a brother who was a naval officer.

Madigan, O'Madagain

Pat Madigan of Carhooearagh, Jas. of Carhoonakilla and Mary of Clieveragh are given in Co. Kerry.

Magane, Mac Canna

Wm. Magane of Tooracladdane is given in Kerry, and J. King gives the name as more anciently coming from MacCanna.

Magee

Tom Magee of Dromgower, and Con of Tieraclea are given in Co. Kerry.

Maginn, Mac Finn

Jos. Maginn of Barrack lane, is given in Co. Kerry.

Maher, Meagher, O'Meacair

John Maher of Ballintogher, John of Knockadirreen, Mary of Dysert, Pat of Trieneragh, Tom of Laharan, Mary of the Rock, Wm. of Abbey street, Harry of Bridge street, Tom of Abbeylands, Jas. of Farran, Margt. of Ballycarnahan, and Rev. P. Maher of Lixnaw were all given in Co. Kerry. (see O'Meagher).

Mac Mahon

Some 66 families are given in Co. Kerry. Mac Mahon is given as chief of Corco Baiscinn in Co. Clare. Turlogh of Ardferte, Co. Kerry, son of Dermott, son of Tiegue of Sroghe in Limerick, was high Sheriff of Co. Kerrye and died in 1639. Marshal Mac Mahon was President of the French Republic.

Among those who have dropped the Mac prefix before the name was Andrew Mahon of Tralee, Co. Kerry.

O' Mahoney Mahony

A very well known family of Co. Kerry, and one of the most numerous surnames in that county as well, with 271 families given there.

The O'Mahoney's were a Munster clan in Cork before the Norman invasions. The name Mahoney was given to be derived from Mahon or Mathghamhain of the Eoganacht Cashel, who died in 1034. Dermod of Ivagha settled in Kerry before 1355; his son John m. a dau. of Aodh O'Connell, having Dermod 1422, who m. Sabit, dau. of O'Sullivan Mor, having Conor and Donal. Conor 1471, m. a dau. of Geoffrey O'Donoghue, having Teig mergach, or angry looking who was seneschal to the Earl of Desmond in 1536, and he m. Honora O'Sullivan Beare having eight sons, Dermod, Conor, Donal, Fineen, Maolmuach, Eoghan, Donogh and Sean. Donal Mac Teig mergeach of Tubrid in Iveragh, was chief officer to Mac Carthy Mor in 1588.

The Mahoney family of Dunloe Castle were Dan, 1676-1747, John d.1780, Dan d.1832, Dan d.1871, John dsp. 1908.

The Mahoney family of Dromore Castle were: Denis, John, d.1743. Denis John d.1817 (?), Rev. Denis d. 1851, Richd. d.1892, Harold 1867-1905 unm., and his sister Nora m. 1900 Edward Hood.

The Mahoney family of Castlequin were: Myles, 1726, Kean.

The Mahoney family of Cullina were Florence, 1751, Myles, Kean, Kean d.1862, sp., his bro., Dr. Myles d. unm.. Burkes Landed Gentry gives details on many of these families.

Count Bartholomew O'Mahoney, 1749-1819, was a general in the French army, his ancestors being Michael, Owen, Teig, Dermod Donogh, Dermod,

O' Mahoney Mahony

Florence 1568, Donal, Teig, meirgeach. Count Daniel O'Mahoney of Cremona d. 1714; his ancestry is given as Dermod, John, Dan, Dermod, Dan, Conor, John, Dermod, Finghin 1450. Count John Francis O'Mahoney, 1815, General in the French army, was son of Dermod, son of Donal of Dunloe.

In 1639 MacDermot O'Mahoney was sheriff of Kerry. The family lands were confiscated by the Cromwellians, and many of the clan served in the Irish Brigades in Europe. John Mahony, of Dromore, was a delegate at Dungannon in 1782. His son, Rev. Denis (m.1827), had a son Harold Segerson. (k2 142)

Knockawinna, in Brosna parish, in 1695 was the residence of the O'Mahoneys. Con. O'M. lived there in 1722. His son John, and his son James of Loughvalla, succeeded. Andrew of Cloghane, was heir to James.

In Caher parish at Castlequin in 1846 was the seat of a branch of the O'Mahoney family.

Dunloe Castle was bombarded by Ireton. D. Mahony resided there in 1864. It was one of O'Sullivan Mor's forts, but was built by Maurice Fitzgerald. It was usually in charge of the Sugrue O'Sullivans. Dunkerron was O'Sullivan Mor's chief seats.

Dromore (1846), was the O'Mahoney residence. (Templenoe parish).

The Mahoney and Hart families lived at Batterfield in Kilnanare parish in the 18th century.

Col. Dermot O'Mahoney, who fell fighting at the battle of Aughrim in 1691, was a brother of Count Daniel O'Mahoney, the hero of Cremona. They were grandsons of Lean, son of Theig Meirgeach O'Mahony, ancestor of the Dunloe and Dromore lines.

O' Mahoney Mahony

Mahony of Kilmorna

Kean, 12th Lord of Kinealmeaky was 24th in descent from Olioll Olum, king of Munster, in the 3rd century. From this line sprang Dermod, who settled in Desmond in 1335. His son was John Mergagh, whose son was Dermod (1442), whose son was Conor (1477), whose son was Teigue (1536), whose seventh son was Donogh, whose son was Kean, from whom the 4th in descent was Con, whose son was David, whose son was Pierce (b. 1750), whose son was Pierce of Kilmorna (b. 1814), whose son was George (b. 1842).

O'Mahony of Brosna

The first of this branch of the family came from Ivagha, West Carberry, through a family dispute. They became magnates of Brosna and Mt. Collins. Dennis Mahoney, b. 1680 was High Constable for the barony of Upper Conelloe (Glinquin), in 1746. The family tomb is found at Brosna. His lands were lost as a result of this branch not conforming to the Protestant religion during the Penal years and the government lease was not renewed. This Dennis was son of Cornelius Mahony of Knockawinna, and grandson of Gerald Fitzgerald, Knight of Glin. One son of this Dennis was James, Mahony, of Batterfield and he married Margaret Meredith of Dicksgrove.

An extensive article on the family found in the Kerry Archaeological Magazine, October 1917 issue gives 5 minor branches of the family; (1) Clann Fineen (2) Clan Conogher (3) Ui Floin Luadh (4) Sliocht Donal of Kilnaglory and (5) the Sliocht Dermod Og of Kerry.

Only Ui Floin Luadh can be traced past the 17th century, through Cornelius O'Mahoney in the Spanish Army, who d.1776 and Count Dermod O'Mahoney.

Main, Mac Maine

Wm. Main of Spunkane and Bridget of Ballinskelligs are given in Co. Kerry.

Mair, O'Midir

Jas. Mair of Farranreagh, in Co. Kerry.

Malachy

Ferdinand Malachy of Clooshguire, Co. Kerry.

Malley, O'Maille

J. King gives general notice of the O'Malley family of Mayo and then lists several families of the Malley name in Co. Kerry, including: Jas. of Dungeel, Mce. and Mce. of Bohereencael, Dan of Tinnahally, Jas. and Pat of Callinafercy, Pat of Ballymacprior, John of Tulligmore, Ml. and Dan of Laharan, Pat of Killirglin, and Ml. of Curraheen.

Malone

Several of the name are given in Co. Kerry including Eoin of Brawney in W. Meath; Margt. of Ardnamweely, Ml. of Listowel, John and John of Coumeenole, Hanoria of Lough, Ml. of Emlagh, Geo. of Dingle, Pat of Cloghaneduff, John of John street, Wm. and Tom of Rahinane, and John of Ballintlea.

Malvey

Given in Co. Kerry were Pat and Jas. and Pat of Tarmons, Mce. of Darrynane, Pat and Pat of Droumakilla, Mary of Cahersavane, Crohan of Spunkane, and Julia of Gleesk.

Manaher

Given in Co. Kerry were Ml. Manaher of Cloonbrane, and Ellen of Tieraclea.

Mangan, O'Mongain

There were some 67 families of the Mangan name given in Co. Kerry. The Rev. John Mangan, bishop of Kerry, 1904-17; was P.P. of Glengariffe, Sneem, and Kenmare; b. 1852 at Bedford, he completed Killarney cathedral which was designed by Pugin in 1840; and he was buried beside Bishops Moriarty and Coffey in the cathedral; he lift his books to form the nucleus of an episcopal diocesan library.

Mannering

A settler family on estates near Tralee, from the coming of the Elizabethan undertakers to the rebellion of 1641.

Manning, O'Mainnin

(see also Mangan) Several Manning families are given in Co. Kerry, as listed by J. King.

Mannion, O'Mainin

John and Ml. Mannion of Demesne are given in Co. Kerry. Both Manning and Mannion are given as coming from the same ancient spelling of O'Mainin.

Mannix

Several of the Mannis name are given in Co. Kerry, as listed by J. King.

Mansell

John and Wm. Mansell of Rhodes, Co. Kerry are given.

Mansfield

Several of the name are given in Co. Kerry, including John of Knockavrogeen, John of Strand Road, Sam and Sam of Poulawaddra, Tom of Inchinaleega, John of Driminamore, John of Waterville, Wm. of William Street, and Jos. of Kenmare.

Mac Manus

The Rev. Bro. P. B. Mac Manus of Balloonagh, Co. Kerry.

Mareschall

The Castle of the Island of Kerry was built in 1226 by Geoffrey de Marisco, and taken by Sir Ralph Ufford in 1345 from the Geraldines. The lands were delivered to Walerond Fenton after the death of Wm. Mareschall, Earl of Pembroke. (see Marshall)

Marisco

Geoffrey de Marisco, justiciary of Ireland; in 1216-19, led an army into Kerry and Desmond, spoiled the corn, encamped at Athnahuamha, built a castle at Maighe Ruathe, and intruded John of Emly as bishop of Ardfert, but he resigned in 1225.

The Castle of the Island of Kerry was built in 1226 by Geoffrey de Marisco, and taken by Sir Ralph Ufford in 1345 from the Geraldines.

Marshall, de Marascal

Several of the name are found in Co. Kerry. In 1298 Elias le Marshall was juror at the manor de Insula or Castleisland. Tristram Marshall, 1602, married Mary Fitz Gerald of Bally Mac Adam. Ralph Marshall, had issue Eliz. who m. 1820 Robt. Leeson, son of Earl Milltown, having Rd. Leeson Marshall, who m. 1858 Rebecca Power, having Markham Rd. who m. Mabel Godfrey, having Mary, and he m. Meriel Hodson in 1907.

The Castle of the Island of Kerry was built in 1226 by Geoffrey de Marisco, and taken by Sir Ralph Ufford in 1345 from the Geraldines. The lands were delivered to Walerond Fenton after the death of Wm. Mareschall, Earl of Pembroke. (Castleisland parish).

Also given as the name (Marshall) of a Cromwellian settler granted lands in 1667 in Co. Kerry.

Martel

Given as the name of a family settling in Co. Kerry, subsequent to the 1641-42 rebellion.

Martelli

Given were Francis and John and Horatio Martelli, of Sunday's Well, Co. Kerry, in 1831.

Martin, O'Martain

Some 24 Martin families are given in Co. Kerry. One Wm. Martin was parish clerk of Dingle in 1683. Rev. Austin and Robert Martin are given in Tarbert in 1831, and M. Agnew (Martin) in Tralee. Roger Martin of Killorglin is given in 1821.

Martin is found as the name of a settler family, given on estates near Tralee, from the coming of the Elizabethan undertakers to the rebellion of 1641. Homeland: Of Sussex.

In 1831 we find Austin Martin, Clk. Tarbert, J.P.; Robert Martin of Tarbert, M. Agnew Martin of Tralee. In 1908 we find Austin, Bernard, Daniel and Leo Martin in Tralee.

Mason

A settler family on estates near Tralee, from the coming of the Elizabethan undertakers to the rebellion of 1641. This family was originally of Cambs..

Wm., Pat, John and Wm. Mason in Tralee in 1908. By his wife, Catherine O'Hara, Pierce Power had a dau. Catherine, who m. James Mason, of Ballymacelligott and Ballydowney. This James Mason was the son of John Mason of Ballymacelligott, and his wife, Avis MacLoughlin. John Mason and Avis McLoughlin, besides the son James, the husband of Catherine Power, had a son Richard and three daughters. Catherine Mason, the eldest m. Francis Spring, third son of Thomas Spring of Ballycrispin. John Mason, the brother of those daughters had three sons, John, James and Richard, and a daughter Elizabeth. John Mason the eldest of these three sons, and the proprietor of Ballydowney, and of considerable property round Ballymacelligott, married his cousin german Avis, but died childless. The family property passed to his second brother, James Mason. He m. Elizabeth Austin of Cork, and left an only son, (circa 1908) St. John Mason, and a daughter m. to Edward Bishop M.D.. Richard Mason, the third son of James and Catherine Power, m. his cousin-german Alice, only daughter of his uncle Richard Mason, before mentioned, and had a son John, m. to Jane Gorham, and three daughters from whose line would come the ill-fated Robert Emmett. Thus Emmet had scores of Kerry cousins, i.e. Masons, Blennerhassetts, Hewsons, Hilliards etc..

James Mason lived at Ballydowney in 1757.(Aghadoe Parish)

St. John Mason in 1799 wrote against the Act of Union, and in 1845 against Chris Gallway concerning Cleeny lands.

Mason (cont'd)
Fred mason of Fealeview is given in 1821, Oliver of Aghamore is given in 1818. Robert of Ballinduganig and Wm. of Kilmore, Co. Kerry.

Mathews
Joseph Mathews of Clovers lane and James of New Street, all in Co. Kerry.

Matson
John Matson of Valencia Road, Co. Kerry.

Maunsell
Several families of the name are given in Co. Kerry, including one Rev. John Maunsell of Kilemly in 1831.

Mac Maurice
(see Fitzmaurice, Morris, Morrice etc..)

Mawe, Mac Maige
Mary Mawe of Kilmore and Maria Mawe of Inch are given in Co. Kerry. John D. was b. 1832 at Lixnaw, Co. Kerry; to the U.S.A. in 1852, served in the U.S. Army in Civil War, also at Ridgway; at Danville, Illinois in 1909. Dr. Tom Mawe of Tralee, m. 1804, Anne Lett. Rev. Mce. Mawe, in 1779 at Beaufort, m. Miss Cossart. In 1710, John of Barrow and Wm. of Ballymaquin are given in Kerry. J. King gives the Irish form of the name as Mac Maige.

Maxwell
Hy. Maxwell of Kenmare, Co. Kerry.

May
Tom May of Fenit, John May of Cross Lane and Seabourne May of Abbeylands, Co. Kerry.

Maybury, Mayberry
Given in Co. Kerry were: Mrs. Maybury of Ballyheigue, Geo. of Gearhanagoul; James of Churchground, James and Aug. of Cahir, Dan and Geo. of Kenmare, Arisia of Gortagass, Catherine of Tubrid, Helena of Mucksna, Dr. Francis of Riversdale.

One John Maybury was parish clerk of Kilgobbin in 1758. Francis and William are found in 1783. Dr. Rd. and Geo. of Killarney and John of Greenlane are given in 1821. Dr. Thomas Maybury m. Isabella Day, having Geo., Robert, Kate, Eliz., Harriette. Aug. of Cleady had Dr. Wm., who had Drs. Aug., Wm., Aurelius, Horace, and Lysander.

Augustus Maybury of Cleady, Kenmare, had a son William Augustus Maybury, surgeon of Ceadar Lodge, Frimley, who had (1) Augustus Constable Maybury DScl, d. 1908, aged 65. (2) Dr. William Augustus Maybury, Colchester. (3) Dr. Aurelus Victor Maybury, Portsmouth. (4) Dr. Horace Mansell Maybury, London. (5) Dr. Lysander Maybury, Southsea.

Maynard
Given as the name of a family settling in Co. Kerry, subsequent to the 1641-42 rebellion. Homeland/ descent: Of Herts., Midx. Francis Maynard had a son William, b. 1702. Barry Maynard of Ballyvelly, Co. Kerry, given in 1751.

Meade
Several of the name are given by King, including Francis Meade who was law and land agent in Kerry 1760-1784; his mother was a Miss Langford of Keel; he m. 2 Miss Collis of Monaree; he resided at Fenit and d. at Carrigafoyle; his will 1784 and of Anne 1797 are given in the Public Record Office earlier.

Meagher

Justin Meagher of New Street, Killarney, Co. Kerry is given. It is also noted that Ua Meacair was chief of Ui Cairin in Tipperary.

Meara, O'Meadra

Some 43 Meara families are given in Co. Kerry and it was also noted that Tuaim Ui Mheara or Toomavara in Ormond was the clan cemetery. Rev. William O'Meara, deacon of Waterford cathedral, was bishop of Kerry 1743-52, and exchanged to Killaloe.

Meehan, Meahan

Several families of the name are given in Co. Kerry. It was also noted that the Meehan of Ballymeehan in Leitrim had custody of the Gospel of St. Molaise of Devenish in the 6th century.

Meek

Henry Meek, of the Mall, in Kerry.

Mehigan

Con Mehigan of William street is given in Co. Kerry.

Melville

W. Melville is given in Kings History of Kerry as serving 46 years in the London police force, becoming a chief detective and escort to Royalties.

Mercer

Jerh. Mercer of Nelson street is given in Co. Kerry. Also given as the name of a Cromwellian settler granted lands in 1667 in Co. Kerry.

Meredith

Given as a family name settling in Co. Kerry, both prior to and subsequent to the 1641-42 rebellion.

Meredith of Dicksgrove.- Richard Meredith, second son of David of Gowress, Co. Montgomery, came to Ireland being related by marriage to Lord Herbert of Cherbury and Castleisland. He died in 1752, and left Richard of Tierneygore; and William of Dicksgrove who was sheriff in 1766, and his son was William, sheriff in 1803. His son Richard, b. 1803, had a son William, whose son was Richard Meredith of Dicksgrove, high sheriff in 1886.

When given as a settler family, on estates near Tralee, from the coming of the Elizabethan undertakers to the rebellion of 1641 we find origins listed as Wales.

Also given separately we find Dicksgrove (1846) was the residence of the Meredith family in 1756.

Parkmore was the residence of Richard Meredith in 1846 (Both in Killeentierna parish).

More extensive genealogy is given in the works of J. King.

Mernagh

Denis Mernagh of Fybough, Co. Kerry

Meskill

Tim Meskill of Tieraclea, Co. Kerry.

Mac Michael

Geo. Mac Michael of Ballinskelligs, Co. Kerry.

Mihigan

John and Nora Mihigan of Kenmare, Co. Kerry are given.

Miles
John Miles of Farranakilla; Tom and Tom of Milltown and John of Craig are given in Kerry in 1821. The Dr. Miles memorial at Dingle, took the form of a tablet outside the courthouse in Dingle and the endowment of a bed in the Mercy Hospital in Cork.

Milner
Henry Milner of Boherbee, Co. Kerry.

Milward
Hanoria of Cordal, Mary and Fanny of Ballyegan, Co. Kerry. John of Ballyegan is given in Kerry in 1821.

Minchin
Catherine of High Street, Co. Kerry.

Mingane
Kate Mingane of Killnagore, Co. Kerry.

Minogue
Con Minogue of Rattoo, Co. Kerry.

Mitchell
Flor. of Gortshanavogh, Flor of Cragg, Mary of Moanmore, Pat of Ferriters quarter, Robt. of Goat street, Ml. of Kildurrihy, John and Sylv. of Ferriters quarter.

Mochlehayn
John Mochlehayn in 1397 was a priest assigned Dayngyn church, Dingle, held by the Augustinian prior and convent of Killagh Belloloco, Kilcoleman. (Might this name today be found as MacIlhaney ? Pure speculation, of course.)

Molloy
Michael Molloy of Montanagay, Co. Kerry.

Moloney, Molony, Maloney
With some 50 Moloney families given in Kerry, O'Maoldomnaig is cited as chief of Cuilteran in Tulla, Co. Clare. The Hon. M. T. Moloney b.1849 at Listowel, was Attorney General at Ottawa in 1892: his brother, Rev. W. Moloney was missionary in Vancouver.

Molyneaux
Several families of the name are given in Co. Kerry in the works of J. King.

Monahan, O'Manacain
Tom Monahan of Kealid and Wm. of Moyderwell, Co. Kerry.

Monson
Castlemain gave the the title of viscount in earlier days to the family of Monson, and afterwords the dignity of earl to Roger Palmer, Esq., so created in 1661.

Andrew Monson of Ballinclemesig, Co. Kerry is also given.

Montgomery
Robert Montgomery of Strand Street.

Mooney
Tom Mooney of Clounmackon, Co. Kerry.

Moore, Moor, More

There were 53 Moore families listed by J. King in Co. Kerry. O'Morda was given as an old form of the name by J. King. In 1609 the Moore family was transplanted from Queen's Co., and 102 came to Tarbert, Co. Kerry, with Patrick Crosby as tenants. In 1408 Richard de More of knightly race was rector of Annagh and Clockorbryan. In 1588 Richard Moore of Castle Moore claimed lands at Ballydavid; Gerrat claimed Ballymore; Rd. More, alias Mac Morris of Cyaltady, prayed for relief from conye and livery. In 1689 Ambrose Moore of Kilgulban was provost marschal and died in 1620. Edward Moore of Kilgobban had Tom, b.1713, Rd. 1715; Wm. had Wm. b.1721, and Sarah b.1726; Rd. d.1729. Garrett Moore of Teeravane d. 1773, leaving Nicholas.

Canon Moore of Paris left a stipend for a Latin School in Donquin. Wm. Moore d.1797, m. Eliz. Hilliard, leaving John of Kilfenora, Anne and Eliza. The father of Tom Moore, the poet, was John Moore of Kerry, and a grocer in Aungier st. in Dublin, 1779-1800, who had a brother Garrett of Finuge and Newtowndillon. Moore's Melodies will survive as long as Irish history.

Moorhead

Samuel Moorhead of Waterville, Co. Kerry.

Morahain

James Morahain of Moyeightragh and Peter of Ardshanavooly, Co. Kerry.

Moran

With 92 families given in Co. Kerry, Moran is a fairly numerous family here. It is also noted that Ua Morain was chief of Crumthan in Killian barony, Galway.

Morgan

In 1666, Capt. Robt. Morgan was granted lands in Glanneroughty at Dromrouke, Carrigeene, Inceancouse, Cameene, Glangory, and Gortnimacry. Archdeacon Edward of Ardfert is given in 1669.

Morgell

Philip of Dingle d.1738, his wife m.Capt. Magee. Ann Morgell, dau. of Crosbie of Rathkeale, a solicitor who was M.P. for Tralee; she m. 1791 Sir Barry Denny, and 2 Sir John Floyd.

Moriarty

Descended anciently through Heber and Eoghan Mor (Owen Mor) we find the family of Moriarty (O'Muircheartagh). The name is said to be taken from muir (the sea), and ceurt (right chieftain), taken to mean the chief in rightful possession of the sea coast according to the works of J. King.

Traced from Eoghan Mor, to Aodh Benan d. 619, to Muirceardoig of loch Lein in 1068, whose district was seized in 1107 by MacCarthy Mor and given to O'Donoghue Mor. In 1014 the son of Moriarty was slain at Clontarf in battle. In 1019 Joanna m. O'Connor Kerry; in 1068 Muircertaig was wounded by the O'Connors; in 1110 Moriarty was captured by O'Connor; in 1192 the Moriarty was slain by the O'Donoghues. They held sway over Eoghanacht Loch Lein until 1107 A.D., when it was taken by MacCarthy, king of Munster, and assumed by the O'Donoghues. In 1169 the MacCarthy Mor and the O'Sullivans established themselves also in Kerry fighting against the Norman Fitzgeralds until 1583 with some success, holding Desmond lands until the Cromwellian confiscations.

The O'Moriartys held on to Castlemaine and Castledrum (Killorglin) with the aid of the Earls of Desmond, and afterwards against Conway. Before the invasion of the O'Donoghues and MacCarthys, the Moriarty clan lands ran from the lakes of Killarney along the banks of the Laune and the Mang or Maine, with the lands of Dunkerron and Templenoe also included.

Moriarty obtained the land of the Aes Iste of the Tuath sen Eran in west Cork, and in 1200 obtained the cantred belonging to Humurierdac was granted to Meyler Fitz Henry. (Killarney -

Moriarty

Yoghenacht Lokhelen) which rightfully belonged to O'Moriarty. (see Irish State Papers).

By the 16th century the clan no longer held Upper Laune, but still held extensive lands as vassals of the Earl of Desmond, in Garrinclondrig, Trughanacmy. Sliocht Murry was held by Ferris in 1641. In 1578 Moriarty was prior of Kilcolman; in 1583 Owen Moriarty captured the Earl of Desmond; and was granted some land in 1588 at Strahenmartle; in 1582-1601 pardons were granted to several Moriarty's; in 1620 Dermot had leased Ballinacourty from Lord Cork; in 1635 Teigue had Ballyristin; in 1641 Donnell of Castledrum and Dermot of Ballinacourty were at the siege of Tralee; in 1653 Rev. Tadg Moriarty, prior of Tralee was executed and his brother Rev. Thos. Moriarty of Castledrum; Rev. Denis Moriarty 1653-1737 was P.P. of Dingle and Bishop of Kerry; in 1657 the Moriarty lands were granted to Coote, Jones, etc..; in 1689 Edward Moriarty was in Maryland; in 1723 Thomas was a linen mftr. in Dingle; in 1724 Dr. Mce. was in Brittany; in 1725 Rev. Ignatius was P.P. of Killarney; In 1742 Richard was shipping cruits to the French army; in 1763 Redmond of Killorglin claimed Farrentorine.

The arms of the family are given by King as: Argent, an eagle displayed sable; crest on a helmet an arm embowed in armour holding a sword, the blade environed with a snake; Motto: Scandit Sublimia Virtus. It should be noted that some families omit the snake altogether.

The Annals of Ireland hold numerous mention of the family. In 1641 while Owen Moriarty was shut up in Tralee Castle during the siege, while several 'MacMoriartys' of Kerry were among

Moriarty

those attacking the castle. They are all given to be of the same O'Moriarty family, despite the 'Mac' before some of the names at that time. The Book of Survey and Distribution, noting forfeited lands under the Cromwellian settlement, 1657, gives several of the name.

Moriarty's Hotel, Limerick, was a celebrated hostelry, found mentioned in the works of Lever. In the 1821 census they had a man cook, 4 men waiters and 5 maids. Mrs. Eliza Moriarty was innkeeper.

An extremely numerous family of Co. Kerry, 436 Moriarty families are given here by J. King.

One line of the family is traced to America in 1688 through Edward Moriarity of Ann Arundel Co. in Maryland, and his wife Honora in 1701, mention in their wills, their children. In 1776 Tim was in 5 Penn.; Dennis was in Washingtons Guard in 1780; Eugene of Castlemaigne d. 1907 was editor of the Worcester Evening Post. Others of the name are given in Chicago, Boston, Brooklyn, Springfield, Holyoke, Norwich, Minneapolis, Montreal etc.. Wills in the Public Records Office included those of Wm. of Milltown in Co. Kerry 1781; Tom of Dingle 1785..

Derryvrin (1814) was where Bishop Moriarty was born. (Kilcaragh parish).

Ballyneanig castle in Marhin parish was a Geraldine stronghold, afterwards the residence of the Moriartys', often mentioned along with the Moriarty family by the noted author J. King. Smith gives Ballymalus Castle as said to have been built by the Moriarties, seated on the river Lane. He also gives the ruins of Castle Drum 3 miles west of Castlemain, as being built by the Moriarties according to the Irish, but others say it was built by an English

Moriarty

family called Murrie, by an heiress of whom the ancestor of all the FitzGeralds got their possessions in Co. Kerry. This castle was demolished in the wars of 1641.

By the time of the 1821 census 600 Moriarty householders were in Kerry; in 1908, there were 425 householders are found in Kerry. Miss L. E. Moriarty, at one time of 35 Manor Park, Lee, London, S.E., made many researches on the family down to the year 1919.

In the works of J. King we find the following families noted; (1) that of Admiral Sylverius Moriarty 1735-1809, with several sons noted as distinguished commanders in the West Indies, Tasmania, etc.. He had six sons, Peter, R.N.; Sylverius R.N., d. 1850; Merion, R.N. and M.D.; Martin d.s.p. Redmond left issue, Edward, d.s.p., and Lucinda, d. 1903; Merion, left issue a large family in Sydney. Also of this line was Major Sylverius Moriarty, Royal Irish, Buttevant, Cork.

(2) Another family of Moriarty, connected in some way with the above, is traced back to 1772 and Thomas Moriarty who married E. Trant about 1772, living in or near Tralee.

(3) The family of Matthew Moriarty, R.N. -1761. Who appears to have been the first of the family to go into the Royal Navy. He and his brother Michael joined HMS Rochester, Oct., 1739. He was probably born around 1710 as the son of James Moriarty of Cork, who in 1708 married Margaret, daughter of Michael Gould, d. 1733. Margaret married 2nd, Redmond Moriarty, the Admirals father. The pedigree of the branch of the family name is from Matthew then Edmund Joshua, Matthew, and then James. From James we have Jas., Robert, from

Moriarty

whom are Jas. W. Pomeroy, Lieut-Col. Marshall Pritchard and Elizabeth Marshall, as given in the works of J. King.

(4) Maurice Moriarty, the Dean of Ardfert, b. 1760. His son was Denis of Dingle, b. 1784 and d. 1839. Of this branch is given Henry (Moore), son of Ethel Moriarty and Henry J. Moore, who was in the U.S.A. prior to 1910.

(5) Moriarty of Boston, U.S.A. About 1700 Moriarty married Mary Trant, and had a son Daniel Moriarty of Cork. Of this line John Moriarty of Cork, m. Peggy Moriarty, and emigrated to Salem, Mass., U.S.A. in 1775, leaving in Ireland two sons, John and Daniel as well as six daughters. Of this line were the brothers John and Joseph Moriarty, both M.D.'s in Boston.

(6) Moriarty of Cork. From Daniel Moriarty of Cork who in 1762 m. the widow O'Connor, of Kerry.

(7) Moriarty of Limerick. In the late 18th century was James or John Moriarty at Castleisland, who had two sons', James and John. James, the eldest son left Kerry in 1824, settling at Grange in Limerick. He died in 1868, aged 80 leaving seven sons.

(8) Sir Thomas Moriarty. From Henry Moriarty, of Dingle, who m. Helena, daughter of Edward Fitzgerald (her nephew, Bishop Edward Fitzgerald, of Little Rock, Arkansas, USA died in 1907. Of this line were 3 sons who all went to New York, and all were priests.

(9) Moriarity of Ballymalis who descend from Mortough Moriarty who had a son Thade who had at least two sons John and Eugene. Thade Moriarty of Gneeves, married Elizabeth Foley in 1831 and left 5 sons - John, Eugene, Michael, Edward, and Daniel.

(10) The Matthew Moriarty family of Dingle descend through Dr. Melchoir Moriarty d. 1747 and Matthew Moriarty of Dingle who m. Eleanor Trant, from whom sprang Blaise, Alexander and Constantine Moriarty. Of the last family was Matthew Moriarty who died in Belgium in 1854, leaving some young children. The Family Of Bishop David Moriarty of Derivrin are of this line.

(11) Patrick Moriarty of Dingle, also of Australia.

(12) Moriarty of Ballintarmin. (Timothy b. 1774.)

(13) Moriarty of Glanahira (Timothy d. 1834)

Various wills and graduate listings of those of the name of Moriarity was also found in a separate booklet (The Moriarty Book), originally offered by the publishers of J. Kings 'History of Co. Kerry', of which I know nothing more.

Morley, Morly

Several families are given in Co. Kerry; Dan of Lisnagrave, John of Doocarrigbeg, Pat of Tinnahally, John of Farrantooreen, Pat of Aghanboy, Catherine of Main street, John of Callyhearney, Dan of Coomakilla, Tom of Main Street, and Tim and Jas. of Pound Lane.

Moroney, Maroney, Morony

Some 20 Moroney families are given in Co. Kerry. It is further noted that O'Maolruanaid was chief of Crumthan in Killian barony in Galway.

Morphy

John Morphy of Mt. Prospect d.1799; his will was in the record office. John Stephen Morphy of Kerry was an Australian police magistrate; his daughter m. Mr. Bligh who in 1900 succeeded as Lord Darnley. Charles J. Morphy, Crown Solicitor for Kerry, d.1913.

Morrice

John Morrice of Northal in Essex,, was the first of this family to settle in Ireland. Francis Morrice, the eldest son, and his father came to Ireland 'having spent' their fortune in England. He came to Ireland during Queen Elizabeth's wars.

Morris

A settler family on estates near Tralee, from the coming of the Elizabethan undertakers to the rebellion of 1641. Descent / homeland: Of Essex. John Morris is given in Tralee in 1908. Joseph Morris. The grandson of the first settler of his name in Kerry, who took a lease of the lands of Urltemp Elizabeth. He died and his brothers eldest son was styled 'of Ballybeggan', which estate was in the possession of Walter Hussey until 1639, who mortgaged it in that year to an Englishman named Exham.

Col. Arthur Morris had a youngest son, Mr. F. W. Ambrose Morris who passed away in Litchfield, England a few years prior to 1910. Col. Morris was the youngest son of Col. Samuel Morris, of Lizelton House, who had three sons- Sam who lived at Ballybeggan Castle, Tralee; Arthur at Ballylongford: and George who was a distinguished officer of the rank of Colonel, with service in the West Indies 1795 - 1801. His brother Sam, lived in Ballybeggan Castle, Tralee. The Morris family are related to the Peerages of Southwell and Ventry. One of the few members left (1910?), a grand-daughter of Col. Arthur Morris m. Mr. Taaffe, agent of the Bank of Ireland, Charleville. One Samuel Morris sold Ballybeggan and Castle Morris to James O'Connell, brother of the Liberator, and died 1838.

In 1831 we have record of Samuel of Tralee, Arthur of Ballylongford, Wm. C. of Carrow, Robert of Tralee, John of Tralee and Lt.-Col. George Morris.

Ballybeggan Castle, Ratass parish, did not surrender to the Irish Army in 1641-3, but was burned in the war of the revolution. The new house was built by the Morris family after the revolution.

A name settling in Co. Kerry, both before and after the 1641-42 rebellion.

Morrison

Tom Morrison of Bridge street, and Geo. Morrison of Spunkane, Co. Kerry.

Morrissey

Some 17 Morrissey families are given in Co. Kerry. Edm. and David and Edm. of Knocknagoshel, John and Jas. of Gortroe, Ml. of Ahane, Rachel and Mary of Brosna, Pat of Canguilla, John of Chapel lane, Ellen of Castleview, Edw. of Meenleitrim, John of Knock,nacrohy, Jas. of Mastergeehy, Kate and Ml. of Oulagh, and John of Scarteen, all of the preceeding are of Co. Kerry.

Morrogh

The Morrogh Bernard family of Fahagh was a joining of the Morrogh family of Cork with the Bernards of Ballynagare, Kerry, in 1816, by the marriage of Edward Morogh to Martha Bernard. Their son John took the name of Morrogh Bernard and died in 1866. His son was E. J. Bernard.

We also find Walter Morrogh of Cork, Jas. of Ards, 1776; Jas. of Killarney 1821.

Mosley

Timothy Mosley of Canuig, Co. Kerry.

Moylan

Mary Moylan of Boherbee and Mary Moylan of Ballybunion, Co. Kerry.

Moynihan Monighan

One of the more numerous family names in Co. Kerry, 183 families are given there. In 1776 lived Arthur of Stagmount, Malaky of Knockaliffan, Thady of Rhabeg, Darby of Carrum, Thady of Newbridgt. Humphrey Moynihan of Rathbeg, m. Catherine O'Connell, sister of the Liberator.

Spellings of the name are numerous with Moynihan, Monighan, Monaghan and Monahan given.

Muirlihy

The Rev. Donatus Muirlihy, O.S.F., was killed at Muckross in 1589 by soldiers.

Mulcahy

The following Mulcahy families are given in Co. Kerry: David of Doolaigue, Tom of Knockafreaghane, Tom and Frank of Chapellane, Jas. of Mangerton View, Tom of Brosna, Ml. and John of Farranmanagh, Pat of Cloonafineela, John of Church-street, John of Abbey-street, Tom of Ballinknockane and Wm. of Brogue-lane.

Mulcare

Dan and Eugene Mulcare of Ahanagran, and Ml. of Knockavallig, Co. Kerry.

Mulchinock

Ml., son of Ml., b.1779, d.1828, m. Mary, dau. of John MacCann, attorney at Tralee in 1804; Nicholas in 1782 was shot in Tralee during a military riot; John, son of Nicholas, was baptized March 2, 1781; had a draper's shop in Castle Street, he became a Catholic in mid life, left money to the Convent of Mercy and Christian Brothers, died unmarried, leaving nephews Edw. and Wm. P.. In 1908 Mary, widow of the late Edward Mulchinock of Tralee, and 53 Pembrook Road in Dublin, died at 56 Wellington road in Dublin. Wm. Pembroke Mulchinock wrote poems for the "Nation" and American papers, edited the "Irish Advocate" and published his poems in New York in 1851.

Mullally, Mulally, Lally

John Mullally of Tieraclea, Pat of Listowel, Sarah of Coolnanoonagh, Ml. of Boherboy, are all given in Co. Kerry. The Marquis Lally Tollendal of France is noted in 1817. It is also noted that O'Maolalaid was of Moenmoy in Galway.

Mullane

Mce. of Droumroe, Ml. of Knockanaroor, Mary of New-street, Tom of Farranmanagh, John of Ballylongford, John of Clountubrid, Johanna of Ardroe, and John of Main street are all given in Co. Kerry.

Mac Mullen

Frank Mac Mullen of Spunkane, Co. Kerry.

Mulligan

Pat Mulligan of Droumyrourke, Co. Kerry.

Mullins, Mullens, Moleyns

Given as the name of a family settling in Co. Kerry, subsequent to the 1641-42 rebellion. Descent/ Homeland:

Of London. Mullins - Ventry family.- Col. Frederick William Mullins, of Burnham, England, purchased land in Kerry in 1666, and settled at Burnham, near Dingle. He was M.P. for Dingle, 1692-5, and died in 1712. His son, Frederick, d. 1695, leaving a son William, whose son Thomas Mullins, 1st Baron Ventry d. 1824. His son Wm. d. 1827. His nephew, Thomas, assumed the surname of Moleyns, by royal license in 1841 and d. 1868. His son, Sir Dayrolles Blakeney Eveleigh De Moleyns, was 4th Baron Ventry.

Also noted are: Fred Mullens of Ballingolin in 1679, Hon. Fred Mullins 1801, Wm. 1790, Hon. and Rev. Fred of Beaufort 1828.

In 1831 lived Hon. Edward Mullins; Hon. Frederick, Clk., of Beaufort; and Frederick, Wm., and Allurid Mullins.

Burnham House was the residence of Lord Ventry in 1846. Mullins of Burnham, in England, settled here in 1666, in Rice's Castle of Ballingolin. (Dingle Parish). (215)

Killorglin Castle and Manor reverted to the Fitzgeralds from the Knights Templars. It was then granted to Capt. Conway, and later bought by the Mullins family from the Blennerhassetts. Florence MacCartie More caused the castle to be burned around 1600, fearing that Sir Charles Wilmot would settle there. (218)

Variant spellings given: Mullins, Mullens, Moleyns, DeMoleyns.

Mullis

Thomas Mullis of Carhoona, Co. Kerry.

Mulquinn
John Mulquinn of Caherulla, Matt of Dromgower, John of Ballyheigue, all given in Co. Kerry.

Mulvihill, Mulvehill
A numerous family in Co. Kerry, some 91 families of the name are given. It was also given that Ua Maelmhicil was of Corca Eachlinn in Connacht in 1416 and Doon Maolmichial was noted in Clare in 1653.

John, N.T. of Ballincrossig school, d.1923, and was buried in Rahelia cemetery; his son Michael died with the O'Rahilly in Dublin in 1916 and was buried in Glasnevin.

Munchas
J. H. Munchas of Fenit without, Co. Kerry.

Munro
Rev. James Munro of High street, Co. Kerry. King gives Mac an Rotaic or O'Maolruaid as the Irish form of the name.

Murdock, Murdoch
Wm. of Main Street, Co. Kerry.

Murhill
Pat of Gortahoonig, John of Muckross, Pat of Carrigeencullia, Hanoria of Gortagullane, and John of Gortdromakiery, all in Co. Kerry.

Murnane
Tim Murnane of Rathmore, Ml. of Annaghmore, Sarah of Greenview tce, and James of Dromatouk, Co. Kerry.

Murphy, O'Murcada
One of the most numerous of all families in Kerry and in all of Ireland, some 656 Murphy families are given in Co. Kerry alone. In 1871 Rev. Eugene Murphy, C.C., of Kilcrohane, compiled an Irish Dictionary, but not published as he died young; the M.S.S. was left to Bishop MacCarthy's executor.

Murray
Norah Murray of Deepark, Pat of Ballyheigue, Amos of Tieraclea, Dan of Francis street, Mce. of Connors lane, Albert of Waterville, Jerh. of Ardtully, Pat of Coologues, Nat of Tooreenasliggaun, and Margt. Murray of Dromnycolman are all of Co. Kerry.

Muschamp
Denny Muschamp, muster master general of Ireland died in 1700; he had a grant in 1665, fro the services of his father, Agmondisham, lieut. of ordenance in Munster.

Musgrave
Hy. Musgrave of Ralapane, and Stewart and Thos. Musgrave of Castle-street are given in Co. Kerry.

Myaghe
James Myaghe of Cork was sheriff of Desmond in 1586; sent to London the cloth, painted in Rome, which was set up on stakes when Dr. Sanders said Mass in the field.

Myers
Dan and Edmond Myers and Dan and Edm. and Dan and Edm. of Barleymount, and Bridget and Edm. of Killeagh, Wm. of Sheans, and Dan of Curragh, all of these are given in Co. Kerry.

Myles, Mac Miles
Among the several Myles families in Co. Kerry were; Wm. of Moyderwell, Ml. of Caherfealane. Z. Myles of Limerick had Dr. George, m.1868, Marion, dau. of Wm. Marshall Saunders of Carker, she d.1916, leaving Letitia, m.1904 W. T. Englefield; George, M.B., b.1871; Margaret d. young; Wm., M.B., m. 1904, A. Lloyd, having George, Marion, Frances; Henry b.1873; Marion, m. 1910 L.S. Palmer.

Nagle, Nangle, de Nogla

Only 29 families of the name are given in Co. Kerry. It is noted that Gilbert de Angulo, an Anglo Norman invader of 1172, was granted Maghery Gallen, Navan and Ardbraccan; the Costelloe and Nagle and Jordan families trace back to Gilbert de Angulo.

Richard and John and Pierce of Cork were Stuart supporters, 1640-90. In 1685, Sir. Rd. Nagle was attorney general, secretary of war and speaker in 1689; and secretary of state at St. Germains; the Nagle estates in Ireland were confiscated in 1700. In 1451, Margaret, daughter of David Nagle of Monahinny, m. John O'Connor, Kerry, who founded Lislaghtin friary, where he was buried in 1485. Nano Nagle, 1728-84, founded Presentation Order of Nuns. John D. Nagle of Dingle, in 1874 took an active interest in Corca Duibne antiquities.

Nally, Mac Nally

James Nally of James Street, is given in Co. Kerry.

Mac Namara

It is given to refer to the story of the MacNamara sept by N.C. Mac Namara. Given in Kerry were Julia of Craughdarrig, Ml. of Tieraclea, Tom of Kilomore, Mary of Inch, Mary of Dromclogh, John of Toor, Jas. of Doon, Poon, John of Beale, Jas. of Ahanagran, Mo. of Bromore, Ml. of Ballyhadigue, Magt. and Tom and John and John of Guhard, John of Daly's lane, and Tom of Rae Street.

Nammock

John Nammock of Kilaspictarvin; Pat and Wm. of Mary Street; Wm. of Roe Street; and James of Abbey street, are all given in Co. Kerry.

Nash, de Nais

There were 21 Nash families given in Co. Kerry. Included were; Rev. Edward Nash, of Ballycarty in Ballyseedy, 1828; Clementia died 1891; Edward Leahy Nash; Eleanora, dau. of Rev. Edward, m. Rd. Leahy; lt.-col. Nash of the Ridge, Corsham, Wilts, in 1923.

Ballycarthy was also found as the residence of the Rev. Mr. Nash in 1846. There was a Geraldine fortress here in 1584. It is mentioned during the siege of Tralee in 1641. (Ballyseedy parish).

Natt

A settler family on estates near Tralee, from the coming of the Elizabethan undertakers to the rebellion of 1641.

Naughton

Several of the name are given in Co. Kerry. The Rev. Rd. Naughton was P.P. of Brosna, 1840-64; his brother Rev. John, was P.P. of Boherbee. Mrs. Naughton made the first mould candles in Tralee. It was also noted that O'Neactain of Maonmagh in Hy Maine gives rise to the name of Naughton in modern times.

Naylor

Sarah Naylor of Listowel and Sam Naylor of the Mall, both of Co. Kerry.

Neenan

Ml. of Crotta, Pat of Gullane, Margt. of Edward street, all of these Neenan households are found in Co. Kerry.

Neilan, Nealon, O'Niallain

Mce. of Knoppogue, Dan of Benmore, Edm. of Ballyhorgan, Denis of Lacca, John of Ballincrossig, Ml. of Ballinglanna, Mce. of Farran, Pat of Rathmorrell, John and Tom of Ballyronan, John of Commons, Denis and Denis of Ballinascreena, John of Gortnaskehy, and James of Liscahane, are all given in Co. Kerry.

Mac Neill
Geo. Mac Neill of Canal new road, Co. Kerry.

Neill O'Neill O'Neal
One of the more numerous families in Co. Kerry, some 212 Neal families are given in that county in Ireland. It was further noted that Ua Neill of Oileach and cinel Owen and Clannaboy was ard ri in 943. "The land of clan Dealvaoi of the poets is governed by O'Neill lord of Fionluaraigh; to his residence come the hosts of Tradree, warriors of flaxen tresses." In 1679, Rev. Walter O'Neale of Ballinvoher; in 1821, Rev. Connolly and John and Connolly O'Neill of Killorglin are given in Co. Kerry.

Anglont House, Killorglin parish, was the home of the Foley family, earlier Connelly O'Neill lived there in 1821.

Neilson, Nelson, Nellson
Magnus Neilson of Boulenshare, Co. Kerry. Bridget Nelson of Coolroe, Co. Kerry is given by J. King.

Brigadier Nellson received the surrender of Ross castle in 1652.

Neligan Nelligan
Not a numerous surname in Ireland, some 34 Neligan (O'Niallagain) families are found in Co. Kerry. This may be encouraging to the family researcher who finds the name missing from the 1890 birth index of Ireland, as compiled by Matheson.

Sir John Chute Neligan, K.C., born 1826, had a good circuit practice in Munster from 1849; was county court judge from 1866 in Louth, Leitrim, King's Co., Derry, Fermanagh, and Cork, for 40 years; died 1911, a.85, in Tralee; left £14,811 estate to Garratt Thos. Nagle; his son Major Wm. John d.1902. Rev. Mce. P.P. of Beaufort, Co. Kerry.

Neville
Several Neville families are given in Co. Kerry, including those of Tom and Pat Neville of Leanamore, John of Bedford, Jerh. of Dromloughra, Tim of Aughrim, Ellen of Addergown, Tom of Knockavota, Eliza (of) Glenerdallive, and Tom of Ballymullen. We quote from J. King: 'All of the Alltraighe return two kings of the plain of Ciarraighe, a tribe which is ready in the point of difficulty, O'Neidhe (Neville) and the clann Conaire (King).'

Nevin
Wm. Nevin of High street, Co. Kerry.

Newton
Eva Newton of Main street is found in Co. Kerry. Frances Newton of Cottage is given in 1821. Mary, of Woodville in Kilcolman m.1799, Edw. Twiss of Stealroe in Killorglin.

Nicholas MacNiocoil Nichols
Alfred Nicholas of Boherbee, Alfred of William street, and James of Driminamore, all given in Co. Kerry.

Nihill
A settler family on estates near Tralee, from the coming of the Elizabethan undertakers to the rebellion of 1641.

Patrick Nyle, given in Tralee in 1908.

Nihilly
Rory Nihilly is given and his burgage in Tralee was owned in 1641 by Chris. Walsh and Celia his wife.

Nixon
Lce. Nixon of Gortgower, Co. Kerry.

Noble
Samuel Noble of the Mall, Co. Kerry.

Nolan, O'Nuallain

A fairly numerous family in Co. Kerry, some 109 households are given there. A Mrs. James Nolan of London left £14,000 to her children, Eliza, Ellen, Margt., Agnes, Catherine, Johanna, David and James. It is also noted that Ua Nuallain (O'Nolan) was chief of Fotharta in Carlow in 1133.

Noonan

Several Noonan families are given in Kerry, including Mary and David and Pat of Ardfert, Tom of Minard, Denis of Tawlaght, Jerh. of Istatlea, John of Cooraquanish, Cappanacush, Wm. and Pat and Peter and Martin of Rossdohan.

O'Nunan was given as chief of Tullaleis in Duhallow. Rev. James Nunan, D.D. b.1872 at Ardfert d. 1898, was of the St. Augustine diocese in the U.S.A.

Norris, Norreys

A settler family, given on estates near Tralee, from the coming of the Elizabethan undertakers to the rebellion of 1641. Descent / homeland: Of Lanc.

Of Lord President of Munster's family, related to Carews. John Norris, servant to the ward of Ballycarty, was killed in 1641. Geo. Norris is in Tralee in 1908.

George Norris of Ballymullen, Wm. Norris of Knockeens, Rd. of Castleisland are given in 1821. John Norreys, Lord President, in 1585, assigned custodian of Tralee and Moally or Mallow.

Northcott

The name of a Cromwellian settler granted lands in 1667 in Co. Kerry.

Norton

Hanora Norton of Ballykissane and John Norton of Tralee, Co. Kerry.

Norval

Archibald Norval of Spunkane, Co. Kerry.

Nott

John Nott of Tarbert Island, John of Ardcost, John of Dunkerron, given in 1821 in Co. Kerry.

Noughane

John Noughane of Lissyvigeen, Co. Kerry. O'Neachtain given anciently.

Noughton

John and Tom Noughton of Knockaclare, Co. Kerry.

Nugent

Mce. Nugent of Listowel, Co. Kerry.

Nurse

John Nurse of Cloghaneanode, and John of Coolroe, are given in Co. Kerry.

Nye

Henry Nye of Dromatoor, Co. Kerry.

Nyle, Nihill, O'Neigill

Pat Nyle of Keane's Lane in Co. Kerry.

Oaks

H. Oaks of Spunkane, Co. Kerry is given. Given anciently as Mac Darac.

Oatts

James Oatts of Ballymullen, Co. Kerry.

Ogg

Edwin Ogg of Ardfert, Co. Kerry.

Oliver

Given as the name of a family settling in Co. Kerry, subsequent to the 1641-42 rebellion. Homeland/ descent: Of Corn., Herts., Kent.

One Wm. Oliver was churchwarden in Listowel in 1771; Hy. of Ballinahoune is found in 1821, Hy. and Robt. of Castleisland found in 1831; in 1876 Major Oliver of Cork owned 1369 acres in Kerry, and R. S. of London 4804 acres; in 1913 Richardson Oliver.

Ormsby

Oliver Ormsby (1666) was granted Kinard, Togherighmore, Lisdargane, Garfenagh and Dunsheny, in 'Corgaginny' barony.

Orpen

Ardtully given both in Kenmare and Kilgarvan parish was said to be the residence of the Orpen family in the works of J. King. (217)

Richard Orpen was the leader of the Protestant settlement in Kenmare, 1688-'9. Abraham Palmer of Ashgrove would in later times come to marry Margaret Orpen of Killowen, leading to the Orpen-Palmer of Killowen line.

The Orpen family of Ardtully is given to have come to Ireland from Norfolk, and Robert Orpen lived at Killorglin in 1661. His son, Richard of Kenmare, joined the Orange party. His son, Rev. Thomas, was Rector of Kenmare, whose sons were Rev. Richard, d. 1770, and Rev. Francis, of Kilgarvan, d. 1805. The son of the latter, Richard (Sir) Knt., of Ardtully, b. 1788, d. 1876, left Richard Hugh Millerd Orpen, of Ardtully, b. 1829.

In 1876 Sir Richard (Orpen) had 12,873 acres in Kerry, and R. H. (Orpen) of Killaha had 4348 acres. Robt. of Killorglin in 1661 had Rd. of Kenmare, who had Rev. Thomas of Kenmare, who had Rev. Rd. d.1770, and Rev. Francis of Kilgarvan who d.1806 leaving Sir Rd. of Ardtully who left Rd. Hugh Millerd Orpen of Ardtully b.1829. In 1688 the Rev. Thos. Palmer and Rd. Orpen the agent to Lady Petty gathered the Protestant Orange party to Killowen house and Kenmare, and after getting terms from the Jacobites, embarked to Bristol until the war was terminated.

In 1764 the Rev. Richard Orpen was rector of Valencia, and had Rd. . Rev. Raymond was Bishop of Limerick and Kerry 1906-21. The Orpen wills in the record office are Rd. of Ardtully 1740, Thomas of Killowen 1768, Rd. of Valentia 1770, and Rd. of Ardtully 1810.

Osbaldiston

W. B. Osbaldiston, of John Street, given in Co. Kerry.

Otnonia

Mark Otnonia, priest, was assigned the vicarage of Killrochayn in 1396, void by death of Dennis Ossulluayn. (per King.)

Ovens

Alexander Ovens of Knockreer, Co. Kerry.

Owens

John Owens of Rathea, John Owens of Ballyhorgan, given in Co. Kerry. Also give as the name of a Cromwellian settler granted lands in 1667 in Co. Kerry.

Ozzard

Allen Ozzard of Main Street, given in Co. Kerry.

Page

A settler family, given on estates near Tralee, from the coming of the Elizabethan undertakers to the rebellion of 1641. Of Essex, Norf., Suff., Devon. J. Page is given in Tralee in 1908.

Pails

A. E. Pails of the Mall, in Co. Kerry.

Palmer

A settler family on estates near Tralee, from the coming of the Elizabethan undertakers to the rebellion of 1641.

Arms (per J. King) - Sable, a chevron or, between three crescents, argent.

Crest: A wyvern, or, armed and langued, gules.

Motto: (1) Anciently - Pour apprendre oblier ne puis.
(2) Par sit fortuna labori.

J. King gives the Palmer families as dating back to the times of the crusades, taken from those of the religious houses who returned from the Holy Land with palm branches carried in the palms of their hands as a passport wearing a religious habit.

The family is further given to descend from a crusader who was knighted on the field under Richard I, as Sir Ralph 'le Palmer'.

In 1574 Thos. and Jas. Palmer were in Castle Maine garrison. In 1624 Augustine Palmer was in Tralee.

In Ireland, the Rev. Thomas Palmer was Judge of the Admiralty Court of Munster and of the Consistorial Court of Ardfert and Aghadoe. (By patent in the Rolls Office, Dublin, 4th August., 1678). The first Protestant rector of Kilmare, Kilgarvan, Templenoe, Kilcrohane and Caherciveen, in 1689 he was elected Gov. of the fort called the 'White House of Killowen', into which were crowded 42 Protestant families besieged by Capt. Phelim MacCarthy and 3,000 Irish soldiers. Accounts of the affair were penned by Richard Orpen and by Macauley in his 'History of England'.

The Rev. Thomas Palmer m. Jane, sister of Sir Richard Aldworth, of Dunhallow; and secondly Shelah, dau. of the O'Sullivan Mor. By the former he had 4 daughters and two sons of which George Palmer, the second son, was rector of Castlemaine, and m. Jane White, having issue of 4 sons of whom George was Governor of the Bank of Ireland in 1800. Thomas, the eldest son of Rev. Thomas Palmer, m. Sarah Coakley of Co. Cork. They had 3 sons, of whom the eldest, Abram m. Isabella Duckett; and his eldest son, Caleb, m. Jan. 22, 1782, Dorcas, dau. of William Twiss of Ballybeg.

Abram, son of Caleb, was b. Dec. 10, 1782, and in 1805 m. his cousin Margaret, dau. of Major Ed. Orpen. William Twiss Palmer, brother of Abram, b. 1784, was a clergyman and married his cousin Catherine Twiss.

George Palmer, brother of Abram, b. 1786, m. Miss Giles. Caleb Palmer, brother to Abram, b. April 10, 1793 is also given.

The Palmer family given to be of Devon, through the line of Augustine Palmer of Tralee in 1624 is also given, along with R. J. Palmer at Banemore and George Palmer of Milltown both living in 1831.

The life of the Rev. Thomas Palmer was said to have been spared through the entreaties in Irish, of his second wife, the daughter of O'Sullivan Mor, from the onslaught of victorious Jacobites.

Killowen House (1846) of Kenmare parish, was owned by Revd. Abraham Palmer.

A Genealogical and Historical Account of the Palmer Family of Kenmare, Co. Kerry, by Rev. A. Henry Herbert Palmer, was published in 1872.

Panorma

F.C. Panorma, Tralee, 1854-56, published the Kerry Magazine.

Paradine

Given as the name of a family settling in Co. Kerry, subsequent to the 1641-42 rebellion. Homeland/ descent:

James Paradine gave name to James Street, Tralee. His sister Nancy, m. Daniel Shea, a famous Tralee schoolmaster. Ellie Paradine m. John Flynn of Ballyvelly. There is a family of the name near Castleisland in 1908.

Pat Paradine of Ballypylimouth, Co. Kerry is given. In 1828 died Jas.; who was a builder in Tralee; gave his name to James street; his sister Nancy m. Dan Shea, a schoolmaster in Tralee; Ellie m. John Flynn of Ballyvelly.

Park

William Park of Spunkane, Co. Kerry.

Parker

Given in Co. Kerry were; Jas. of Culleenymore, Rd. and Catherine of Nelson street, Ellen of Russell street, Margt. and Eliz. and Robt. of Fenit, Ellen and Margt. and Edm. and Eug. and Robt. of Tawlaght, Eug. of Listrim, Tom of Ballymacegogue, C.P. of Spunkane, Ml. of Lissaniske, John of Tarbert in 1821.

Leslie Lodge (1846) is given with F. V. Parker.

Parkes

R. Parkes of Listowel, Co. Kerry.

Parkinson

Several Parkinson families are given in Co. Kerry. They are also given as related to the Benson, Williams, Goggin, Fitzell, Wharton, Staughton, Jones, Pollard, Hurley, O'Neill, Latchford and Mac Cowen families.

Families given include Rd. of Carhoonakinealy, John and Francis of Tullig, Arthur of Knocknakilla, Wm. of Ballyconnell, Sarah of Nelson street, and Wm. of London. Arthur of Newcastle West m. Miss Benson having issue.

Parr

Given as the name of a family settling in Co. Kerry, subsequent to the 1641-42 rebellion. Homeland/ descent:

Henry Parr was the eldest son of Rev. Henry Parr, of the Church of England, who according to Capt. John Blennerhassett in his book of genealogies drowned when going to one of his parishes services.. He was Rector of Kilmoe and Scull in 1677. Henry Parr, was noted as the grand juror of 1711. William Parr, son of Rev. Henry Parr, m. Mary, dau. of Rev. Thos. Connor of Ardfert.

Parsons

Wm. Parsons knt., in 1621, was granted the lands of James Rice of Dinglecuishe, Ardfert, Tralee, Ballemacphillip etc..

Partridge

Arthur Partridge of Spunkane, Co. Kerry.

Patt

There were 11 households of the Patt surname given in Co. Kerry; Bridget and Ml. of Leanamore, Margt. and Dan of Lislaughtin, Ml. of Kilpadogue, Richard of Dooncaha, Mary of Asdee, Martin of Cloonamon, Wm. of Ahanagran, John of Listowel, and Wm. of Kimego.

Patterson

Tom Patterson of Spunkane, Co. Kerry is given. Tarbert House (1846), is given as the home of J. D. Patterson.

Pattison

Rev. John Pattison of Listowel, Co. Kerry.

Patwell

Tom Patwell of Carhoona, and Richard. of Kilpadogue, Co. Kerry.

Paulin

Robert Paulin of Farranreagh, Co. Kerry.

Payne Paine

A family name found settling in Co. Kerry, both prior to and subsequent to the 1641-42 rebellion.

Some were Cromwellian. Note that C. Payne is given in Tralee in 1908.

A settler family, given on estates near Tralee, from the coming of the Elizabethan undertakers to the rebellion of 1641, was given originally of Norf., Sussex, Herts, Essex. In 1831 we find Robert, Thomas and Nathaniel Payne, all of Tralee.

Given in Co. Kerry also were Cornelia Payne of Canal new road; Edw. Payne 1674; Hardinge Payne of Tralee in 1821; Robt., Tom, and Nath. Payne of Tralee in 1831.

Peacocke, Peacock

Mary Peacocke of Charles street, is given in Co. Kerry.

Pearson, Pierson

Ellen Pearson of Kilkeaveragh, Co. Kerry.

Peet

Hastings Peet of Meanus, FitzMaurice Peet of Ballybrenagh, John of Gortshanavally, Jas. of Ardfert; Hastings of Arabella, d.1913, a.86. Francis of Currens 1821. In 1912 J. St. Leger Peet of Shanavalla wrote that in 1798 his great grandfather, Rev. John Murphy, chaplain to the Countess of Moira, accompanied Pamela, Lady Edward Fitzgerald to London, and for this kindness she gave him a miniature of herself; his church in Dublin, the Magdalene, was closed against him, and he lived at Castle Forbes until 1808, when he became rector of Kiltallagh, and married Miss St. Leger of Dublin, having Selina, who m.Francis Peet of Currens, grandfather of J. St. Leger Peet, to whom Lady Pamela's miniature passed.

Peevers

Wm. of Poulawaddra and Mary of Commons, Co. Kerry.

Pegum

Stephen Pegum of Glin, Co. Kerry.

Pelham

William Pelham was agent to Lord Lansdowne, 1792-1801, and made survey of Kerry for the county surveyor's office where his sketch maps are, and from which in 1811 Larkin prepared the maps of Kerry; in 1798 he fortified Lansdowne Lodge with shutters in black oak, and had a spring well in the basement; in 1801 Charles Spread was appointed agent, and Lord Lansdowne wrote off Pelham's arrears. Pelham later helped erect a Martello tower tower at Bere Island, where he died.

Pelham's mother was the widow of Copley, the portrait painter, father of Lord Lyndhurst. The widow, Mary Copley, was a tobacconist in Boston and married Peter Pelham, a writing master. Their son, Henry Pelham, made many drawings to illustrate a history of Kerry, and his papers passed to the Rev. Wm. Godfrey of Kenmare. Henry Pelham m. Miss Butler of Castlecrine in Limerick, having Peter and Wm., who d. unmarried.

Pelican, Pellican

One James Pelican was parish clerk at Ardfert in 1696; Rev. Wm. in 1721 was rector of Killahin and Kiltomey, and of O'Brennan in 1710; was B.A. of T.C.D. in 1702. Robt. m. Frances Fuller in Cork. Wm. Harnett of Ballyhenry d.1727, m. a sister of Rev. Wm. Pellican, his executor.

Pembroke, de Pionbroc

Ml. and John of Ahaneboy, Jas. of of Fahaduff, Ml. and John of Dooneen, Edm. of Bawnluskaha, Bridget of Farranlickeen, and John of MacEnery's Lane, all are found in Co. Kerry.

Pendred
A settler family on estates near Tralee, from the coming of the Elizabethan undertakers to the rebellion of 1641. Homeland: Of Kent, Northants, Herts.

Peppard
Alice Conway of Killorglin m. Pat Dowdall of Cappa in Limerick, having Katherine, who m. Pat Peppard of Kilmacow in Limerick. In 1743 Herbert bought lease of Muckross Abbey and Dinish Island from Peppards, who resided at Cappa. Pat's grandson was Robert, who had John, from whom was Mrs. Dowdall Cooke, her dau. Alice Maud Peppard Cooke of Cappagh, Ballingrane, Limerick, given in 1910.

Pepys
A settler family on estates near Tralee, from the coming of the Elizabethan undertakers to the rebellion of 1641. Descent / homeland:
Of Norf., Essex. Related to the Groomes and Blennerhassetts in Norfolk. Thos. Pepys resided in Tralee in 1624.

Thomas Pepys was sheriff of Kerry in 1619; son of Fermor of South Creake in Norfolk; b.1594; m. dau. of Sir John Dowdall; d. at Ballinhow in 1623; his sons Fermor and Knevett died young; his bro. Francis d.1620 sp. Ballingowan in Ratass had a castle called Hollenhone in 1608 map. Ballynahow in Cloghane was tierna Houssaye or Hussey's land.

Periman, Perryman
A settler family, on estates near Tralee, from the coming of the Elizabethan undertakers to the rebellion of 1641. Descent / homeland: Of Devon.

The following are found with the spelling of Perryman: Jerh. of Acres, Wm. of Beale, Pat of Meenagohane, Mary of Montanagay and John of Ballynoneen are given in Co. Kerry.

Perry, de Poire
Sam Perry of Mangerton View, Co. Kerry.

Pery
Rev. Wm. Pery, is given as the Prot. bishop of Ardfert, 1784-94.

Petty
Sir Wm. Petty 1623-87 made a survey of Irish lands and was granted or purchased 50,000 acres in SW Kerry; he wrote several tracts. His wife Eliz., dau., of Sir Hardress Waller, was created Baroness Shelbourne of Wexford; his son Hy. was Baron and Earl of Shelbourne and Viscount Dunkerron; the Marquis of Lansdowne is given as head of the family by J. King.

Phaire
Kilmurry Castle was taken from the Fitzgeralds by Col. Phaire in 1650.

Also found are the Rev. J.P. Phair of Ballyheige in 1914 and the Rev. G.C. Phair m. Dorothy Eve in 1914.

Phelan, O'Faolain
Julia Phelan of Main street, and Pat Phelan of Edward street, in Co. Kerry.

Phelips
Thomas Phelips in 1666 was granted Cleadaghrea, 7 acres, in Agunnyhy barony.

Philip
Philip, canon of Ardfert, was elected bishop of Ardfert in 1257. Philip, bishop of Ardfert, died in 1493.

Philips, Phillips
A settler family on estates near Tralee, from the coming of the Elizabethan undertakers to the rebellion of 1641. Originally of Cornwall, Wales.

Jas. and Chris. Philips of Inch and Mrs. Philips of Day place, Co. Kerry.

Pickford
Charles Pickford of Knoppogue, Co. Kerry.

Pierse, Pierce, Piers

Some 45 families are given in Kerry. John Fitz Maurice 5th Lord of Kerry, c.1350, m. Elenor, dau. of Garrett Fitz Pierce, having Gerald of Duagh and Robert. In 1604 Nicholas Mac Shane Perse of Dromartin was attainted. Richard Pierce of the Austrian army was the son of Patrick of Ballincrossig and Aghamore, the son of Gerard. Thomas Pierse, the elder brother of General Richard was the great grandfather of Dr. Gerard J. Pierse of Bushmount, Ballyduff, Kerry, 1925; Pierse, or Peter, was younger son of Fitz Maurice, baron of Lixnaw.

Thomas Pierse was captain in the Irish Brigade in Spain, and m. Phyllis O'Leary of Charleville; he resided and died at Meenagahane; he was brother of Gen. Richard Pierse; his eldest son, Garrett, m. Lucy Church of Listowel, dau. of the agent to Lord Listowel, having Thomas Garrett who m. Mary Hodgins of Rushin, Mountrath, having Dr. Gerard of Bushmount and John Hodgins., M.R.C.V.S., of Listowel and Meenogahane.

In 1653 Patrick Pierse and his wife, Joan Hussey, forfeited Aghamore, which went to T.C.D.. In 1924, Dr. Gerard J. Peirse of Bushmount got extracted in Vienna war office the army record of Major Gen. Richard de Pierce, who d. 13, April, 1774 in Wien, b.1718 at Ardfert, a Catholic who entered the Austrian army in 1736, and had a brilliant record of service; the extracts give full details from the archive records, which also contain the record of 6 other officers named Pierce; viz: Thomas, Thomas, Johann, Petritius, Petritius and Richard, besides 11 officers named Piers; Rev. Garrett Pierse, professor, Maynooth College, 19241 Ballykeely castle near Ardfert was held by the Pierce family. In 1580, the bishop of Ardfert was James Fitz Richard Pierse Fitz Maurice.

David Pierse lived at Ballynoe (1846) in 1821. (Killury parish).

Pierse, Pierce, Piers, Fitz Maurice, Geraldin, were all given in the same heading as sort of a variant spelling group by J. King.

Pigott, Piggott

Jerh. and Jerh. of Meenbannwane, John of Brasby's lane, Tom of New street, Mary of Bawnluskaha, James of Raccommane, Wm. of Knockeenduff, Pat of Breahig, Andrew of InchinascarthyPat of Knockaneglass, Andrew and John of Rineen and John and Andrew of Tooreenealagh, in Co. Kerry.

Pilcher

Stephen Pilcher of Farranreagh, Co. Kerry.

Pinchin

George Pinchin of Dingle, Co. Kerry, given in 1321.

Plowman

James Plowman, lieut. in Carlow militia, had a son Thomas, b.1807.

Plummer

Given as the name of a family settling in Co. Kerry, subsequent to the 1641-42 rebellion. Homeland/ descent: Of Norf., Berks.

John Plummer lived at Tralee in 1754, and with his brother Edward, refused to toast the Pretender in John Ginnis's house, the "Kings Arms". In 1831 lived R. Plummer, clerk, Tralee.

George, son of John, b.1771.

Plunkett, Pluinceid.

William Plunkett of Dublin in 1618 was granted Lislaughtie Abbey with 12 acres, rent 71s. Patrick d.1780, a.70; his tombstone (is) in Molahiffe churchyard; of Ballymaceagogue in Ballynahaglish in 1742-67; Jane, dau. of Sir Nicholas Plunkett, m. Sir Valentine Brown, who d. 1694. In 1776 Rev. Thomas Plunkett was priest in Killarney.

Poff

Wm. Poff of Lissataggle; Wm. of Cahermore; John of Flemby; Mary of Castleview, are all given in Co. Kerry.

Pollard, Polard

Francis Pollard of Ballyaukeen, Ed. of Keelduff, and Mary of Tonreigh, all of Co. Kerry.

Ponsonby

Given as the name of a family settling in Co. Kerry, subsequent to the 1641-42 rebellion. Homeland/ descent:

Of the Cromwellians of the name, Henry Ponsonby in 1666 was granted Stackstown, alias Crotto.

Thomas Ponsonby, the second son of the first settler of the name in Kerry, was an officer in Cromwell's army, and the brother of Sir John Ponsonby, ancestor of the Earl of Bessborough. They claimed to descend from an ancient Cumbrian family, lords of the manor of Ponsonby, near Whitehaven. According to Smith the three combs in the Earl of Bessboroughs coat of arms are from serving as barber surgeons to royalty. Crotta, the estate of Thomas, passed to the son of his sister Rose, wife of William Carrique of Glandine, who assumed the name of Ponsonby. From him descended the late Thomas Carrique Ponsonby, a Captain in the Royal Navy. Thomas and his brother John were among the 'Galway prisoners' of '88. In 1831 lived W. Ponsonby, J.P., and Wm, jr., at Crotto.

Seperately, we find Capt. Henry Ponsonby in 1666 granted lands in Kiltomy and Kilflyn, and d. in 1681; his brother Col. John, settled in Tipperary; Hy. m. Rose Weldon of Athy, having Thomas, who m. Susanna Grice of Ballgahan in Limerick, having Rd., disp. 1764. Rose Ponsonby m. John Carrique of Glandine, having John Carrique Ponsonby, whose successors were William and Capt. Thomas, who sold Crotto and the estate.

Crotto House (1846) was the residence of T. Ponsonby. It is illustrated in Neale's Views of Seats, 1824.(Kilflynn Parish).

Port

Bernard Port of Emmet's Terrace is given in Co. Kerry.

Potter, Potar
Fred Potter of Tarbert Island and David Potter of Castlemaine street.

Pottinger
Thomas Pottinger, precentor of Ardfert, Co. Kerry, 1669.

Powell
James Powell of Clashganniv; John of Dooneen; John of Ballinakilla; Wm. of Sandville (in 1821).

Power, de Poer
There were 25 Power families in Co. Kerry. In 1607 Sir Henry Power is on record as being granted the rents and services due to Mac Carthy Mor for a rent of £6. In 1641 Sir William Power was granted Listrim trim, near Ardfert. See also the History of the Powers by G. O'C. Redmond, M.D., 1897.

Also given as the name of a Cromwellian settler granted lands in 1667 in Co. Kerry.

Prendergast, Pendergast
There were 19 Prendergast families given in Co. Kerry. The Rev. Jarleath Predergast, O.F.M., 1840-1900, in 1868 was a friar at Killarney, he was author or editor of many devotional books and wrote articles on Muckross Abbey in the Franciscan Annals. One Edw. Prendergast, a painter, died 1812.

Prendergast, Pendergast, and de Priondargas were given as variants.

Prendeville, Pendeville
There were 46 Prendeville families given in Co. Kerry. Wm. de Prendeville in 1299 was a juror at the manor de insula or Castleisland. Thomas Prindeville's poems on Donough O'Moriarty, Bishop of Kerry, is in the British Museum, Egerton MSS 154. In 1621, Rd. Prendeville held Killinganane, the Short castle and another stone house with two gardens in Tralee, Gortinvoher, Gortfadda, Gortoola and Gortayhngrour, which he demised to Wm. Trant Fitz Edmund of Dingleicuish, whose son was Garrett Trant. Thomas S. Prendeville of Castleisland had Rev. J., Rev. Edw., and Jos., M.B., m.1913 Kathleen Evans of Glenbeigh.

Prendeville, Pendeville and de Prionnbiol were given as a variant spelling group.

Preste, alias Fletcher
A settler family, given on estates near Tralee, from the coming of the Elizabethan undertakers to the rebellion of 1641. Homeland: Of Devon.

Price, Pris, Rice, Rhys
Edward Price and Ml. Price of Crohane; John of Kylebeg; John of Agheebeg; John of Caher; Hy. of Sheheree; and John and Johanna of Shanacloon, are all given in Co. Kerry. The variant spellings of Pris, Rice, and Rhys are those listed by J. King. (see also Rice)

Procter, Proctor
Henry Procter of Henry Street, is given in Co. Kerry.

Prossor, Prosser
Fred Prossor of Baltygarron and Eliza of Nunstown 1776, given in Co. Kerry.

Purcell, Pursell

Given as the name of a family settling in Co. Kerry, subsequent to the 1641-42 rebellion. Homeland/descent: Of Bucks.

Theobald Purcell, perhaps also the Tobias Purcell on the list of Commissioners for 1699, was member for Ardfert from 1695 - 1703. Col. Nicholas Purcell, titular Baron of Loghnane, m. the dau. of Sir Valentine Brown. The Pursell family generally followed the Jacobite standard, but Col. Thomas Purcell distinguished himself in the service of William III, and after the Boyne received a grant of lands in Tipperary.

There were 17 Purcell families given in Co. Kerry.

Tobias was M. P. for Ardfert 1695-1703. J. Purcell is given in Tralee in 1908. Edm. of Killarney is found in 1776. Richard was rector of Kilflin in 1771. Edward of Tralee found in 1821.

Purdon

James Purdon of Kirklington in Cumberland, had Simon of Tallaght in Dublin, who had John of Tulla in Clare, who had Nicholas in 1657, who had Batt of Ballyclough in Cork d.1695, leaving Capt. John who had Batt of Dysert, who had Gilbert who m. Cherry Rowan having Rowan, Rev. Rd.; had Rev. Geo, Rd., Wm. b1784, and 3 daus. of whom Dr. Rowan had Thos. and Rowan. Rev. Rd had Rev. Geo., Rd., Watson, and Charlotte who m. Rev. Geo. Hickson having R.R. Purdon Hickson. Rev. Geo. m. Mary, granddaughter of Sir Rowland Blennerhassett having Rowan, Rowland 1838-83, Letitia m. Rev. John Collins of Ballyheigue.

Purtill, de Portuil

Jerh. and Tom of Banemore, Jerh. of Dromcloughra, Catherine of Ballynoe, Edm. of Ballydonoghue, and Ml. of Dean's lane, are all given in Co. Kerry.

Mac Quaide, Mac Quade

Pat Mac Quaide of Burnham, Co. Kerry. Spellings given include: Quaide, Mac Quade, Mac Uaid.

Quane

Pat and John of Kilmoyley, John of Kilconly, Nano of Lerrig, Ml. of Ardfert; Ml. of Dublin m. E. FitzGerald of Mile Height.

Quill

There were 30 'Quill' families given in Co. Kerry. They were said to derive from the Eoghanaght Caisil, through Aodh Dubh, Fingin, Leacnusa, Reactabra, Flan, Inderact, Maorig, Brian, Mulfotard, Donoch, Flan, Cuill, Hugh, Donoch, Cristfaolad, Hugh, Mahon, Christfaolad, John, Donogh, Mac Cuill, son of the hazel, was one of the three last kings of the De Dannan according to legend. Mac Cuill, St. Maughold of the Isle of Man, was converted by St. Patrick. In 1821 lived Mce. and Tom and John of Tralee, Rd. of Mayglass, Pat of Rathscannell. In 1818 Mce. Quill and William Twiss fought a duel at Rathnoonane, without injury. Lieut.-Col. Berkeley Crosbie Quill, C.B., 1902, b.1852, third son of Jerome of Tralee, entered Army in 1872, York and Lancs. regt., of Ballycarty. Albert Wm. Quill, M.A., B.I., son of Thomas, m. Margt. Chute; edited Landowners' Guide; history of Tacitus; poems; of Carriganas castle in Bantry. O'Cuil was also given as chief poet of Munster in the 12th century.

Quillinan

Michael Quillinan of Listowel, Co. Kerry. (see also Cullinane - O' Cuileannain).

Quilter, de Cuitleir
There were 24 Quilter families given in Co. Kerry, including Tom of Carguilla, John of Dromlough and Tom of Tullahinnett.

Quinlan
There were 45 Quinlan families given in Co. Kerry. Mce. Quinlan was was clerk of Tralee Union for 16 years, and county secretary for 14; his son, Ml. Jos., d.1918, a.28, was also secretary to the Kerry County Council. Dr. Mce. Quinlan, son of P.M., was tuberculosis medical officer for Kerry. Rev. John Quinlan, son of John of Killarney, resided in Lancashire.

Quinliven
Pat Quinliven of Main Street, is given in Co. Kerry.

Mac Quinn, Quinn, Quin
Those of the Mac Quinn spelling given in Co. Kerry were Dan of Fiddane, Pat of Gurranedarragh, John of Ballyheige, Ml. of Ballinclemesig, John of Lackamoer, Mary and Martin and Dan of Banna, Mary of Ballinahoulart, Wm. of Listellick, Pat of Brogue lane, John of Bridge Street and Mrs. Mac Quinn of Boherbee.

There were also 17 'Quinn' families given in Kerry. It is noted that Ua Cuinn was chief of Muinter Gillagain in Annaly, of magh Lugad in Ulster, and of clann Iffearnan in Thomand. Bridget, relict of Alfred Quinn, d.1913 at Bridge House in Dingle, leaving £4,756 to her sister, Mrs. Sarah E. Kennedy.

Variant spellings are numerous, with MacQuinn, Quinn, Quin, Mac Cuinn and O'Cuinn given.

Quinnell
Those of the name of Quinnell in Co. Kerry included Edw. of Garryrooth, Albert of Castle Street, John of Prince's street, John of Spa, and John of Ballymacegogue. John H. Quinnell, d. Dec.24, 1912, was owner of the Kerry Weekly Reporter, the Killarney Echo and the Kerry News, as well as the printing works in Tralee; he was born in Russell street in 1837; his brothers were Geo. and Ned; he left four sons and three daughters. His son John Busteed Quinnell, resided at Spa Lodge, and later at Edenburn, which he purchased from Sam Hussey.

Quinty
John Quinty of Dreemnacurra, Co. Kerry.

Quirke, Quirk
There were some 51 Quirke families given in Co. Kerry. We are also reminded that O'Cuirc, was chief of Muscraighe in the year 1043.

Rae, Rael

Rae is given in one instance as the name of a family settling in Co. Kerry, subsequent to the 1641-42 rebellion. Homeland/ descent:

Of Rail. Essex. Given to be a Cromwellian family. F. and G. Rael are given in Tralee in 1908.

Giles Rae lived at Keel, in Kilgarrylander parish, in 1821. Also given are John of Keel, Wm. of Boolteens; ; Edw. Rae m. a dau. of Rev. Stephen Giles, having Giles of Derrymore who m. Ellen Day of Lohercannon, having John of Derry who m. Sarah Day and Edw., who m. Anne Langford of Keel, having Anne who m. Catherine Rochfort, and Giles of Keel, in 1818 who m. Debora Langford, having Edw., John, Langford, Francis and Sarah. Mac Rait and O'Riabaig are two possible Gaelic family roots of the name of Rae given by J. King. From his listings we are given to believe that Rael has been simply shortened to Rae at times, as Rael is listed with Rae and as a seperate name unto itself.

There were 24 families of the Rael name given in Co. Kerry as well, including Tom of Killahan, Ellen of Dromkeen, Denis of Baltovin, Margt. of Kilgulbin, Pat of Banna and Pat and Ml. and Stephen and Julia and Garret of Farrantooreen.

O' Rahilly of Slieve Luachra

An account is given in Kings work of the family and descendants of John Mor Ua Raghailligh (O'Reilly), the son of Owen O'Reilly of Clare (who was confiscated in 1653), in Crosserlough Parish, Co. Cavan, who m. Hanora Daly of Aghacreevy. John Mor was educated for the priesthood in Kerry but "having killed one of a party of footpads who had waylaid him" he returned to the south where he settled in the district of Slieve Luachra. He was a poet of some note, and a precursor to Egan O'Rahilly, born at Scrahanaveal around 1678, d. 1747 at Tomies and buried at Muckross abbey, who was a gaelic poet of the first order. (see King for detail) He married a Miss Egan, having Egan O'Reilly, or O'Rahilly and Morgan. (The Egan O'Rahilly mentioned above b.1678.) Several descendants are given as emigrating to Melbourne.

In 1834 in the Irish Monthly Magazine, Dominick Ronayne, M.P., described Patrick Rahilly, a schoolmaster, as grandson of Egan; and this article was reprinted in the Cork Journal in 1917.

From the same family descend the Rahillys of Tullig, Killarney, and the Reillys (formerly Rahillys) of Knockburrane, near Listowel. The O'Rahilly was noted as being killed in the Dublin rising in 1916.

There were 45 families of the name of Rahilly given in Co. Kerry. It is noted that Ua Raighillagh, O'Raghallaigh or O'Reilly, was chief of muintir Maelmordha in 1162, and chief of Breffny in 1449.

Mac Raith, Mac Rae

Mac Raith was the chief poet of Munster who died in 1098.

Raleigh
A settler family on estates near Tralee, from the coming of the Elizabethan undertakers to the rebellion of 1641. Descent / homeland: Of Devon.

Andrew Raleigh, tailor, was killed during the Siege of Tralee in 1641.

Ramage
George Ramage of Denny street, Tralee, Co. Kerry.

Randal, Randall, Randle
A settler family on estates near Tralee, from the coming of the Elizabethan undertakers to the rebellion of 1641. Descent / homeland: Of Devon, Cornw., Kent, Berks.

Geo. Randal of Spunkane, Co. Kerry is given. A possible gaelic origin for the name is given as Mac Ragnaill. (see also Randles)

Randles
Tom and Con and John of Ardtully, Pat of Gortnaboul, Pat and John of Fussa, Ml. of Churchground, John of Inchmore, Pat of Letter, and Margt. of Duckett's lane are all given in Co. Kerry. (see also Randal)

Rattray
David Rattray of Gortnaskehy, Co. Kerry.

Rawleigh, Raleigh
Andrew Rawleigh was a tailor killed in Tralee siege in 1641; Sir Walter Raleigh, of Smerwick fame, beheaded in 1618, sold his Irish Estate to Lord Cork.

Rawlins
Wm. and Margt. of Tralee, Co. Kerry.

Ray, Mac Rait
Matt Ray of William street, given in Co. Kerry.

Raycroft
Francis Raycroft of Sunny hill, given in Co. Kerry.

Raymond
Given as the name of a family settling in Co. Kerry, subsequent to the 1641-42 rebellion. Homeland/ descent:

Of Devon. A Cromwellian family. Samuel Raymond, the grandson of the first settler of the name at Ballyloughran, in North Kerry, who, according to Archdeacon Rowan in the Kerry Magazine, vol. iii, p. 169, was an attorney of the Star chamber. This commissioner m. Ellen, dau. of Capt. O'Lavery, of Moyce, Co. Down. Samuel Raymond is found styled as Esquire in 1699, in 1694 he is placed among the 'gentlemen', his father or elder brother likely being alive in the 'latter' year.

Raymond of Ballyloughran had a grandson given as Samuel. In 1831 lived at Riversdale, Geo., Rev. S., J., and S. Raymond, and Wm. of Bedford; also given are Geo. of Killarney in 1783; John of Rockfield in 1795; Geo. of Woodmount, and John of Kilhenny in 1821; W. Raymond in 1841 printed the Kerry Examiner, and later the Kerry Evening Post to 1918.

In 1831 we find given separately, J. Raymond of Riversdale, J.P.; Wm. of Bedford; G. of Riversdale; S., (Clk.), Riversdale,; S., junior of Riversdale. In 1908 we find G., R., and J. Raymond of Tralee.

Spraymount (1846) was the home of Capt. W. Raymond. (Killehenny parish).

Riversdale (1846) was the home of George Raymond in 1821, (Kmockanure parish).

Bedford House (1846). W. M. Raymond lived here in 1831. (Listowel parish).

Reading
The name of a Cromwellian settler granted lands in 1667 in Co. Kerry.

Reany, O'Raigue
John Reany of Boherbee, Co. Kerry.

Reddin, Redin
Tom Reddin of Kilmore, and Pat Reddin of Killorglin, both in Co. Kerry.

Redmond, Redmon
Wm. Redmond of Strand Street, given in Co. Kerry.

Reen, O'Rinn
Several of the name are given in Co. Kerry including: John of Shinnah, and those of Islanderagh, Rathbeg, Gortnahaneboy, Knockysheehan, Rathmore, Annaghillymore, Shronebeg, Shronemore, and Doocarrigmore.

Reeves, Reaves
Pat Reeves of Ballyoutragh, Co. Kerry.

Regan, Reagan, O'Riagan
There were 69 Regan families given in Co. Kerry. It is noted that Ua Riagain, heir of Teamair in 1059, and chief of S. Breagha 1034, and one of the four tribes of Tara, was chief of Hy Riaghain or Tinehinch barony in Queens County (Leix), Ireland.

Reid, Reed, Read
Given in Co. Kerry were Jas. of Ballycasheen, Jas. of Droumyrourke, Rd. of Carrigafoyle, Jas. of Ennismore, Louis of Nelson Street, Helena of Castle street, Tom of Callinafersy, Robt. of Dromquinna, and Wm. of Dunkerron. Rd. Tuohill Reid, L.L.D., T.C.D., of Killarney, Indian Civil Servant, d.1883 at Rome, left £7,000 for educational purposes, including the Reid professorship for penal legislation in T.C.D..

Reidy, Ready
There were 120 Reidy families given in Co. Kerry, making Reidy a fairly numerous name in this county. It is also noted that Ua Riada, was chief of Arada in 1129.

Reilly, O'Rielly, Riley
There were some 54 Reilly families given in Co. Kerry. It is also noted that Ua Raighilligh was chief of Breifne in 1583; see also Rahilly, also given are Rev. Robert of New York; Rev. D. F. of Kansas; Rev. Daniel of New York; Sarah, L.L.A., of Glasgow, daughter of J. Lissivigeen. Reilly, O'Rielly, Riley, and Really were all given.

Relf
R. G. Relf of Nelson Street, is given in Co. Kerry.

Relihan
The following Relihan households are given in Co. Kerry: Tom and Jerh. and Tom of Knockadirreen, Ml. and Tom of Kilcaramore, Con of Ballinclogher, Jerh. of Tullahinnell, Ml. of Toor, Jerh. of Tullahinnell, Ml. of Toor, Jerh. of Ardoughter, John of Kylebwee, Denis and Dan of Tullig, Julia of Knockreagh, Dan of Beenanaspuck, and Eliza and Mary of Mountcoal.

Restrick
Tom Restrick of Main street, is given in Co. Kerry.

Revington
Jos. and Wm. and John of the Mall, and Georgina of Princess quay are given in Co. Kerry. Revington, Ltd., drapers in Tralee since 1857, is also be noted.

Reynolds, Mac Ragnaill
The following Reynolds families are given in Co. Kerry: Mce. of Shanavally, Pat of Tarbert, Rd. of Skrillagh, Dan of Listowel, Ml. of Rock St., and Stephen of Brogue lane.

Rezin
John Rezin of Cloonbegh, Co. Kerry.

Rice, Rhys

The Rice family of Bushmount and Lord Monteagle's, descend from a common ancestor, Edw. Rice of Dingle. Several of this line are found with the personal name of Dominick, residing at Bushmount. Bushmount (1846) was the seat of the Rice family in Rattoo Parish.

Burnham House was the residence of Lord Ventry in 1846. Mullins of Burnham, in England, settled here in 1666, in Rice's Castle of Ballingolin. (Dingle Parish).

Burnham was formerly called Ballingolin, and is near Dingle, where a castle belonged to the rice family before the wars of 1641. It lay a small English mile from the harbor of Ventry in Kerry, and is well situated on the SW side of Dingle harbor.

Smith gives this family as that of 'ap Rees' or Price, as they were called in Wales, with some of the family arriving with Strongbow in Ireland in the reign of Henry II. Several of the name were mayors of Waterford city in the 1400's, and one James Rice built a chapel near Christchurch in Waterford. (see *The Ancient and Present State of the County of Waterford* by Smith). see also Price.

Some 27 'Rice' families are given in Co. Kerry. Rice, ap Rees, Rhys, Price, of Wales and Ireland is a widespread family now, as noted by J. King. In 1232, Thomas Fitz Rhys, juror, Kilmallock; John Rice of Fidden in Kilkenny, 1291; John, was treasurer of Ireland in 1294; Sir John of Buttevant 1307-57, arms in Ulster Heralds; Pat was mayor of Cork in 1413; Peter was mayor of Waterford 1483-88; Peter or Piers of Smerwick and Dingle is given in 1579; Rice of Ballymaceidal and Ballingolin in 1587; Capt. John Rice drowned off the Blasquets, when the Spanish ship, Our Lady of the Rosary, was wrecked in 1588; Rd., son of Dominick, of Dingle 1603, had wardenship of Mce., son of James Traunt in 1605 who was to be educated in the English religion and habits in Trinity College in Dublin from the 12th to the 18th year of his age; Richard of Gallerus given in 1614; Ellen Rice was the wife of Pat Fitz Rd. Trant in 1618; Stephen of Dingle was pardoned in 1624, his heir was James, whose sons were Robt. and Andrew; his other sons were Dominick and Thomas; Lieut. Rd. Rice of Dingle 1627; George and Robert were burgesses of Dingle in 1629.

Rhys is a possible variant spelling.

A much more extensive listing appears in the History of Kerry by J. King.

Richards

Francis Richards of Lahard, Geo. of Boherbee; and Rev. John Richards of Tralee is given in 1683.

Richardson

Hanora Richardson of Cloonb'rane, Wm. of Ballymullen; in 1649 Edw. was granted Kilbonane.

The name of a Cromwellian settler granted lands in 1667 in Co. Kerry.

Riney

Dan and John of Clonee, John of Coornagillough, Jerh. of Cooryeen, Ellen and Ml. and Ml. of Clogherane, Denis of Rossacoosane and Tim (or Tom) of Lehud, are given as Riney households in Co. Kerry.

Ring, Rinn, O'Rinn

Jerh. of Valentia cable station for 45 years; Canon Ring of London, 1884, pioneer priest in Silvertown. Said to possible have derived from O'Rinn.

Rinuccini

G. B. Rinuccini was Papal Nuncio, and landed at Kenmare, Co. Kerry, in October 1645, on the way to Kilkenny.

Riordan, Reardon

One of the more numerous families in Co. Kerry, there were some 266 Riordan families given in Co. Kerry. Dr. O'Reardon, d.1866, aged 90, at Killarney; became a physician in 1802, was in France until 1814, in charge of Cork Fever Hospital until 1848, lived at Mt. Prospect in Killarney afterwards.

Roachford

John Roachford of Tullaghna, Co. Kerry.

Roberts

The Following Roberts families are given in Co. Kerry: Francis and Jas. and Robt. of Clovers lane, Robt. and Mary of Pound Row, Mary and Dan and Francis of Callinafercy, Tim and Tom of Killorglin, and Mary of Bohercael.

Robinson

The following Robinson families were found in Co. Kerry: Wm. of Langford street, Jas. of Canal new road, Anne of Faha, Jas. of Drimnamore, Jas. of Garinish, and Sarah of Main street.

Roche, de la Roche

There were 78 Roche families given in Co. Kerry. It is also noted that Sir Boyle Roche was M. P. for Tralee 1790-8; Jerome W. Roche, solicitor, d.1893 at Tubbermaing aged 45, son of Redmond, m. Miss Uppington, having 2 sons and 2 daus., was buried in Kilsarkin. In 1821 lived John of Sandville, Wm., Edw. and J. H. of Killarney.

Rodd

Frederick Rodd of Emlagh, Co. Kerry.

Roe

A settler family on estates near Tralee, from the coming of the Elizabethan undertakers to the rebellion of 1641. Descent / homeland:

Of Cornwall, Devon. The first settler of the name noted as m. in 1612 to the dau. of Jenkin Conway. Hugh Roe of Tralee, barber, was killed at Ballinskelligs in 1641. Edward Roe resided in Tralee in 1624.

The town of Tralee was incorporated in 1612, and its charter named Edmond Roe among the first provost and burgesses.

Edward Roe in 1619 was granted by Arthur Denny the castle, town and lands of Cloghanemacerne(sp?), and Ballydunlea, rent £11. Edw. Roe's daughter m. James Conway in 1632. Edm. Roe of Clohane m. Alice Conway.

Rogers

John Rogers of Ballymullen, Co. Kerry.

Rohan

The following Rohan families are given in Co. Kerry; Tim of Ballyhonen, Tom and John of Ballyduff, Pat of Farranskilla, John of Glenahoe, Pat of Aughacasla, Martin and Mary and Ml. of Deelis, Pat of Gurrane, Tom of Laharan, Ml. of Goat street, Tom of Blackloon, Pat of Caher, Johanna and John and James of Farrantooleen, Ellen of Lisnamoovane, Julia of Kilmurry, and Pat and Pat of Gowlane.

Ronan, Ronayne,

The following Ronan families are given in Co. Kerry: Ml. of Strand street. Magrath O'Rontain, was bishop of Ardfert, d.1099. Maelbhrenainn Ua Ronain, bishop of Ciarraighe Luachra, d.1161, buried in Ardfert. Cailte Mac Ronain was a Fiann leader at the battle of Ventry. Ua Ronain was chief of Cairbre Guara or N. Teffia. Roynane's island is found in Killarney Lake.

Rooke, Rook

Rev. Chas. Rooke of Gortnaspiddal, Co. Kerry, was rector of Ardfert in 1914.

Rookes

A settler family, given on estates near Tralee, from the coming of the Elizabethan undertakers to the rebellion of 1641. Descent / homeland: Of Kent.

Roome

Given as the name of a family settling in Co. Kerry, subsequent to the 1641-42 rebellion.

Rooney

Bridget Rooney and Edm. Rooney of Doonimlaghbegh, James of Ballydwyer, Mary of Dean's Lane, and Dan of Killeen are given in Co. Kerry.

Roper

Sir Thomas Roper was appointed constable of Castle Mayne and he had grants of confiscated lands in 1612 and was constable 1608-37.

Rose

Henry Rose, M.P. for Ardfert, 1703-34, m. Catherine Crosbie; and was Justice of the Kings bench.

Rosney

Tom Rosney of Castleview, and Mary Rosney of High street, are given in Co. Kerry.

Ross, Mac Aindreis

Eliz. Ross of Droumyrourke, Kate Lacca, James of Kilmore, Edm. of Knoppogue, James of Rae street. Geo. of Main street, and Mary of Blennerville are given in Co. Kerry.

Rourke

There were 47 Rourke families given in Co. Kerry. It is also noted that Ua Ruairc (O'Rourke) was chief of Dartraighe and Dealbhna and Conmhaicne and Breifne. Cathal O'Rourke was weirsman on the Laune to Teig na Mainisterah Mac Carthy Mor; and Manus to Earl Donald in 1584. Rev. Dermod O'Rourke was P.P. of Listry in 1776. Edmund Falconer O'Rourke wrote the song 'Killarney'.

Rowan

Given as the name of a family settling in Co. Kerry, subsequent to the 1641-42 rebellion. George Rowan m. Mary Blennerhassett, grand daughter of Capt. A. Blennerhassett. His son George, had a son George, whose son William had A. B. Rowan, D.D., whose son was William Rowan of Belmont. The Rev. Arthur Blennerhassett Rowan wrote Lake Lore in 1853, b.1800, d.1861, having Anne Margaret 1832-1913, and Col. Wm. b.1830. In 1831 lived G. Rowan, J.P. Rathany; and A. B. Rowan, of Tralee in 1908.

Ua Robhachain, as given by J. King is given as O'Rowan, Dunchadh, was successor of Colum Cille and Adamnan in 983. Rev. Andrew Rowan was rector of of Dunaghy in Antrim in 1661, and ancestor of Hamilton Rowan, his son, Capt. Wm., raised a company of foot for William and Mary, and was granted half pay pension in 1710.

Belmont (1846) in Tralee parish, was the home of the Rev. A. B. Rowan in 1831.

Rowe
Lce. Rowe of Killerisk, Co. Kerry.

Rowland
George Rowland of Ballymullen, Co. Kerry.

Ruachtain
Mac Cairthig Ruachtain of Kilgarvin, Co. Kerry.

Rubin
Solomon Rubin of James Street, given in Co. Kerry.

Rudd
Given as the name of a family settling in Co. Kerry, subsequent to the 1641-42 rebellion. Homeland/ descent: Of Norf., Shrops.

Ruddle
Two individuals of the name of David Ruddle are given of Glanawillan, Co. Kerry.

Rumney
Given as the name of a family settling in Co. Kerry, subsequent to the 1641-42 rebellion. Homeland/ descent: In 1831 Thos. W. Rumney lived in Tralee.

Rumsby
Harry Rumsby of Tarbert Island, Co. Kerry.

Rusk
Robert Rusk of Connor's lane, given in Co. Kerry.

Russell
There were 33 Russell families in Co. Kerry. Anthony Russell of Ballytrasna, Co. Kerry is given in 1797, along with his son Francis.

Ruttle
Ellen Ruttle of Castle street, Tralee, Co. Kerry.

Ryan
There were 47 Ryan families given in Co. Kerry. It is also noted that Ua Riain was chief of Ui Drona, or Idrone in Carlow in 1015.

Rycroft
A settler family, given on estates near Tralee, from the coming of the Elizabethan undertakers to the rebellion of 1641. Descent /homeland: Of Devon.

Ryder
A settler family, given on estates near Tralee, from the coming of the Elizabethan undertakers to the rebellion of 1641. Descent / homeland: Of Berks.

Thomas Ryder was rector of Stradbally, in Co. Kerry in 1722.

Ryeves, Ryeeves, Reeves
A settler family, given on estates near Tralee, from the coming of the Elizabethan undertakers to the rebellion of 1641. Descent / homeland: Of Kent.

Col. Jas. Ryeves, of Carrignafeely, Co. Kerry, m. Alice Spring of Castlemagne, whose father was Constable there. William Ryeves appears on a document as the late or forfeiting proprietor of the lands of Carrignafeely alias Carrignabruisher and Wm. Ryeves of Carrignafeely is given in the year 1700., and of a part of Ballymack Ulick O'Brennan, out of which lands Edward Denny, Esq., claimed by descent.... It appears he held those lands however, as he bequeathed on his death to his sisters children. A nephew of his, Thomas Ryeves, the grandson of Col. David Crosbie, after the surrender of Limerick, followed James the Second to France in 1692

Ryle
There were 21 Ryle families given in Co. Kerry. It is also noted that Maurice P. Ryle, editor of the Kerry People, wrote the Kingdom of Kerry; 2nd edition in 1903.

Sadler
Minard Castle, built by the Knight of Kerry, was blown up in 1650 by Cols. Le Hunt and Sadler. Its' defender Walter Hussey of Castlegregory was killed.

Sampson, Samson, Samsun
Tom Sampson of Listowel, Martin of Rathpogue and Mary Sampson, a nun, daughter of Tom, d. 1913.

Sandes of Sallow Glen
Sallow Glen (1846), was the residence of the Sandes family. Wm. Sandes of Cumberland came to Ireland in 1649 with Cromwell, and got portion of the Connor lands. His son was Lancelot of Carrigfoyle, d. 1668, had a son, John, of Cloonbrane, whose son was Thomas of Sallow Glen, whose son was William, b. 1736, whose son was Thomas William, b. 1771, whose son was William, whose nephew was Thomas William Sandes, b. 1842.

Pyrmont (1846) was the seat of S.C. Sandes, and the Rev. F. Sandes is given at Carrunakilla (1846). All 3 of the above are in Kilnaughtin parish.

Oakpark (1846), was the Bateman residence since 1697. Now Collis Sandes lives there (according to J. King, circa 1908). Tralee parish.

Sankey
Sankey's Regt. of horse was granted nearly 8,000 acres of land in 1667, near Tralee, confiscated from Mac Conroi, O'Connor, Mac Ellistrum, Walsh, Roche, etc..

Saunders, Sanders
The family vault of one Saunders family line was found in Castleisland Prot. church and was inscribed 'this is the burying place of the Saunders family of Braehig, 1696.' Among those Saunders families in Kerry were those of: Robt. Saunders of insula de Kerry in 1679, who had Wm. of Tullig, who had Eliza and Arthur of Currens, who had Rev. Wm. around 1777, who had Dr. Wm., John of Cork, and Arthur of Tullig. Arthur of Killarney was sheriff in 1842. Saunders of Carker had Col. Rd., Susan, Anne, Mary, Margt.; and Wm. of Carker, d.1883 aged 87.

Savage Savadge
Some 31 families are given in Co. Kerry. Sir Arthur Savage, in 1613 was granted lands in Co. Kerry. A history of the Savage family of Ards, in Ulster, by G.F.S.A. was published in 1906.

Savin
Jas. Savin of Killarney, Co. Kerry.

Sawers
Garrett Sawers of Islandgan --, Co. Kerry.

Sawyer
A settler family, given on estates near Tralee, from the coming of the Elizabethan undertakers to the rebellion of 1641. Descent / homeland:
Of Norf., Camb, Northants, Berks.

Sayers
Garrett of Listowel, Tom and Garrett and Martin of Derrymore, Tom of Lat--emore, Tom of Knockavrogeen, Jas. of Milltown, Pat of Kilcooly, and Pat of Gortbreagogue, all given in Co. Kerry.

Scaife
Wm. of Farranreagh, Wm. and James and Arthur of Cable tce. in Valentia, Co. Kerry.

Scanlan, O'Scannlain

Some 119 Scanlan families are given in Co. Kerry, making them one of the more numerous families in this county. It is also given that in 1914, Eocha, son of Dunadhach, chief of clann Scannlain, and Scannlan son of Cathal lord of Eoghanacht locha Lein, were killed at the battle of Clontarf. In 1414 Donald Oscannlayn was canon of Ardfert. Edm. O'Scanlan of Fusan is given in 1776, and Ml. and Jas. of Ballylongford in 1821.

Scannell O'Scannail

There were 57 Scannell families given in Co. Kerry. The Rev. Cornelius Scannell, 1845-1913, bro. of John of Bunagara, o. in 1870, was pastor of Visalla, and Pasadena, in Southern California.

Scargill

Frank Scargill of Beaufort house, in Co. Kerry in 1914.

Scollard

There are 15 Scollard families given in Co. Kerry, including Ellen of Castleview, Mary at Knockeen, Mary of Tonebwee, Nich. of Farranmanagh, David of Knockardtry, Ml. of Kilmaniheen, Barry of Cordal, Garret of Castleview, Nich. and Mce. of Kilbulbin, Pat of Ler-ig, John and Nich. of Ballybranagh, John of Gallinorig, and the Rev. Patrick Scollard of Currahee, are all given in Co. Kerry.

Scott

There were 9 Scott families given in Co. Kerry. including Batt of Boolacullane, Pat and James of Rusheen, Edm. and Edm. of Rossmore, James of Coracow, Peter of Carrigeencullia, Robert of Ardfert, and Richard of Tralee.

Sculles

James Sculles in 1605 was granted Lislaughtie abbey, houses and gardens, 12 acres, the creek fishings, 20 acres of land, and two ferries across the Shannon river, at Begh to Bingannon, and at Carrickfoile to Kilrush, at fixed tolls.

Scully

There were 18 Scully families given in Co. Kerry, including Denis and Philip of Nantinane, Kate of Chapel lane, Pat of Demesne, John of Moyeightragh, Pat of Bohereencael glebe, Honoria of Lahard, Ml. of Ardrinane, Jerh. of Ballymullen, Margaret of Rathass, John of Kenmare, Philip of Kilnabrack, John of Shanacashel, John and Denis and Pat of Beaufort, and Pat and Batt of Dunloe.

Seaganstown

Seaganstown is given in 1846, in the works of J. King. (volume 3 of Kings History of Co. Kerry).

Sealy

Given in Co. Kerry were: Wm. Sealy of Ballymalis, Catherine of Cromane; Cam of Maugh 1768. Uriah and Mary had a dau. Mary 1772. Uri of Maugh d.1797. John of Moyglass d.1799. Wm. son of Sam, b.1802. Sam of Maglos in 1809 m. a dau. of R. Hilliard of Listrim. Wm. Sealy of Rockfield in 1818 had a duel with Edw. Harnett of Sandville, Uria of Killaly and Eusebius of Mullamarka, Wm. of Brickfield, and John of Glenville, in 1831. Sam, son of Arthur H. R. Sealy, died 1913 at Killarney.

Sears

Eleven Sears families are given in Co. Kerry, including Andrew and Garrett and Johanna of Lack; Batt of Lativemore, Garrett of Ballybeg, Pat of Glenfahan, James of Knockavrogeen, Kat and Tom of Ferriters quarter, and Tom and Pat of Vicarstown.

Seary
Robert Seary of Castleview, Co. Kerry.
Seaward
William Seaward of Finuge, Co. Kerry.
Sedgewick
Thomas Sedgewick of Gallowsfields, Co. Kerry.
Seekins
Wm. Seekins of Ballinskelligs, Co. Kerry.
Seever
John Seever, burgess of Tralee, Co. Kerry in 1611.

Sandes of Greenville, Co. Kerry
Extract From The Irish Book of Arms.
(IGF) 1988.

Segerson, Sigerson
There were only 8 Segerson families given in Co. Kerry, including John of Kinard, Pat of Ballinskelligs, Jas. of Cloghaneanad, Rd. of Dungegan, Ml. of Laharn, Jas. of Derreen, Jas. of Rinneen and John of Ardcost.

The surname of Segerson was said to have come from the Norseman Sigurd, who fell at the battle of Clontarf; from the family of merchants at Liverpool, Bristol, Dublin, Cork, etc.. from 1,000 - 1600 a.d..

Rd. Harding had a grant of Ballinskelligs abbey which he passed to Chris. Segerson of Dublin in 1615. In 1653 Chris. of Valentia and Rd. of Ballinskelligs were confiscated, and Thos. heir of Chris., had a lease in 1697 from Henry Petty. In 1776 among the chief Kerry Papists were Chris. Segerson of Kinard, Jas. and Chris and John of Cahirbarnagh, and Edw. of Cove. In 1779 Jas. of Ballinabloun, being aged, made a transfer, to his son John, of Cahirbarnagh, Killerelig, Canuge, etc..

The Segersons married with the local families of O'Connell, O'Mahoney, Conway, O'Sullivan, Sugrue, etc.. John Segerson of West Cove in 1825 left his property to his daughter Lucinda Mahoney of Dromore castle who had Harold and Nora. In 1821 Thomas Segerson resided at Dungegan, and John at Castle Cove. In 1810 Alice O'Connell of Glenville, widow of John Segerson, had Aghatubrid, etc.. D. O'Shea wrote a poem on Francis Segerson

Selick
David Selick of Ballybrack, Co. Kerry.
Sellers
Ezard Sellers of Nelson street, given in Co. Kerry.

Selles
Thomas Selles of Ballinvoher, Co. Kerry.

Sewell
Mary Sewell of Henn street and John of Main street are given in Co. Kerry. Wm. Suell of Milltown in 1797 m. Eliza Twiss of Ballahantouragh

Sexton
John Sexton of Brosna and James Sexton of Gortdromagownagh, Co. Kerry.

Shade
Rev. Wm. Shade of Kilbanivan, Co. Kerry.

Shanahan
There were 77 Shanahan families given in Co. Kerry. It is also noted that Ua Seanacain (O'Shanahan), was chief of Tulla in Clare and Hy. Rongaile in Tipperary.

Shannon
Bartley Shannon of Knockanarney, Co. Kerry.

Sharkey
John Sharkey of Spa road, given in Co. Kerry.

Shaughnessy
Edm. of Beeheehagh, John of Kilelton, Tom of Baltovin, Ml. of Lisardboola, Rd. of Listowel. It was also noted that Ua Seacnasaig was chief of cinel Ada, and Kinelea in Galway in 1224. Edward O'Shaughnessy of Caherciveen, d.1905, aged 38 journalist of Press Gallery in London, and the 'Irish Independent'.

Shaw
John Shaw of Inch and Chas. Shaw of Farranreagh, Co. Kerry.

O' Shea (O'Seadha)
O'Shea is given as one of the chiefs of Iveragh by O'Heerin. Many of this line are found as notable Gaelic poets. (Noted separately as chief of Ui Raehach, in Corca Duibne, of the clan Conaire and of the tuath sen Eran.) After 1261 the clan Cashel, Mac Carthys and O'Sullivans, driven out of Tipperary, settled in Desmond on the lands of the tuath sen Erann. The O'Shea sept of the clan Conaire remained in the old homesteads of Iveragh, and several of the name are found on the old lands into the 20th century.

Before the Normans came to Munster the O'Shea's and O'Falvey's were principal families in Kerry. Subsequently the O'Shea's were broken, for they did not own a single acre of land in Kerry according to the list of landowners drawn up in 1653 by order of the Cromwellian government.

There were 900 'Shea' families listed in Co. Kerry. This makes the Shea family one of the largest to appear in this county. In J. Kings work it was given that 'O'Shea' was the spelling of the name used by James of Ballyfinane, Dan of Cleeny, Arthur of Ballyvirrane, John of Bishops lane, Dan of High street, Pat of Ardfert, Tim of Ballynamanagh, Tim of Bortahoonig, Mary of Listowel, Roger of Tullamore, T. of Bedford, and several others.

P.J. O'Shea was a pioneer of the Irish language revival and wrote several books in Gaelic. The Rev. Thomas O'Shea, Archbishop of Wellington, N. Zealand, was born at Hawera, the son of Kerry emigrants, his mother being Johanna O'Sullivan of Lahern, who lived to the age of 85.

Sheehan, Sheahan
There were 275 Sheehan families in Co. Kerry, making Sheehan one of the more numerous family names there.

Mac Sheehy, Sheehy, Joy
There were 135 Sheehy families given in Co. Kerry, and that relies upon the spelling of Sheehy that was prominent at that time. Mac Sheehy is also a noted spelling of the family name. (see also Sheehy and Joy) Edmund Mac Sheehy was constable to the Geraldines 1568.

Sheeres
Wm. Sheeres was vicar of Marhin and Minard, Co. Kerry, in 1679.

Sheldon
Lieut. Wm. Sheldon, 1666, was granted Cledereagh, in Co. Kerry.

Sheridan
Tom Sheridan of Pound lane, is given in Co. Kerry.

Shiell
Grena, in 1839, was the seat of John O'Connell, in 1864 of D. Shiell. (Aghadoe Parish).

Shine
There were 18 Shine families given in Co. Kerry, including John of Glangristeen, John of Killaha, Tim of New street, Tim of Ardteegalvin, Mary of Knocknagoshel, Pat of Carrigeenwood, Dan of Listowel, Pat of Carhoona, Pat and Con of Grotdromas--hy, Con and Dan of Killaha, John and Conn and Dan of Moyvane, Dan of Cahir, and Stephen and Stephen of Slaheny. Rev. T. Shine is given in 1776. Rev. Batt Shine is given in 1757-1827, Brosna.

Shirley
John Shirley was parish clerk of Listowel in 1696.

Shortal, Shortall
Kate Shortal of New St., Killarney, Co. Kerry.

Shortcliffe Shiercliffe
A settler family, given on estates near Tralee, from the coming of the Elizabethan undertakers to the rebellion of 1641. Descent / homeland:
Morris and Edmond Fitz Gerald, the sons of Edmund Fitz John, forfeited Behinagh, Glandyne and other lands in 1641, which were divided between John Carrick, a Cromwellian Commissioner, for surveying forfeited estates, and Capt. Welstead, a Cromwellian officer, ancestor of Thomas Welstead of Ballywalter, Co. Cork. Capt. Welstead sold his grants in Kerry to Anthony Shortcliffe, also a Cromwellian officer, whose name in old records is variously spelt Shiercliffe, or Sutcliffe. Thomas Shiercliffe was the owner of a considerable property around Castle Gregory. The name is frequently spelt Shortcliffe in old records, with Shiercliffe and Sutcliffe given as variant spellings.

(Also found separately, Anthoney Shortcliffe of Castle Gregory in 1674, and Tom Shortcliffe of C. Gregory had a dau. who m. Edward Rice.)

Shortis
The Shortis family of Ballybunion, Co. Kerry, is given.

Shuel, Shuell
Wm. and Jas. and Annie and Margt. of Caherciveen and James of Cloghanelinaghan, Co. Kerry are given.

Shute Chute
Given as the name of a family settling in Co. Kerry, subsequent to the 1641-42 rebellion. Given to have originated in Dorset and a Cromwellian family settling here. (see also Chute)

Silles
Thomas Bolton Silles (or Silies) of Ballinvoher, Lixnaw, d.1914, aged 74, and was buried at Kiltomey.

Simms
Anne Simms of Gortagullane, Co. Kerry.

Simon
Albert Simon of Spunkane, Co. Kerry.

Sincox
Hy. Sincox of Shelbourne St., and John Sincox of Gortamullen are given in Co. Kerry.

Singleton
Con Singleton of Mausrower, Margt. of Pawn office lane are given in Kerry. M.C.C. of Tralee is given in 1821.

Sinnette
James Sinnette of Commons, Co. Kerry.

Skinger
Henry Skinger of Demesne, Co. Kerry.

Skinner
John Skinner of Boherbee, Co. Kerry.

Skipworth
A settler family, given on estates near Tralee, from the coming of the Elizabethan undertakers to the rebellion of 1641. Homeland: Of Norf., Herts.

Slattery
There were 74 Slattery families given in Co. Kerry.

Sleath
Thomas Sleath of Kenmare, Co. Kerry.

Sleator
Samuel Sleator of Kenmare, Co. Kerry.

Sloan, Slone
Rd. Sloan of Spunkane, Co. Kerry.

Smith, Mac Gowen
There were 27 Smith families given in Co. Kerry including Tom of Brosna, Wm. of Rockfield, John of Ballycasheen, Geo. of Mangerton view, Pat of High street, Jas. of New street, Robt. of Moyvane and Caleb of Carhoonakineely. One John Smith in 1669 was archdeacon of Aghadoe. In 1821 Marmaduke lived at Tarbert and Benjamin in Dingle, Co. Kerry.

Smithworthe
Edward Smithworthe in 1612 was granted the confiscated lands off Donell Mac Cartie of Dungeele, of Daniel Mac Fearris of Bealahamalismore, of Daniel Mac Finnin of Artulihie, and of Daniel O'Suillevane of Tomies, in Co. Kerry.

Smyth
Thomas Smyth was a Prot. Bishop 1695-1725, in Co. Kerry.

Somers
Ml. and Pat of Curraknockaun, Ml. of Killeentierna, Lucy and Chris. of Knockreagh, Edm. of Ballinorig, Ml. of Coolaruane, John of Dromclough, Edm. of Irremore, and John of Castlegregory.

Sparks
Edward Sparks of Tralee given in 1789.

Speart
Richard Speart and others on Dec. 16, 1583, asked for 160 plough lands in Desmond country, and to press 100 mariners.

Spicer
George Spicer of Dominick street, given in Co. Kerry.

Spillane
Noted as the chief of Hy. Lughaidh of swords, is O'Spellan of the bright spurs. Some 76 families were noted in Co. Kerry. It is given that Hy Lughaidh in Tipperary and Ballyspellane in Kilkenny and in Cork were owned by this clan, according to J. King.

Spotswood

Frank Spotswood, attorney in Tralee in 1782; his daus. Elinor b.1781 and Caroline in 1786; John, Theo, Mce, Rd., of Valentia in 1839; Dr. Mce. of Caherciveen in 1876 owned 295 acres.

Spratt

A settler family, given on estates near Tralee, from the coming of the Elizabethan undertakers to the rebellion of 1641. Descent / homeland:

Of Devon. Daniel Spratt, clothier in 1643, deposed to his losses during the siege of Tralee. The Rev. Devereux Spratt wrote an account of the siege of Tralee in 1641. He was tutor of Sir. Edw. Denny's three sons.

Spring

Given as the name of a family settling in Co. Kerry, subsequent to the 1641-42 rebellion. Said to be originally from Suffolk. The Springs had grants near Kilcoleman from Queen Elizabeth. A.; and F. Spring are found in Tralee in 1908.

One Spring family came from Lavenham, in Suffolk, where their ancestor was joint builder of a fine church described in Weaver's Funeral Monuments. Capt. Thomas Spring was the first of the name in Kerry. In 1592 he was sheriff, and he held the Constableship of Castlemagne until his death in 1597. Walter Spring, the eldest son of Capt. Thomas, was high sheriff of Kerry in 1609. Walter Spring, having forfeited a large estate in 1641, was commonly called 'the unfortunate'.

Thomas, the 2nd son of the original settler, succeeded to the constableship of Castlemagne fortress. He had three sons, Thomas, Walter and Edward. Thomas the eldest son had Thomas, who was a lawyer of great eminence, being called to the bar in 1762.

Of the same family given above, the Rev. Edw. Spring was rector of Kilcoe, Co. Cork.

To the east of Castlemain is Ballycrispin (1846) which was the seat of Counsellor Thomas Spring in 1756. (Kiltallagh parish)

Kilcolman Abbey (1846) was the residence of Sir W. D. Godfrey. Thomas Spring resided in 1588 at Kilcolman, granted to him at the dissolution of the churches.

Eight Spring families were given in Kerry, including Edw. of Ballinavarrig, John of Gortatlea, Hy. of Gortavullen, Wm. of Gorttanedan, Arthur of Spa road, Francis of Waterloo lane, Robert of Ballygrameen, and Edw. of Ballinvarrig.

In 1586 Capt. Thomas Spring of Lavenham in Suffolk, was constable of Castle Maigne, with a lieutenant, and 16 privates; he m. Annabella Browne of Awney, having Walter, who m. Mary Crosbie dau. of Patrick, having Edw., who m. Anne Browne of Ross, having Walter who m. Julia Fitz Gerald having Thomas, etc..

In 1876 Edward Spring of Farranfore owned 77 acres in Kerry.

Stack, Stak, Stake

There were 180 Stack families given in Co. Kerry. Stak and Stake were variant spellings of the day given by J. King.

In 1308 William Stak was rector of Fyndtrahig. In 1424 Philip Stake was rector of Cuoygnys, vicar of Rynbera, and rector of Kylbertan. In 1427 Mce. Stack was canon of Ardfert. In 1488, Rev. John Stack, bishop of Ardfert, was buried in the cathedral. In 1217, Mar. 21, Petronilla Bloet, wife of Dermot Magarthy, king of Cork, was granted the marriage portion which her brother gave her, some accounts, (according to Abbe MacGeoghegan) given her as a Stack.

Stackstown, or Crotto, was granted to Henry Ponsonby in 1666. Stack's mountain is a townland in Kilflyn parish. Wm. Stack in 1422 was archdeacon of Ardfert. In 1285, Alexr. Stake, to have peace, paid the sheriff £4. In 1596 Maurice Stack and his brothers may be trusted, writes Carew, and that Garrett Duff Stack of 1592 was of English descent. Garrett Roe Stack, in 1603 was besieged in Ballingarry castle. Mce. Stack was killed at Beale in 1600, after his service at Liscahane. John Stack of Ballyconry, m.1780, Bridget Studdert having Dinah, Ann, Isabella, Eliz., Col. Geo. d.1855, John m. 1802 Catherine Massy having Eyre d.1856, John, Nathanial manor-genl. b.1811, d.1874, m.1858 having Geo., Eyre, Maria, Agnes.

General Edward Stack, lieut. in French army in 1777, entd. British army as lt.-col. of Irish Brigade in 1794, col. 1801, general in 1830, died at Calais in 1833. Thomas de Stack translated Irish poems. Rev. John Stack was P.P. of Brosna 1776. Austin Stack, T.D., is son of Wm. d. 1899, son of Hy. d.1839, son of Patk. 1800.

Liscahane Castle was held by Stack

Stack, Stak, Stake
against the Geraldines in 1600. Before 1599 the place belonged to Daniel Gray, an English Colonist under Sir Edward Denny. In 1641 it appears that the Gun family settled there, while Gray likely moved on to Tralee for better security. A new stone house erected by Gray is described by King. (Ardfert Parish).

Beale Castle, in Kilconly parish, was once a residence of Lord Kerry. It was dismantled in 1600, and Maurice Stack was killed there in the same year.

Stackpoole, de Stacabul
Ml. of Glenalappa, Tom and Jas. and Pat of Aughrim, Co. Kerry; Mrs. Stackpoole of Aughrim, d.1913, aged 103. The spelling of de Stacabul is one given by J. King.

Stainstreet
Sydney Stainstreet of High street, is given in Co. Kerry.

Stanley
Sir Wm. Stanley was in pursuit of the Earl of Desmond in 1583, who was killed by Daniel Kelly; Edward Stanley was captain of 40 footmen in Dingle in 1583; Michael Stanley was granted Nedeene in 1666, 10 acres.

Steele
J. Steele of Fenit, and G. of Day place.

Steere
Rev. John Steere, treasurer of Ardfert in 1612, and bishop 1622; his dau. m. Col. David Crosbie of Ballingarry; his bro. Rev. Wm. Steere was vicar of Ballineglisse and Kyrieleeson or O'Dorney in 1618, and bishop of Ardfert and Aghadoe in 1628-37, with the right to hold in his hands commendams to the value of £100 a year.

Stephens
There were 13 Stephens families given in Co. Kerry, including Andrew of Listowel, John of Lisardboola, Wm. of Chute's lane, Wm. of Day place, Robt. and John and Thos. of Main street, John of Kilderry, Francis of Kilburn, Jos. and Wm. of Rathpogue, and Joseph of Callinafercy. Tom of Cappagh, Thos. and Anne Stpehens had Robert b.1789, and Samuel b. 1797. Hy. of Blennerville is given in 1821, and Robt. of Curragraigue; Sam had a bro. Hy. who had a son Robt.; Mary, dau. of Wm., b.1808, Jessy, dau. of Henry., m. m. John Day Stokes. The Rev. W. P. Stephens, vicar of Gt. Ashfield in Suffolk, was son of Jos. Stephens of Tralee.

Stephenson, Stevenson
In 1583, Oliver Stevenson was constable of Glin castle, and was granted Dunmoylan manor; his son Thomas, m. Una, dau. of bishop John Crosbie, having Rd., Una, and Anna, and he died in 1636; Thos.. had a bro. Oliver, who m. Elinor, dau. of Sir Valentine Brown and d.1642; Rd. Stephenson, m. Cicely Peppard having Oliver, John, Patk., Rd., and Frances. In the chancel of Muckross abbey is a stone marked 'pray for Donald MacFineen and Elizabeth Stephenson, 1631, Oliver Stephenson caused this to be made'.

G. Stephenson of Spunkane, Co. Kerry is given.

Sterne
The name of a Cromwellian settler granted lands in 1667 in Co. Kerry.

Stewart
Walter Stewart was rural dean, 1787, Tralee, Co. Kerry.

Stiles, Styles

The town of Tralee was incorporated in 1612, and its charter named the following as among the first provost and burgesses; John Stiles.

A settler family, given on estates near Tralee, from the coming of the Elizabethan undertakers to the rebellion of 1641. Descent / homeland:

Of Kent, Essex, Suff., Sussex. John Stiles resided in Tralee in 1622.

Given as a family name settling in Co. Kerry, both prior to and subsequent to the 1641-42 rebellion.

Tom Styles of Caherulla, John of Ballyronan, Simon of Tonreigh, Jas. of Balleightra. John of Tralee in 1611. Simon Styles of Drishane in 1758.

Stoughton of Ballyhorgan
From The Irish Book of Arms. (IGF) 1988.

Stokes deStokke Stokys

The Stokes family is of Anglo-Norman descent, and they are found throughout Ireland and England. One of the principal settler families in Ireland in 1172, the family name is found written as de Stokes, de Stokke, and Stokys in the middle ages. Other spellings include that of Stock.

The Kerry branch of the family may descend from the Devonshire family of the name in England, from John Stokes of Dunmoylan, circa 1622. His father the first of the family to settle in Munster held property at Stokesfield, and was buried at Askeaton. It is given that the first of the name in Ireland was an army officer who settled in Limerick. Oliver Stokes is found married to Margaret Creagh of Ballybunion, leaving a son George, who married in 1771, Bridget Cooke of Skehenerin. His son Oliver d. 1844, leaving George Day Stokes of Mounthawk, b. 1800, whose third son, Maj. Gen. George Baret Stokes, was born in 1831.

Much genealogical information, including those who settled abroad is to be found in Kings History of County Kerry, including Robert Yallop Stokes b. 1836 who settled in New Zealand.

Askive, in the parish of Kilcrohane, was the home of Henry Stokes, C.E.; now home to S. Fraser, C.E.. Reverts to owner of Derriquin Estate upon lease expiration. -per the works of J. King.

There were 11 Stokes families to be found in Co. Kerry, including Edw. of Mounthawk, Mary of New Street, John of Gartdromagowna, Tom of Banemore, John and Pat of Listowel, John and Eliza of Tralee, Eliza of Mounthawk, and Letitia of of William St. in Kenmare.

Stone

Harold Stone of Ballinskelligs, Co. Kerry.

Stoughton

A settler family on estates near Tralee, from the coming of the Elizabethan undertakers to the rebellion of 1641. Descent / homeland:

Of Kent, Northants, Glouc.. Anthony Stoughton, the father-in-law of William Sandes, was not as has sometimes been stated, the first settler of his name in Kerry. His father, Anthony Stoughton, the elder, obtained lands in Clanmaurice in the reign of Elizabeth, or very early in the reign of her successor. This Anthony was the Clerk of the Star Chamber in Dublin Castle. His funeral certificate there presented gives the date of death as Sept. 5, 1626, leaving two sons, Anthony and Arthur, to whom he left the lands of Kilnaghtin and Rattoo. The Deering family is further given as connected to the Stoughtons of Rattoo.

Henry Stoughton was the son of the first settler of his name at Rattoo. The name of Nicholas Stoughton, Esq., of Stoughton, appears in the 'list of Adventurers for the land and sea service', for a sum of $600, one of the largest subscriptions on the list. A London merchant of the same name was also a subscriber on that list.

In 1831 lived, Thomas Stoughton of Ballyhorgan, JP.; Anthony, Clk,. of Ballynoe, J.P.; and Wm., of Ballyhorgan, JP.

Also given as a family name settling in Co. Kerry, both prior to and subsequent to the 1641-42 rebellion. Rose Stoughton sold her Iveragh lands to the tenants.

Strange

Alex of Kilbride in Lanark, 1757-1840, m. Lucinda Orpen of Killowen, having Lieut Alex. b.1793; Capt. Thomas m. Eliza Taylor having Capt. Alex, Col. Harry, C.B. m.Emily Ormsby having Editti; Thos. Geo. of 65th Regt.; Mary; Lucy m. Thos. Ducket. Alex and Lucinda had a third son, Col. Hy. Francis Strange, 1798-1879, m. Mary Bland leaving Major Alex, 1830-70; Major Gen. Thos. Bland, b. 1831, m.Elinor Taylor, having Major Harry Bland, Capt. Alex b. 1866, Alice, Kathleen, Hilda. Alex. and Lucinda also had Cadet Geo. 1803-24; Capt. Charles b.1805; Dorothea 1791-1818, m. Lieut. C.M. Christian; Barbara 1792-1878.

Street

A settler family, given on estates near Tralee, from the coming of the Elizabethan undertakers to the rebellion of 1641. Descent / homeland: Of Beds.

Stretton

Wm. Stretton of Knockroe, Mary of Francis St., John of Clahane, Mary of Feoramore, Tom of Capagh, and Jas. of Srugreana, all of Co. Kerry.

Stritch

Edm. Stritch of Booleenshare, Co. Kerry.

Stuart

Louisa Stuart of Lisardboola, Co. Kerry.

Studdert

Thos. of Strand street ; in 1821 Thos. of Banemore, and Hugh of Listowel, in Co. Kerry.

Stundon

Johanna and Catherine of Ballinglanna, Dan of Ballyheige, Tom of Mweevuck, John of Parknageragh, John of Dromkeen, John of Ballinascreena, Pat of Dromthacker, and Mary of Muing are all given in Co. Kerry.

Sugrue O'Sullivan

There were 160 Sugrue families given in Co. Kerry, making it one of the more numerous surnames in that county. It was also given that O'Siocfrada, was of clan Cashel, and of Knockgraffon in Tipperary. The Rev. Charles Sugrue was bishop of Kerry, 1797-1824, and was buried in Killarney chapel.

Dunloe Castle was bombarded by Ireton. D. Mahony resided there in 1864. It was one of O'Sullivan Mor's forts, but was built by Maurice Fitzgerald. It was usually in charge of the Sugrue O'Sullivans. Dunkerron was O'Sullivan Mor's chief seats.

O' Sullivan

O' Sullivan

In 1193 the Anglo Norman invaders drove the O'Sullivans of Clan Cashel out of their rath at Knockgraffon, and built a stone castle there; some of the O'Sullivans migrated, with the MacCarthys, into Desmond and settled on the lands of the tuath sen Eran in Corco Duibne, particularly in Iveragh and Beara, when the Eoghanacht Caisil return to Tipperary, the O'Sullivans to Knockgraffen, and Cashel, the clan Conaire and tuath sen Eran will will restore the temair Eran, on Catair Conroi, for iar Muman. After 1261 when they defeated the Geraldines at Callan in battle, they seized the Anglo Norman castles, and held the country until they were confiscated in 1653. The farmer owners, the tuath sen Eran, remained as farmers, ant the MacCarthys did likewise after 1653.

Of the 2,135 O'Sullivan families given in Co. Kerry, 1,150 were in the South, 480 in the East, 330 in the West, and 175 in the North of the county.

Cappanacoss Castle was built by Carew in 1215. It was the residence of the MacCrah, or senior, branch of the O'Sullivan clan, from 1261 - 1661.

O'Sullivan Bere

Ardea Castle, an O'Sullivan fortress where a Spanish ship landed supplies in 1602. The O'Sullivan Bere (Beare) tanist had this castle. (Tuosist parish)

O'Sullivan Mor

Lord Herbert reported in 1673 that the Irish of the area were all branches of a few families, and 'chiefly of the Sullivans and Carties'(MacCarthy's), but 'mostly of the Sullivann, they having been of late proprietors of most of the lands here.'.

The O'Sullivan lands were subject to O'Sullivan Mor of Dunkerron and Dunloe castles, whose over-lord was

O' Sullivan

MacCarthy Mor of Castle Lough, Pallis, and Ballycarberry. The nine branches of O'Sullivan were given to be:
MacGillicuddy;
O'Sullivan Cumurhagh or Mac Muirrihirtigg;
O'Sullivan of Glenbeigh;
O'Sullivan of Caneah and Glanacrane;
O'Sullivan of Culemagort;
O'Sullivan of Cappanacuss;
O'Sullivan of Capiganine;
O'Sullivan of Fermoyle and Ballycarna;
and O'Sullivan of Ballyvicillaneulan.

Dunloe Castle was bombarded by Ireton. D. Mahony resided there in 1864. It was one of O'Sullivan Mor's forts, but was built by Maurice Fitzgerald. It was usually in charge of the Sugrue O'Sullivans. Dunkerron was O'Sullivan Mor's chief seat.

Dunkerron Castle belonged to O'Sullivan Mor. It was built by Carew in 1215 according to the works of Jeremiah King. Smith says that the barony of Dunkerron took its name from this ancient castle, which was the chief seat of O'Sullivan Mor, which stood near the bottom of the Kenmare river. Camden said the castle was built by Carew as well, but Smith believes Camden to be wrong on the two following points. (1) Camden said the castle was possessed by Donald Mac Carty Mor, but it was always the principal residence of the O'Sullivan Mor, and (2) it was likely erected by the same house.

Smith also gives the ruins of the Cappanacushy castle in the parish of Templenoe as belonging to a younger branch of the O'Sullivan Mor family - said to have been built by MacCrath, brother to O'Sullivan Mor, from whom the MacCraths of this area took their name. That family was given as always succeeding to the lands of O'Sullivan Mor when their was no heir, and a branch of that family still resided near the castle when Smith wrote his *History of Kerry*. The Mac Crehans of Iveragh are also given as descended from the O'Sullivans.

It was also given in the above work that the O'Sullivans, given to have built the parish church of Templenoe, held a tradition of coming anciently from Knockgraffin in Co. Tipperary.

The Sullivans are also found buried at Templenoe in the tomb having the crest of the O'Sullivan arms.

Sunderland

Arthur Sunderland of Spunkane, Co. Kerry.

Supple, Suipeil, de Capella

Edw. and Jerh. Supple of Knockacree, Batt. of Ballyronan, David of Ballyheigue, Edward Kerry of Carhoona and Ripon, N.G. of Woodroyd, Witherby land Harrogate. Wm. Supple of Aghadoe is given in 1624.

The de Capella or Chappelles of Youghal, were called Sheapallh and Supple also. Philip De Capella in 1172 had lands at Ahadoe near Killeagh in Cork, and Wm. Supple had the old deed in 1636. Capel and de Capel are variations of the surname. Geo., son of Dan was born in 1806. Edw. h. p. 10th foot,, and Kerry of Ballyhennessy given in 1821. Daniel Supple, in 1828 held lands at Molahiffe in dispute between Ellen Fagen and Mce. De Courcey. Jerh. Supple of Tralee in 1829 m. Catherine, dau. of John Harman. Mary Supple, 1826-1911, dau. of Kerry Supple of Ballyhorgan, m. M.J. Collis, solicitor, of Tralee.

Prospect Hall, Jas. Supple lived at Prospect Hall in 1756. Wm. Denny was born here in 1744 and Thomas Denny in 1746.(Aghadoe Parish). It is a name found settling in Co. Kerry, subsequent to the 1641-42 rebellion too.

Sutton

Thos. of New street, Killarney, Co. Kerry.

Swanzy

The Rev. H. B. Swanzy of Omeath, Newry, 1910.

Swayne

Michael Swayne of New St., given in Co. Kerry.

Mac Sweeney, Sweaney

A numerous family of Co. Kerry, some 143 families are given there by J. King. There are several spellings of the name including Sweany, Sweeny, McSweaney, McSweaney etc..

Mac Sweeney of Tiernaboul

The MacSweeney family came from the North of Ireland in the 13th century, becoming auxiliaries of the MacCarthy's. Their lands were confiscated in 1698, and they became Rapparees. In the glen of Ahahunnig the bashee of Margaret Barry, the white maiden of Tiernaboul, is heard once a year, near the hanging tree and the stone on which is inscribed, 'McSweeney took me from my place, may he, like me, meet due disgrace.'.

Owen Mac Sweeny, constable of Desmond, died 1582. The Marquis Mac Suibne Mag Seana Glais, b. 1871, son of Valentine, son of Dr. Valentine, was of Kerry origins. (see the record of his services to the Papacy and to Ireland; he organized the Irish section of the Vatican Library.

Sweetman, Sweatman

Paul Sweetman of Ballygologue, Co. Kerry. Given also as the name of a Cromwellian settler granted lands in 1667 in Co. Kerry.

Swift

A settler family on estates near Tralee, from the coming of the Elizabethan undertakers to the rebellion of 1641. Descent / homeland: Of Hereford.

Swindel

Rd. Swindel of Tullaree; Catherine, dau. of Ellen and Edm. b.1784; Rev. Rd. F. of Castle Gregory given in 1821.

Switzer

Tobias Switzer and A. of Tralee, Co. Kerry.

Swords
Ml. Swords of Castle Gregory.

Synan, O'Sionain
John and Nich. Synan of Drera; Bessie of Clounmackon and John of Dromore, all given in Co. Kerry.

Synge
Edw. Synge as Prot. bishop of Ardfert, 1660-63. John M. Synge wrote a sketch of life in the Blasket Islands.

Syvrac
De Marquis Syvrac, m. a dau. of Lord Kenmare and her son d.1774; her dowry was £35,000.

Tackaberry
Jerh. Tackaberry of Charles street is given in Co. Kerry.

Taite
Robert Taite of Killerisk, Co. Kerry.

Talbot
There were 26 Talbot families given in Co. Kerry, including Thomas and James of Ballyhar, John of Dromdoohigbeg, Tom of Cloghermore, Tom of Coolroe, Ml. of Dromin, Chas. of Gortaree, Boyle of Killalee, Boyle of Aghacurreen, Tom of Culleenybeg, Henry of Kilmanihan, and John of Lackabet.

Tangney
There were 50 Tangney families given in Co. Kerry.

Tansley
Jos. Tansley of Fenit, and Bridget of Tawlaght, are given in Co. Kerry.

Tapper
Thomas Tapper of Gortgower, Co. Kerry.

Tarrant
Sam Tarrant of Glounawaddra, Rd. and Rd. of Knocknaboul, and Ellen of Pound road are given in Co. Kerry.

Taylor
There were 16 Taylor families given in Co. Kerry, including Stephen of Ardnamweely, Walter of Bridwell lane, John of Beenaspuck, John of Killorglin, Tom of Mac Enery's lane, Bessie and Jos. and John and Wm. and John of Lyranes, James of Gowlanes, Tom of Ardtully, Sam and Wm. and John of Gortmaloon, and Pat of Derrynafeana. The Rev. Isreal Taylor in 1611 was rector of Bally Mac Elligott, Molahiffe, Kilcummin.

Teahan
There were 79 Teahan families given in Co. Kerry.

Tedmarsh
Johanna Tedmarsh of Knockavahig and Mary of Addergown, are given in Co. Kerry.

Teer
William Teer of Tooreenascarty, Co. Kerry.

Thistall
Isabella Thistall of Tralee, Co. Kerry.

Thomas
There were 10 Thomas families given in Co. Kerry including the Rev. John of Knoppogue, Wm. of Cloghane, Pat and Ml. and Rd. of Dingle, John of Acres, Wm. of Coumlanders, Pat of Droum, Geo. of Waterville, Herbert of Spunkane. Edwin Thomas was rector of Kilflynn in 1787.

Thompson

There were 12 Thompson families given in Co. Kerry, including Tom of Tubbermuing, John of Killarney road, John of New street, Tom of Knockbrack, John of Rockfield, Tom of Ballyrameen, Jas. of Denny St., Jas. of Abbey street, Robt of Franis Street, Wm. of Garryrooth, and Wm. and Geo. of Farranreagh.

In 1821-31 lived Alex of Molahiffe, Wm. of Rockfield, Wm. of Parknagera, Peter and David and Wm. of Tralee, and Jas. of Aunascaul. Peter, treasurer of Tralee, built Belmont, Ballyard, and Spring lodges.

Thomson

Robert Thomson was parish clerk of Killarney in 1683; Blennerhasset of Tralee in 1831. M. P. Thomson m. a dau. of Geo. Fitz Gerald of Meenascarty, having Nora who m. E. Helliwell of Vancouver.

Thornhill

John Thornhill of New St., and Francis of Bishop's lane are given in Co. Kerry.

Thornton

There were 13 Thornton families given in Co. Kerry including, Kate of Rathbeg, Francis of Knockburrane, Tom of Knockreagh, Myles and Jas. of Kilbaha, John of Croughtoosane, Tom of Ballinorig, Dan of Clashmealcon, Pat of Tullaghna, Francis of Ballinclogher, Jas. of Ballincrossig, Jas. of Abbey street, and Francis of Derry. Thos. of Tralee d.1829. Rd. opened the Denny Arms hotel in Tralee, Co. Kerry.

Thurston, Thryston

A settler family on estates near Tralee, from the coming of the Elizabethan undertakers to the rebellion of 1641. Descent / homeland: Of Suff., Kent.

Thwantes (sp? Thwartes)

Rd. of Bunnow given in 1821.

Tidings

Mce. of Ballynoneen, Ml. of Glanawilliam, John of Carrigane, and Ml. of Leitrim, all given in Co. Kerry.

O' Tiegrnach

Cornelius O'Tiegrnach (O'Tiegerneach etc..) was bishop of Ardfert in 1372.

Tierney

Stephen Tierney of Dromalivaun and Ml. of Ballylongford are given in Co. Kerry. It is also given anciently that O'Tigearnaig was of Carra.

Timmins

James Timmins of Brackhill, Co. Kerry.

Timony

Sarah Timony of Chute's lane, Co. Kerry.

Tisdall

Was rector of Kenmare in 1808, m. Mary Jameson, having Ml. of Clifton in 1863, Fitz Gerald, George, Mary, and Jane; he was shot in 1809.

Tobin, Tobyn

Ml. and John Tobin of Lackbroder, Dan of Brosna, Rd. of Bally Mac Jordan, Mary of Kllconly, James of Beale hill and John of Brogue's lane are all given in Co. Kerry.

Tong

James Tong of Spunkane, Co. Kerry.

Tooher

John Tooher of Dromore, Co. Kerry.

Topham

Robert Topham of Reen, Co. Kerry.

Topping

Frederick Topping of Ballinskelligs, Co. Kerry.

Tough

James Tough of Ballymullen, Kerry.

Towell
A settler family on estates near Tralee, from the coming of the Elizabethan undertakers to the rebellion of 1641. Descent / homeland: Of Devon.

Townes
John Townes of Feaghmaun, Co. Kerry.

Townsend
R. Townsend, rector of Nohoval Daly in 1758; R. O. of Ardtully in 1831; Eliza. of Kilshenane and Irramore 1900.

Tracey
Dan Tracey of Bishops court, John of Poulnahaha, Mce. of Kiltean, Hanora of Finuge, Ml. of Ballymacquin, these are all given in Co. Kerry.

Tranfield
Fred Tranfield of Waterville and Edw. of Spunkane, Co. Kerry are given.

Trant Trowent Treawant
The Trants are of Danish extraction and are found in the barony of Cocaguiney on Ortelius' Map, and it is almost certain that they descend from followers of Strongbow who settled at Dingle soon after the Norman invasion.

Caheratrant was given as Trant's Castle. A Phillip Trant family is found on documents dating back to the year 1272 in Ireland. In 1580 Garrett Trant was a merchant of the 'best reckoning' in Dingle. Richard Trant was the first Sovereign under the Dingle charter in 1585. Several are found under the forfeiting proprietors of Corkaguiney and under the transplanters certificates. (From the latter 17th century onwards many are found in the West Indies). Five of the family name are found in the Spanish army from 1718-77.

Dominick Trant, Esq., published a book in 1787 concerning the tithes war in Munster. He was a B.L., and M.P., and ancestor of the Trants of Dovea.

In 1846 we find Ellen Trant of John Street, and Patrick and Bridget Trant of Main Street in Dingle, and in 1910 in Corkaguiney we find Maurice of Gowlane and Catherine of Foheraghmore.

Trant Arms
The Trant of Dovea arms are given as; Per pale az and gu., two swords in saltire, hilts in base ppr., between three roses, one in chief and two in fesse arg. Crest: A demi eagle displayed ppr. Motto: Aquila non capit muscas.

Trant of Queen's County., Bart,. attainted 1690. Patrick Trant, son of a London merchant was created a Bart. of Ireland, 1686, forfeited for his adhesion to James II. Arms: crest a demi eagle or., holding in the beak a rose or slipped vert.

Trant of Rathmile, Co. Roscommon -

Trant Trowent Treawant

confirmed 1816 to Henry Trant, Esq., of Rathmile, and descendants of his grfather Dominick Trant, Esq.,. Arms: crest out of a ducal coronet or. an eagle rising ppr., holding in the beak a sprig of laurel vert. Motto: Non Capit Muscas.

Of the various branches of this family we find Trant of Fenit; the line of Sir Patrick Trant who went with James II to France and lost over 23,000 acres in Kerry; William Trant of Cork; Henry Trant of Dingle; Richard Trant of Dingle (Will 1748); John Trant of Dovea; Dominick Fitzwilliam Trant and Sir Nicholas Trant of Ballintlea, Ventry, Co. Cork and later descendants of Dingle; and the Trant family of North Kerry who claim descent from the Dingle family.

Of the North Kerry family, two brothers left Dingle obtaining lands on both sides of the River Feale, from Ennismore to Listowel on one side and from Finuge to the Bridge Listowel on the other side. One brother lived at Ennismore, the other at Finuge, and from them spring the present North Kerry Trants.

Also given are the Trant families of Lisanerla and of Listowel under separate pedigrees in J. Kings work.

Extensive coverage of the Trant Family is given in the Kerry Archeaological Magazine, including the April and October 1914 issues. Here the family is covered in detail, including Trant of Barbadoes, the pedigree downwards of Nicholas Trant b.1768, and a review of other accounts of the family by D'Alton, etc.., Trants of Cork, Trants of Clare, and various wills and records.

Some 21 families were given in Co. Kerry. Spellings of the name given in older works include Trant, Trowent, Treawant, Trante, and Traunte, and as Teraunt in a journal written in 1580.

Some of the family emigrated to the West Indies and settled in Antigua and Montserratt, where many of the name lived during the 18th century and part of the 19th century, although reported not found there by the start of the 20th century. Several interesting photographs of noted Trant family members are found in the Kerry Archaeological Magazine, March 1914.

Trassy

A settler family on estates near Tralee, from the coming of the Elizabethan undertakers to the rebellion of 1641. Descent / homeland: Of Devon.

Trawdsome

A settler family on estates near Tralee, from the coming of the Elizabethan undertakers to the rebellion of 1641. Descent / homeland: Of Cornw.

Treddle

A settler family on estates near Tralee, from the coming of the Elizabethan undertakers to the rebellion of 1641. Descent / homeland: Of Cornw.

Trench

G. Trench of of Abbeylands, Ardfert, given in Co. Kerry.

Tretton

John Tretton of Cloghaneanode and Eug. of Cloghanesheskeen, Co. Kerry.

Trimlet

Alfred Trimlet of Kilfarnogue, Kerry.

Tristam

A settler family, given on estates near Tralee, from the coming of the Elizabethan undertakers to the rebellion of 1641.

Lawrence Tristam of Traly, gaoler, was hanged, at the siege in 1641.

Trodden

John Trodden of Ballymullen, Co. Kerry.

Truman
A settler family, given on estates near Tralee, from the coming of the Elizabethan undertakers to the rebellion of 1641. Descent / homeland: Of Notts.

Tubriddy
John Tubriddy of Bridge Street, given in Co. Kerry.

Tucker
Rd. Tucker of Dromatoor, Co. Kerry.

Tuff
Samuel Winters, Provost of T.C.D., visited the college estates in Kerry in 1655, and in Tralee baptized Eliz. Sullivan, Mary Nicolls, Ed. Smith, and Mary Tuff.

Tuite
Rd. Tuite of Kilnabrack, Co. Kerry.

Tuohill
Catherine Tuohill, dau. of Jas. of Killarney, m. 1829 J.D. Martin; Rev. James d.1845, was P.P. of Brosna, Carran Tuohill, 3,414 ft. peak of Erin.

Tuohy
There were 17 families of the Tuohy name given in Co. Kerry, including John and Mary and John of Cloghane, Mary of Brogue lane, Ml. and John of Tulligbeg, John of Brogue lane, Edw. and Edw. of Gortaglassa, John of Kilpatrick, Mary of William St., Ml. and Pat and John of Meallis, and Ml. and John and Dan of Gortloughra.

Tuomey
There were 60 Tuomey families given in Co. Kerry.

Turner
A settler family on estates near Tralee, from the coming of the Elizabethan undertakers to the rebellion of 1641.

John Turner, yeoman, was killed during the siege of Tralee in 1641.

John Turner of Listanavally, James of Clounalour, V.J. of Denny St., Thomas was rector of Killarney in 1686. John, son of John of Tralee, was born in 1830.

Twiss of Killeentierna
The first family of the name in Ireland in the reign of Charles I, was Richard Twiss (agent to Earl Herbert, of Powis), who lived in Castleisland castle. His son was Francis, whose son was Martin, whose son was Robert, d.1771, whose son was George of Cordal, who m. Honoria Meredith in 1773. His son, Robert, b.1777, had a son George of Birdhill, Tipperary, heir to Arthur Ormsby of that place. His brother Hastings succeeded in 1878 and left Robert of Birdhill, Tipperary, b.1856.

Twohig
Dan Twohig of Farranreagh, Co. Kerry.

Tyler
John Tyler of Bridge Street, Tralee, Co. Kerry.

Tyndall
Mary Tyndall of Blennerville, Kerry.

Tyter
Norah Tyter of Dromcunnig and Anne of Farna, are given in Co. Kerry.

Ufford
The Castle of the Island of Kerry was built in 1226 by Geoffrey de Marisco, and taken by Sir Ralph Ufford in 1345 from the Geraldines.

Underwood
Rd. Underwood was M.P. for Tralee in 1775.

Usher
Rd. Usher of Ardoughter, Co. Kerry.

Vale

Jas. of Oakview tce., John of Abbey street, and Mary of Boherbee, are all of Co. Kerry.

Valle

John de Valle was bishop of Ardfert in 1348. Philip was archdeacon 1363.

Vauclier Voakley Vauckler

A settler family on estates near Tralee, from the coming of the Elizabethan undertakers to the rebellion of 1641.

Edmund Voakley, gentleman, left Tralee Castle during the 1641 siege, and lived at Ballycarthy. This Vauclier was brother-in-law to O'Sullivan Mor. He led a party to harass O'Sullivan Mor at Dunkerron in 1641, but 40 were killed, and two others escaped with him. He saved his life by leaping into the sea, having 14 wounds, and swimming a mile to his ship. He was later taken prisoner at Adare, but exchanged for an officer in the Irish Army. The town of Tralee was incorporated in 1612, and its charter named Edward Vaucleere, among the the first provost and burgesses.

Also given as the name of a family settling in Co. Kerry, subsequent to the 1641-42 rebellion.

Mrs. Isabella Vauckler lived in Tralee in 1665.

Variant spellings of the name given include Vauclier, Voakley, Vauckler and Vaucleere.

Vaughan

John Vaughan of Nelson street, given in Co. Kerry.

Vesey

John Vesey was Prot. Bishop of Ardfert, 1672.

Vicars

Sir Arthur Edward Vicars, C.V.C., cr. 1896, was Ulster King of Arms from 1893; b.1864, son of Col. W.H. Vicars of 61st Regt. and of Jane, dau. of R. Gun Cuninghame, and widow of P. K. Mahoney of Kilmorna; published the index of prerogative Wills of Ireland 1536-1810.

Vickery

Tom Vickery of Kenmare, Co. Kerry.

Vincent

Arthur Vincent of Muckross, son of Col. Vincent of Limerick, married the daughter of a Californian millionaire, who bought Muckross for her dowry, from Lord Ardilaun.

Vynes, Vine

A settler family on estates near Tralee, from the coming of the Elizabethan undertakers to the rebellion of 1641. Descent / homeland: Of Glouc., Wilts.

Michael Vines, shoemaker and British Protestant of Tralee made a deposition in 1643, about the siege of the castle in 1641. Elizabeth Vine, widow, was killed 1641. S. Vine is given in Tralee in 1908. Separately we find Sarah Vines of Princes Quay.

Wade, Mac Uaid

Pat Wade of Church St., Julia of Gortalicka, Dan of Lissyclerig, Tom of Gortnadullah, and Wm. of Ardfert, are all given in Co. Kerry.

Walker

John Walker of Castleview, John of Caherscullibeen, Charlotte of Meanus, George of Spunkane, M.W. of Faha, Tom of Gurranearagh, are all given in Co. Kerry. Lieut. John of 1641 army m. Lucy Blennerhassett of Ballyseedy.

Wall

James Wall of Crotta, Pierse of Kilmeany, John of Francis St., and John of Mary street are given in Co. Kerry.

Wallace

There were 16 Wallace families given in Co. Kerry, including Small Wallace of Dromatoor, John of Tarmons, Mce. and Johanna of Commons, Rd. and John of Ballyline, Wm. of Rusheen, Pat of Cloghane, Pat of Ballynoneen, John of Ballymore, Tom of Garfinny, Ml. and Pat of Acres, Wm. of Pembroke St., Wm. of the Mall, and Rd. of the Wood.

Waller

James Waller, M.P. for Tralee in 1692, son of the famous Cromwellian, had grants of forfeited lands in Kerry.

Walpole

Jonathan Walpole of Ballyea, Co. Kerry.

Gallerus Castle

Walsh

There were 330 families of the surname of Walsh in Co. Kerry, making it one of the most numerous families in the county. This is not surprising as Walsh is one of the most numerous names in the country as a whole. The Teutons call their bordering nations Walsche or foreigners or Welshmen; e.g. Wales, Wealande, Armorica now Brittany.

In 1176 David Walsh, nephew of Raymond le Gros, was at the siege of Limerick. (See Giraldus 2, v.8, p.263). The Walsh family settled in Iverk in Kilkenny and in Kerry with the FitzMaurice and Fitz Gerald invaders and were called Brannagh or Welshmen.

Chris Walsh was a lessor in Kerry in 1603 and died in 1620, leaving Nicholas; they held the lands of Castle Mac Ellistrum, Ballymacrobert and the burgage of Rory O'Nihilly in Tralee in 1641. In 1686 Thomas Fitzgerald of Ballymullen was called the MacRobert of Trughe'nackmy. Nicholas Walsh forfeited the Boulteens or east of Strand street, Gortinacashlane, etc..in 1656, which lands were given to Col. Sankey and Capt. Bateman; Walsh was to be restored his lands in 1670 by the King, but the Cromwellian grantees retained them. Rev. Ml. Walsh P.P. of Sneem, was the 'Father O'Flynn' of the song by Graves of Parknasilla.

Warburton

Chas. Warburton, Prot. Bishop of Ardfert, 1806-20, in Co. Kerry.

Ward

Peter Ward of Knockachur, John of Knockbrack and John of Cloghane are all given in Co. Kerry.

Wardell

John of old Abbey, Shanagolden, 1915, had collections of local family histories.

Warden
Charles Warden of Derryquinn, Co. Kerry. Col. Wm. Warden was given as sheriff in 1913.

Derriquin Castle, for many generations the seat of the Bland family; became the property of Colonel Warden.

Ware
A settler family, given on estates near Tralee, from the coming of the Elizabethan undertakers to the rebellion of 1641. Descent / homeland:

Of Essex, Suff., Devon.

John Ware of Kileton, Tom Ware of Dooncaha, Co. Kerry. James in 1613 was granted Geraldine lands and advowsons in Killury, Ballyheige, Kilnaughtin, Bally Mac Elligott and Oughvaille.

Warham
A settler family, given on estates near Tralee, from the coming of the Elizabethan undertakers to the rebellion of 1641.

Robert Warham of Tralee was killed at Ballinskelligs in 1641.

Warner
Robert Warner of Main street, Wm. of Bridge Street.

Warren
A settler family, given on estates near Tralee, from the coming of the Elizabethan undertakers to the rebellion of 1641. Descent / homeland:

Of Essex, Herts, Norf., Camb, Devon, Cornw.

There were 9 families given in Co. Kerry, including Pat and Pat of Arnaghilymore, Johanna of Mausrower, Ml. of Annaghbeg, Ml. of Dodd's lane, Tim of Knocknagoshel, John of Slaghts, John of Gortamullen, Tom of William St.: Rev. J. Warren of Caherciveen, until it was joined to Valencia. Rev. Joshua was rector of Prior in 1683. J. King also gives that O'Murnain may have been an old Irish surname changed into Warren.

Warwick
Walter Warwick of Spunkane, Co. Kerry.

Waterson
Ralph Waterson of Ballinskelligs, Co. Kerry.

Watkins
A settler family, given on estates near Tralee, from the coming of the Elizabethan undertakers to the rebellion of 1641. Descent / homeland:

Of Glouc. Wales. Related to the Fleetwoods.

Watson
Gerald Watson of Clahane, Jane of Clonbeg, Wm. and Gerald of Church St., and George of Ballinskelligs are all given in Co. Kerry.

Watters
Countess Watters, nee Rice, of Paris in 1789, had a dau. with her at Maisonfort 1790, Co. Kerry.

James Waters of Gearhameen, Co. Kerry, is given.

Watts
A settler family, given on estates near Tralee, from the coming of the Elizabethan undertakers to the rebellion of 1641. Descent / homeland:

The Watts are given to be connected with the Lynnes of Essex. Walter Watts lived in Tralee in 1622.

Weatherup
Richard Weatherup of Tralee, Kerry.

Webb
Wm. Webb of Tooreennablaha, Rd. of Ardrinane; Ezekial in 1696 was Archdeacon of Aghadoe.

Weekes Weeks
The name of a family settling in Co. Kerry, after the 1641-42 rebellion. Originally of Devon, Kent, Glouc. and noted of Cromwellian origins. John Weekes is given in Tralee in 1831. One John Weekes, coroner of Tralee, 1759 - 1828, had a son Wm. b.1782. Nat of Tralee had a dau. Eliz. b.1789.

Weir
John and John of Tuhig, Wm. of Cloonametig, John of Mountcoal, Anne of Ballyrehan, George of Dean's lane, Jas. of Tawlaght, and John of Waterville are all given in Co. Kerry.

Weldon
William Weldon of Ballymullen, Co. Kerry.

Welland
William Welland, of Ballyheigue, Co. Kerry.

Wellings
Elizabeth Wellings, of Inch, Co. Kerry.

Welstead
Morris and Edmond Fitz Gerald, the sons of Edmund Fitz John, forfeited Behinagh, Glandyne and other lands in 1641, which were divided between John Carrick, a Cromwellian Commissioner, for surveying forfeited estates, and Capt. Welstead, a Cromwellian officer, ancestor of Thomas Welstead of Ballywalter, Co. Cork. Capt. Welstead sold his grants in Kerry to Anthony Shortcliffe, also a Cromwellian officer.

Welton
David Welton of Langford St., is given in Co. Kerry.

West
Given in Co. Kerry were the following West households, those of: Arthur of Flemby, Wm. of Ahane, Wm. of Anglont, Tom of Carhoonakilla, James of Callinafercy, Tom of Tinnahally, Anne of Banshagh, Edw. of Waterville, and Rd. of Aghatubrid. Sir Raymond West, 1832-1912, son of Fredk West and Frances Raymond, in Indian Civil Service 1856-92, wrote the Bombay code and Hindu Law at Cambridge University; he m. Clementine dau. of Wm. M. Chute and Sara Nash.

Westbrook
Edward Westbrook of Ballinskelligs, Co. Kerry.

Westcombe
A settler family, given on estates near Tralee, from the coming of the Elizabethan undertakers to the rebellion of 1641.

Edward Westcombe, shoemaker, was shot during the siege of Tralee in 1641.

Wharton
Rd. Wharton of Ballyhar, Wm. of Poulnamuck, Tom of Dromin, Wm. of Tullahinnell, Jos. of Clooncarrig, James of Ballyseedy, Robt. of Valencia road, Jos. and Robert of Aghatubrid, are all given in Co. Kerry. In 1832 Joseph of Caher m. Eliz. Huggard.

Whelan
There were 20 Whelan families given in Co. Kerry, including Jerh. of Gortagurrane, Ml. of Montanagay, Ml. of Banemore, Ml. and Tom of Kilmore, Jas. of Commons, Ellen of Glouria, Martin of Finuge, Hanoria of Ballyrehan, Catherine of Glenerdallive, John of Sleveen, Mce. of Ballinageragh, John of Garrynagore, John of Lacca, John of Boherbee, Mce. and Tom and Mce. of Manor, Kate of Spring's lane, and Mary of Canal new road.

Whiston
Patrick Whiston of Boherbee, Co. Kerry.

White
There were 46 White families given in Co. Kerry. In 1641 Peter White was provost of Tralee; and in 1683, John was parish of Castleisland. One Lt. Col. White is noted in 1913.

A settler family, given on estates near Tralee, from the coming of the Elizabethan undertakers to the rebellion of 1641. Descent / homeland:

P. and W. White, are found in Tralee in 1908.

South Hill (1846), in Killarney parish, was the residence of the White Leahy family.

Whitson
Samuel Whitson of Lisardboola, Co. Kerry.

Whittaker
Ben of Ballygarron, and Ben of Rock Street, are given in Co. Kerry.

Wholly
John Wholly of Driminamore, Co. Kerry.

Wilde
John Wilde of Glandine, and Hy. of Derrymore, Co. Kerry are given.

Wilkie
Peter Wilkie of Duckett's lane is given in Co. Kerry.

Williams
Given as the name of a family settling in Co. Kerry, subsequent to the 1641-42 rebellion. Of Cornw., Kent, Suff., Wales. In 1831 lived John G. Williams of Blennerville; John of Milltown; Ephraim of Milltown; & John, jr. of Bunnow.

In 1908 we find R., R., J., and J. Williams, all of Tralee. There were some 30 Williams families given in Kerry.

Willis
John Willis of Killarney; Rd. 1853-1905, son of Jos., and Jane Mac Carthy, painter, was master of Manchester and Dublin Art Schools, m. Miss Twiss of Steelroe, having a son Oscar.

Willmore
Louisa Willmore, 1744-1828, was Prot. Teacher in Killarney for 50 years.

Willoe
Chris 1674; Rd. of Bandon 1710; Chris of Tralee 1797; his wife d.1819; Capt. Sam, 8th foot, 1801; Chris of Prospect Hall in 1821, all of Co. Kerry.

Willove
Given as the name of a family settling in Co. Kerry, subsequent to the 1641-42 rebellion. Noted as a Cromwellian family.

Wilmot

Ardfert Castle, built in 1312 by Nicholas Fitz-Maurice was taken in 1600 by Sir Charles Wilmot. It was rebuilt in 1637 by Patrick, Lord Kerry. It was demolished in 1641 by the Irish Army. (Ardfert Parish)

The Knight of Kerry Castle in Dingle parish, was given up to to Sir Charles Wilmot around 1600, who for some time made it his headquarters.

Listowel Castle, built by Carew in 1215, was captured in 1600 by Sir Charles Wilmot who put the entire garrison to the sword. This Fitz Maurice castle and manor was purchased from the Earls of Kerry by the father of the first Earl of Listowel.

Ratoo Castle was taken in 1600 by Sir Charles Wilmot. In 1756 it was the seat of Townshend Gun.

Also given in Co. Kerry were Dan of Glashananoon, Catherine of Inchymagilleragh, Edw. and Mce. of Listowel. Sir Chas Wilmott in 1614 was granted confiscated lands in Kerry at Ardea castle.

Wilson

Rev. Jas. Wilson of Poulnamuck, Edw. of Listowel, Edwin and Mary of Ballygarron, Pat of Spunkane, Chas. of Waterville, Thos. of Killarney, Rev. Mce. of Macville in Ontario. In 1679 Rev. S. was rector of Castleisland; Rev. R. was vicar of Killarney in 1683; Rev. Nathanial was Prot. Bishop of Ardfert in 1691-95. Wm. Wilson, attorney, had Edw. b.1784, Jane b.1789 m. Barry Gun of Ploverhill.

Wimpris

Archibald Wimpris of Moyderwell, Co. Kerry.

Windele Windle

John Windele, born in Cork in 1801, belonged to a Kerry family that styled the name as Windle, and originally came from England.

There are 10 families given in Kerry including John of Tarbert, Tom of Tieraclea, Nic. and Hy. and Pat and John and Nic. of Aughrim, Pat of Glenalappa, and Tom of Leitrim. J.F. Windle and T.M. are given as solicitors; J.F. Windle as an engineer of Tarbert, Co. Kerry.

Winters

Samuel Winters, Provost of T.C.D., visited the college estates in Kerry in 1655, and in Tralee baptized Eliz. Sullivan, Mary Nicolls, Ed. Smith, and Mary Tuff.

Wise

Nellie Wise of New St., is given in Co. Kerry.

Witherall

Lindsay Witherall of Beaufort, Co. Kerry, is given in 1821.

Woodhouse

Kate Woodhouse of Shelbourne Street given in Co. Kerry. Geo. and Edw. of Dingle are given in Co. Kerry in 1821.

Woods

Wm. Woods of Ballinvarrig, and Wm. of Tubbermuing, and Jas. of Spunkane are given in Co. Kerry.

Worthington

James Worthington of Mac Enery's lane, given in Co. Kerry.

Woulfe

There were 11 Woulfe families given in Co. Kerry, including Mce. of Knockeen, John of Kilmaniheen, Bridget of Brosna, Jas. of Ballyoneen, Rd. of Dromclough, Johanna of Finuge, Mce. of Irremore, Pat of Gortdromagownagh, Tom of Beale west and James of Beale hill.

Wreil
Charles Wreil of Tarbert Island, given in Co. Kerry.

Wren, O'Rinn
The name of a family settling in Co. Kerry, subsequent to the 1641-42 rebellion, noted as a Cromwellian family with Sussex origins. Charles Wren was the son of a Cromwellian officer, who m. the dau. of Thomas Blennerhassett.

Separately given was Charles Wren, the son of Capt. Thomas Wren, the Cromwellian officer in Col. Ingoldsby's regiment. He had a son, John, styled 'of Littur', who was living in 1733.

John Wren was sheriff in 1732. He m. Honora, dau. of Thos. Ponsonby of Croto. In 1831 lived Geo. and William Wren of Littur. M. Wren is found in Tralee in 1908. There were 40 Wren families given in Co. Kerry.

Wright
Sarah Wright of Clooncarrig, and Wm. of Mac Cowen's lane, all in Co. Kerry.

Wrixon
James Wrixon of High street, given in Co. Kerry.

Wyk
Robt. de Wyk was sheriff for Kerry in 1290.

Wyllie
Wm. Wyllie of Spunkane, Co. Kerry.

Wynne, Winn
Jas. of Castletown, John of Ayle, Robin and John of Ballyhorgan, Jas. of Derryabeg, Edw. was R.M. of Tralee and d.1923 in Cornwall. Rev. Geo. was rector of Killarney; b.1838; he left for Limerick rectory in 1904. Sir Geo. Wynne, M. Miss Blennerhassett of Balliseeda in 1783. Rowland Winn, and Lord Headley, his nephew, owned the Glanbehy estate and castle.

Yeeden
The name of a Cromwellian settler granted lands in 1667 in Co. Kerry.

Yeilding
Given as the name of a family settling in Co. Kerry, subsequent to the 1641-42 rebellion. The Yeilding family was represented by Col. W. R. Yielding, C.B., DSO, CIE, and his sister Mary Stokes Eagar of Bedford, Galey. In 1597 Rowland Bateman leased land between Loghercannon and Strand Street to James Yielding, where there was a fine dwelling house erected, known as 'Volunteer Hall'.

In 1831 lived J. Royse Yielding of Tralee, and Augustus Richd. Yielding of Spa, Co. Kerry. Lohercannon (1846), Tralee parish, was the Yielding home since 1697, leased from Bateman of Oak Park.

Rd. of Cloghers d.1804, and Theo. of Cahireina in 1805; J.R. and Augustus lived at Tralee in 1831.

Young
John Young of Ballinorig, Pat of Knockbrack, Wm. of Tieraclea, John of Reen, Tom of Knockeens, Andrew Young was M.P. for Ardert borough from 1692 - 1709. Andrew Young is also given as a schoolmaster in Tralee in 1738. Mrs. Young made gifts to Ballybunion church funds. Young's Island is found in Dunquin parish.

Zouche
John Zouche, captain of English army in Kerry; in 1580 at Smerwick massacre; had 400 footmen and 50 horse, but most of them died of fever at Dingle; raided Aghadoe in 1581; hanged the Baron of Lixnaw's pledge at Ardfert in 1582; returned to England and was killed there in a duel.

Appendix

√ Bibliography & Suggested Reading

√ Kerry Families Found In *The Master Book of Irish Surnames*

√ 1876 Landowners List Extract

√ Some Castles illustrated

√ Co. Kerry Place names from the *Master Book of Irish Placenames.*

√ Household lists of some families of Co. Kerry, believed taken from the 1901 Irish census. (or the works of J. King).

Bibliography
Suggested Titles from The IGF Library

√ Ancient and Present State of the Co. of Kerry. Smith, Charles. 1756.

√ MacCarthy People and Places. A. St. Leger. Whitegate, Co. Clare.

√ O'Connell Family Tracts. O'Connell. 1946 - 1950.

√ Irish Family Names. O'Donovan, Peadar. 1991 Skibbereen, Co. Cork.

√ A guide to Tracing your Kerry Ancestors. O'Connor, M. H. 1990.

√ 49er Irish. One Irish Family in the California Mines. McGuire.

√ Headley Papers of Co. Kerry Estate.

√ The Brosnans of Glounlea, Co. Kerry. Brosnan, Donald P. 1988.

√ Co. Kerry Past and Present. a handbook to the local and family history of the county. King, Jeremiah. 1931 Dublin

√ Kings History of County Kerry. part III. King, J., 1910 Tralee, Ireland

√ Kings History of County Kerry. part II.. King, J., 1909 Liverpool, Eng.

√ Kings History of County Kerry. part IV., King, J., 1910 Tralee.

√ The Last Colonel of the Irish Brigade- Count O'Connell and Irish Life at Home and Abroad 1745-1833. O'Connell, Mrs., 1892 London.

√ (Kerry) 'Twixt Skellig and Scattery. Book 1., 1932 Tralee.

√ A Popular History of East Kerry., Donovan, T. M., 1931 Dublin.

√ (Fitzgerald) Earls of Kildare, and their ancestors; from 1057 to 1773

√ Kings History of County Kerry., King, J., 1909 Liverpool, Eng.

√ Killarney, Land and Lake. O Catail, Domnall., 1931 Tralee.

√ Legends of Killarney., Croker, Crofton.

√ Discovering Kerry., Barrington, T.J., 1986.

√ Kerry Magazine. (#4. 1992-3...) Kerry Arch. & Hist., 1992. Ireland.

√ The History of Ireland. (O'Mahoney, translator.)., Geoffrey Keating., (1856) 1980 reprint. Kansas City, MO., U.S.A., IGF.

√ Book of Irish Families, great & small., M. O'Laughlin. 1992. K. C. MO., U.S.A., IGF.

√ Kerry Archaeological Magazine., 1912 - . various dates. Ireland.

√ Historical Essays on the Kingdom of Munster., MacCarthy Mor., 1994. Kansas City, MO., U.S.A., IGF.

√ The Annals of Innisfallen. Dublin.

√ The Kenmare Manuscripts. Dublin.

√ Corca Dhiubhne, its People and their Buildings. 1977. Ballyferriter. (i.e. the O'Sheas and O'Falveys were of this ancient tribe.)

√ The O'Donoghue Book. IGF. 1980.

√ Antiquities of the County of Kerry. J. O'Donovan. Royal Carbery Books. 1983. Cork.

√ O'Kiefe, Coshe Mang, Slieve Lougher and Upper Blackwater in Ireland, multiple vols., Dr. A. E. Casey. Birmingham.

√ The Fitzmaurices, Lords of Kerry and Barons of Lixnaw. Snamha. Lixnaw.

√ Historical Essays on the Kingdom of Munster. MacCarthy Mor. 1994. Kansas City, MO.

√ *OLochlainns Journal of Irish Families*. 1985 to present. monthly. various issues. Box 7575, Kansas City, Mo. 64116. U.S.A.

√ see also, sources, page xxii, xxiv, of this book.

Family Names in Coumty Kerry, Ireland
As Found in the Master Book of Irish Surnames (O'Laughlin. IGF. 1993)

McAdams	McBryen	Connor	Dally	O'Duane	Fitzharris
Allman	OBryen	OConnor	Daly	Duhig	Fitzherbert
Almes	Buckley	Conway	O'Daly	ODulinge	Fitzmaurice
Amery	Burns	Cony	McDaniel	O'Dunady	Fitzmorrice
MacAndrew	Cahalane	Conyers	Mc Daniell	O'Dunnady	Fitzmorris
Archer	Cahane	Corcoran	McDauid	Dwane	Fitzmorrish
Arnalds	OCahane	Corkery	McDavitt	Dwyer	Fitzwalter
Ashe	Cahassy	McCormack	O'Day, O'dea	Eager	Fizzell
Ashton	OCahesey	Corridon	ODayly	Edmond	Flaherty
Bambury	Cahill	Corrodan	O'Dea	McEdmond	Floyd
Bambury	Callaghan	(o)Counihan	Deady	McEligod	OFlyne
Barrett	Cantillon	(o)Cournane	Deatick	MacElligott	O'Foley
Bastable	Carey	Courtney	Dennehy	McEllygott	Foley
Bateman	Carmody	Craddock	Denny	Ellyott	OFowlue
Beamish	Carrick	McCreagh	Denny	Enright	Fuller
OBegley	O'Carroll	O'Creagh	McDermod	O'Fallon	Galleghor
Behan	Carther	Crean	Devane	Faluey	Gallivan
Bland	McCarthy	Cremin	O'Devoy	Faluy	Gallway
Blennerhasett	MacCarthy	Cremin	Diggin	Falvey	Galvin
Bourke	Casey	McCrohan	Dillane	O'Falvey	O'Galvin
Bowler	O'Casey	Cromwell	ODillane	Farley	OGarvan
Breen	Chambers	OCroneene	Dinnahane	Fenton	MacGarvey
OBreene	Chappell	Cronin	O'Donaghoe	Fenton	Garvey
Brenagh	Church	OCronin	McDonnogh	McFergus	Geaney
McBrenan	Chute	Crosby	McDonogh	Feris	Gentleman
O'Brenan	Clifford	Crosby, Crost	Donoghue	Ferriter	Gerrald
OBrenane	Clifford	Culloty	ODonoghue	Finch	McGillicuddy
OBrennan	McCnoghor	Cunningham	O'Donoghue	MacFinneen	MacGillicuddy
O'Bric	Coffey	Curan	MacDonough	McFinneen	MacGillycudd
Brick	Coinyn	OCurnane	O'Doolan	O'Finnerty	Glanvill
Brinagh	OColahan	Curran	O'Dorohy	MacFinnucane	Glavin
Broder	OCollaghane	O'Curran	Dowd	Fitz-henry	O'Gleason
OBroder(ick)	Collis	Currane	O'Downey	Fitz-maurice,	Gloster
Broderick	Colthurst	OCurrane	Downing	Fitzedmd.	Godfrey
O'Brosnahan	Condon	McCurtaine	Doyle	Fitzelle	Godfrey
Brosnan	Connell	OCurtaine	O'Drea	Fitzgerald	Goggin
Browne	O'Connell	Curtin	O'Driscoll	Fitzgibbon	Gold, Golden

Family Names in Coumty Kerry, Ireland (cont'd)

Golden	Hoard	Kyery	Maybury	Reen	MacSheehy
Grady	Holland	O'Lalor, Lawlc	O'Moore	Reidy	Shewell
O'Grady	Holly, Holley	Landers	O'Moran	Relihan	Shine
Greaney	Holmes	Latimer	O'More	Rice	O'Shine
Greany	Horan	Leaghy	Moriarty	McRichard	Shorttliffe
Gregory	Hord	Leahy	O'Moriarty	ORiedy	Sigerson
OGriffen	Horgan	O'Leahy	MacMorrice	Rierdane	Slattery
Griffin	Hoskins	Leane	McMorrice	Riordan	OSpillane
Groves	Houlihan	Leary	Morris, Mauric	O'Riordan	Spillane
Gunn	Howard	O'Leary	McMorrish	Roch	Spring
O'Hagarty	Howard	Leehey	Moynihan	Rodgers	Stack
Hallissey	OHowrane	Lehane	Mulchinock	Rohan	Stokes
Hallissy	Hudson	Lency	Mullineux	Rourke	Stoughton
Hambery	Hurd	OLency	Mulvihill	Roydy	Studdert
OHanafane	Hussey, O'hos	O'Lennon,	O'Mulvihill	Rumny	Styles
Hanafin	Huston	Leonard	OMurphy	Ryerdane	Sugherne
Hanifin	Justice	Leslie	Murphy	Ryle	Sugrue
Hanlon	McKeanan	Leyne	O'Nedi	Sandford	Sulleuan
Harding	Keane	Linane	Neill	Sands	Sulliuan
Harnett	Keating	Linnane	O'Neligan	Sands	Sullivan
Harold	O'Keefe	Loue	Newlin	Sanford	O'Sullivan
Harrington	Keeffe	Lovett	Ormsby	Sayers	Sullivane
OHartnett	O'Keeshan	Lucey	Orpen	Sayers	Suvane
Hartnett	Keith	OLyne	McOwen	OScanlan	Sweeney
Harty	Kelleher	Lyne	Palmer	Scanlan	McSweeney
Hassett	O'Kelleher	Lyons	Peet	Scanlon	Sweeny
OHea	Kelliher	Mack	Petty	O'Scanlon	Tangney
O'Hea	McKenna	McMahony	Piers	Scannell	Taylor
OHealy	MacKenna	Mahony	Ponsonby	O'Sexon	Teahan
Healy	O'Kennedy	O'Mahony	Potter	Shagroe	McTeige
Heerd	Kerin	Mahowny	O'Quill	Shakelton	McThomas
Herbert	OKerins	Mangan	Quinlan	Shanahan	Trant
Herbertt	Kerrisk	O'Mangan	O'Quinlan	Shea	Twomey
Herlihy	Kevane	Mannix	McQuinn	O'Shea	O'Twomey
Hickson	Kinveton	Mansfield	Quirk	Sheahan	Walker
Hickson	Kirby	Marshall	Quirke	Sheehan	Warren
Hilliard	Kissane	Massy	Rahilly	O'Sheehan	Welsted
Hilly	Knight	Matthews	Raymond	Sheehy	Whelton

Landowners in Co. Kerry in 1876

The total for 1,166 landowners in Co. Kerry was 1,153,373 acres.
Given here as: Name of landowner / place of residence/ # of acres owned.
Note the absentee landowners, and which families retained lands.

Aldwell, mary Kenmare, 294 Ac.
Barry, Col. J. Mallow, 740 Ac.
Barry, John Caherciveen, 1,964 Ac.
Bateman, John Dublin 2,406 Ac.
Bateman, Row. Tralee, 1259 Ac.
Bernard, Edw. M. Sheheree, 7,136
Blacker, St. John Thomas Armagh, 8,159
Blackwood, Sir Henry London, 1,940
Bland, Ven. Archdeacon Knockane, 2,960
Bland, Francis C. Derryquin, 25,576
Blennerhassett, Arthur Ballyseedy, 12,621
Blennerhassett, John Ballymacelligott 1,352
Blennerhassett, Sir Rowland Beaufort, 8,390
blennerhassett, Rowland Kells, 6,234
Blennerhassett, Thomas Shanavally, 5,995
Bourke, Maj.- Gen. Thos. Cork, 940
Bowen, Robt. Kenmare, 835
Brennan, Daniel Drumhall, 2,200
Browne, Rev. Geo. Nottingham, 1,477
Browne, John Geneva, 432
Browne, J. P. Crotta, 2,065
Beale, T. Tarbert, 206
Busteed, Isabella Dublin, 704
Busteed, Mary Dublin, 1,685
Butler, Arabella Waterville, 790
Butler, James Waterville, 1417
Butterly, Lau. Listowel, 1052
Church Rep. Body Dublin 211
Church Temp. Body Dublin, 1,500
Chute, Algernon Dublin, 1,606
Chute, Charles Tralee 1,141
Chute, Francis B. Chute Hall, 10,328
Chute, Rev. G. T. Shropshire, 5,094
Chute, Rich. B. Tralee, 433
Chute, Capt. R. R. Tralee, 406

Chute, Capt. Thos. Glenville Camp, 248
Collis, S. E. Tieraclea, 3,598
Coltsmann, Catherine Dublin, 2,016
Coltsman, Daniel Glenflesk Castle, 10,316
Cork, Earl of, Somerset, 11,531
Corkery, D. O'B. Kenmare, 6,439
Creagh, Francis and John Tarmons, 394
Creagh, William Mallow 829
Crosbie, Maj. James Ballyheigue, 13,422
Crosbie, Margaret Glandahalin, 848
Crosbie, W. T. Ardfert Abbey, 9,913
Crumpe, Francis, M. D. Tralee, 568
Curtayne, J. D. Belleville, 1,165
Curtin, John Mullaghive, 619
Cuthbert, Thos. England, 3,407
Darley, Henry Dublin, 663
Day, Catherine Dublin, 309
Day, Very Rev. Dean G. Monkstown, 138
Day, Francis Milltown, 1,704
Day, Rev. John F. Beaufort, 2254
Deane, Jas. Cork, 1,753
De Courcey, Wm. Tarbert, 312
De Moleyns, Wm. Killorglin, 477
Dennehy, Mary Killarney, 1,574
Dennis, M. C. Baltinglass, 3,550
Denny, Ven. Archd. Kilgobbin, 271
Denny, Collingwood England 701
Denny, Sir Edward, Bart. London, 21,479
Denny, Maynard Dublin, 163 Acres
Dodd, W. H. Killorglin, 1,000
Donovan, Nicholas Tralee, 1295
Donovan, Patrick 785
Downing, F. H. Killarney, 1803
Downing, McCarthy Skibbereen, 601
Drew, Rev. B. Castlemaine, 677

Landowners in Co. Kerry in 1876

Drew, Sarah Castlemaine, 498
Drew, Sarah Waterford, 172
Driscoll, John Valentia, 1346
Drummond, Robt. London, 29,780
Duckett, Thomas M. Dublin, 418
Dunraven, Earl of Adare, 1005
Eagar, REv. E. Tralee, 1005
Eagar, E. M'G. Cara Castle, 6404
Eagar, F. J. Dublin, 157
Eagar, J. H. Tralee, 348
Eagar, Oliver S. 360
Eagar, Rev. Thos. Ashton, Lanc., 349
Elliott, Alex. Tarbert, 435
Elliott, Mary Listowel, 557
Fagan, Capt. W. A. Cork, 840
Fitzgerald, Jas. Goulanebeg, 502
Fitzgerald, John Camp, 195
Fitgerald, J. G. Limerick, 41
Fitzgerald, Knight of Kerry Glanleam, 5,372
Ritzgerald, REv. Richard Tarbert, 1349
Fitzgerald, W. N. F. Clare, 2,400
Fitzmaurice, O. Dublin, 2170
Foley, E. H. Ballyard, 1604
Foley, Jas., Killorglin, 1603
Fosbery, Mr. Limerick, 1437
Gallwey, Edw. Queens Co., 1571
Galwey, M. Dingle, 605
Gentleman, G. Ballyhorgan, 741
Godfrey, Sir. J. F. Kilcoleman Abbey, 5986
Goff, Jos. Salisbury, 2625
Gough, Jos. Eng., 799
Gun, T. G. Ratoo, 453
Gun, W. Ratoo, 11819
Harenc(?), H. B. London, 5879
Harman, T. Kenmare, 32
Hartnett, Wm. England, 1489
Harnett, Wm. Listowel, 813
Harte, Mahoney Tralee, 1682

Hartopp, e. B. Leicester, 24,222
Headley, Lord Aghadoe, 12,769
Herbert, A. E. Killintierna, 118
Herbert, REv. E. Killarney, 1
Herbert, Henry Cahirnane, 3016
Herbert, A. Muckross, 47,238
Hewson, Rev. F. Killarney, 1772
Hewson, Geo. Ennismore, 1208
Hewson, G. M. Tralee, 690
Hewson, Miss Killarney, 843
Hewson, REv. R. Killarney, 547
Hickie, Wm. C. Kilelton, 3368
Hickson, Capt. R. M. Tralee, 413
Hickson, R. A. London, 2031?????
Hickson, R. C. Fermoyle, 13,443
Hickson, R. C. E. Barrow, 199
Hickson, Rg. Killarney, 1183
Hickson, Wm. England, 590
Hilliard, H. Ardfert, 242
Hilliard, J. Causeway, 254
Hilliard, B. H. Tralee, 211
Hilliard, G. Tralee, 211
Hudson, E. Tralee, 456
Huggard, Stephen Lismore, 609
Hurley, Conway Tralee, 2559
Hurley, John Fenit, 9675
Hussey, Edw. Grove, Dingle, 3954
Hussey, Sam M. Edenburn, 3526
Julian, Sam Cheltenham, 3711
Kenmare, Earl of Killarney, 91,080
King, Nicholas, M. D. Dublin, 1058
Kitson, G. L. Dublin, 1040
Lansdowne, Marquess of. London, 94,983
Lawlor, D. Shine Grenagh, 1374
Lawlor, Martin Killarney, 1075
Leahy, Col. Arthur Flesk Lodge, 1068
Leahy, John White South Hill, 5511
Leonard, Dan Listowel, 377

Landowners in Co. Kerry in 1876

Leonard, Rev. S. B. **Banteer,** 1212
Leslie, R. **Tarbert House,** 1747
Leyne, Jerh. **Limerick,** 109
Listowel, Earl of **Mallow,** 25,964
Lombard, D. **Dublin,** 420
Mc Carthy, Alex. **Cork,** 2979
Mc Carthy, Dan. **Srugreana,** 1033
Mc Carthy, Dan. **Headfort,** 2203
Mc Elligott, Wm. **Ballyoneen,** 46
M' Gillycuddy, The **White Field,** 15,518
Magill, Capt. James **Beaufort,** 1638
Mahony, David **Wiltslane,** 1370
Mahony, Edw. **Dublin,** 11668
Mahony, Eliza **Killorglin,** 523
Mahony, Geo. P. Gun **Kilmorna,** 5020
Mahony, John **Dunloe Castle,** 8229
mahony, John H. **Kenmare,** 1723
Mahony, Kean **Dublin,** 1024
Mahony, Kean **Beaufort,** 3104
Mahony, Richard **Dromore Castle,** 26,173
Mahony, T. McD. **Killarney,** 7322
Marshall, R. J. **Callinafercy,** 5955
Mason, J. **Gortbrack,** 116
Mason, Susan **Gortbrack,** 173
Mason, W. B. **Gortbrack,** 62
Maybury, Geo., M. D. **Kenmare,** 3160
Maybury, Thos. **Clahane,** 606
Maybury, Wm. **Kenmare,** 12
Meredith, R. **Dicksgrove,** 1839
Monteagle, Lord **Limerick,** 2310
Moriarty, Anne, **Killarney,** 206
Morphy, Edw. **Tralee,** 664
Morrogh, W. **Cork,** 318
Mulchinock, Edw. **Rathmines, Dublin** 606
Mundy, Maj. Gen. **London,** 5898
Nash, C. F. **Tralee,** 1531
Neligan, J. C. **Tralee,** 357
Neligan, W. J. **Tralee,** 1087

O' Brien, J. **Cork,** 748
O' Callaghan, G. **Listowel,** 432
O' Connell, C. D. **Bantry,** 9807
O' Connell, Dan. **Derrynane Abbey,** 17,394
O' Connell, D. J. **Grenagh,** 605
O' Connell, Sir M. J. **Lakeview,** 18,750
O' Connell, M. J. **Cashel,** 496
O' Connell, Thos. **Deerpark,** 611
O' Connor, Francis **Germany,** 290
O' Connor, Gerard **Tralee,** 431
O' Connor, Mrs. H. **Ankail,** 520
O' Connor, John, M. D. **Causeway,** 778
O' Connor, Rev. M. **Tralee,** 383
O' Connor, Thos. **Beal,** 366
O' Donoghue, The **Summerhill,** 9463
Oliver, Maj. **Cork,** 1369
Oliver, R. S. **London,** 4804
Orkney, Earl of **England,** 1642
Ormathwaite, Lord **Berks,** 8907
O' Rorke, C. D. **Galway,** 1047
Orpen, Sir Rd., **Dublin,** 12873
Orpen, R. H. **Killaha,** 4348
O' Sullivan, Dan'l. **Droaghs, Killorglin,** 2160
Palmer, Caleb **Dublin,** 348
Palmer, E. Orpen **Killowen,** 258
Palmer, John **Tralee,** 1427
Palmer, R. S. **London,** 2104
PAul, Sir R. **Waterford,** 708
Peet, Francis **Tralee,** 636
Pope, W. **France,** 821
Quill, Eliz. **Tralee,** 812
Rae, Edw. **Keel House,** 564
Rae, Langford **Keel House,** 5870
Rae, Wm. L. **Ard- - -iel,** 835
Railway, G. S. and W. 496
Raymond, Anne **Dublin,** 314
Raymond, Geo. **Dublin,** 1756
Raymond, James **Listowel,** 272

Landowners in Co. Kerry in 1876

Rice, J. Ballybunion, 284
Rice, Justice D. Bushmount, 1233
Roche, Catherine Charleville, 1007
Roche, Redmond Castleisland, 1256
Roche, Redmond junr. Maglass, 252
Roche, Stephen Dublin, 1007
Rowan, Maj. W. Belmont, 1556
Ryan, Jas., M. D. Germany, 623
Rynd, W. R. Italy, 548
Sandes, C. Dublin, 327
Sandes, Geo. Listowel, 803
Sandes, M. F. Oakpark, 11172
Sandes, Thos. Sallowglin, 7147
Sandes, W. G. Listowel, 449
Saunders, A. L. Cloughjordan, 2221
Saunders, Rev. W. H. Cork, 734
Scanlan, Maria Tralee, 13
Sealy, Deborah Tralee, 94
Simpson, R. A. Dublin, 631
Simpson, S. Dublin, 4609
Southwell, Visc. Rathkeale, 329
Spotswood, Mce., M. D. Caherciveen, 295
Spring, Edw. Farranfore, 77
Stack, Maj. Gen. N. M. Caragh, 1205
Stokes, E. D. Tralee, 826
Stokes, G. D. Tralee, 2747
Stokes, J. D. Cork, 420
Stokes, Capt. O. R. Cork, 59
Stokes, Capt. O. D. Torquay, 901
Stokes, R. B. Derry, 484
Stokes, Wm. England, 211
Stoughton, C. W. London, 2495
Stoughton, T. A. Ballyhorgan, 11710
Strange, Miss B. Kenmare, 1387
Studdert, T. Bunratty, 656
Sugrue, Chas. Cork, 4622
Sugrue, Jas. Coolmagort, 640
Sullivan, John Dromcahan, Kenmare, 69

Sullivan, T. Bandon, 2303
Supple, E. K. Dundalk, 909
Tuohill, R., M. D. Dublin, 1164
Twiss, E. Dingle, 77
Twiss, Francis Tralee, 301
Twiss, J. R. Ballahantouragh, 358
Twiss, R., M. D. Killarney, 250
Twiss, Wm., Tralee, 103
Usburne, T. M. Cork, 2560
Ventry, Lord Burnham, 93,629
White, Geo. P. London, 984
Williams, F. E. Waterville, 3804
Winn, Hon. Roland Rossbehy, 13913
Wise, Francis Cork, 9636
Wren, Leslie Tralee, 2466
Yielding, Samuel Kinsale, 434
Fitzgerald, J. F. Caherciveen, 836
Maybury, J. K. Kenmare, 355

Ruins of the Crosbie Family Mansion, Ardfert, Co. Kerry

Togher Castle

Ballycarbery Castle

Ballyheigue Castle, built by the Cantillon Family

Kanturk Castle

Some Kerry Placenames
Taken From 17th - 20th Century Records
including Modern Parishes, Unions & Registrars Districts

Also shown are other counties where placename is found.
(Counties may be abbreviated thus; Clare = Cla)
as compiled by the Irish Genealogical Fdtn. and the Irish Family Journal,
see also the *Master Book of Irish Placenames*, IGF, 1994.

KEY: Tl = Townland   Pl = place   pm = modern parish   par = parish
Ker = Co. Kerry   Rgd. = placename found in the registrars district of....

Abbey O Dorny, tl. Ker.
Agha McCrime, tl. Ker.
Aghadoe Pm Ker.
Aghadoe, tl. Ker.
Aghamore, tl. Ker.
Aghanagraune, tl. Ker.
Aghavalin, par. Ker.
Aghavallen Pm Ker.
Aghebegg, tl. Ker.
Agherim, tl. Ker.
Aghgort, tl. Ker.
Aghtoburid, tl. Ker.
Aglish, Ker.
Aglish Pm Ker.
Aglish, tl. Ker.
Annagh, Ker.
Annagh, Ker.
Annagh Pm Ker.
Annaghbegg, Ker.
Annagullymore, tl. Ker.
Ardae, tl. Ker.
Ardcanaght, tl. Ker.
Ardcullin, tl. Ker.
Ardd, tl. Ker.
Ardea, Ker.
Ardfert Pm Ker.
Ardfertt, Ker.
Ardglasse, Ker.
Ardglasse, tl. Ker.
Ardguonigh, tl. Ker.
Ardmoniell, tl. Ker.
Ardoughter, tl. Ker.

Ardtinllihy, tl. Ker.
Ardtullyhy, Ker.
Arduonoge, tl. Ker.
Arguill, tl. Ker.
Arniloagh, tl. Ker.
Arres, tl. Ker.
Asdy, tl. Ker.
Atrohis, tl. Ker.
Auenagarry, tl. Ker.
Aulane, tl. Ker.
aunemore, tl. Ker.
Ayle, tl. Ker.
Ballenskealigg, Ker.
Ballim Luine, tl. Ker.
Ballimessie, tl. Ker.
Ballimickine, tl. Ker.
Ballinae, tl. Ker. Wex.
Ballinaulort, tl. Ker.
Ballinbrenagh, tl. Ker.
Ballinclimeasig, tl. Ker.
Ballincloghir, tl. Ker.
Ballincrispin, tl. Ker.
Ballincrossig, tl. Ker.
Ballincurrigh, tl. Ker.
Ballincuslane Pm Ker.
Ballinehan, tl. Ker.
Ballingambon, tl. Ker.
Ballingare, tl. Ker.
Ballinglanny, tl Ker. Wat.
Ballingowlin, tl. Ker.
Ballingowne, tl. Ker. Wat.
Ballinnahigg, tl. Ker.

Ballinnasigg, tl. Ker.
Ballinpriora, tl. Ker.
Ballinrudeligg, tl. Ker.
Ballintaggort, tl. Ker.
Ballinvoher Pm Ker.
Ballinvohir, Ker. Lim.
Ballirieghans, tl. Ker.
Balliriogane, tl. Ker.
Ballshanragane, tl. Ker.
Ballvaccassy, tl. Ker.
Bally Broman, tl. Ker.
Bally Henry, tl. Ker.
Bally McAdam, tl, pl. Ker, T
Bally McCoine, tl. Ker.
Bally McCruttery, tl. Ker.
Bally McDannell, tl. Ker.
Bally McElligott, tl. Ker.
Bally McIdoyle, tl. Ker.
Bally McJordan, tl. Ker.
Ballyarde, tl. Ker.
Ballyargane, tl. Ker.
Ballybane, tl Ker Wex Ros Dub
Ballybeggane, tl. Ker.
Ballybonane, tl. Ker.
Ballybracke, tl. Ker. Wat.
Ballybrenagh, tl. Ker. Lim.
Ballycahill, tl. Cla Ker Lim Tip
Ballycarbery, tl. Ker.
Ballycasslane, Ker.
Ballyconnell, tl. Ker. West. Sli.

Taken from the Master Book of Irish Placenames. ©1994 I.G.F.

Co. Kerry Placenames

Ballyconnery, tl. Ker.
Ballyconry Pm Ker.
Ballyduff Pm Ker.
Ballyduffe, tl. Ker. Wex.
Ballyduhigg, tl. Ker.
Ballyduny, tl. Ker.
Ballyduynleagh, tl. Ker.
Ballyea, tl. Cla. Ker.
Ballyegan, tl. Ker. King.
Ballyeghna, tl. Ker.
Ballyenaghta, tl. Ker.
Ballyferriter, tl. Ker.
Ballyfinora, tl. Ker.
Ballygarrott, tl. Ker.
Ballygawnyne, tl. Ker.
Ballygrenane, tl. Ker.
Ballyguine, tl. Ker.
Ballyhauragane, tl. Ker.
Ballyhea, tl. Ker.
Ballyheige Pm Ker.
Ballyheige, tl. Cla. Ker.
Ballyherny, tl. Ker.
Ballyleadir, tl. Ker.
Ballyleagh, tl. Ker.
Ballylongane, tl. Ker.
Ballyloyne, tl. Ker.
Ballymaceagog, tl. Ker.
Ballymacelligott Pm Ker.
Ballymanuge, tl. Ker.
Ballymore, Ant. Cor. Tip. Lond. Ker. West. Wex.
Ballymorerigh, tl. Ker.
Ballymullin, pl, tl. Cork, Ker
Ballynacourty Pm Ker.
Ballynageragh, tl. Ker.
Ballynaha, tl. Ker.
Ballynahaglish Pm Ker.
Ballynahagulsy, Ker.
Ballynahally, tl. Ker.

Ballynahunty, tl. Ker.
Ballynalaken, tl. Ker.
Ballynecourty, tl. Ker. Lim. Wat.
Ballynorigge, tl. Ker.
Ballyoughtragh, tl. Ker.
Ballyrnaghane, tl. Ker.
Ballyruobucke, tl. Ker.
Ballyseedy Pm Ker.
Ballystragh, tl. Ker.
Ballytrasny, tl. Ker.
Ballyvauldeir, tl. Ker.
Ballyvoige, tl. Cork, Ker.
Balthosidy, Ker.
Baltogarrane, tl. Ker.
Banebialboy, tl. Ker.
Banemore, tl. Ker.
Barnanstockigg, Ker.
Barnynstackigg, tl. Ker.
Barrow, tl. Ker.
Bealafinane, tl. Ker.
Bealamalis, tl. Ker.
Beale, tl. Ker.
Behins, tl. Ker.
Bennagh, tl. Ker.
Billaghcomane, tl. Ker.
Binecree, tl. Ker.
Bohernaballue, tl. Ker.
Bohiruo, tl. Ker.
Bolteenes, tl. Ker.
Brackell, tl. Ker.
Brom, tl. Ker.
Brosna Pm Ker.
Brosnogh, Ker.
Bruvadery, tl. Ker.
Bunnane, tl. Ker.
Buolilienagh, tl. Ker.
Buollycurrane, tl. Ker.
Burgessland, Ker., Tip.
Caharagh, Cor. Ker. Lim.

Caher Pm Ker.
Cahermare, tl. Ker.
Cahir, Cor. Ker. Lim.
Cahir Boshiny, Ker.
Cahir Bulligge, tl. Ker.
Cahir Doniell, tl. Ker.
Cahir Trant, tl. Ker.
Cahirbearnagh, tl. Ker.
Cahircrohan, tl. Ker.
Cahurhuny, tl. Ker.
Cappaclogh, tl. Ker.
Cappagh, Cla. Ker. Lim. Wat. Kilk. West. Cla.
Cappana Cossy, tl. Ker.
Caraghane, tl. Ker.
Carehey, tl. Ker.
Carhew, tl. Ker. Tip.
Carrigafeile, tl. Ker.
Carriganfrieghane, tl. Ker.
Carriggeene, tl. Ker.
Carryfioght, tl. Ker.
Caru Ieragh, tl. Ker.
Carue, tl. Ker.
Castlegregory, tl. Ker.
Castleisland Pm Ker.
Castlemanig, tl. Ker.
Caunegully, tl. Ker.
Cippagh, tl. Ker.
Claddaneanure, tl. Ker.
Clanmorice, Ker.
Clanmorrice, Ker.
Clasganiffe, tl. Ker.
Clasmelcon, tl. Ker.
Clauloght, tl. Ker.
Cloghan Lysie, tl. Ker.
Cloghan McQueine, Ker. tl.
Cloghane Pm Ker.
Cloghane Cahane, tl. Ker.

Taken from the Master Book of Irish Placenames. ©1994 I.G.F.

Co. Kerry Placenames

Cloghane Duffe, tl. Ker.
Cloghane, tl. Cla. Cor. Ker. Tip. King.
Clogherbrien Pm Ker.
Clogherbrien, tl. Ker.
Clogherbrine, Ker.
Clohir, tl. Ker.
Cloincorha, tl. Ker.
Cloinmore, tl. Ker.
Cloniclogh, tl. Ker.
Cloune Idonogane, tl. Ker.
Clounemelane, tl. Ker.
Clounetiburide, tl. Ker.
Cluhir, tl. Ker.
Clunagh, tl. Ker. Sli.
Cluonduglassie, tl. Ker.
Clynis, tl. Ker.
Cnockes, tl. Cork, Ker.
Cnocknegassull, tl. Ker.
Cnocknymuckully, tl. Ker.
Colowes, tl. Ker.
Comego, tl. Ker.
Conenennagh, tl. Ker.
Conyger, tl. Ker.
Coolecleiffe, tl. Ker.
Corbally Dow Cla Cor Ker Lim C. West Ros
Corcaguiny, Ker.
Corelacka, tl. Ker.
Corrigrage, tl. Ker.
Corrumore, tl. Ker.
Coumannassy, tl. Ker.
Coumbeg, tl. Ker.
Coume, tl. Ker.
Crohane, Cor. Ker. Tip.
Crottoe, tl. Ker.
Cryuyne, tl. Ker.
Cuile, tl. Ker.
Cuileneline, tl. Ker.

Culcow, tl. Ker.
Culecasleagh, tl. Ker.
Culecluhur, tl. Ker.
Culecurrane, tl. Ker.
Culemagort, tl. Ker.
Culenagearigh, tl. Ker.
Culereagh, tl. Ker.
Culicke, tl. Ker.
Cullie, tl. Ker.
Culliligh, tl. Ker.
Cullybogie, tl. Ker.
Curecrine, tl. Ker.
Currabegge, tl. Ker.
Currachore, tl. Ker.
Curraghcronyn, tl. Ker.
Curranes, tl. Ker.
Currans Pm Ker.
Currens, Ker.
Curriell, tl. Ker.
Currihenmore, Ker.
Deehs, tl. Ker.
Dereeneanvirrige, tl. Ker.
Desert, Cla. Cor. Ker.
Dingle, Ker. Pmo
Dingle Pm Ker.
Direene, tl. Ker.
Dirrinduffe, tl. Ker.
Dirrygomligh, tl. Ker.
Dirveene, tl. Ker.
Disert, Don. Cor. Kild. West. Ros. Ker. Tip.
Dooneard, tl. Ker.
Doonecaha, tl. Ker.
Doonekerran, tl. Ker.
Doontis, tl. Ker.
Dramguine, tl. Ker.
Droman, tl. Ker. Lond.
Dromartin, tl. Ker.
Drombegg, Cor. Ker. Lim.

Dromcarrabane, tl. Ker.
Dromconigge, tl. Ker.
Dromdisart, tl. Ker.
Dromin, Dow. Ker. Lim.
Dromiruorke, tl. Ker.
Dromleggalsh, tl. Ker.
Drommatewcke, tl. Ker.
Dromod, Ker. Tip.
Dromod Pm Ker.
Dromore, tl. Ker. West. Sli.
Dromoughty, tl. Ker.
Dromragh, tl. Ker.
Droumackee, tl. Ker.
Droumaltare, tl. Ker.
Droumevally, tl. Ker.
Droumkenny, tl. Ker.
Drumhumper, tl. Ker.
Duagh, Ker. Wat.
Duagh Pm Ker.
Duah, tl. Ker.
Dughill, tl. Ker. Ros.
Duglassy, tl. Ker.
Dune Sheane, tl. Ker.
Duneguile, tl. Ker.
Dunekerran, Ker.
Dunemaneheene, tl. Ker.
Dunequeene, tl. Ker.
Dunevrlane, Ker.
Dunkerran, Ker.
Dunquin Pm Ker.
Dunurlin Pm Ker.
Durene, tl. Ker.
Durie, tl. Ker.
Durrinane, tl. Ker.
Dyrrymore, tl. Ker.
Dysert Pm Ker.
England, Ker Lim Mea West Pmo

Taken from the Master Book of Irish Placenames. ©1994 I.G.F.

Co. Kerry Placenames

Erribegg, tl. Ker.
Errimore, tl. Ker.
Fagha, tl. Ker.
Fahaduffe, tl. Ker.
Farren McWm, tl. Ker.
Farrennagat, tl. Ker.
Farrennamracke, tl. Ker.
Farrenruoge, tl. Ker.
Faun, tl. Ker.
Fenit Pm Ker.
Fienett, tl. Ker.
Finuge Pm Ker.
Fleskebridge, tl. Ker.
Fraction, tl. Ker.
Funug, Ker.
Funuge, tl. Ker.
Galey Pm Ker.
Gallaris, tl. Ker.
Galy, Ker. Ros.
Garfinagh, tl. Ker.
Garfinny Pm Ker.
Garineskie, tl. Ker.
Garranerouerice, tl. Ker.
Gearyhudveene, tl. Ker.
Glanbehy, Ker.
Glanbehy Pm Ker.
Glanlogh, tl. Ker.
Glannerdallune, tl. Ker.
Glannesmagh, tl. Ker.
Glanotrassna, tl. Ker.
Glantis, tl. Ker.
GlauneballySherune, Ker. tl.
Glauneoroghty, Ker.
Glaunlap, tl. Ker.
Glauntine, tl. Ker.
Glovry, tl. Ker.
Gort Dromagauna, Ker.
Gort Dromasyllyhy, Ker. tl.

Gort Religge, tl. Ker.
Gortacappull, tl. Ker.
Gortancollipy, tl. Ker.
Gortancunigh, tl. Ker.
Gortdromkiery, tl. Ker.
Gorteene Ruo, tl. Ker.
Gortfadda, tl. Ker.
Gortglasse, tl. Ker.
Gortnacloghy, Ker.
Gortnaraha, Ker.
Gortnivohir, tl. Ker.
Gortnycloghane, tl. Ker.
Gortroe, tl. Cork, Ker
Goulane, tl. Ker.
Gowlane, tl. Ker.
Gurane, tl. Ker.
Gurteens, tl. Ker.
Imelagh Padin, tl. Ker.
Immelagh, tl. Ker.
Inch, Dow Wex Ker Kilk Car Que
Inshy, tl. Ker.
Insyancomue, tl. Ker.
Iraght I Connor, Ker.
Island, Cla. Cor. Ker.
Iveragh, Ker.
Kappamore, tl. Ker.
Keanburren, tl. Ker.
Kenmare Pm Ker.
KERRY, Ker. Pmo
Kilbanauane, tl. Ker.
Kilbonane, Ker.
Kilbonane Pm Ker.
Kilboune, tl. Ker.
Kilcaragh Pm Ker.
Kilcarhae, tl. Ker.
Kilcaskan Pm Ker.
Kilcolman Pm Ker.
Kilcomyn, Ker.
Kilconly, Ker.

Kilconly Pm Ker.
Kilcoulaght, tl. Ker.
Kilcredane Pm Ker.
Kilcrohane Pm Ker.
Kilcummin Pm Ker.
Kildrum, Ker.
Kildrum Pm Ker.
Kilfeighny Pm Ker.
Kilfloine, Ker.
Kilflyn Pm Ker.
Kilfreghna, Ker.
Kilfuntin, tl. Ker.
Kilgarrenlander, Ker.
Kilgarrylander Pm Ker.
Kilgarvan Pm Ker.
Kilgobban, Ker.
Kilgobban Pm Ker.
Kilgolbin, tl. Ker.
Kilgortanny, tl. Ker.
Kilgrauane, tl. Ker.
Kill Bally Ker. McSheenickine, tl.
Killaghine, Ker.
Killaha Pm Ker.
Killaha, tl. Ker.
Killahan Pm Ker.
Killahy, Ker.
Killalyny, tl. Ker.
Killanea, tl. Ker.
Killarney Pm Ker.
Killarny, Ker.
Killarone, tl. Ker.
Killbunnane, tl. Ker.
Killcloghane, tl. Ker.
Killcolman, Ker. Wat.
Killcomyn, tl. Ker.
Killcroghane, Ker.
Killdurrihy, tl. Ker.
Killeene, Cla Cor Ker Lim Kilk

Taken from the Master Book of Irish Placenames. ©1994 I.G.F.

Co. Kerry Placenames

Killeentierna Pm Ker.
Killegh, tl. Ker.
Killehenny, Ker.
Killehenny Pm Ker.
Killelane, Ker.
Killeltin, tl. Ker Wat
Killemlagh Pm Ker.
Killenan, Ker.
Killenterna, Ker.
Killgaruane, Ker.
Killilly, Ker.
Killimleegh, Ker.
Killinane Pm Ker.
Killiney Pm Ker.
Killkeavragh, tl. Ker.
Killmackilloge, Ker.
Killmaneeheene, tl. Ker.
Killmare, Ker.
Killmena, tl. Ker.
Killmore, Arm. Cla.
  Ker. Wat.
  Kild. Ros.
Killmurry, Cla. Tip. Ker.
  Lim. Wat.
  Kild. Kilk.
Killnaghtin, tl. Ker.
Killnanea, Ker.
Killoghane, tl. Ker.
Killorglin, Ker.
Killorglin Pm Ker.
Killowen, Cor. King.
  Ker. Wat.
Killrourally, tl. Ker.
Killshaningge, tl. Ker.
Killshenane, Ker.
Killtinleagh, tl. Ker.
Killuny, tl. Ker.
Killurly, tl. Ker.
Killury, Ker.
Killury Pm Ker.
Killy Killie, tl. Ker.

Killyghran, tl. Ker.
Killynnura, tl. Ker.
Killynny, Ker.
Killyvinine, tl. Ker.
Kilmalkedar Pm Ker.
Kilmelcadder, Ker.
Kilmoholane, tl. Ker.
Kilmoily, Ker.
Kilmoyly Pm Ker.
Kilnaghtin, Ker.
Kilnagleriegh, tl. Ker.
Kilnanare Pm Ker.
Kilnaughtin Pm Ker.
Kilpadoge, tl. Ker.
Kilquane, Ker.
Kilquane Pm Ker.
Kilsara, tl. Ker.
Kilshenane Pm Ker.
Kiltallagh Pm Ker.
Kiltoan, tl. Ker.
Kiltollogh, Ker.
Kiltomy, Ker.
Kiltomy Pm Ker.
Kiluane, tl. Ker.
Kinard Pm Ker.
Knock McIliun, tl. Ker.
Knockanaulgirt, tl. Ker.
Knockane, Cla. Wat.
  Cor. Tip. Ker.
Knockanure Pm Ker.
Knockbreake, tl. Ker.
Knockelasse, Ker.
Knockennery, tl. Ker.
Knockinnis, tl. Ker.
Knocknane Pm Ker.
Knockornaghta, tl. Ker.
Knockouleegane, tl. Ker.
Knockree, tl. Ker.
Knockyly, tl. Ker.
Knoppoge, tl. Ker.

Krecoman, tl. Ker.
Kyeryes, Ker.
Kynard, Ker.
Lackabegg, tl. Ker.
Lackacroneene, tl. Ker.
Lackamore, tl. Ker.
Lacky Roe, tl. Ker.
Laghane, tl. Ker.
Laghard, tl. Ker.
Laugharne, tl. Ker.
Leamnagehy, tl. Ker.
Leateene, tl. Ker.
Lerrigg, tl. Ker.
Letrim, Don. Cor.
  Ker. Long.
  Ros.
Letter, Don. Cor.
  Ker. Leit.
  King.
Lettir, tl. Ker.
Liscarny, tl. Ker.
Liscullane, tl. Ker.
Liseltin, Ker.
Lisha, tl. Ker.
Lislaghtin, tl. Ker.
Lismaghane, tl. Ker.
Lismebane, tl. Ker.
Lismore, Dow. Ker.
  Wat. Long.
Lisnagaune, tl. Ker.
Lisnakelivey, tl. Ker.
Lisnegoinny, tl. Ker.
Lisselton Pm Ker.
Listowel Pm Ker.
Listowhell, Ker.
Listry, tl. Ker.
Listrym, tl. Ker.
Lixnaw, tl. Ker.
Logherbegg, tl. Ker.
Loghertcannan, tl. Ker.
London, Ker.

Taken from the Master Book of Irish Placenames. ©1994 I.G.F.

Co. Kerry Placenames

Lough, Ker. Wex
Loughort Feramer, tl. Ker.
Manner, Ker.
Maquinihy, Ker.
Marhin Pm Ker.
Marhine, Ker.
Mauligh, tl. Ker.
Meanus, Ker.
Milcon, tl. Ker.
Minard Pm Ker.
Minemore, Ker.
Mineogalane, Ker.
Molahiffe, Ker.
Molahiffe Pm Ker.
Monaree, Ker.
Moybilly, tl. Ker.
Moyge, tl. Ker.
Moynish, tl. Ker.
Moyvane, Ker.
Muccorus, tl. Ker.
Mullins, tl. Ker.
Murher Pm Ker.
Murhur, Ker.
Murrirrigane, tl. Ker.
Mynard, Ker.
Myniskie, tl. Ker.
Nauntenane, tl. Ker.
Neadeene, Ker.
New Manner, tl. Ker.
Noghauale, Ker.
Nohaval Pm Ker.
Nohavaldaly Pm Ker.
O Brenan, Ker.
O Dorny, Ker.
O'Brennan Pm Ker.
O'Dorney Pm Ker.
Pallice, Cor. Tip.
    Ker. Lim.
Prior Pm Ker.
Pullin, tl. Ker.
Quilearrymoy, tl. Ker.
Quilly, East, tl. Ker.
Racommane, tl. Ker.
Rah, tl. Ker.
Rahanane, tl. Ker.
Rahannagh, tl. Ker.
Rahen Vegge, tl. Ker.
Rahennye, Ker.
Rahindirry, tl. Ker.
Rahmurrill, Ker.
Rahonyine, tl. Ker.
Ratass Pm Ker.
Rathasse, Ker.
Rathnalcon, Ker.
Rathnalogh, Ker.
Rathoe, Ker.
Rathpouke, tl. Ker.
Rattoo Pm Ker.
Rinard, tl. Ker.
Rineconnell, tl. Ker.
Ross Temple, tl. Ker.
Rossnacartin, Ker.
Ryne, Cork, Ker.
Sanavogh, tl. Ker.
Shandrome, tl. Ker.
Shrone, Ker.
Skekanagh, tl. Ker.
Srone Birrane, Ker.
StradBally, Ker. Wat.
    Lim. Cty.
    Dub. Que.
Stradbally Pm Ker.
Tarbert, tl. Ker.
Tarmon, Cla. Ker.
Teereruane, Ker.
Templeno, Ker.
Templenoe Pm Ker.
Thomies, tl. Ker.
Tibbridd, Ker.
Toburhine, tl. Ker.
Toghirbane, Ker.
Tonekilly, tl. Ker.
Tonevane, Ker.
Tralee Pm Ker.
Traly, Ker. Pmo
Triemeragh, tl. Ker.
Trughanac, Ker.
Tullabegg, tl. Ker.
Tullacrummyn, Ker.
Tullaghine, tl. Ker.
Tullahivill, Ker.
Tulligg, Ker. Lim.
Tulligibbin, Ker.
Tuosist Pm Ker.
Tynahally, tl. Ker.
Tynefagh, Ker.
Tyre Sanaghane, tl. Ker.
Tyrenagouse, tl. Ker.
Urlee, Ker.
Valencia Pm Ker.
Valentia, Ker.
Ventry, Ker.
Ventry Pm Ker.

Taken from the Master Book of Irish Placenames. ©1994 I.G.F.

MacCarthy Households

Donnell Mor, who died in 1206, whose son was Dermod, who died in 1230, whose brother Cormac died in 1248, leaving his son Donnell, who died in 1302, his grandson being Cormac Mor, who died in 1359, his son Donnell died in 1391, leaving his son Tadhg, who founded Muckross Abbey, leaving his son Donnell, who died in 1468, having Tadhg, whose son Donnell died in 1508, and his brother Cormac died in 1516, leaving a son Donnell, whose son was Donnell, the Earl of Clancare, in 1566, whose daughter Ellen married Florence MacCarthy Reagh, and the lordship of MacCarthy Mor came to an end in 1596. The following list gives the succession of the MacCarthy chiefs: Carthagh, 1045; Muireadhach 1092; Tadhg, 1118-24; Cormac, 1124-7; Donough, 1127; Dermod, 1151-85; Cormac 1177; Clan Shane, Donnell, 1206; Finghin, 1209; Tadg Roe na Sgairte, Dermod, 1229; Cormac, 1248; Donnell, 1251: Reagh of Carbery, Dermod, 1234; Duhallow, Donnell Fionn, Donnell Roe, 1302; Donnell, 1303; Dermod Duhallow, Cormac, 1359; Donnell, 1391; Dermod Muskerry, Eoghan Cashmaing, Cormac, 1516; Tadhg, 1514; Tadhg, Donough Ardcanaghty Tadhg, Donnell, 1468; Cormac Dunguile, Dermod, 1489; Tadhg, Donnell, 1508; Donnell, Cormac, Tadhg, Donnell, Cormac, Tadhg, Donnell, 1596; Tadhg, Ellen. In the first edition of this book at pages 235-41 is given the history of this family and its chief branches in Kerry. A list of the 604 householders now in the county is given in this article, and it should not be difficult to trace their cousinship if they elected a council for that purpose. Donnell MacCarthy Mor, first Earl of Clan Carthy left an only daughter, Ellen, who married Florence MacCarthy Reagh of Carbery, who took the title of MacCarthy Mor, which was used by his sons and grandsons until 1770. Judge Samuel Trant MacCarthy of Srugreana has recently assumed the title of MacCarthy Mor as descendant of Cormac of Dunguile. The 604 MacCarthy householders in Kerry, and their location, are as follows: Jerh. and John of Coolnacalliagh, Pat of Toormore, Denis of Knockmanagh. Tim and Denis and Tim and Andrew and Tim of Mastergeeha, Chas. and Andrew of Maulyarkane. Denis of Tournanounagh, Edm. of Tullorum, John and Ml. and John of Ballahacommane, Ml. of Ardaneanig, Jerh. of Coolcaslagh, Jerh. of Kilbreanbeg, John of Tiernaboul, Ml. of Minish, Edw. of Maglass, Tom of Mweenalaa, Martin and Con of Aunaskirtane Owen of Beheenagh. Margt. and Kate of Knockaninane, Denis and Chas. and Dan of New-street. Stephen of Pawn Office Lane, Charles and Dan of Duckett's-lane. John and Pat of High street, Felix of Bishop's lane, Denis of Main street, Pat of Inch, Dan and John of Green lane, Tim of Henn street, Pat and Denis and Roger of Aglish, Eugene of Ballytrasna, Pat of Carker, Denis of Canguilla, Pat and Ml. of Glanlea, Jas. of Dungeel, Jerh. of Ardmeelode, Hanoria of Coolick, Johanna of Knockancore, Chas. of Glounbane, Tim of Gurranedarragh, Wm. of Knockeenalicka, John of Kilbreanbeg, Rd. of Cloonteens, Dan and John of Inchycullane, Con of Gortnatona, Con of Cummeenabuddoge, Pat of Clydaghroe, Flor. and Denis and John of Knocknagown, Ellen of Leamyglissane, Hannah of Maughantourig, Mary of Knocknaseed, Andrew of Knockauncore, Denis of Knockacullig, Pat of Inchycullane, Dan of Bohereenagown, Tim of Inch, Ml. of Fleming's lane, Con of College street, Ml. of New street, Dan of Twohill's lane, Jerh. of Bohereenagown, Wm. of Henn street, Johanna of Meentogues, Johanna of Stagmount, Ellen of Knockdooragh, Ml. of Ballinalane, Mary and Mary of Bohereencael, Ellen and Phoebe and Julia of Henn street, Hannah of Inch, Mary of Pound row, Denis and Chas. and Pat and Ml. of Gullane, Ml. of Scrahanaveal, John and Pat and Ml. of Gneeveguilla, Denis of Maughantourig, John and Denis of Knocknaseed, Con of Tooreenamult, Tim of Lisheen, Catherine and Jas. and Catherine of Gortnaleaha, Pat of Maghanknockane, Redmond of Knockeen, Dan of Camp, Jas. of Ardagh, John of Bawnluskaha, Jerh. and John and Pat of Meentogues, Pat of Ballycullane, Denis and Pat and Tim of Knockdoorah, John and

MacCarthy Households

Jerh. and John of Stagmount, Ellen of Gurranedarragh, Mary of Tiernaboul, John of Inchycullane, Chas. of Rockfield, Flor. of Gortgloss, John of Breahig, Ellen of Shronedarragh, Flor. of Knockdown, Rd. of Cragganoonia, Margt. of Bawnluskaha, Pat of Knockachur, John of Ballyhar, Margt. of Gearha, Mary of Coom, Chas. of Knockaninane, Ml. of Knockbrack, Flor. of Killaha, Jas. of Scart, Julia of Mastergeeha, John of Gearha, Ml. of Knockaderry, Tim of Graffeens, Pat of Shronedarragh, Jas. of Aughacurreen, Tom of Mulloghmarkey, Mary of Ballybeg, Rd. of Coolavoorheen, Wm. of Brosna, Dan and Eugene of Slievegaura, Dan of Listry, Dan of Ballinprior, Eugene of Caheraun, Dan and Standish and Dan and Eugene of Banna, John of Currahane, Flor. and Pat of Ballymacquinn, Wm. of Deerpark, Wm. and Pat and Ml. of Liscullane, Wm. of Clogher, John of Lixnaw, John of Pulleen, Tim of Tarmons, Francis of Lissahane, Pat and Tim of Ballintogher, Tom of Knockburrane, Dan of Ballyhennessy, Mce. and Rd. of Listowel, Edm. of Clounaphuca, Tim of Rahoonagh, Pat and Jerh. of Doon, Pat of Ballybunion, Tim and Denis of Tieraclea, Tim of Ballylahive, John of Ballyrobert, Ml. of Kilgubbin, Rd. of Ardrahan, John of Garrynagore, Jas. and Denis of Ballincloher, Johanna and Mary of Banna, Margt. of Ballymacquin, Rev. Florence of Dromkeen, John and Rd. and Ml. of Ballinglanna, Con and John of Knoppogue, Ml. of Dromcloughra, Tom of Gortnaminich, Wm. and Tom of Finuge, Pat of Killocrim, Dan of Curragheroneen, John of Bromore, Margt. of Knopogue, Pat of Glenoe, Denis of Kilfeighney, Catherine of Ahanagran, John of Ahabeg, Rd. and Hanora of Ballyheige, Flor. of Kilcooly, Bridget of Finuge, Ml. of Rathea, Hanora of Trieneragh, Denis of Ballysheen, Margt. of Cloonafineela, Ml. of Kealid, John of Listowel, John of Ardfert, Hanora of Dromlegagh, Mary of Ballysheen, Jas. of Pilgrim hill, Jerh. of Rathoran, John of Graigue glebe, Margt. of Knockundervaul, John and Denis and Ml. and Dan of Ardagh, Tom and Pat of Cloghane, Rd. of Listowel, John of Inchangallary, Tom of Toor, Jerh. of Lacca, John of Bunglasha, Chas. and John of Ballymacassy, Mce. of Baltovin, Chas. of Ballymacquin, Tom of Kilbrickane, John of Knocknacrohy, Flor. of Ballynagraigue, Dan of Ballynamuddagh, Stephen of Lixnaw, Wm. of Liscullane, Tom of Ballyoneen, Ml. of Lisroe, Kate of Coolnaleen, Ml. of Coilbee, Dan of Glashmacree, Eugene of Laharan, Pat of Farrantooreen, John of Iveragh road, Pat and Denis and Pat and Dan and John and Pat and John of Cromane, Ml. of Gurrane, Jerh. of Killorglin, Eugene of Laharn, John of Main street, John and Denis of Monaree, Tim of Knockavrogeen, Denis of Ballymore, Eugene and Eugene of Carhoonaphuca, Flor. of Milltown commons, Denis of Glens, John of Annagh, John of Ballingamboon, Julia of Ballymacprior, Flor. of Rock street, Tom and Pat and John of Brogue lane, Tom of Strand street, Ml. and John and Ml. of Boherbee, Ml. of Spa road, John of Mary street, John of Caheranne road, Ml. of Abbey street, Mce. of Moyderwell, Wm. of Ballymullen, Dan of Connors' lane, Jas. and Thos. and Wm. of Castle street, Tom of Edward street, Con of the Mall, Denis of Nelson street, John of Blennerville, Denis and Ml. of Main street, Tim and Chas. of Green lane, John of John street, Denis of Grey's lane, Pat of Tralee, Ml. of Tawlaght, Dan of Barrow, Tim and Robt. and Hugh of Fenit, Rev. Jeremiah of Glebe, Anne of James street, Mary and Eliza of Rae street, Johanna of William street, Mary and Eliza of Dean's lane, Flor of Church street, Tim of Mung, Andrew of Ballydunlea, Jos. of Clahane, John and John of Poulawaddra, Ml. of Lisardboola, Justin and Florence of Brackloon Bridget of Cromane, Ml. of Mounthawk, Flor of Cloonmore, John and Jas of Milltown, Pat and Pat of Knockanush, Dan of Knockahaha, Pat of Lisheenashingane, Chas. of Lissivane, Julia of Lohercannon, Tim of Curragraigue, Bridget of Barrow, Eliza of Miles lane, John of Gurrane, Margt. of Poulawaddra, Pat of Boolteens, John of Castledrum, Dan of † Knockglassbeg, Eugene of Lougher, Justin of Inch, Mary of Martramane, Margt. of the Wood, Eliza of Main street, Pat of Cummeenole, Tim of Aughacasla, Tom and Eugene of Kilballylahive, Johanna of Shan-

174

MacCarthy Households

talliv, John of Ballynira, Dan of Liscarney, Hannah of Brackloon, Denis of Inchaloughra, John and Dan of Loughbeg, Chas. and Con of Leath, Jas. of Brackloon, Ml. of Tahilla, Margt. and Ml. of Claddanure, Bridget of Portmagee, Mary of Doory, Ml. of Kilmackerrin, Jerh. of Canuig, Denis of Spunkane, Tim of Tarmons, Pat of Reen, John of Derreenavarrig, Ml. of Derreendrislagh, Flor of Derrynacollaha, Ellen of Dungegan, Catherine of Ballard, Dan of Sillahertane, Eugene of Kilfadamore, Bridget of Inchinaleega, Chas. of Gortloughra, Tim of Barranastooka, Pat of Greenane, Kate of Kilkeehagh, Julia of Dromagurteen, Sylvester of Rath, Eug. of Crinagort, Annie of Gortnaboul, Dan of Dauros, Jerh of Killah, Ellen of Droumquinna, Jerh. and Denis of Ballintleave, Catherine of Laharan, Bridget of Corabeg, Ml. of Lisbane, Samuel Trant of Srugreana, Edw. of Dromore, John of Capparoe, Jerh. and Dan of Derryquin, Mary of Gortnagree, Nora of Cahereikthrush Jas. of Behaghane, Rev. Ml. of Ballycarnahan, Nellie of old Bridge street, Ellen of William street, Mary of Downing's row, Annie of William street, Hanora of Derrynaconalagh, John of Fustane, John of Caher, Dan of Derreencahill, Dan and Jerh of Killanbuonia, Dan and Con of Ballard, Matt and John of Fermoyle, Ml. of Glanrastal, Ml. and Felix of Glantrasna, Eugene of Lauragh, Batt of Eskadawer, John and Tim and Dan and Dan of Cahereighterush, John of Liss, Ml. of Cahernamon, Tim of Reencaheragh, John and Jerh. and John and John of Doory, Dan of Portmagee, Pat of Kilkeaveragh, John and Jerh. of Knockeens, Denis of Lounahan, Edw. of Coologues, Denis of Slaghts, Denis of Dromacoosh, Edw. of Churchground, Dan of Mangerton, Jerh. of Lehud, Ml. of Kilmackillogue, Ml. of Ardea, Felix of Derreenacloig, Chas. of Derreen, Jerh. of Tragalee, Felix of Loughanacreen, Felix of Cummers, Tim of Knockacullig, Ml. of Laharan, Jas. of Liss, John of Nedanone, Dan and John of Ballinskelligs, Ml. of Meelagullen, John and John of Kildreelig, John of Kinard, Wm. of William street, Flor of Killowen, Alex of Gortnagass, Dr. Randall of Kenmare, Denis and Tom and Denis and Flor of Henry street, Edw. of Istalea, Jerh. of Carhoomeengar, Ml. and Pat of Laharan, Jos. and Tim of Farranreagh, John and Denis of Tinnies, John of Coaramore, John of Corabeg, Ml. of Ballyhearney, John and Denis and Tim and Pat and Tim of Emlaghnamuck, Ml. and Chas. of Reenroe, Tim of Emlaghmore, John of Mweelin, Dan of Looscanaugh, Pat of Cordal, Mary and Mary of Reenard, Bridget of Ohermong, Mary and Eliza and Julia of Laharan, Mary of Old road, John of Quay street, John and Pat and J. and Jerh and John of Laharan, John and Denis of Kilcolman, Ml. and Tim of High street, John of Church lane, Ml. of Main street, Denis and John of Valencia road, Tim of Gurranearagh, Flor and Dan of Liss, Jas. of Killeen, John and Pat of Glenlough, Pat of Gleesk.

Mac Clintock, Thomas of Ballyheige.

Mac Clure, Mac Giolla Uidir; Anthony of Poulnamuck, Robt. and Robt. of Denny street, Robt. of Kenmare; tomb in Tralee churchyard is marked Anthony Mac Clure, 1817.

Mac Cluskey, Mac Bloscaid; John of Connors lane, Geo. of Chapel street.

Mac Coluim, Fionan, Gaelic language pioneer since 1898.

Mac Conarchy, Donald, bishop of West Munster, died in 1193.

Mac Connell, Mac Conaill; Robert of Mangerton view, David of Edward street.

Mac Conroi, King, clan Conaire, which see; 49 gamilies in Kerry.

Mac Cormaic, Mac Cormack; John of Ahane, Sam of Ballinruddra, Alex of Tarbert, Mary and John of Tiduff, Robert of Gortnaskeha. Catherine Mac Cormac married Lord Thomas Fitz Gerald who died at Rouen in 1420; see Thomas Moore's poem on the Desmond, by the Feale's wave benighted, etc.

Mac Cowen, Mac Comdain; Wm. and Wm. of Clounalour, Robt. of Cloghers, Mary of Barrow, Edwin of Nelson street, R. A. of Denny street, Thos. of Tralee in 1831, Robt. and Sons, Ltd., merchants in Tralee.

Mac Coy, Mac Aoda: Ml. of Clountubrid.

Mac Crohan; 28 families in Kerry, viz.: John of Killahane, Jas. of Killorglin, Mary of Roxborough,

O'Connor Households

Donnell, O'Donnell, O'Domnaill: families in Kerry, viz.:—Ml. and John and Wm. of Coolgreane, John of Clogherclemin, Pat and Dan Brosna, Mary of Doonimlaghbeg, Eliza of Ashhill, Matt of Ballycollig, Dan of Chapelquarter, Jas. and Jas. of Carrigeen, Jas. Ahane, Jas. of Knockalough, Martin and Dan and John Trieneragh, Tim of Lacca, Tom Creggane, Dan of Meenahorna, P. of Shanafona, Ml. of Moynsha, Co. of Ballyegan, John of Lahardane, Wm. of Tullamore, Bridget of Tubridmore, Wm. and Geo. and John of Kilgarvan, Mce. of Cahoona, Tom and Hanoria Tieraclea, Eugene of Tonaknoc, John of Meevoo, Wm. of Coola, John of Clounmackon, John Keelballylahive, Ml. and Ml. Cappananee, Jas. and Tom Carrigaha, Jas. of Deelis, Pat and Jas. of Ballyglasheen, Mago and Thos. and Jas. of Dromavally, P. of Brackloon, Ml. and Thos. of Aunascaul, Jas. of Maumnahalton, John and Jas. and John and Ja. and Mago and Ml. and Kate and Jas. and Tim of Slieve, Tom Killorglin, Eugene and John Glenmore, John of Curracullena, Robt. of Mountoven, John Foilatresnig, Francis of Glounaga, Ml. and Pat of Doonore, John Glandine, Denis and Jas. Clahane, John of Clounalour, John of Buntaloon, Francis of Moydewell, John and John and Ellen and Eliza and Bridget and Hannah of John of Bridge street, John Rock street, Pat of Gowlane, Alex. of Farrantooleen, Ml. of Aghama, John of Kilmore, John of Knocknagower, Ml. of Liscarney, Eugene of Maghanaboe, John and John Tawlaght, Eugene and Francis Derrymore, John of Tralee, Jas. Ardcanaght, John and Alex. Feohanagh, Tom of Curragraigue, Ml. of Ardroe, Robt. of Gortbreagogue, John and Kate and Johanna of Martramane, Ml. of Killiney, Pat of Kilmalked, Alex. of Knocklossmore, Margt. of Curragrague, John of Ballycullane, Ml. of Cloghane, Wm. Ballyenaghty, Mary of Carriga, Bridget of Dromavally, Nora Brackloon, Wm. of Drimnab...

Connelly, Connolly, O'Congaile, O'Conghalaigh; "O'Conghaile of the slender swords, over the bushyforted magh o g Coinchinn, a hazel tree of branching ringlets in the Munster plain of horse-hosts;" of Magunihy; of the Corco-Duibne, Degad, and tuath sen Eran; 12 families in Kerry, viz:—Pat of Ardoughter, Mary of Doonard, John of the Wood, Geo. of Fenit, Tom and John of Edward street, Mary of Kenmare, Pat of Drombane, Dan of Letterdunane, Ml. of Baureauragh, Pat of Mucksna, and Ml. of Shelburne street.

Connor, O'Connor, of the clann Conaire. 1371 families in Kerry, viz:—Bryan and John of Cragg, Pat of Farranbrack, Thos. and Batt of Tullig, John of Kilcow, Pat of Bawnluskaha, John of Cahereens, John and John of Knockeen, John of Dooneen, Jas. of Tonebwee, Tim and Denis of Castleview, Denis of Kilcow, Con and Lce. of Camp, Ml. of Caheragh, Tom and Jerh. and Tom and Dan and John and Dan of Shronebeg, Ml. of Doocarrigmore, Ml. of Gortnagane, Dan of Brosna, John and Tom of Knocknagoshel, Lce and Batt and Denis and Chas. and Ml. of Gortroe, Jas. and Chas. of Ahaneboy, Ml. of Mausrower, Dand. and Jerh. of Lisheen, John of Tooreenamult, John and Pat, and Jerh. and John of Greeveguilla, John of Coom, Wm. of Reanasup, Hugh of Gortacoppul, Bryan and Philip of Gortgloss, Edm. and David of Dromultan, Con of Breahig, Con of Scartaglin, John of Inchinapoagh, Bryan and Con and Denis and John and Ml. and David and Con and Denis of Knockbrack, Dan and Jas. and Dan of Brosna, Hugh and Denis and Tim and Denis and Mortimer and Denis and John and Denis and Tom and Ml. and David of Kilmanihan, Pat and Philip of Derra, Tom and Bryan of Ranaleen, Denis and John and Jas. of Glandeagh, Dan and Con of Curraaross, Pat of Inchincummer, Pat and Tom and Ml. of Bawnaglanna, Chas. of

O'Connor Households

Killeentierna, John of Dromulton, John of Faha, Jerh. of Coolroe, John of Flintfield, Tim and Jerh. of Coolbane, Jerh. and Ml. of Laharan, Denis and John and Denis of Cordal, John of Glanowen, John of Ballinvarrig, Pat of Bushmount, Chas. and Tom and Chas. and Jas. and Pat and Denis and John and Thos. and John and Dan and John and Con and Mary and Julia of Knocknagoshel, Matt and Tim of Ballyduff, Pat and Mary of Ahaneboy, Chas. of Tooreenamore, Batt of Beheenagh, Pat of Gortroe, John and Ml. and John of Gneeves, John and Ml. of Knockafreghane, Jerh. of Meenvoughane, Denis of Carrigeenwood, Denis of Ardagh, Denis and John of Droumyrourke, John of Cloghereen, John and Mce. and Matt of Doolaigue, John and Jerh. and John of Broughane, Ml. and John and Jas. and Jerh. and Thade and Bryan of Muingvatia, Mce. of Mulloghmarkey, Ml. and Denis and Ml. and Denis and Tim of Knockaninane, Jas. and Jerh. and John and Jerh. of Ballahacommane, Jas. of Coolacorcoran, Jas. of Clasheen, Jas. and Jas. of Ardananiz, Ml. of Minish, Ml. of Knockeenduff, Wm. and Con and Dan and Simon and Dan of Ballinahulla, Jerh. and John and Pat and Tim and Edm. of Knockrour, Pat and Bryan of Flemby, John of Grenagh, Denis of Gortatlea, Batt of Knockavinnane, Thomas of Kilkerry, James of Coolnadead, John and Rd. of Well lane, Con and Tom and Con of Brasby's lane, John and Tim and Pat and Tom of Bohereencael glebe, Pat of Fair hill, James of High street, Ml. and Ml. of Inch, Terence of New Market lane, Wm. of Church lane, Pat of Barry's lane, Ml. of Fleming's lane, Jerh of Crahane, John of Bohereenagown, Tom. and Ml. and Ml. and Ml. and Tim of Knocknahoe, Bryan and John and Bryan of Glanageenty, John of Maglass, John and James of Reenagown, Bryan of Clogher, Bryan of Knocknacurra, Ml. of Tooreenastooka, Jerh. of Muingnaminane, Denis of Ardagh, John of Cloonteens, Pat and Ml. of Doonryan, Ter and Tim and Margaret of of Coolbane, John of Cleedagh, John of Dromadeesert, Con of Coolick, James of Canguilla, John and Jerh. of Ballahantouragh, Ml. of Kilsarcon, James of Carker, James of Inchocorrigane, Pat and Ml. of Maulyarkane, Jerh. and James of Mastergeeha, James of Toornaounagh, James of Knockdoorah, Pat and Pat of Shinnagh, Jerh. of Gortnahaneboy, Dan of Rathmore, Ml. of Readrinagh, Anne of Knockreigh, Margt. of Corbally, Mary of Catleview, Hanoria of Toanbwee, Kate and Thomas of Cragg, Margt. of Bawnluskaha, Mary of Kilbannwane, Thomas of Lacarhoo, Pat of Kilnanare, Thade and aJmes of Tralia, Dan and Mce. and John of Farrandoctor, Ml. of Coolbane, Tom and John and John of Dromin, Kate of Gortdromerillagh, Mary of Firies, Mary and Johanna and Tim of Meenleitrim, Jerh. of Coolgarrive, Tom of Fiddane, Pat and Tom of Scart, John and Ml. of Knockatee, Mary of Glanowen, Batt. and John and Jerh. of Meenleitrim, John and James and John of Killeens, Bryan of Urrohogal, Simon of Pallas, John of Tralee, Jerh. of Glenlaharn, Terence of Lyre, Dan of Ballybrack, John of Shone, John of Ballincarrig, Ml and Tim of Knocknagown, Jas. of Shanaknock, Pat of Barleymount, James and Tim of Rocommane, Johanna of Meenavoughane, Kate of Greeves, Chas. and William of Kilcusnan, Mary of Huggard's lane, Ellen of Coffey's lane Ellen of Doocarrigbeg, Con of Annaghillymore, John of Lisbabe, Pat of Shronedarragh, Ellen of Gortnahaneboy, Ellen of Shinnagh, Pat of Knockauncuddoge, Pat of Gortalee, Pat of Crohane, James and John of Leannaguilla, Pat of Scart, Ellen of Kilquane, Bryan of Clogher, Mary of Crosstown, John of Fahaduff, Margaret of Killeagh, Margaret of Mullen, Tom of Cloghane, Kate of Brosna, Julia of Ahane, Kate of Kilsarcon Dan of Balivmalis, Con of Glenawaddra, Kate of Glanageenty, Ellen of Coolnageragh, Mary of Farranspig, Denis o' Gortagullane, John of Gortdromakiery, Jerh. and Mce. and Edm. and Pat of Leagh, John and Pat and William and Ml. of Knocknacree, Ml. of Knoppogue, Bryan of Derrico, Dan of Bishopscourt, Ml. of Rathmorrell, Con and Jerh. of Feans, Jerh. of Ballynoe, John of Lisduff. Tom and Tom and Pat of Mcenagohane, Pat of Dromnacurra, Lce. of Lissycurrig, Tom

O'Connor Households

of Cleanderry, Mce. and John of Cloonclogher, Hy. of Sleveen, Pat and John of Slieveawaddra, James and Bryan of Coolkeragh, Dan and John and Denis of Gortnaskeha, Ml. of Ahinma, Pat and Ml and Batt. and Tom and Ml. and John of Doon, John and Dan and Ml of Farranpierce, John of Ballybunion, Tom and John and Edm. and John of Cloghane, James and Ml. of Clashmealcon, Con of Kilmore, John of Bawnmore, Dan of Garrynaneaska, Martin of Ballinvoher, Tom and Tom of Ballincloher, Jas. of Garrynagore, John and Pat of Buncurrig, John and Michael of Booleenshare, David and Ml. and Pat of Tiershanaghan, James and Wm. of Listowel, Stephen of Convent lane, Mce. and John and James of Curraghtoosane. Ml. and Thomas and Pat and Edm. and Jas of Kilcoleman, Tim and Ml. of Larha, Batt and James and Ml. of Asdee, Morgan of Cloonamon, Harry of Curraghdarrig, James of Carrigane, Bridget of Shanaway, Mrs. John of Dooncaha, Ml. and Dan of Dungh, Geoffrey of Foildarrig, Con and Tim and Dan of Lisroe, Tom of Knockeenderraul, Batt of Kilcarabeg, Tom of Shronebeirne, Jas. and William and Tom of Listowel, Wm. and Pat of Croughatoosane, David of Garryantanavalla, John of Dromin, Michael and R.i. and Edm. of Gertacurreen, John of Coolnalought, Pat of Ballymacassy, Pat and Wm. and Denis of Leanamore. James of Ballylongford, Jerh. of Ballyline, Tom of Dromlivaun, Mary of Clahane, Kate of Kilmore, Tom of Shronebeirne, Jerh. and Pat and Wm. of Ratoran, Martin and Geo. of Bunagara, Ml. of Kilmeany. Pat of Ballycoury, John and Ml. of Ballydonoghue, David and Mce. of Moybella, Edm. of Gortagurrane, James and Pat of Asdee, Pat of Carrigane, Jerh. of Litter, Tom and Tom of Ardrahan, Wm. of Kilgulbin, John and Thomas and Denis of Tubridmore, Tom of Lerrig, Ml. of Dreenagh, John of Glenderry, Ml of Ballylongane, James of Dromatour, Thomas of Slievebwee, Mary and Mary of Gortdromagowna, Mary and Margt. of Lissaniska, Bridget of Beenaspug, John of Leitrim, Edm. of Glenalappa, John and Con of Gortdromasillahy, John and Pat of Cloonbrane, Wm. and Pat of Kilbaha, James of Shanaway, John and Tom and Ml. of Dooncaha, Con of Turmons, Tom and Con and Pat of Moyvane, Mary and Johanna of Asdee, Margaret and Mary of Larha, Denis of Dromcunnig, John of Boherroe, Batt of Drocunnig, Tom and James of Gortdromagownagh, Jerh. of Lissaniska, James of Finuge, Denis of Poulnahaha, Pat and John and Dromclough, Jerh. of Carhoonakineely, James and Martin of Kilcolgan, John and Thomas of Meen, Jerh. of Coolaclarig, Mary of Boherroe, Julia of Lissereen, Pat of Farranwilliam, Pat of Commons, Pat of Lyracrompane, Tom of Carrigcannon, John of Dromaddamore, James of Kilshenane, Pat of Irremore, Pat and John and Edm. of Droomkeen, David of Ballynagraigue, John of Meenahorna, John of Toor, John of Trieneragh, Tom of Lahaserough, Thomas of Lacca, John of Ballinorig, Thomas of Kilcooly, Johanna and Maria of Farranwilliam, Kate of Cloonclogher, Mary of Tulaghna, Kate of Dromartin, John of Gortanare, Mce. of Ballinprior, Batt of Guhard, Deela of Dreenagh, Ml. of Trippul, Thomas of Bromore, Mary of Murhur, Mary of Rea, James of Moyessa, Mary of Ballybunion, Margaret of Derreendaff, Mary of Benmore, Ml. of Ahabeg, Mary of Coolbeha, Margaret of Lenamore, Tom of Castlequarter. Manoria and Catherine of Ballydonaghue, Margaret of Rathroe, Edm. of Cloghaneliskart, James of Curraghcroneen, Ellen of Meenanare, Margaret of Dromkeen, Pat of Ahanagran, Pat of Crotta, Thos. of Convent street, Deborah of Ahamore, Jerh. of Garryard, Nora of Dromin, Tim and Pat of Cloonbeg, Ml. and Pat of Carrigaday, James of Shantallive, Mce. and Tim of Glanmore, James and John and Jas. of Scrallaghbeg, Pat of Glounagalt, Jerh. of Cloonmore, Ml of Ballyoughtra, John of Milltown, John and Tom of Church street, Dan of Bleach road, Annie of Cloghane, Edw. of Kilcooly, Mce. and Mce. of Murreigh, Thomas of Camp, Charles of Poulawaddra, Pat and Dan of Dromavally John and Batt. and John and John of Faha, Pat and Tom of Mullaghveal, Dan of Cloghane, John of Ballybeg, James of Glenfahan, James and Michael of

O'Connor Households

Kilwickadownig, John of Coumaleague, Ml. of Cloghers, Thomas of Killerisk, Mce. and John of Clahane, Kate of Tulligbeg, Nora of Reenu, Nora of Bansha, Bridget of MacCowen's lane, Ellen of Moyderwell, Mary of Castle Mac Ellistrum, Margaret and Kate and Margaret of Bridge street, Hanoria of Nelson street, Norah of John street, Nora of Russell street, Kate and Ellen of Mary street, Margaret of Strand street, Mary of Rock street, Mary of Spa road, Mrs of Caheranne road, Margaret of Francis street, Ml. and Jerh of Kilshanig, Tom and Edm. and Tom and Ml. of Fahamore, Tom of Maherabeg, Thomas of Kilshanig, John of Cloghanesheskeen, Ml. of Clooshguire, John of Illancoum, Kate of the Mall, Mary of Green lane, James and John and Bryan and Ml and Pat and Ml. of Curraheen, John and Tom and John of Derrymore, Margaret and Mary of Cromane, Kate of Bansha, Bridget of Laharan, Mary of Tullibeg, Bessie of Douglas, Johanna of Main street, Mary of Ballygamboon, Ellen of Lisnanoul. Ml. and James and Ml and John of Ballyviheen, Pat and Mce. and Pat of Kilcummin, Ml of Scraggane, Jerh. of Farrantooleen, James of Taulaght, John and Ml. of Monaree, Con of Doonsheane, Edward and Ned of Ballinavownig, James and Andrew of Ballyameenbought, Pat of Dingle Commons, Pat of Knocknahow, Mce. of Ballyheabought, John of Killehane, Jerh of Farransteenig, Pat of Cloghane, Pat of Ballyhea, Ml. of Carhoonaphuca, John of Emlagh, Mce. of Ballycurrane, John and Pat of Ballinknockane, Thomas of Ballinabuck, Ml. of Ballinloughig, John of Ballybrack, Pat of Ballydavid Hugh of Clash, Mce. and John of Ballyroe Ml and Ml and Ml of Ferritersquarter, Tom and James and Tom and Tom of Lassaboy, James of Gortaleen, James of Shanakeale, Jerh of Gortnahulla, John and Pat of Keel, James of Shanahill, Dan of Tulligbeg, James and Ml of Gurrane, John of Douglas, Dan of Laharan, James of Dromavally, Pat and John of Cromane, John of Knockyline, Mary and Ellen of Kilshanig, Ellen of Tullaree, Mary of Castlegregory, Mary of CloghaneSheskeen, Bridget of Cloghaneanode, James and Jerh. and Ml of Ballygamboon, Pat of Meanus, John of Ballyard, Pat of MacCowen's lane, Wm. of Chutes lane, Terence of Ballymullen, John and Pat and John of Brogue lane, John of Francis street, Batt and John of John street, Mce. of Market place, Jerh. of Strand street, John of Bridge street, Ml. of Blennerville, Con and Tim and Matt and John of Caheranne road, Mce. of Green lane, John of the Rock, Henry of Cronin's lane, Pat of Abbey street, Dan and Tom and Francis of Brherbee, Philip of Mary street, John of Rock street, Jerh. of Farrantooreen, John and Pat of Main street, John and Denis of Ardmoniel, Dan and Rd. and Pat and Eugene and Ml. of Laharan, John and Jas. and Stephen of Tulligbeg, John and Pat and Eugene of Tulligmore, John of Knockyline, Ml. and Ml. and Ml. of Rangue, Ml. of Iveragh road, Jerh. and John of Cromane, John of Lonart, Ml. of Dromavally, Eliza. of Clashaphuca, Mary of Clogherbrien, Jerh. of Lack, Ml. of Ballyarkane, Tom Joe. of Caheranne road, John and Jas. and Chas. and Jas. and Tom of Moyderwell, John and Tom and John of Boherbee, Pat of Bridge street, John of Edward street, Con of Princes street, John of the Rock, Chas. of James's street, Wm. of John street, Dan of the Square, John nd Philip of Abbey street, Jerh. and Florence and Pat of Strand street, Ml. of Market place, John of Denny street, Pat of Castle street, Tom of Brogue lane, Thade of Tierbrien, Denis and Denis of Droum, Ml. of Ballyiniry, Chas. and John and Dan and Jerh. and Ml. and Tom and Dan of Coolroe, John and Pat and John of Derrygorman, Tom of Kilduff, Tim of Ballintaggart, Tom of Brackloon, Ml. of Main street, John and John of Green lane, Mce. o fSpa road, John of Goat street, Jas. of Strand road, Tom and Tim and Jas. and Tom of John street, Ml. of Green street, Pat of Gortonora, Mce. of Dingle, Mce. of Graigue, Pat and Denis of Ballyaglisha, Con of Ballyenaghty, Con of Kerries, Peter of Liscahane, John of Cloghmakirkeen, Thos. of Knockanush, Mary of Kilmore, John of Boolteens, Tom of Ballybeggan, Pat and Denis and Thos.

O'Connor Households

of Camp, Michael of Tonevane, Johanna of Ballyroe, Pat of Gowlane, Kate of Kilvickadownig, Bridget of Ballyviheen, Mary of Ballintarmon, Bridget of Killeagh, Mce. of Ballinvogig, Thos. of Lisnakeelivee, Ellen of Cloghane, Kate of Ballinalackon, Pat of Gortacurrane, Mary of Coolroe, Johanna of Ballycarthy, Pat of Derrynaclough, John of Droumanassig. Tim and Tom and Ml. of Kenmare, Jas. of Gortagass, John of Killowen, Tim and Thos. of Goulane, Pat of Carrigahihilan, Jerh. of Downings lane. Ml. and John and Pat of Gortnagulla, Jerh. and John of Coulagh, John and Con of Garrydine, John of Kells, Ml. and Tim and Pat of Kilnabrack, John of Curra, Pat and Jerh. of Ballinakilla, Pat and Jerh. and John of Droum. Jerh. of Coolnabarrigill, Mce. and Tim of Doolahig, Denis and Jerh. of Ballintleave, Jerh. and Denis of Dooaghs, Tom and Mce. of Knockaunglass, Pat of Commaun, Jerh and Ml. and Jerh. of Glounagillagh Martin of Treanmanagh, Tim of Callahaniska. Mce. and Tim and Mce. and John and Jerh. and John and Tim of Cooleanig, Ml. and Jerh. John of Lisliebane, Ml. and Tim of Gortbov, Jerh. of Coolroe, Con of Shanacloon, Jerh. and John and Dan of Lateeve. Tim and Pat of Doory, John and Tim and John and Con of Cool. John and Ml. and Dan of Tinnies, Ml. of Coarabeg, Tim of Coaramore, Ml. of Maulcalee, John and Hugh of Dromlusk, Jerh. and Ml. of Rossdohan, John of Derreenamuckla, Tim of Letternadarrive. Hugh of Dromlusk, Con and John and Pat of Knockroe, Pat and Pat of Coomleagh, Mary of Killurly, Ellen of Deelis, Dan and Denis of Tooreenmore, Dan and Pat of Church lane, Silvester of High street, Bryan of Caherciveen, Pat of Fair green, Bryan of Valencia road, John of the Quay, Humphrey and Pat of Main street, Pat of Derreen, Pat of Gurranearagh, Con of Killoe, Jas. of Letter, Ml. of Gurranebane, Jerh. of Curragraigue, Jerh. and Dan of Innishfoyle, John of Coolnagoppogue, Jerh. of Baurearagh, Jerh. of Gortnagoppul, Chas. of Kilbonane, Ml. of Milleens, Margt. of Farranreagh, Johanna, of Cool, Jerh. of Roads, Denis and Tom and Dan and Tom and Con of Kimego, John and Pat and John of Killurly, Con of Deelis, Jas. of Ballycarbery, Pat of Laharan, John and Pat and Jerh. of Coars, Humphrey of Gurrane, Jerh. of Islandboy, Ml. and Con and Ml. of Cappagh, John of Ardlahas, Pat of Whitefield, Crohan and John of Rineen, Ml. of Inchee, Mary and Maria of Old Bridge street, Bridget of Victoria terrace, Nellie of Pound lane, Jerh. of Ballinakilla, John and Pat and Edw. and Pat and Rd. of Droum, Con and Dan and Tom and Jas. of Carhoonahone, John and Jas. of Alohart, John and Tom of Tullig, Tim and Ml. of Killoughane, Batt of Churchtown, John and Dan and John and Ml. of Gortfadda, Ml. and Pat of Maulagullane. John of Derryquin, John and Ml. of Driminamore, Ml. and Dan and John and Tim of Keel, Jerh. of Bunglasha, Pat and Matt of Creveen, John of Derreenaryagh. Ml. of Letter, Jerh. of Lacka, Denis and John and Tim of Rossacoosane, John and John of Gearha, Dan of Derrygurrane, Ml. of Scarteen, John of Inchinglanna, Eugene of Gortbrack, John and Tom and Jas. of Dunloe, Con and Tim of Cullinagh, Jas. of Coolmagort, Stephen and John and Pat and John of Shannera, Tim of Coomlettra. Denis and Ml. and Florence of Tooracladdane, Pat of Cloonaghlin, Tim of Coomaspeare, Martin of Maulnabrack. Pat and Ml. and Denis and Ml. of Toorslaeen, Denis of Derreen, Batt of Coomavoher, John of Lissantanuig, Tom and Johanna and Dan of Curraghbeg, Pat of Capnantanavally, Tim and John and Johanna and Bridget of Shanacashel, Pat of Sussa, Tom of Fermoyle, Jerh. of Killoluaig, Pat of ₋mlaghpeasta, Julia of Ballintᵢeave, Annie of Dooaghs, Bridget of Commaun, Mary of Treanmanagh, John and Batt and Denis of Kealafreaghane, Humphrey of Bunaderreen, Pat of Breahig, Pat and Tim of Tarmons, Ml. and John and Pat of Curravaha, Tim of Lettergarriv, John and Jerh. of Shroneahirreemore, John and Pat of Derreenavarrig, Pat of Canuig, Michael of Boolakeel, Tim and John of Kilpatrick, Ml. of Aghatubrid, Ml. of Cloghanecarnahan, Jerh. of Meanus, Tim of Ardacluckeen, John of Gortloughra, Mary of Doiminamore, Bridget of Inchin-

O'Connor Households

aleega, John of Maulnagower, Tim of Coomnakilla, Hanoria and Hanoria of Greenane, Kate and Mary of Kilnabrack, Bridget of Gleensk, Mary of Knockaneyouloo, Dan of Ballycarnahan, Jas. of Coad, Norah of Keel, Hanoria of Farranreagh, Mary of Laharan, Pat of Glounagillagh, Abbey of Lounaghan, Bridget of Curravaha, Ml. of Cahernageeha, Johanna of Coomlettra, Mary of Shannera, Dan of Curraghbeg, John of Derrylahan, Ml. of Claddanure, Ellen of Strandsend, Bridget of Reenard, Mary of Inchinlough, Mary Knockroe, Julia of Coomaspeare, Mary of Doory, Margt. of Cullenagh, John of Killanbuoina, Mary of Rossmore, Julia of Loher, Mary of Kealafreaghane, Julia of Emlaghnamuck, Tim of Killoughane, John of Caunteens, Mary of Cools, Ml. of Bohocogram, Dan of Derreengarinshagh. The following spell the name O'Connor:—John of Castleisland, John of Ballymacadam, Bryan of Castleview, Mce. and Wm. of Cahereens, Peter of Cliddaun, Jas. and Jas. of Highstreet, Jerh. and John and Jerh. and Denis of New-street, Dan of College-street, John of Demesne, Jas. of Well-lane, Thaddeus and Ml. of Moyeightragh, John and Chas. and Denis of Inch, Dan of Mainstreet, Tim of Cordal, Hanoria of Cloonkeen, Julia and Johanna of Knocknagoshel, Mary and Mary of Fahaduff, Wm. of Greeveguilla, Wm. of Tooreenamult, Nora and Lizzie of Moanmore, Mary of Tonebwee, Eliza of Knockeen, Anne of Caheragh, Mary and Hanoria and Nora and Hannah of New-street, Kate of High-street, Edw. of Headfort, Geoffrey of Annaghillymore, John of Shronedarragh, Jas. of Fahaduff, Kerry and John of Knocknagoshel, Jerh. of Fossa, M. of Ballydwyer, Eugene of Knockatagglebeg, Bella and Anne of Kilmaniheen, John of Grenagh, Dan of Mullaghmarkey, Batt. of Meenleitrim, Anne and Annie of Cragg, Ellen of Lyre, Mary and John of Rathanny, Tim of Gurrane, Mce. of Inchincummer, Deborah and Hannah of New-street, Jerh. of Laharan, Ml. of Coilbwee, Michael of Kylebwee, Pat of Gortnaminich, Pat and Con of Kealed, Pat of Ballylongford, Ml. of Ballymacassy, Tim of Bawnmore, Tim of Ballymacquin, John of Glanaphuca, Ml. of Killehenny, Johanna of Barraduff, Ellen and Edm. of Tullamore, Edm. of Derrindaff, Humphrey of Rathea, Tom of Dromaddamore, Ml. of Ballinclemesig, Pat of Cloonamon, Tim of Larha, Margt. of Rahoonagh, Julia of Doon, Hy. of Sleveen, Ml. of Listowel, David and Wm. of Ballyhadigue, Thos. cf Shrone, Hanoria of Larha, Ml. of Rathoran, Mce. and Thaddeus of Dromkeen, Rd. and Hanora of Ahanagran, Mary and Mary of Listowel, Rd. and Thos. of Loughancs, Jas. and Pat and Ml. and Wm. and John of Tieraclea, John of Kilcolgan, Tim of Tarbert island, Dan of Lisroe, Batt. and Edm. and John and Batt. of Duagh, Morgan of Clogher, John of Lixnaw, Ml. of Ballinageragh, Ml. and Rd. and Ml. of Tarmons, Jerh. of Gurteenooelig, John of Pulleen, Ml. and Thos. and Ml. and Pat and Ml. and Jerh. of Listowel, Denis of Convent-lane, Tom of Market-street, Jas. and Thos. of Meenahorna, Jerh. and Tim of Knockmeal, Wm. of Coolanealig, Johanna of Tarmons, Mrs. John of Dooncaha, Mrs. Tim of Tarbert island, Sarah of Kilcolgan, Kate of Leanamore, Jerh. of Gransha, Hannah and Mary and Hanoria, and John and Tom and John and Mary and John and Mary and Tom and Eliza and Kate and Hanoria of Main-street, Mary of Killorglin, John of Holyground, John of Castle-street, Jas. of John-street, Thos. of Green-lane, Jos. of Bridge-street, Flor. and Tom of the Mall, Tim of Russell-street, Tim of the Square, John of Ballymullen, Flor. of Martramane, Batt. of Clooshguire, Ml. of Fahamore, Mce. of Ardamore, Nora of Ballinknockane, Pat of Ballinraha, Mary of Kilmalkedar, Ml. of Cloghane, Tim of Graigue, Jas. and Tim of Lisanoul, Tim and John of Aughacasla, Martin of Gortagass, Mary of William-street, Mary of Kilnabrack, Tim of Dereenaclaurig, Jerh. of Dooaghs, Eliza and Francis of Caherciveen, Ml. and Hanoria of Main-street, Tim of Quay-street, Jerh. and Chas. and David of. Henry-street, Michael of William-street, Jerh. of Tubrid. There are references to O'Connor, O'Conchobhair Ciarraighe, in the Annals of Ireland at the years 1019-67-9-86-93-5, 1103-7-10-15-38-42-51-2, 1154-65-6-83-96, 1405-31-45-70-85, 1516-24-62-68-73-83-99, 1600-1-2-52.

O'Connell Households

In 1201 Wm. de Burgh held the lands of Castle Connell. In 1244, John Fitz Thomas Fitz Gerald held a charter of free chase and warren in Okonyl, Muskry, Kery, Youach, and Orathat, i.e., Co. Kerry, W. Cork, W. Limerick or most of West Munster under the tuath sen Eran. In 1215 King John granted Daniel Connell English liberty and laws. In 1211 Donogh Cairbreach O'Brien held Carraig o g Coinell. In 1604 Theobald Burke, baron Bourgh of Connell or Castleconnell, was granted the lands of Cloghankeanige and Inishfearglin, held by Morishe Mac Richard O'Connell, yeoman, who died in rebellion. In 1650 Richard O Connell was bishop in Killarney, Connell was in Kilarney, and Tiegue served in Colonel Courtenay's regiment. In 1656 Peter lived at Cloghanmacquin Morris at Cahirbearnagh, Charles at Beginis, John at Ballyheirny, John at Caherciveen, Daniel Mac Geoffrey, the ancestor of the Darrynane branch, Ellin, alias Lyne, at Durrinemore, John at Ballinahow and Ashtown, Morrogh at Va.entia and Daniel at Bailyhirney. Geoffrey, son of Maurice of Ballinehaw, nephew of John of Ashtown, dsp. in 1699; Charles, of Ballynacleragh and Canburren, was brother of John of Ashtown, and was living in 1700. Colonel Maurice, son of Jeffrey, and heir to John of Ashtown, was killed at Aughrim, dsp.; John, son of Jeffrey, bro. to Col. Maurice, dsp. before the surrender of Limerick, Richard, nephew of John of Ashtown, dsp. 1693, and his brother, John, living in 1700, dsp. Maurice of Dunmaniheen, nephew of John of Ashtown, was living in 1700. In 1776 the following O'Connells took the oath of allegiance: Con, M.D. of Carhen; Dan of Comego, Dan of Tarmons, Mce. of Daurinane, Mce. of Ballinaclaun, Morgan of Carhen, and Richard of Comego. Daniel Charles lived 1745-1838. Daniel 1775-1847, John 1810-58, Sir Mce. Chas. 1812-79, Sir Mce. Chas. Ph. 1848, Morgan 1804-85, Baron Moritz 1740-1830. In 1876, Kerry landowners included C. D O'Connell of Bantry 9,807 acres; Dan of Derrynane 17,394; D. J. of Grenagh, 603; Sir M. J. of Lakeview, 18,752; M. J. of Cashel, 496; and Thomas of Deerpark, 611 acres. The O'Connells were connstables of Ballycarbery castle for MacCarthy Mor, and Sir James of Lake View bought the castle and adjacent lands. Richard, of Ballycarbery, had Mce. of Caherbarnagh, John of Ashtown, and Rickard bishop of Kerry: John of Ashtown in Dublin was seneschal to the Duke of Ormond, and l. in 1680, being buried in St. James' church in Dublin. Bishop Rickard, b. 1575, travelled in Spain, France, and England, was educated at Bordeaux, was bishop of Kerry in 1643-1653 and is mentioned in the State Papers. Maurice of Caherbarnagh in 1656 was transplanted to Briantree, Lisdoonvarna, Clare, but died en route, leaving issue (1) Batt, ancestor of Dunmaniheen (Tralee) and Darrynane branches, and (2) Charles, ancestor of Ballinabloun branch. (1) Batt had (a) Mce. of Briantree in Clare, (b) Geoffrey (Sheara), and (c) John, author of the dirge of Ireland, died 1702. This poem of 244 stanzas is in the Br. Mus. MSS. 33,567 addl., and in Egerton 129, and in addl. 18,951, it was published by M. A. O'Brennan in 1858, see also Mr Clarke's dirge in 1827, and Admhuim fein by Rev. P. S. Dinneen in 1900. Geoffrey (Sheara) had two sons, Mce. and Daniel. Maurice of Dunmaniheen, lieut.-colonel in Lord Slane's infantry, d. 1715, leaving a son Jeffrey of the vast herds, d. 1722, aged 38, buried in O'Connell tomb in Caherciveen old churchyard, and by his wife, Eliz., dau. of Edmund Conway of Glenbeigh, had a son Maurice, of Imlaghmore, who m. Jane Blennerhassett, having issue Thomas and Edward. Thomas, M.D., had a dau., Mary, who m. 1802, Daniel O'Connell, the Liberator; and a son, Rickard, capt. and adjutant in the Kerry militia in 1816. Rickard O'Connell, lieut. 89th reg., m. 1801, Eliz. Tuohy. Edward, son of Maurice of Imlaghmore, had issue John, Dan, and Rickard; John, lieut., 43rd reg., died at San Sebastian; Dan, "splinter," an attorney, m. Ellen, sister of the Liberator, having a dau. Catherine, who m. Denis Mac Cartie of Headfort, having a son, Dan, who m. Mary, dau. of Mce. O'Connell of Darrynane, leaving issue; Rd., surgeon, 43rd regt. Geoffrey, of Kilkaveragh, had a son, Chas., of Maghera in Clare, whose son, Rickard, was a captain in the Irish

O'Connell Households

Brigade and later in the Dutch service; in 1785 he was lieut. in Walsh's regt.; he m. Mary, dau. of Jas. Burke of Clonkelane in Clare; in 1777 he entered the Irish Brigade; his father was tenant of Briantree in Clare to Lord Inchiquin; his grandfather was Geoffrey the great herds; in 1782 he was at Fenloe in Clare; in 1783 he visited the O'Connell tomb at Inagh, near Briantree; he wrote to Dr. Mce. Leynes of Tralee about the O'Connell pedigree. In 1782, Morgan, P.P., Killarney, was uncle of Capt. Rickard. Dan, son of Geoffrey, settled at Darrynane or Aghavore, having a son John, Jacobite captain, and d. 1741, having Dan of Darrynane, d. 1770, and Mce. of Tarmons, father of Baron O'Connell. Chas. of Ballinabloun, son of Philip, had a son Sir Maurice Charles, lieut.-general, C.-in-C. in N. S. Wales, col. of 80th reg., d. 1848, m. Mary Bligh, having Mce., Chas., Wm. and Eliz., who m. Henry, son of Lord Wm. Somerset, having issue: Wm. m. Mary, dau. of Genl. Sir P. Stuart; Sir Mce. Chas. dsp. 1878, capt. in 28th reg., and of British legion in Spain, president of legislative council in Queensland. Chas., son of Dan of Ballynabloun, 1805-77, m. Kate, dau. of the Liberator, having issue Dan, Chas. F. K., 1846-75; Mary, a nun, dec.; Theresa, dec.; Kate, nun, dec.; Betsy, dec.; Eileen, m. 1870, K. Cullen; Teresa, m. 1876, T. Downes. Dan, son of Chas., b. 1842, m. (1) Milly Curtis of Cork, having 2 daus. dec.; m. (2) Helen Mac Kenna of Cork, having Chas., staff surgeon, R.N.; Donald, b. 1879; Mce., b. 1885; Esther; Ellen, m. 1910, G. Moorhead of Enniskillen; Teresa, Jeffrey, of Ballycarbery, d. 1635, had Mce. and Dan. Mce. of Brentree in Clare, had Mce. and John. Mce. of Briantree, grandson of Mce. son of Batt, had 3 sons, Mce., Brigadier, d. at Aughrim in 1691; Richard, dsp., 1748, in London; John, lieut., dsp. at Derry, 1689. Dan of Ahavore, son of Jeffrey, m. Alice Sigerson, having 2 sons John and Mce; he rented Darrynane from Lord Cork, and his grandson built part of the present house. Mce., d. 1715, had a grandson, Richard, Captain in the Legion of Maillebois in Holland. John, son of Dan, served under Col. Mce. at Aughrim,

m. in 1709 Eliz. Conway of Cluhane, d. 1741, having 3 sons, Dan, Mce. and Jeffrey; Mce. of Tarmons, m. Mary O'Sullivan Beare, having Mce and a dau. who m. Chas. O'Connell whose son was Genl. Sir Mce., whose son was Sir Mce. Chas. dsp. 1878. Mce. of Tarmons, had a son Morty or Mce, 1740-1831. Baron Moritz O'Connell of the Austrian service, Colonel, Chamberlain to Maria Theresa, and Governor of Praigue Jeffrey was son of John; Daniel, son of John, m. Mary O'Donoghue of Anivys, who d. 1794, having issue 22 children, he d. 1770, and built Darrynane house in 1745-51 4 sons and 8 daus. grew up. John son of Dan, was b. 1725, m. 1748 Mary O'Falvey of Faha, and d. 1751, leaving a dau. Abigail who m. Jas. Gould of Clonakilty, having a dau. in 1776. Mce. m. Mary Cantillon, dsp. a. 97, his heir being the Liberator, and his estate of £54.000 was divided between 3 nephews, Connell, 1741-65, son of Dan, navigator, was drowned at sea; Daniel, 1745-1833, Count, Colonel of IrishBrigade, sub-lieut. 1761, 1st lient 1766, aide major in Clare regt. 1769, lt.-Col. 1779, col. 1783, Count in 1788, outlawed by the French Convention, Col. of 4th regt. of Irish Brigade in British army in 1794, m. Marthe Gourand, Comtesse de Bellevue in 1796, in 1817 at French Court, died July, 9, 1833, and was buried in Coude cemetery, Madon leaving his title to his godson (the son of a stepdau.), Daniel Charles d. Etchegoyen O'Connell, Eliz. O'Connell m. 1744 Tim MacCarthy of Ougthermoney. her grand-dau. was Evelina. Joan m. Chas. Sughrue of Fermoyle. Abigail m 1766 Major O'Sullivan of the Austrian army, and the Empress Maria Theresa was godmother to their first child. Mary m. Jas. Baldwin of Chohina, near Macroom, in 1762, and had six children. Ellen m. (1) O'Connor of Firies, and (2) Arthur O'Leary, and wrote a poem on his outlawry. 1773. Catherine, m. Mortogh O'Sullivan of Coulagh; Anne or Nancy m. 1773, Capt. Mce. Geoffrey O'Connell, of France and Ballinablown, sold Lative, and settled in Killarney, having no issue. Alice m. 1750, Thos. John Segerson of Ballinskelligs. Morgan O'Connell of Carhen, 3rd son of Daniel, m. 1771,

O'Connell Households

Catherine O'Mullane of Whitechurch, having issue 4 sons and 3 daus.; he kept a general and export store in Caherciveen and salt puns at Carhen, and leased lands from T.C.D. and Lord Shelbourne; he d. in 1807; his eldest son was Daniel the Liberator. Maurice, 1776-1797, lieut. in Serrants regt. of Irish Brigade, and died at St. Domingo, in the British army. John of Grenagh, 1779-1859: m. 1806, Eliz. Coppinger of Ballyvolane, having 2 sons and 2 daus. Morgan of Ballyglean in Clare, 1811-75, B.L., M.P., m. Mary Bianconi, having a son John b. 1871 m. 1894 Arabella Hayes, having three daughters. Rev. John D. P. of Grenagh, 1828-72. Jane of Grenagh, m. (1) Chas. O'Donoghue of the Glens, and (2) Mac Carthy O'Leary, having issue Catherine of Grenagh, m. Samuel Vines. Sir James of Lake View, son of Morgan of Carhen, was created a Baronet in 1869, m. 1818 Jane O'Donoghue of the Glens, having 5 sons, Sir Mce., Dan, Chas. 1828-93, James 1832-55, Morgan 1833-70; he bought Ballycarbery castle and lands, b. 1786, d. 1872, Daniel 1823-88, son of Sir Jas. m. 1863, Frances Shine Lawlor, having 6 sons and 5 daus. Jas. b. 1864, Donal b. 1867, Mce. b. 1876, Morgan 1880-1902, Edw. d. 1881, Conail b. 1882, Isabel, Eva, Clare, Mary, Dorothy. Sir Maurice, 1821-96, 2nd Baronet, m. 1855 Emily O'Conor, having 4 sons and 1 dau., Ellen, m. 1902 Genl. Sir Chas. Tucker, Jas. Ross, son of Sir Mce. 2, b. 1863, major, 1st Shrops., served in Egypt 1896-8. Sir Daniel, 1861-1905, 3rd Baronet. Sir Morgan, 4th Baronet, b. 1862, m. 1884, Maria Hickie of Slevoyre, having Mce. b. 1889, lieut. 6th R. Fusiliers; Donal, b. 1893; Basil, b. 1900; Lucila; Callister, d. 1895. Mary, dau. of Morgan of Carhen, m. Jerh. Mac Carthy of Woodview in 1791. Honora, dau. of Morgan, m. Dan O'Sullivan of Reendonegan in Cork. Catherine, dau. of Morgan, m. H. Moynihan of Rathbeg. Ellen, dau. of Morgan, m. Daniel O'Connell of Tralee. Bridget, dau. of Morgan, m. Miles Mac Swiney of Kenmare. Alicia, dau. of Morgan, m. 1820, W. F. Finn, M.P. for Kilkenny. Daniel O'Connell, the Liberator, 1775-1847, m. 1802, Mary, dau. of Thos. O'Connell, M.D., of Tralee, having 4 sons and 3 daus. Morgan, 1804-85, son of Daniel, m. 1840, Kate Balfe; was M.P. and Registrar of Deeds for Ireland. John, son of Daniel 1810-58, m. 1838, Eliz. Ryan, having 3 sons and 5 daus.; he was M.P. Clerk of the Hanaper in Ireland, and wrote the Argument for Ireland, Recollections, etc. Dan, son of John dsp. 1872. John, son of John, b. 1843, m. 1873 Mary Baldwin, having John, b. 1875, Dan. 1879, Hy. b. 1881. Morgan, 1845-81, son of John, Captain in 1st Hampshire regt., d unm. Eliz., dau. of John, m. 1861 Jas. Sullivan. Mary, dau. of John m. 1867, A. N. Comyn, and d. 1910. Eily, dau. of John, a nun, dec. Kathleen, dau. of John, m. 1885 Major M. J. Balfe of Castlerea. Alice, dau. of John. Daniel, son of Daniel, b. 1816, m. 1866, Ellen Foster, and d. 1897, leaving Daniel, son of Daniel, b. 1873, Mce. b. 1874, Geoffrey b. 1876, Eily, Mary, Morgan b. 1879, Edm. b. 1885, Jas. b. 1888. Ellen, dau. of Daniel the Liberator, 1805-83, poetess, m. C. Fitzsimon of Glancullen. Catherine, dau. of Daniel, m. 1832 Chas. O'Connell of Ballynabloun, and d. 1891 Elizabeth, dau. of Daniel, m. N. J. Ffrench. Maurice, 1803-53, son of the Liberator, poet, M.P., m. 1832, Frances Scott of Cahercon in Clare having 2 sons and 2 daus. John son of Mce., b. 1839, m. 1873, Mary Mac Cartie, having Daniel 1878-93 Mce. b. 1888, and 4 daus. Fanny d unm. 1878. Mary, m. 1858 Daniel Mac Cartie of Headfort. Daniel son of Maurice, of Darrynane, b. 1816, m. 1861, Isabella Shine Lawlor of Grenagh, having Isabella Kathleen, Margaret, Eileen, Frances. The literature about Daniel O'Connell, the Liberator, is very extensive; and biographies of him have been written by M. Mac Donagh, W. J. Fitz Patrick, John O'Connell, T. C. Luby, W. MacCabe, Canon O'Rourke, R. Dunlop, C. O'Keeffe, M. F. Cusack, J. Fagan, W. Daunt, W. Phillips Connll, O'Conntall, O'Conghaile O'Conaill; 376 families in Kerry viz.: Pat and Dan of Inch, Dan of Main-street, Dan of Duckett's lane, Ml. of Knockreer, Ml. of Brewery lane, Denis and David of Ahaneboy, John of Tooreenmore, Ml. of Moanmore, Denis and John of Tullig, Jerh. of Readrinagh, Denis and Mce. of Gortnahaneboy, Jerh.

O'Connell Households

of Lissyconnor, Thos. of Knocknagown, Mce. of Beheenagh, Dan of Knockrour, Denis of Knockeenahone, Ml. of Knockearagh, John of Park. Bridget of Hogan's-lane, Julia of Inch Margt. of Bishop's-lane, Jas. and Ml. of Fahaduff, Ml. of Faughcullia, Tim of Gortagullane, Con. and Ml. of Brosnu, Ml. Kilmanihan, John of Gortalee, John of Derreenaculig, Wm. and Tim of Knockawinna, Edm. of Gneeveguilla, John of Reanasup, Tim of Knockanes, Marv of Canguilla, Mary of Coom Mary of Ballymalis, John of Gortahoonig, Mce. of Kilcusnan, John of Dromadeesert, Margt. of Kilmore. Pat of Cordal, Tim of Graffeens, Dan of Ardteegalvin, Mary of Rathbeg, Mary of Mullen, Mary of Doolaigue, John of Gortatlea, Jas. and Ml. of Liscullane, Ml. of Deerpark, Thos. of Ballinageragh, Pat of Liscullane, Ml. of Banna, Pat of Currahane, Ml. of Killeacle, Ml. of Gortadrislig, Dan of Gransha, Mary of Dromlegagh, Margt. of Bally Mac Jordan, Kate of Ballynagraigue, Edm. and Pat of Crotta, Ml. of Kilfeighney, Ml. and Con. and John of Kilbaha, John of Ahalahanna, Ml. of Heirhill, Pat and Pot of Ballyheigue. Denis of Dreenagh, Tom of Glenderry, Ml. and Pat of Tiduff, Dan of Ballymacquin, Denis and Pat of Cahernead, Mce. and Jerh. of Ballyhennessy, John of Irremore, Ml. and David of Aughrim, John of Creegovane, Pat of Commons, Ml. of Kilteen, Denis of Killarida, Dan of Slievewaddra, Dan of Tullaghna, Ml. of Lackamore, John of Lissireen, Margt. and Kate of Carrahane, John and Mce. of Ahabeg, John of Rahavanig, Julia of Dromkeen, John of Muckenagh Kate of Dromclought, John of Ardcullen, Ml. of Farranawanna, Wm. of Ballinorig, Dan of Clashnanoon. Ellen of Rea, Joan of Grogeen, Jas. of Curraghcroneen, Kate of Ballinorig Pat of Clounmacon, John of Dromloughra, Kate of Moyvane, Ml. of Murhur, Ml. and Chas. of Rock-street, John of MacCowen's lane, John of Strand-street, Ml. of Mary-street, Tim of Island of Geese, Tim of Abbey-street, Chas. of Church-street, Jas. of Russell-street, Tim and Ellen of Boherbee, Ellen of Rock-street, Mary of Moyderwell Tim and John and Ml. and Jas. of Barrow, Dan of Baltygarron, Dan and Ellen of Ballymeenboght. Morgan of Doon, Mce. of Curragraigue, Pat of Gurrane, Mce. of Curragraigue, Pat of Gurrane Mce. of Mill road, Ml. of Ballineanig, John of Carrigadav, Ml. of Milltown. John of Knockenagh, Mce of Tullig John of Fahamore, Pat of Tonevane, Ml. and Dan and Ml and Pat of Main-street, Pat of Carhan, Pat and John of High st. Rd. of Old road, Thos of Reenard, Tom of Valencia-road, John of Gurteen, Mce. of Inchimateigue, Geoffrey of Commanes, Andrew of Glanbeg, John of Beenbane, Mce. of Breahig, Mce. of Kealgurteen, John and Pat of Cloghvoola, Michael of Waterville, John of Reencaheragh, Pat and Tim and Ml. and Tom and Tim of Kilkeaveragh, Denis and Tim and Dan and Ml. and Dan and John of Doory, Denis and Ml. and John of Portmagee, Ml. of Lateeve, James and John of Knockeenawaddra, Mce and Pat and Dan of Bray, John of Feighmane, John of Laharn, John and Pat of Corabeg, John and Kate and Ml. and John of Tinnies, Jerh. of Farranreagh, John of Kilbeg, Mary and Bridget and Mary and Mary of Coarhabeg, Abbey of Farranreagh, John and Wm. and John of Beginish, Dan of Dooneen, Mce. and Ml. of Inchintrea, John of Laharn, Pat of Mountluke, Pat of Ballycarbery, Ml. of Killelan, Pat of Kimego, Dan of Liss, Roger of Caherlihellan, Morgan of Knockaneybouloo, Dan and John and Ml. and John of Fermoyle, Pat and Tim of Aghaneboy, Kate and Mary of Tarmons, Dan of Downing's row, Felix of Droumanasig, Dan of Kilmurray, Ml. of Kenmare, Mary and Kate of Castlequin, Julia and Kate of Ballycarbery, Mary of Mountlunke, James of Caherciveen, John and Pat of Letter, Denis of Reenard, Ml. and John of Carhan, John of Gurranebane, Mary of the Quay, Mary of the Old road, Mary of High street, Mary of Kilcolman, Maurice of Farranearagh, Pat of Emlaghlea, Geoffrey and Tom and Pat and Ml. of Emlaghmore, Mce. and John and Malachy of Coomataukane, Pat of Cahernageeha, Denis and John of Dungegan, Dan of Kinard, Jas. of Bolus, Pat of Canwig, Pat and Mce. of Ballinskelligs, John of Dungegan.

Donnelly & Donoghue Households

Donnelly, O'Donngaile; chief of Muscraighe tire in Ormond; 41 families in Kerry, viz.:—David and Denis of Gneeveguilla, Dan of Coom, Francis of Killarney, Ml. of Ardcrone, Ml. of Rockfield, Dan of Gortavullen, Dan. of Knockaderry, Batt of Kilfeighney, Tom and Dan of Dromkeen, Ml. of Fahamore, John of Furrancarriga, Ml. and Denis and Sylvester and Denis and John and Norah of Eigthercua. John and Mary of Raheens, Pat of Shanaknock, John of Bridge street, Ml. of Mucksna, Pat and Flor of Coomatloukane, Con and John of Derrynane, Denis of Gurranebawn, Crohan and Humphrey and Ml. of Spunkane, Tim of High street, Denis and Ml. of Meelagulleen, Ml. of Dirrenedin, Mary of Derrynane beg, Ml. of Rath, Denis of Ardcost, Ml. of Tooracladdane, James of Rossacoosane.

Donoghue, O'Donncada; Ua Donnchadha of Cashel; O'Donoghue; 363 families in Kerry, viz:—Geoffrey the O'Donoghue of the Glens, Con and James of Rusheenbeg, Denis and Denis and Roger and John and John of Curreal, Pat and Tim and Flor of Shroneboy, Denis of Garries, Jerh. and Denis and Roger of Killaha, James of Derreenacullig, Pat of Rusheenmore, Pat of Gortalee, Ml. and Pat and Sylvester and Tim and James and Tim of Gortdromakiery, John of Faughcullia, Dan of Coolies, John and Flor of Sheheree, Pat of Annaghmore, John and Ml. and John and Jerh. and John of Killeen, Roger of Knockanes, Tim of Annaghbeg, Dan and Pat of Carrigaveema. Dan and Flor of Inch, Dan and Jerh. of Islandmore, Ml of Carrigavannia, John of Ardteegalvin, John of Emmett's tce., Dan of Bridewell lane, Dan of Brasby's lane, Sylvester and John of College street, Edward of Barry's lane, John of Tooreenagown, Nicholas and Tim of Kilmurry, Mort of Lackbroder, John of Tooreenagown, Nicholas of Lyre, Pat and Con of Gortalicka, Flor and John and Dan of Coomacullen, Denis and Roger and Jerh of Derryreag, Con of Gortalicka, Pat of Derrymaclavode, Dan and Pat and Hugh of Barraduff, Tim and Ml of Shronedarragh, Dan of Headfort, John and Denis of Lisbabe, Tim of Gortnahaneboy, John and Pat of Shinnagh, Pat of Rathbeg, Pat of Rathmore, Ml. of Meentogues. Denis of Readrinagh, Dan of Gortnaprocess, Pat of Carrigeencullia, Hugh and John and Hugh of Knocknahoe, Ml. and Tim of Kilquane, Tim and Dan of Doocarrig, Hugh of Sheans, Hanoria and John of Tiernaboul, Kate of Tullig, Margt. and Hanoria of Lissivigeen, James of Coolcaslough, Pat of Coolcorcoran, Jerh of Knockaninane, Tom of Gortnacarriga, Pat of Knockasartnett, John of Lisheen, Pat of Maughantourig, John of Bawnard, Tim of Greeveguilla, Dan of New street, Dan of Brewery lane, Con of Brasby's lane, Bridget and Ellen and Dan and Ellen of Annagh, Pat and Jerh. of Toornanounagh, John of Gortatlea, Mary of Gortdromakiery, Ellen of Faughbane, Ellen of Dromickbane, Anne of Faughcullia, Jas. of Knockrour, Mce and Denis of Knocknaboul, James of Ballinard, James of Knockatee, Denis of Tooreenascarthy, Ellen of Inch. Ellen of Dromcarbin, Ellen of Gortahoosh, Jerh of Corbally, Flor of Killeagh, Denis and Denis of Carker, Pat and Denis of Knocknagoshel, Ellen of Luckabane, Margaret of Kilmurry, Ellen of Killaha, Johanna of Curreal, Denis of Killarney road, Tim and Tom of Faha, Tim of Ballinahalla, Con of Breahig, Mary and Mary of Carrigeencullia, Mary of Ballyfinane, Mary and John of Clounmelane, Ellen of Inchicorrigane, Ml of Ballybrack, Ellen and Johanna of Gortderrig, Con of Maglass, John of Mweenalaa, John of Barleymount, Margaret of Coolavoorheen, Ml of Incheens, Con of Ballybeg, Wm. of Dromroe, Ellen of Droumavranka, Con of Corbally, Dan of Knockreagh, Mary of Well lane, Hugh of Sheans, Ml. of Knockacullig, Pat and Tom of Meenagohane, Tom and John and Mce of Dreemnacurra, Ml and Geoffrey of Ardydonegan, Dan of Tooreen, Mort and John of Knockaclare, Tim of Dromaddra, Matt of Clountubrid, Pat of Coolaclarig, James of Clounmacon, Dan and John of Ballyoneen, James of Rathea, Ellen of Dromadamore, John of Poulnahaha, James

186

Donoghue Households

of Garrynagore, Dan of Libes, John of Bedford, James of Dromartin, John of Duagh, Tom of Aughacasla, Ml of Fahamore, Ml. and Jerh. of Lisnagree, Tom of Deelis, Mary of Ml and Ml of Ballinabooly, Anthony Callenafeicy, Mce and Mce of Glens, of Martramane, John of Ballinclare, Deborah of Clounalour, Julia of Dromavally, Ml. of Rathass, Pat of Aughanna, Garrett of Brackhill, John of Old Chapel lane, Dan of Farranlickeen, Bridget of Strand street, Johanna of Mac Cowen's lane, Tom of Brogue lane, Ml. of Francis street, John and Flor of Boherbee, Tim of John street, Mary of Goat street, John and Dan of Main street, Jerh. of Killorglin. Dan of Douglas, Pat and John of Tulligmore, Ml. of Laharan road, Ml. and Ml. of Laharan, James and Dan and James of Reen, John of Ballykissane, Pat of Castle Conway, Jerh of Canburrin, John and Dan and Ml. of Reenard, John of Pound lane, John and Tim of Main street, Ml. and John of Garranereagh, Jas. of Killoe, Dan of Knockaunrory, Ml of Letter, Roger and Ml. of Sallahig, James and Pat of Dromkeare, Ml. of Gortgower, Pat of Coorhabeg. Ml of Tinnies, Peter and John of Bray, Peter and Ml. and Molachy of Dohilla, James and John of Feighmane, Francis of Ballymanagh, John of Ballyharney, Pat of Corabeg, Denis and Pot ond John of Clohermoosh, Denis of Uallis, Pat of Kilgariffe, John of Collogues, Daniel of Churchground, John of Knockeens, Ml of Inchincocsh, Tim of Fusso, Tom and Tom of Lomanagh, Dan of Gullaba. Dan of Gurteen, John of Coolmagort, Denis of Cullinagh John and Ml and James and Dan of Castlequin, James and Pat and Tim and Mart of Coomnahincha, John of Ballycarbery, James of Killurly, John and James and John and James and Tom of Coomatloukane, John of Darrynanebeg, Pat and Dan and Tom of Derrynafoyle, Tim of Ankail, Tim of Gartlahard, Flor of Coolknoohill, Jerh. of Inchees, Dan of Kilfadamore, Tim of Rosseightragh, Ml and Roger of Cahir, Geoffrey of Inchinaleega Ml. of Caherdaniel, Dan of Ballycarnahan, Pat and Ml. and Pat of Rath, Nora of Main street, Mary of Laharan, Kate of Ohermong, Bridget and Ellen of Reenard. Jerh. and John of Skehanagh, Ml. of Dungegan, Ml of Curraghnanov, Batt. of Reenanallagane, Tim of Curraheen, Hanoria of Clcon, Tim of Loher, Hanoria and James of Ballinabloun, Mary of Gortgower, John of lllaunstookagh, Jane of Pound lane, Nano of Coomdeeween, Pat of Murieigh, Mary of Cloghernocsh, Tim of Kilcoolaght, the following use the prefix, O, Tim of Moyeightragh, Fred of New street, Fred and James of College street, Dan of Inch, Dan of Pound row, John of Henn street, James and Dan of Dromdoohigbeg, Dan of Lissyvigeen, John of Clash, Dan and Pat of Carrigeencullia, Hannah of Henn street, Mary of Boherkeale, Julia of Fair hill, Hanoria of New street, Tom of Dingle. Matt of Ballyheabought, Tom of Glins, Flor of Cahir, Geoffrey of Cuhig, Bridget of Main street, Tom of Farranreagr, Ml. of Reencaheragh, Tom of Kilmurry, Con of William street, Ml. and Jerh. of Main street, Dan of Valencia road. The O'Donoghue of Eoghanacht Cashel are from Oiliol Ollum, Eoghan, Fiacha, Oiliol, Lewy. Corc. Eochy, Criomhthan. Hugh, Conaing, Hugh, Muldoon. Conail. Blathno. Conail, Hugh, Clothna. Cinaeth, Amblaoomh, Danal, Hugh, Cathal Donchadha. Aongus, Hugh, Amhlaomh, Cathal, Dudavoren. Amhlaomh, Thomas, Amhlaomh. Tadg, Hugh, John. Tadg, Rory (1560). Eoghanacht Cashel is in the plain of Cian, O'Donoghue is its lineal inheritor; its name in other days was Feimhin, which extended to the border of the brown-nut plain. In 1014, Dungal O'Donoghue was king of Cashel, his successor Magrath died in 1043, and Donchadh in 1057. The chief seat of their lands in Ossory was at Gowrau. The man who is elected to govern Magh Mail is O'Donoghue of the fair Gabhrain. Jerpoint Abbey was founded in 1180 by Donogh O'Donoghe. The O'Donoghue Mor lived at Ross castle in loch Lene to 1560, and his pedigree is traced from Corc, king of Munster, through Cas, Eochaidh, Crimthan, Laeghaire, Aodh, Cairbre, Cloranach. Dunlong, Eladhach, Dunlong, Altan. Flaithrigh. deneas. Dubhdabhoireann, Donal, Donal, Donal, Cathbha. Conor. Davoren,

Donoghue Households

Donal, Donoch 1057, Conmhighe, Cathal 1063, Donoch. deneas, Amhailgadh, Cathal, Davoren. Amhailgadh, Thomas, Ambailgadh. Teige. Aodh. Shane, Teige, Rory. Rory. Rory, Geoffrey 1759, Donall 1790, Cathal 1808, CCharles b. 1806. The O'Donoghues of lough Lene and of the Flesk, ruled over the clan Sealbuidhe. O'Donoghue of loch Lene is chief of that eoghanacht, which extended from the Roughty to the loch Lene, and to Lios Ui Conchobhair, and contained 45 ploughlands, while the O'Donoghue of the Glens had 20. In 1060, chief of the Eachii or cinel Eoghaidh died. In 1158, the O'Donoghue Mor rebuilt the stone church of Aghadeo. In 1161, Amhlaomh and his son Hugh died. In 1163, Muircheartach of loch Lene died. In 1175, Conor and Cathal were living; they died in 1178. In 1180, Maolduin took Innisfallen monastery. In 1208, Murchadh, son of Murchadh, son of Auliffe Mor, died. In 1231(Hugh, son of Conor, son of Aulige Mor, died and was buried in his own tomb in Aghadeo. In 1238, Geoffrey and his wife, and his brother, and his three sons, died. In 1320, Tadg an enig, son of Auliffe, was chief, and a poem by Cathan O'Dunin was read and is still extant. In 1399, Hugh died. In 1613, Valentine Browne, of Molahiffe, got a grant of the O'Donoghue Mor. lands, forfeited by Rory O'Donoghue during the Geraldne confiscations. O'Donoghue, of the Glens is chief of Glen Flesk from the younger brother of Cathal O'Donoghue Mor, viz., Conor ancestor of Aedh, Jeoffrey, Conor, Donall, Jeoffrey 1520, Donall Jeoffrey, Rory. Donal, Jeoffrey Teige. Jeoffrey, Teige, Jeoffrey; Jeffrey of Killaher, attainted in 1603. restored in 1609, left a son Teige of Glenflesk, 1628 whose son Geoffrey of Killaher d. 1655; his son Daniel 1700, had Geffrey, whose son Daniel d. 1800, whose son Charles had a son Charles whose son Charles had a son Daniel, 1833-89, whose son Geoffrey b 1859, had Geoffrey b 1896. Donoch or Donnchu, d. 1057, gave the clan name to the O'Donoghues. Jeffrey O'Donoghue, of the Glens, who d. 1758, m. Elizabeth, dau. of Randal Mac Carthy Mor having a son, Daniel, who m Margt. Mac Mahon of Clonina in Clare, having a son Charles, who d. in 1808, leaving Charles who m. Jane O'Connell, and d. 1833, having Daniel, 1833-89, a political leader; he m. Mary, dau. of Sir John Ennis, having issue Geoffrey, Charles 1860-1903, Daniel d. 1888, John, Angus d. 1908, Florence. Geoffrey b. 1859, m 1895 Maud Charlton having Geoffrey b. 1896, Maud Mary, and Nora Kathleen. In 1688, Captain Daniel and Lieut Calixtus O Donoghue were in Mac Elligott's regiment. In 1712, John Florence O'Donoghue of Glanfleska, K.S.L., second son of Owen, was created Marquess of Cleinchamps and La Ronce; he m. Lady Mary Drummond, dau of Edward, Duke of Perth, having Jean Joseph, second Marquess brigadier and colonel, who d. 1782, leaving a son Joseph Ambrose. Conor O'Donoghue, elder brother of the 1st Marquess, was ancestor of the O'Donoghues of Belgium, Lords of Geldorp and Niel, naturalised 27 July, 1716. Helen, dau. of Tadg O'Donoghue of Glanflesk, m Dermod, brother of Florence Mac Carthy Reagh. The wills of Geffry O'Donoghue of Glenflesk 1678, of Dan 1804 and Pat 1808 of Killarney, are in the Record Office. Egan O'Rahilly praises Killaha castle, the house of Geoffrey, and also describes Finneen of the Glen in 1714 as the only bush of refuge left to the bards of Conn. In 1679 Geoffrey of the glen wrote poems in Irish. In 1732 Chas. and Florence of Glanflesk were acquitted from a charge of being tories. The O'Donoghue tomb is in Muckross abbey, and has been used since that church was built by Mac Carthy Mor. The O'Donoghues of Droumcarbin, or Anwys, lived near Brewsterfield; Maire Ni Dhuir O'Donoghue m. Donal Mor O'Connell of Darrynane, and was the mother of Count O'Connell of the Irish Brigade . Her mother was the daughter of Donell Mahony of Dunloe. In 1741, Teigue Mac John Donohue, of Rushen beg, was indicted for harbouring Keadagh Donohue Baccoole a proclaimed tory. Geoffrey of 1655 had a son Geoffrey whose son Donal had a son Geoffrey and a dau. Maure ni dhuiv who m. Donal O'Connell. In 1612, Francis Blundell was granted Killaha, Sowneyboy, Inshie. Cleydagh, Dromecarribane, Bally-

Lynch Households

Lumsden, Madeline of Denny street.
Lunatic asylum, Killarney; see reports of.
Lunham, Annie of Strand street. Robt. of Tralee, had Mrs. Agnes Benner, and Robt. of Chicago, who d. 1913, a. 56.
Lunny, O'Luinig, Jas. of Listowel.
Lupton, Wm. of Ballinskelligs.
Lybes, strips, baile in Duagh parish.
Lyden, O'Liodain, Colman of James street.
Lynch, O'Loingsig; 288 families in Kerry, viz—Tim of Ballahacommane, Pat and John and Ml. of Knockeenduff, Jerh. of Killeen, John of Coolcorcoran, John of Fossa, John of Lissyvigeen, Pat of Cahnane, John of Brasby's lane, John of Bohereencael, Jerh. and Pat of High Street, Rd. of Barry's lane, Ml. of Old Market lane, James of Bishop's lane, Dan of Fleming's lane, Jerh and John of Derrymaclavade, Con of Coomacullen, Dan of Clonkeen, Denis of Derrynafinnia, David and John and Jerh. of Ballynananagh, Ml. of Inchycullane, John of Cloonteens, Pat and John of Coolies, Ellen of Sunny hill, Margaret of Clover's lane, Mary of High Street, Ml. of Inchycullane, Eden of Ballyfinane, Tim of Carker, John of Brasby's lane, Dan of Pawn Office lane, Ml. of Aghacurreen, Pat of Kilnarovanagh, Ml. of Brewsterfield, John of Gortahoosh, Dan of Derrynafinnia, Con of Derrymaclavode, Hanoria of Kilmaniheen, Dan of Fahaduff, Ml. of Annaghillymore Con of Sheans, John of Glenawaddra, Ml. of Rathmore, James of Knocknacurra, Dan of Toormore, John of Killegy, Tom of Ranalough, Tom of Dicksgrove, Mary of Moybella, Margaret of Ahascra, Johanna of Annaghillymore, John and John of Dooneen, Edw. of Castleview, Denis of Coolkeragh, Ml. of Ballinageragh, Tom of Lixnaw, Ml. of Tullahinnell, Pat of Leitrim, Ml. of Cloonanetagh, Geo. of Knockbrack, John of Laccamore, James and Tim and Ml. of Stack's mountain, Tom of Finuge, Ml. of Ennismore, Mce. of Bealkelly, John and Pat of Kilgarvan, John of Kilcock, Tim of Guhard, John of Behins, Ml. of Rathea, Thos. of Mountcoal, Ml. of Ballyduhig, Joseph of Ballymacassy, Dan of Lislaughtin, Tom of Ballyline, James of Kilcolgan, James of Tieraclea, Dan of Kilpadogue, Mary of Cloghaneleesh, John of Kiltean, John of Moybella, John of Knoppogue, Denis of Benmore, Martin of Clashmealcon, Tom and Bridget of Kilmore, John of Caherulla, John of Knockane, Pat and Tom of Dooncaha, Mary of Banemore, Ml. of Murhur, Mary of Tonreigh, Tom and James and John of Lahaserough, Pat of Urlee, Ml. of Kilomeroe, James of Castlequarter, Denis of Kilconly, John of Ballyhorgan, Margaret of Larha, Pat and Ml. of Gortdromagowna, Denis and Pat and Denis of Doon, John and Denis of Ballybunion, John of Ballyeigh, Bridget of Coolnagraigue, Dan of Lyracrompane, Pat and Ellen of Dromaddamore, Jas. of William street, Tim of Clieveragh, Ml. of Listowel, Tom of Ballyconnell, James of Glanoe, John of Tullig, Hanoria of Ballinageragh, Pat of Ardydonegan, Ml. of Tubridbeg, John of Banna, Pat of Carhooeragh, James of Gortdromagowna, Denis of Knockenagh, Jerh. of Affouley, Pat of Rusheen, Tim and John of Ballylongane, Pat of Curraghdarrig Tom and Tom of Asdec, Mce. of Ballynoneen, Eliza of Feans, James of Leansaghane, James of Tullamore, Tom of Moynsha, Tom and John of Abbey St., Pat of Market place, John and Eliza of Brogue lane, Pat and Hanora of Moyderwell, John of Edward street, Mce. of Rock Street, Martin of Cloonsharragh, John and John of Ballyquin, Denis and Pat and Mce. of Cloghane, Ml. of Cappagh, Kate of Ballinabuck, Pat of Gallerus, John and Ml. of Cloghaneduff, Pat of Milltown, Pat and Tim of Garfinny, Tom of Doonsheane, John and Ml. of Kilfountain, John of Listellick, Kate of Fybough, Johanna and Mary of Ballintlea, Wm. of Cloonalour, Tom and Nic and Mary of Kilfenora, Dan of Fenit, John of Curraheen, Ml. of Ballyquin, Margaret of Tawlaght, Pat and Ml. of Ballintlea, Tim of Aghanna, Edm. of Cap-

Lynch & Lyne Households

patigue, Pat and Ml. of Gowlane, John of Ballyveheen, Pat and John of Ballinrannig, Peter of Reask, Batt of Ballineanig, Pat and John of Fahamore, Batt. of Castle Gregory, Tim of Glentane, Mce. of Tralee, Tom of John street, Ml. of Main street, Tom of the Mall, Tim of Dromavally, Bridget of Cullenagh, Mary of Farraneestenig, John of Gurteen, Denis and Dan of Tulligbeg, Tim of Lissivane, Ellen of Dukegate lane, Bridget of Cloghane, Bridget of Ballyquin, Tom of Lisnakealwee, John and James of Murrigane, Denis of Derrynamucklagh, Dan of Lohart, James and Ml. of Coaramore, Pat of Feighmane, Denis of Ballymanagh, Pat of Kilbeg, Ml. and John and James of Tinnies, Denis and Dan of Bansheen, Tom of Meelick, Dan and Humphrey of Coologues, John of Dromacoosh, Dan of Lounaghan, John of Gortnaboul, Ml. of Inchincoosh, Tim and Edw. and James and Edw. of Kenmare, James of Coolroe, Ml. of Gearhadiveen, Dan of Letter, John of Kilgortaree, Pat of Kinneigh, Chas of Spunkane, John of Scariff, Con of Killurley, Denis and Tim of Dooneen, Mce. of Ballycarbery, John and J. of Caherciveen, David of Gurranearagh, Ml. of Derreen, Ellen of Gortgower, Ellen of Tinnies, Kate of Lackaroe, Pat of Tarmons, Ellen of Reen, Patrick of Cappanacush, Dan and Dan of Gortlicka, Eugene and John of Lissantannig, Annie of Moyrick, Dan of Ballagh, Peter of Gortmarraghafincen, Jerh. and Ml. and Bridget of Kells, Johanna of Dooneen, Julia of Valencia road, Batt and Mary of Tulfig, Finian of Kilmackerin, Mary of Ballagh, Mary of Waterville, Jas. of Doory, Ml. of Coolroe, Jerh. and Denis of Barranastooka, Lynch, O'Linchy, O'Loingsigh, Ua Loingsigh, longseach a mariner, chiefs of Uaithne thire inhabit the wood in front of the foreigners or Danes of Limerick at Castle Connell, chiefs of cinel Bacat, lord of Dal Araidhe. In 1402 Cornelius Oloynsig was vicar of Limerick; and in 1411 Alan Olonsigh of Limerick was a canon of Killagh de Belloloco. In 1821 lived Jeffrey and John Lynch at Dromin, Garrett at Killarney, John at Tralee. Diarmuid Lynch and Finian Lynch are prominent Irish scholars. Lyndon, O'Liondain; Thomas of Kilpadogue.

Lyne, O'Laigin, 110 families in Kerry, viz:—Dan and Tim and John of Coolie, Pat and Wm. and John and Tim and Jas. of Knockreagh, Tim of Gortagullane, Stephen of Canguilla, Dan and Tom of Breanshagh, Pat of Gortdromerillagh, Pat of Coolclieve, Denis of Mangerton view, Tim of Sunny hill, Tom of New street, Ml. of High street, John of Tiernaboul, Jerh. of Annaghbeg, John of Knockmanagh, Wm. of Knockinagh, Pat of Gortaguliane, John of Faughcullia, Tim of Coolies, Hanoria of Gearha, Kate of Ballinvarrig, Jerh. of Breahig, Jerh. of Scarttaglin, Ml. and Jerh. of Annaghhillymore, Jerh. of Tooreenamult, Pat of Knockaninane, Hanoria and Tim and Con of Brosna, Pat and Tim of Ahane, Mary of Tooreenmore, Bridget of Henn street, Julia of Bohereenkeale glebe, Jas. of Drumulton, John of Lissataggle, Ml. of Carrigafreaghmore, Pat of Lismongane, Martin of Ballybrack, Catherine of Trippeenagh, Pat of Ballytrasna, Johanna Anablah, Kate of Knockmanagh, Mary of Ballinalane, Ellen of Lisheenbawn, Tim of Gowlane, John of Kilfelim, Tim of Nantinane, Mary of Listry, Tim of Garrynagare, Ml. of Lackabeg, Tom of Ballygarrett, Tom and John of Carrahane, John and James of Banna, Kate of Aunascaul, Pat of Clogher, Eugene of Lisnakeolwee, Ml. of Miles lane, Tom of Coumduff, Mary of Coolroe, Ellen of Knocknamon, Margaret of Main street, Ml. of Strand street, Eneas of Lissvane, Tom of Iveragh road, John of Castle Conway, Pat of Cromane, James of Laharan, John of Cummeenduvasig, Jerh. of Knockeens, Denis and Tim and Jerh. of Slaghts, John of Gortnaboul, Tim of Knockeens, Ml. and Dan of Ballinskelligs, John of Meelagullen, Bridget of Coom, Con of Aghanboy, Flor of Curravolla, Tim and Jerh. of Curraheen, Pat and John of Doory, Denis of Ballyhearney, Con of Cool. Ml. and Tom of Quaybaun, Pat of Ballynahowmore, Pat of Knockaunroe, Mary and Jerh. of Gortavallig, Pat of Carhan, Bridget of Main street, Pat of Boulerdah, Mary of Glounagellagh.

Mahoney Households

Madden, O'Madain of siol Anmchadha in Hy Maine; Ml. of Listowel, Nicholas of Leanamore, Dan of Curraghdarrig, Tom and John of Kilgarvan, Tom of Knockenagh, John of Market place, Tim of Dykegate lane, Tom of Kenmare, Rev. Jos. of Dromhall. Ambrose of Lacken 1700, will in P. Record Office.

Madgett, Nicholas, D.D. 1752, Nov. 10, late of the college of St. Barbara in Paris, to be Bishop of Killaloe; 1753, Feb. 8, exchanged to Ardfert with Wm. O'Meara; he built a residence in a narrow lane off Strand street in Tralee, costing only £16 3s. 10½d.. and occupied it until his death in 1774, when he was buried in Ardfert in the same tomb as Bishops Moriarty 1737, and O'Sullivan d. 1739; he was born in Ballynorig in Kilmoiley, having eight sisters who married locally, having issue, and a brother who was a naval officer.

Madigan, O'Madagain; Pat of Carhooearagh, Jas. of Carhoonakilla, Mary of Clieveragh.

Magane, Mac Canna; Wm. of Tooracladdane.

Magazine, Kerry, 1854-6, Tralee, edited by Archdeacon Rowan, printed and sold by F. C. Panormo at 25 Lower Castle Street, was discontinued from want of support; it has been used in compiling this book, like all these named in Bibliography heading which see.

Magee, Mac Aoda; Tom of Dromgower, Con of Tieraclea.

Magh, macha, lawn, plain, milking field; baile in Bally Mac Elligott.

Maghanaboe, cows' lawn, baile in Ballyduff.

Maghanacoosaun, baile in Killorglin; chuasain, cove, path, cave.

Maghanknockane, baile in O'Brennan.

Maghanlawaun, baile in Knockane, in Laune or Leamhain or elm plain.

Maghanveel, baile in Cloghane; lone tree.

Maghasheela, baile in Killiney; blast.

Magherabeg, little lawn, baile in Killiney.

Magherasrahan, streamlet, baile in Knockane.

Maghygrennane, baile in Dromod; palace.

Maginn, Mac Finn; Jos. of Barrack lane.

Magistrates in 1796 were mainly the Protestant gentry and middlemen of Kerry; in 1896 many Catholics were J.P.'s, 62 out of total of 152; the 4 R.M.'s were appointed under 6 Wm. IV. c. 13; P.C.'s are now selected. A brugaid for each baile to a parish council with the P.P. as chairman, all honorary posts, would be the old Irish way and more democratic and cheaper than having professional justices and police all strangers.

Mag laithimh, Lahiff's plain, see Molahiffe.

Maglass, bailes in Nohoval, Bally Mac Elligott.

Mag luachra Deadad, Trughenaicme, between sliab Luachra and sliab Mis.

Mag uladh, corcach; in the west, near Catair Conroi; Lathair Luingi was north of it.

Magunihy, magh Ui Coincinn, of the Conceannaic or Corca Duibne sept of the clan Conaire and tuath sen Eran; O'Conghaile of the slender swords was over the bushy-forted Magh O g Coinchinn; mag craoib leasac Ua g Concind; in Magunihy barony composed of the parishes of Aghadoe, Aglish, Currens, Kilbonane, Kilcolman, Kilcredane, Kilcummin, Killalea, Killarney, Killintierna, Kilnanare, Molahiffe, and Nohoval Daly were Finn's enemies.

Maher, O'Meacair; John of Ballintogher, John of Knockadirreen, Mary of Dysert, Pat of Trieneragh, Tom of Laharan, Mary of the Rock, Wm. of Abbey street, Harry of Bridge street, Tom of Abbeylands, Jas. of Farran, Margt. of Ballycarnahan, Rev. P. of Lixnaw. See O'Meagher.

Mahon, O'Macain; Andrew of Tralee.

Mahony, O'Matgamna; 271 families in Kerry, viz.: Jerh. of Shinnagh, John of Rathmore, Jerh. of Cloonts, John and Pat and Jerh. and Tim of Gortnahaneboy, Denis of Lissyconnor, Tim of Gortnaprocess, John of Freemount, John of Banard, Jas. of Leamyglissane, John of Bawnard, John of Carhoonooe, Jas. of Coom, Dan of Gneeveguilla, Tom and Jas. of Gullane, Con of Coolbane, Con and Denis of Coolroe, Denis of Flintfield, Ml. and Flor of Faha, Ml. of Seersha, John of Laharan, Margaret of Sheans, John of Brosna, James and Denis of Bawnluskaha, James of Camp, Batt of Cloonacurrig, Cain of Chaplequarter, John of Tonebwee, Ml. of Coolavanny, Dan of Castleview, Denis and Pat of Gortshanavogh, Dan of Ballybane, Jerh.

Mahoney Households

of Farranfore, Rd. of Rathanny, Flor and John and Denis and Flor of Muingnaminane, Dan and Tom of Gortdromerillagh, Myles of Burrane, Bridget of Kilcow, Mary of Camp, John and Flor of Runaleen, Jerh. of Kilbonane, Margaret of Ballinard, Mary of Gortglass, Catherine of Mastergeeha, Pat and Tim of Lackbroder, Abbey and Bessie of Greeveguilla, Ml. of Knockachur, Ellen and Kate and Julia of Gortnahaneboy, Gon or Duckett's lane, Tim of High street, John of Inch, James and Pat of New street, Con and John of old Market lane, Con of Well lane, Jas. of Rockfield, Jerh. of Ballinard, Johanna of Laharan, Eliza of Faha, John of Gurranemore, Margaret of High street, Minnie of Lower New street, John and Con and John of Rahanane, Pat of Leamnaguilla, Denis of Mastergeha, Michael of Incheens, Con and James of Knockeenahone, Ellen of Carran, Flor of Beenageeha, Tim of Meenleitrim, Jerh. of Ballyplimoth, Kate of Glanlea, Tom of Gullane, Rd. and James and Johanna of Asdee, Ellen of Kilcox, Pat of Cloghane, Matt of Clashmealcon, John of Ardoughter, John of Tarmons, John of Dromaddamore, Margaret of Leitrim, James of Murhur, Tom of Moyvane, James of Ahalahanna, Johanna of Clounprohus, Catherine of Cloonbrane, Pat of Rathroe, John of Urlee, Mce. of Doonferris, John of Lisadraun, Tom and Julia of Banna, Garrett and Ellen of Ballinprior, Mce. of Aughrim, James of Leitrim, John and Edn. of Ballybunion, Rd. of Kille henny, Tom of Doons, Ml. of Ballyhorgan, James of Dromakee, Mary of Killahan, John of Curraghtooseane, John of Island ganniv, Johnanna of Kilmoyley, Mary of Ballinageragh, Anne of Rathkenny, Hanora of Dromakee, Margaret of Toornageehy, Denis of Bawnmore, Edm. of Garrynaneska, John of Bawnmore, James of Killahan, Robert of Duagh, James of Knockavallig, Ml. of Gortanare, Pat of Lisnaw, James of Gortacrossane, John of Ballyheigue, John of Cloghanebane, Tim of Heirhill, Pat of Cloghaneleesh, Mce. of Feans, Pat of Droumnacarra, Mary of Ballinorig, Rd. of Ballyline, John of Leanamore, George of Kilmorna, Eng. and Tom of Ahabeg, Ellen of Montangav, Mce. of Meen, Tom of Coolacarig, Mce. of Gortagurrane, Dan of Moybella, Anne of Rahoonagh, Mary of Killehenny, Pat of Ballyegan, Johanna and Bridget of Coolkeragh, Bridget of Carhooeragh, John of Coolard, John of Knockenagh, George of Kilmeany, Ter. of Ballincrossig, Pat of Clooneen, John of Glenderry, Stephen of Dreenagh, Pat of Knockreach, Dan of Tubridmore, Eug. and John of Rathkenny, Pat of Ballybroman, Tim of Dromartin, Tim of Ballinascreena, James of Tcherbane, James of Leansaghane, Pat of Bromore, John of Coolnaleen, John of Gortcurreen, Pat of Derrymore, John of Annagh, Thade of Gransha, Julia of Clounalour, Jerh. of Slievenavadogue, John of Kilfenora, Dan of Skehanagh, Norah of Connor's lane, Julia of Farrantooreen, Nano of Langford street, Deborah of Kilmurry, John of Reask, Tom of Lateevemore, Thos. of Lativemanagh, John of Aughills, Pat of Farrandalogue, John of Cappatigue, Thade and Ellen and Martin of Kilcumminmore, Denis and Ml. of Illauncoum, Pat of Tullig, Pat of Slieveadrehia, Garrett of Rathass, Tim of Gallowsneld, Pat of Lohercannon, Wm. of Tulligmore, Pat of Killorglin, Dan of Rangue, Dan of Cromane, Pat of Mary street, Ed. and James of Rock street, John and James of Brogue lane, James of Castle street, John of Francis street, John of Daly's lane, Tim and John of Connor's lane, John of the Rock, Abel of Goat street, Denis and Dan of Gortamullen, Flor of Pound lane, Ml. of Shelburne street, Pat of Cooracoosane, John of Derrylicka, Con of Drimnamore, Pat of Gearha, John and Pat of Kilmackerrin, Jerh. of Sunkane, John of Beenbane, Jas. of Derreenavarrig, Tim of Coornachaeragh, Clara of Meanus, Con of Ardtully, Ml. and John of Kilnabrack, Dan of Curraghbeg, Pat of Ahane, John of Lyrances, Tom and John of Castlequin, Flor of Cullina, Myles of Main street, John and Dan of Gurranebane, Ml. of Brackaharagh, Jerh. and James and Jerh. and John of Ardcost, Flor and John of Coars, Kate of Castlequin, Mary of Luharan, Jerh. of Dromaclaurig, Ml. of Cannagullen, John of Dun-

Mahoney Households

loe, Myles of Caherciveen, Dan of Clydagh, Mary of Ballybunion, Jas. of Tralee, Florence of Fenit. The name Mahony is derived from Mahon or Mathghamhain, of the Eoganacht Cashel, who died in 1034. Dermod of Ivagha settled in Kerry before 1355; his son John m. a dau. of Aodh O'Connell, having Dermod 1442, who m. Sabit, dau of O'Sullivan Mor, having Conor and Donal. Conor 1471 m. a dau of Geoffrey O'Donoghue, having Teig mergach or angry looking who was seneschal to the Earl of Desmond in 1536, and he m. Honora O'Sullivan Beare having eight sons, Dermod, Conor, Donal, Fineen, Maolmuach, Eoghan, Donogh, and Sean, Donal Mac Teig mergeach ot Tubrid in Iveragh, was chief officer to Mac Carthy More in 1588. The Mahony family of Dunloe Castle were Dan, 1676-1747, John d. 1780, Dan d. 1832, Dan d. 1871, John dsp. 1908. The Mahony family of Dromore Castle were: Denis, John, d. 1743. Denis John d. 1817, Rev. Denis d. 1851, Richd. d. 1892, Harold 1867-1905 unm., and his sister Norah m. 1900 Edw. Hood. The Mahony family of Castlequin were: Myles, 1726, Kean, Kean, Myles m. 1788, Kean, Myles d. unmd.; his sister Mary m. Thos. MacDonogh, having Thos. McD. Mahony. The Mahony family of Cullina were Florence, 1751, Myles, Kean, Kean d. 1862, sp., his bro., Dr. Myles d. unm. The Mahony family of Kilmorna is from Teig Meirgeach, Donogh, Kean, David, Peirce 1750-1819, Peirce 1792-1853, Peirce 1814-1850, Peirce b. 1850, the O'Mahony. Refer to Burke's Landed Gentry for details of above families. Count Bartholomew O'Mahony, 1749-1819, was a General in the French army, his ancestors being Michael, Owen, Teig, Dermod, Donogh, Dermod, Florence, 1568, Donal, Teig, meirgeach. Count Daniel O'Mahony of Cremona d. 1714; his ancestry is given as Dermod, John, Dan, Dermod, Dan, Conor, John, Dermod, Finghin, 1450. Count John Francis O'Mahony, 1815, General in the French army, was son of Dermod, son of Donal of Dunloe.

Maing, Mand, Maine river; deceit, sudden floods; tomaidm Fleisce and Mainne; in cois Mainge; erupted in a.m. 3751; the plain of Magh Luachra Deadhaidh was cleared of forest in a.m. 3790; the Flesk and the Maine drain the plain of Kerry, and are angling resorts for trout and salmon.

Main, Mac Maine; Wm. of Spunkane, Bridget of Ballinskelligs.

Mainister o dtorna, abbey Odorney, church of the monks in 1302 was valued at 13s. 4d. for tithes, in deanery of Othorna and Offlannan, in cantred of Ui Flanannain; see Odorney parish; the Cistercians house of Kiriel, revenue, 73s. 4d.

Mainister oirbhealaigh, Irrelagh, Muckross Franciscan friary, in Killarney parish, founded 1440 by MacCarthy Mor.

Mair, O'Midir, Jas. of Farranreagh.

Malachy, Ferdinand of Clooshguire.

Malicious injuries to persons and property by black and tans and green and tans, in Kerry 1914-24, prove that gunmen of all colours are criminal lunatics, and a danger to democratic rule, by a brugaid for each baile elected as honorary members of a parish council.

Malley, O'Maille of Mayo; Jas. of Dungeel, Mce. and Mce. of Bohereencael, Dan of Tinnahally, Jas. and Pat of Callinafercy, Pat of Ballymacprior, John of Tulligmore, Ml. and Dan of Laharan, Pat of Killirglin, Ml. of Curraheen.

Malone, O'Maoil Eoin of Brawney in W. Meath; Margt. of Ardnamweely, Ml. of Listowel, John and John of Coumeenole, Hanoria of Lough, Ml. of Emlagh, Geo. of Dingle, Pat of Cloghaneduff, John of John-street, Wm. and Tom of Rahinane, John of Ballintlea.

Malvey; Pat and Jas. and Pat of Tarmons, Mce. of Darrynane, Pat and Pat of Droumakilla, Mary of Cahersavane, Crohan of Spunkane, Julia of Gleesk.

Manaanan Mac Lir; of the Isle of Man; sea rover; rolled wheel like on three legs; buried near Loch Orbsen in Moycullen.

Manaher; Ml. of Cloonbrane, Ellen of Tieraclea.

Mangan, O'Mongain; 67 families in Kerry,

Moriarty Households

Moore cont'd

Nic. of Knockanarney, Mce. of Aughacasla, Tom of Laharn, Ml. and Tom and Ml. and Pat and Jas. and Nich and Tom of Lisnakealwee, Pat of Murrigane, Kate of Teer, Nich of Gowlane, Pat of Green lane, Tom of Caher, Tom and Mce. of Curracullenagh, Ml. of Ballinloghig, Tom of Mary street, Tom of Boherbee, Edw. of Pembroke street, John of Dingle, Pat of Ballinglanna, Pat of Vicarstown, Garrett of Tawlaght, Edw. of Ballinskelligs, Rd. of Old road, John of Redtrench. In 1609 the Moores were transplanted from Queen's Co.. and 102 came to Tarbert with Patrick Crosby as tenants. In 1408 Richard de More of knightly race was rector of Annagh and Clockorbryaff. In 1588 Richard Moore of Castle Moore claimed lands at Ballydavid; Gerrat claimed Ballymore; Rd. More, alias Mac Morris of Cyaltady, prayed relief from conye and livery. In 1689 Ambrose Moore of Kilgulban was provost marschal and died in 1620. Edward Moore of Kilgobbin had Tom b. 1713, Rd. 1715; Wm. had Wm. b. 1721, and Sarah b. 1726; Rd. d. 1729. Garrett Moore of Teeravane d. 1773, leaving Nicholas. Canon Moore of Paris left a stipend for a Latin school in Donquin. Wm. Moore d. 1797; m. Eliz. Hilliard, leaving John of Kilfenora, Anne and Eliza. The father of Tom Moore, the poet, was John Moore of Kerry, and a grocer in Aungier st. in Dublin, 1779-1800, who had a brother Garrett of Finuge and Newtowndillon. Moore's Melodies will survive as long as Irish history.
Moorestown, baile in Kilquane parish.
Moorhead, Samuel of Waterville.
Morahain, O'Murcain, James of Moyeightragh, Peter of Ardshanavooly.
Moran, O'Morain; 92 families in Kerry, viz., John of Castleview, Bridget of Inch, John and Tom and John of Ballyline, Jerh. and John of Leanamore, John and Edm. of Listowel, Pat of Kealid, Denis of Dromurrin, John of Billerough, Edm. and John and Con of Lahaserough, Ml. and Edm. and Ml. of Tullamore, Tom of Rahealy, Ml. of Doon, Dan of Tullahinnell, John and Ml. of Ahanangran, Tom and James of Tullamore, Ml. of Derra, Pat of Carhoona, Ml. and Ml. of Knockenagh, James of Lateevebeg, Margaret of Main street, Johanna of Knocknahow, Pat of Ardamore, Eugene of Murreigh, James of Caherboshaina, Pat of Dingle Commons, John of Ballybeg, Mary and John of John street, Mary of Ballinahow, John and Ml. of Strand road, James of Drom, Denis of Abbey street. Ml. and John and Wm. of Strand street, Jerh. of Rae street, Dan of Kealafreaghane, Dan of Murreigh, Pat and Denis of Cooryanaheen, Pat of Cappawee, Pat and John of Sussu, Dan of Inchaleega, Denis of Teeramoyle, Ml. of Gleensk, Denis of Toon, Ml. and Tom and James and Stephen of Kells, John and John of Cahersavane, Ml. and Pat of Mahygrennane, Pat of Farranreagh, Mary and Ml. of Derriana, Kate of Downing's row, Julia of Inchleega, Ellen of Sussa, Mary of Coad, Pat and James of Curraheen, Jerh. of Liss, Johanna of Teeramoyle, Kate of Toon, John of Coomattaukane, Pat of Old road, John of Boolakeel, James of Ballinskelligs, David of Kinnard, Jerh. of Meelageeleen, John of Laharan, Dan and Jerh of Coomnahincha, Michael of Rhodes, Pat of Cloghanelineghan. Ua Morain was chief of Crumthan in Killian barony in Galway.
Morgan, O'Muireagain; in 1666, Captain Robt. was granted lands in Glanneroughty at Dromrouke, Carrigeene, Inceancouse, Cameene; Glangory, and Gortnimacry. Archdeacon Edward of Ardfert in 1669.
Morgell; Philip of Dingle d. 1738, his wife m. Capt. Magee. Anne Morgell, dau. of Crosbie of Rathkeale, a solicitor who was M.P. for Tralee; she m. 1791 Sir Barry Denny, and 2 Sir John Floyd.
Moriarty, O'Muirceartaig; 437 families in Kerry, viz:—Eugene of Kilbonane, Eug. of Ballymalis, John of Greeves, Rd. of New street, Stephen and Stephen of Brasby's lane, Jerh of Fleming's lane, Ml. and Wm. of Bohereencael glebe, Ml. of High street, David of Sunday's well or Droumhal, John of Gortalassa, Chas. of Rossanean, John of Skahies, Eug. of Derrybanane, Ml. and Ml. of Coolies, John of Gneeves, Kate of Coolcorcoran, Ml. and Anne of Brosna, Hanoria of Rockfield, Ellen of Sheans, Kate of Huggard's lane, Margt. of New street, Mary of

Moriarty Households

Coom, Eug. of Toormore, Ml. of Knockafreaghane, Rd. and John and Jas. of Gortatlea, Ml. of Clashatlea, Batt and John of Glanowen, Ml. and Jas. of Knockeenduff, Pat of Tiernaboul, Tim nad John and Ml. of Gortnatona, Tim and John of Leamnaguilla, John and Tim and John and Morty of Rusheen, Jerh of Rathmore, Dan and John and Dan of Dromin, Ml. and Ml. of Dromulton, Dan of Knockeen, Con of Bawnard, John of Kilsarcon, Johanna of Knockrour, Mary of Clashatlea, Mce. of Carrigafreaghane, Jas. of Carrigeenwood, Ambrose of Lissataggle, Jerh and John of Killeens, Tom of Ballyrobert, John of Lerrig, Mce. of Tubridmore, John of Kilgulbin, John of Tullamore, Bridget of Kilconly, Bridget of Acres, Pat of Pulleen, Jas. of Aughrim, Pat of Ballygologue, Ml. and Jas. of Listowel, Catherine of Ballykealy Ml. of Loughanes, Ml. of Lacca, Bridget of Doon, Mary of Kilgulbin, Hugh of Ballyrehan, Mary of William street, Catherine of Farranwilliam, Mary of Lehanes, Eug. of Lehardane, Eug. of Montanagay, Tom and John and Ml. of Ahanagran, Tim of Carrigafoyle, Pat of Rusheen, Ml. of Knoppogue. Tom of Coolard, Jerh of Knockenagh, Eug. and John of Litter. Dan of Dromkeen, Edm. of Cloghaneliskart, Pat of Addergown, Pat of Feans, Denis of Trippul, Dan of Ballinduddery, Margt. of Feans John and Denis of Caheracruttera, Jerh of Aughills, Jas. of Ballyculiane, Jas. of Ballyoughtra, Edw. of Callinafercy, Jas. of Derrymore, John of Curraheen, Dan and John of Listellick, Tom of Ballinahow, Ml. of Ballyard, Dan of Tralee John of Lohercannon, Eug. of Lisardboola, Dan of Poulawaddra. Pat of Caherleheen, Bridget of Tulligbeg, Maggie of Main street, Mary of Cromane, John of Boolteens, Pat of Ballingamboon, Pat of Ballinamona, Margt. of Ballinaboula, Ellen of Ballinahow, Mary of Cloghanesheskeen, Hanora of Castlegregory, Catherine of Martramane, Pat of Farrancarriga, Ml. of Acres, David of Gortacurrane, Pat of Anagap, Tom and John or Ballyviheen, Jas. and John of Reask, Edw. of Lateevebeg, John of Carrigadav, John of Aughacasla, Tom and John of Lisdorgan, John of Boherbrack, John of Deerpark, Pat of Churchfield, Ellen and Eugene of Murreigh, Ellen of Ballyrisha, Kate and Ellen of Smerwick, Ml. of Dingle, Mce. of Glanlick, Tom of Ballylickeen, Mary of Green lane, Margaret of Caheracruttera, Mary of Murrigane, Denis of Mountoven, Jos. of Killenagh, Pat of Caheracruttera, Anne of Brackloon, Ml. of Parkboy, John and James of Ballyenaghty, John of Kerries, Pat of Tonevane, Pat and John of Annagh, Ml. of Curragraigue, James of Ballycaneen, Eug. of Cloghane, Edw. of Ballymore, Anthony of Glinn, John of Doonsheane, John of Ballynahunt, Pat and Robert of Brackloon, Pat of Kilshanig, Ml. of Castle Gregory, James and John and Pat and Pat of Tawlaght, Tim of Ballyea, John of Samphire island, Tom and Ml. of Drom, Tom and John of Lisnakealwee, Ml. and John and Pat and John of Inch, Jchn of Milltown commons, John of Ballycanneen, John of Ballybrack, John of Moore's town, John and Ml. and John of Ballinaveenoragh, Tom of Ballinahow, John of Ballinbuck, Mce. of Curragraigue, Pat and John of Ballinloghig, Michael of Ballynahow, Wm. and Hugh and Wm. of Mac Cowen's lane, John of Boherbee, John and Edward of Cronin's lane, James of Rock street, Dn of Caheranne road, James of Abbey street, Pat of Bridge street, Tom of Mary street, Pat and John of Connor's lane, John of Francis street, Ambrose of Caherina road, Andrew of Caherfealane, Jerh. of Shanahill, Ml. of Strand road, John of the Grove, Tom and James of Main street, John of John street, Michael of Holyground, Tom of Ballintlea, Tim and James and Tim of Rahinane, Tom of Ventry, Denis and Ml. and James of Ballyferriter, Tom and Ml. of Ballyoughtra, Pat of Gortadoo, Ml. of Smerwick, Bridget and Ellen of Castle street, Katherine of Geese island, Margaret of Rackett lane, Mary of Greene lane, Margaret of Mary street, Hannah of Boherbee, Eliz. of Blennerville, Edm. and John of Martramane, Tom of Fahamore, Tim of Castle Gregory, John and John and John of Kilshanig, James of Tullig, John of Coolroe, John and Dan and John of Cappagh, Ml. of

Moriarty Households

Cloonsharagh, John of Mullaghveal, James of Ballynalackon; Tom of Faha, Edm. of Cloghane, Pat and Ml. of Cromane, Dan and Morto of Killorglin, John of Lonart, James of Reen, John and James and Ml. and Batt of Tulligbeg, Ml. and Dan and Tim of Rangue, Tom of Ballymullen, Jerh. of the Rock, Tim of Brogue lane, John of Spa road, David of Blennerville, Pat of Francis street, Jerh. of Rock street, Ml. of Derrygarrane, Rev. Thomas of Scariff, John of Sunkane, Pat of Kells, Dan of Coulagh, Tim and Rev. John of Scariff, Michael of Doory, Ellen of Dromkeare, Mary of Knockeenawaddra, Pat of Cloghanecarhan, Mary and Con of Inchinaleega, Ml. of Maulagullane, Pat and James of Clogherane, Bridget of Emlaghmore, Margaret of Creveen, Pat of Bahaghs, Mary of Coomahaharn, Ellen of Droum, Kate of Derreendarragh, Mart and Mart of Dromteewakeen, Johanna of Clogherane, Michael of Killagh, John of Curraghflugh, Jerh of Shanacashel, Ml. of Lyranes, Edw. of Dromore old, Mary of Lauhir, Julia of Glounagillagh, Mary of Muingaphuca, Bridget and Ml. and Pat and Ml. and John of High street, Ml. of Coomnahorna, Ellen of Glenlough, Mary of Dunloe, Denis of Ballycarbery, Con of Killelan, Pat of Inchintrea, Tim and Denis of Derry, Pat of Moneyflugh, Jas. of Derreenauliffe, Ml. of Glanearagh, Flor of Rathkieran, John of Cloghanecanuig, Con of Killanbuonia, Mary of Doory, John of Parkalassa, John and Thade and Hy. of Meanus, Ml. and Pat of Owenagarry, Jerh of Meelageeleen, Pat of Derreenacollaha, Bridget of Knocknahoola, John of Coss, Dan and John of Maulnahorna, Andrew of Greenane, Ml. and Pat and John of Slieveaduff, Ml. and Jerh of Bunglasha, Con and Dan of Creveen, John of Sallahig, Dan and Batt of Commanes, Crohan of Tarmons, Con of Breahig, Denis of Cullina, Dan and John and Dan and Con and Dan of Dunloe, John of Gowlane, Ml. and Myles of Liss, Denis of Moneyflugh, John of Skehanagh, Denis of Staigue, Ml. of Killeen, Pat and John and Pat and John and Jas. and Mort of Kilmackerrin, John of Glounagillagh, Jerh and Ml. and Jerh of Treangarry, John and Eugene of Muingaphuca, John and Dan of Lauhir, Ml. of Doolahig, John of Reenanallagane, John and Denis and John and Dan of Curraheen, Pat of Rossbeigh, Pat of Kilkeehagh, Jerh and Pat and Batt and John and Pat and John and Jas. and Batt and Tom and Ml. and Batt of Droum, Ml. of Kilnabrack, Pat of Coolnaharrigill, Batt and Jerh of Kilkeehagh, John of Ballinakilla, Dan and Jerh of Cosha, Pat and Ml. of Treangarriv, Denis of Commaun, Tim of Muingaphuca, Edm of Dooaghs, John and John of Commaun, Jas. of Cosha, Ml. of Glounagillagh, John and Morty of Muingagarha, Morty of Magherascrahan, Ml. of Maghanlawn. The Moriarty family pedigree begins with Eoghan Mor, to Aodh Benan d. 619, to Muircheartach, to Muirceardoig of loch Lein in 1068, which district was seized by Mac Carthy Mor in 1107 and given to O'Donoghue Mor. Moriarty obtained the land of the Aes Iste of the Tuath sen Eran in west Cork, and in 1200 the cantred belonging to Humurierdac was granted to Meyler Fitz Henry. In 1014 the son of Moriarty was slain at Clontarf battle; in 1019 Joanna m. O'Connor Kerry; in 1068 Muircertaig was wounded by the O'Connors; in 1107 Mac Carthy Mor expelled Moriarty; in 1110 Moriarty was captured by O'Connor; in 1192 the Moriarty was slain by the O'Donoghues; in 1578 Moriarty was prior of Kilcolman; in 1583 Owen Moriarty captured the Earl of Desmond; and was granted some land in 1588 at Strahenmartle; in 1582-1601 pardons were granted to several Moriarty's in 1620 Dermot had a lease of Ballinacourty from Lord Cork; in 1635 Teigue had Ballyristin; in 1641 Donnell of Castledrum and Dermot of Ballinacourty were at the siege of Tralee; in 1653 Rev. Tadg prior of Tralee was executed and his bro. Rev. Thos. of Castledrum; Rev. Denis 1653-1737 was P.P. of Dingle and Bishop of Kerry; in 1657 the Moriarty iands were granted to Coote, Jones, etc.; in 1689 Edw. Moriarte was in Maryland; in 1723 Thomas was a linen mftr. in Dingle; in 1724 Dr. Mce. was in Brittany; in 1725 Rev. Ignatius, was P.P. of Killarney; in 1742 Richard was shipping re-

Moriarty Households

cruits to the French army; in 1763 Redmond of Killorglin claimed Farrentorine; in 1788 Redmond of Ballyneanig died; Rev. David 1814-77 was Bishop of Kerry; in 1821 census, 600 Moriarty householders were in Kerry; in 1908, 425 householders; it is difficult to trace all the branches of the Sliocht Aedha Beanain; the late Miss L. E. Moriarty of 35 Manor Park, Lee, London, S.E, made many researches down to 1919, details of which are given here. 1. Admiral Sylverius Moriarty, 1735-1809, son of Redmond of Ballyneanig; his sons were Lieut. Peter, Lieut. Sylverius, Comdr. Merion; his daus. were Margaret, Lydia, Ellen, Ann. Redmond, 1790-1853, had Edward and Lucinda. William, 1792-1850, had Aphra, Ellen, William. Sylverius had Beatrice, Ethel, Lieut. Col. Sylverius (who had Merion and Dermod), and Theodore (who had Lewis, Denis Sylvia). Merion had 7 daus. and 4 sons—Lucy, Lydia, Cherry, Agnes, Annette, Charlotte, Sylverius, Edward, Abram; Merion had 3 sons. Abram had Edward, Annette, Merion, Harry, Francis, Alexander, Arthur, Nathaniel, Ada, Harriet, Dorothea. 2. Moriarty of Tralee; Thomas (probably son of James, son of Thomas of Dingle, 1723), m. Ellen Trant, having Stephen and James; Stephen b. 1773; d. 1817 in Rathmines, having Stephen; Commander James 1775-1838, son of Thomas of Tralee; m. Catherine Webb, having Ellen, Mary, Catherine, Emma, James, Hy., Stephen. Henry Augustus, 1815-1906, C.B, Captain R.N; in 1866 he picked up the broken Atlantic cable; he m. 1 in 1852 Lavinia C. Foster having Lavinia E, and Ellen, and Hy. d. 1877; and Rev. James Hy, vicar of Dorney in Bucks, chaplain R.N; m. Edith dau. of Captain David Moore, R.N, having Eileen, Winifred, and Jas. Henry, lieut. R.A., in France, 1914 star, killed 12-10, 1915, a. 22, buried at Bethune. 3. Matthew Moriarty, R.N., d. 1761 had Edm. J., Matthew and James. Comdr. Edm. J.. d. 1833, his son Captain Hy., d. 1852, his dau. Eliza m. Hon. Hy. Dawson Damer. Lt.-Col. Mattew, 1750-1804, had Captain Warren. Capt. James d. 1791, having Margaret, Martha, Eli., Lieut. Jas. Robert, 1790-1852, had James, Lieut.-Col. Marshall P, b. 1840, disp. Eliz. 1816-95, m. 1848 General Sir Orfeur Cavenagh, having Col. Orfeur and Col. W. O. Cavenagh. 4. The Dean of Ardfert, Rev. Thos. Moriarty, 1813-94, son of Denis 1784-1839, son of Mce. of Dingle; he m. Matilda Bailey having 4 sons and 6 daus., Matilda, Margaret, Eliz., Emily, Katherine, Mary, Thomas, John, Matthew, Robert, of whom Rev. Thomas of Mill St. had Dr. Rowland, Cecil, Rev. Thos.; John had John, Lieut.-Colonel Thos., Muriel, Major Oliver, Matilda, Gerald, Major Oisin, Aideen, Emily, Col Matthew, M.D., had Eileen, Kathleen, Captain Gerald, M.D., Donald; Robert, has Constance and Lionel; Rev. Matthew, son of Denis, d. 1888, had Torrens, Rev. Matthew, Rev. George, Rev. Gerald. Rev. Denis, son of Denis, d. 1904, of Castleisland, had Daisy, m. Colonel Banning, Emma m. Col. Corkery, Sybil m. Rev. Robert Rowan, Ethel m. Henry Moore, Henry us U.S.A. 5. Stephen Moriarty of Cork, son of Daniel, son of Daniel, son of Rev. Martin of Glountane, d. 1847; Abbe Maurice 1805-66; Dr. Stephen of Dieppe, d. 1869, having Mce., Louis, Arthur, Gerald, author of a life of Dean Swift. 6. Matthew Moriarty of Dingle; brs. of Dr. Melchior, d. 1747, and of Ellen, m. Robert Hickson; he d. 1737, having Blaise, Alex. and Constantine; Blaise d. 1775, had Ellen, Mary, Eliza, Catherine, and Dominick, Constantine had Matthew and Alex; Matthew d. 1834 having Clarissa; Dr. Alex. d. 1814, having Ellen, Fanny, Chris, who had Chris and Edw., d. 1874, and Matthew d. 1854 in Belgium, leaving issue. Bishop David Moriarty, 1814-77, o. 1837, c. 1854, son of David of Derrivrin, son of David, who m. Catherine, dau. of Blaise of Dingle, having Anne, Ellen and Margaret. David m. Bridget Stokes having John, Catherine, Bishop of David, Edward and Oliver, R.M, who m. Helen Morrogh, having Helen, Kate, David, Oliver, Henry and John. David m. Mary Griffin, having Oliver and Frances; he was Crown Solicitor, and later Clerk of the Crown and Peace, and d. a. 65. 7. Sir Thomas Moriarty, b. 1775; M.D., knt. 1811, m. Eliza Lee, having

Moriarty Households

Capt. Hy. and Rev. Wm.; he was a son of Henry of Dingle, who m. Helena Fitzgerald, having Honora, Anne, Catherine, Sir Thomas, Counsellor Maurice, Captain James, Dr. Fergus, Thaddeus, Edward, b. 1799, m. 1839, Catherine, dau. of Dr. Eugene O'Sullivan, and d. 1864, having Rev. Henry of Baltimore, Rev. Eugene, Rev. James of Chatham, N.Y, Helena, and Catherine, d. 1916. 8. Lord Justice John Moriarty was grandson of James, of Grange, Kilmallock, 1788-1868, who m. Bridget Barry, having John, Mce. 1823-1903, James d., 1864, Rev. Michael of Rockdale 1817-97, Judge Jerh. of Baroda d.. 1865, Major David, d. 1879; Lieut.-Col. Thomas 1837-1912, m. Margt. MacCarthy having Bride, Mary and Sophie. John, 1818-89, solicitor had Mallow, m. Ellen O'Connell, having Mary, James of Sydney; Lord Justice John Francis, who m. 1 Kate Kavanagh and 2 Mabel Dolphin, having Maguerita, Ellen, Kathleen, Frances, Michael, solr. d. 1913; Mce. d. unm. 9. Moriarty of Ballymalis, Mortogh had John. Eugene, Thade, of whom John, b. 1741, had Dr. Mortimer, 1779-1829, Thade. Eugene b. 1785, Edmond 1785-1824; Thade had Tim, Morto and Eugene, b. 1769, and m. Mary Ferris having Thade, who had John, Eugene, Ml., Edw. and Dan. 10. Moriarty of Aunascaul; Tim of Ballintarmin, b. 1774, was seneschal or barony constable of Corcaguiny; he m. Sarah Fitzgerald having Ellen, Marcella, Edw. of Monarca 1805-33, James of Brackloon, 1807-78, Denis 1811-47, John of Minard, Tim of Ballintarmin, 1824-1909. Of these James m. Ellen Gallway, having Sarah, Annie, Mary, Ellen, James, Robert, Pat m. Margaret Thompson, having Eileen, Mary, Evelyn, John m. Marcella Thompson having Sara, Ellen, Emily. Tim was seneschal and m. Mary O'Leary, having Sarah, Eileen, Mary, Edward, Philip, Denis, Robert, Morgan. Edward's son Gerald M.C., was Capt. Aus. Artillery in France 1918; Edward, brother of Tim, 1774, of Minard, m Mary Bagley, having Thomas of Dayton in Ohio. See branch 16. 11. Moriarty of Glanahira. Tim 1777-1834 m. Eliza MacCarthy having Pat 1808-33, a poet; Michael m. 1835 Maria Fitzgerald, having Tim, Marcie, Honora, Ellen; Redmond had Pat, Eliza, Hanna; Thade, b. 1812; Ignatius, b. 1816; Tim, b. 1820; John, b. 1824, Eliza. 12. Moriarty of Kilcrohane. Rev. Owen, 1715-1810, P.P. of Kilcrohane and Sneem, had four brothers—Thade, John, Mce. and Jasper. Thade had 21 sons, of whom Owen b. 1767, m. Mary O'Mahony having Mary, Kate, Ellen, Hanora, Mce., Myles 1877-78, who m. Julia Brennan having Mary, Ellen, Eugene, James. Myles, Maurice, and Batt., of whom Eugene of Wicklow had Julia, Lily, Lee., Rev. Andrew of Dublin, Mce., James, Myles, Eugene. 13. Moriarty of Ventry. Tim 1759-1835, son of Rowland, son of Tim, m. Ellen Rice, having Rowland, James and Edw., b. 1796, who had Rowland, Tim, James and Myles. 14. Dr. Patrick Moriarty of Killarney had Maria and Thomas. Maria b. 1803, m. 1826 John son of Thomas Dennehy of Cork having General Sir Thos. Dennehy, who m. 1859, his cousin Elizabeth, dau. of Thomas Moriarty, 1805-43, and Margaret Fitzpatrick, who had also a son Thomas. 15. John Moriarty of Cork. Count Daniel O'Mahony of Cremona, d. 1714, was the son of Dermod, who m. Mary, dau. of John Moriarty, and his grandfather, John, m. Joan, dau. of John Moriarty of Courtstown, near Cork. 16. Moriarty of Ballinlohig. Dan of 1750 had Kate, John, Dan, Jas. and Thomas; of whom James had John, b. 1820; Mary, Catherine, Eliza; Dan b. 1791 had Mary, Julia, John, James, Dan, and Pat; John b. 1781, had James, Dan and Pat. 17. Pat of Dingle, 1750, m. Magd. Hickson, having Denis, who m. Margaret Kennedy, having John, who m. Johanna Sugrue, having Denis, Charles, Teresa and Helena. 18. Moriarty of Ballycaneen, Thomas b. 1801, had Mce., John, James, Michael Jonathan, Thomas and Bridget. Michael of Dingle had Dr. John and Rev. Thomas. 19. Moriarty of Bandon, Michael d. 1860; Con had Wm., James, Mary m. 1829, Jos. Stanley, having Rev. Abraham. 20. Moriarty of Tralee, John had Hannah, John, Kate, Marion, Eliza, Margaret, Pat and Mce. Pat m. Sarah Mac-

Moriarty Households

Turk having Dorothy, Capt. John, Lieut. Pat, Denis, Edw., Thomas, Louis, Gerald. Mce., bro. of John, of Deeds Office in Dublin, d. 1881, having John, Pat, Tom, Kate, Nellie. 21. Moriarty of London, Daniel, the eloquent, in 1828, was a club member with Jerrold, Thackeray and Dickens, and died 1858, leaing a daughter, Mary. Moriarty family in America, traced by Lieut. Ambrose T. Moriarty, U.S. Army, of Putnam, Conn. In 1688 Edward Moriarty of Ann Arundel Co. in Maryland, and his wife Honor in 1701, mention in their wills their children Dan, Edw. Margt., Eliza and Rachel, of whom Margt. m. Col. Thomas Sprigg, ancestor of Lord Fairfax. In 1776 Tim was in 5th Penn. Dennis was in Washington's Guard in 1780. Eugene of Castlemaine, d 1907, was editor of "Worcester Evening Post." Bro. John of Dingle, and Boston Jesuit College for 46 years, d 1911, a. 77. Col James of 7th Regt. in Sp.-Amn. War, in Chicago 1913. Michael, 1833-1907, son of Batt of Caherciveen, m. Emma Seator having Mary m. Col. Wm. Flynn; Oscar m. Nancy Irvine having Alfred, Oscar and Ruth; Ambrose, lieut. 1887, LL.B., M.L.; Walter; Rd. m. Mary Todd, d. 1905; Oscar's sons Major Alfred and Oscar, in France 1918. 2, John Moriarty d at Salem 1797; his son Thomas d 1783, m. Deborah Bowditch, having John m Abigail Moseley having Dr. John and Dr. Joseph of Boston; Dr. John, 1807-65, m Nancy Andrews having Anne, Caroline, Wm. John, and Geo. who m. Mary Sheffield having George who m. Olga Boker having Lilias. 3. Patrick of Brooklyn, son of Joseph of Tralee, was Captain of the Irish Volunteers, he m. Margt. O'Sullivan having 5 daus. and 6 sons. 4. Eugene of Martara d 1889, having 3 daus. and 2 sons of whom Martin in Brooklyn had Eugene, Harold, and Mildred. 5. Dan, son of John, b. 1830, in Federal navy 1861-4, m. Margaret Foley, having 2 daus. and 5 sons of whom Frank has 3 daus. and 3 sons. 6. Stephen, d 1907, son of Tom, was manager of Edison Phonograph Co. in London. 7. Eugene, 1815-70, of Waterbury, had 5 daus. and 4 sons of whom John had 5 daus. and 3 sons. 8. Dr. Pat of Boston 1902 has 3 daus. and 1 son. 9. Murtach of Holyoke had 1 son dsp. 10. Geo. of Vermont Univy., son of Ml. 11. Denis of Holyoke, son of John, has John and Mary. 12. Mce. of Worcestor, son of Mce. 1848-1910. 13. Mce. of Manchester had 4 daus. and 2 sons. 14. Thomas of Norwich has 3 daus. and 1 son. 15. Tim of Springfield, 1836-99, had 5 sns and 4 daus. 16. Tom of Dayton d 1872, having 2 sons and 1 dau. of whom Pat of Holyoke has 2 sons and 3 daus. 17. Tim of Springfield has 9 children. 18. John of Albany had 2 daus. 19. John of Norwich had 10 children. 20. Mce. of S. Hadley Falls, had 5 sons. 21. John of Holyoke, has 2 daus. and 1 son. 22. John of Granby d. 1898, having 2 sons and 1 dau. 23. Joseph of Phila has 2 daus. 24. Peter of Waitsfield had 5 sons and 4 daus. 25. Jerh. of Brooklyn has 1 son and 3 daus. 26. James of New York has 1 son and 2 daus. 27. Wm. of Brooklyn had 1 son and 3 daus. 28. Thomas of Malden had 5 sons and 2 daus. 29. John of Boston has 2 daus. and 1 son. 30. Dan of Boston has 2 daus. and 1 son. 31. John of Holyoke has 1 son and 1 dau. 32. Denis of Springfield had 5 sons and 2 daus. 33. Ml. 1843-1910 of Worcester had 2 daus. and 3 sons. 34. Mce. of Worcester has 6 sons and 3 daus. 35. Rowland of Phila had 3 sons and 2 daus. 36. Mce. of Holyoke had 7 sons and 2 daus. 37. James of Washington had 3 sons and 4 daus. 38. John of New Bedford had 2 daus. 39. Dan of Oswego had 2 sons and 1 dau. 40. Con. of Waterbury had 9 children. 41. John of Minneapolis had 1 son. 42. John of Washington d 1902, having 1 dau. 43 Rd. of St. Paul had 4 sons and 3 daus. 44. Tom of Springfield had 6 sons and 1 dau. 45. Tom of Clermont 1818-1907 had 10 children. 46. Pat of Granby had James of Montreal. There are many more of the name of Moriarty in America, detailed particulars of whom will be welcomed. Moriarty wills in Record Office in Dublin included those of Tom of Tuoreen in Clare 1719; Ml. of Ballymacalla in Clare 1729; Wm. of Milltown in Kerry 1781; Tom of

Moriarty Households

Dingle 1785; James of Dingle 1799; prerogative wills of Blase of Dingle 1781; Tom of Dingle 1785; Edm. of Ballymalis 1842; Eugene of Ballymalis 1814; John of Scrolough, 1835; Matt of Ballybeg, 1834; Matt. of Ghent 1854; Dr. Mortimer of Killarney 1830; Redmond of Cork in 1852; Sir Thomas of Abbeytown, 1838; Tom of Cork 1839; wills in Ardfert and Aghadoe diocese—Alice of Dingle 1767; Catherine of Boherroe 1818; Dan of Killenare 1836; Rev. Denis of Dingle 1735; Denis of Corrovagh 1795; Fergus of Dingle 1855; Johanna of Dingle 1833; John of Dingle 1824; John of Acres 1826; John of Caharaha 1832; John of Cappagh 1832; John of Annablaha 1835; John of Caherciveen 1842; Mary of Kilbonane 1851; Matthew of Dingle 1743; Mce. of Milltown 1781; Dr. Melchoir of Dingle 1747; Miles of Killarney 1823; Mortogh of Knockaneacoolteen, 1730; Owen of Ballynbeg 1842; Thomas James of Dingle 1799; Thos. of Mulachveal 1826; Johanna of Cork 1854; Ambrose of Cork 1837; Catherine of Cork, 1836; John of Castlecim in Raphoe 1814; Royal Navy wills at Somerset House in London—Thomas 1728; Michael 1742; Daniel 1748; James, 1753; Matthew 1761; Stephen 1764; Edward 1764; John 1779; Daniel 1783; Peter 1785; Daniel 1799; Lt.-Col. Matthew 1804; Sylverius 1804; John 1808; Lieut. Peter 1808; Vice Admiral Sylverius 1810. Moriarty marriage licence bonds in Dublin diocese—Stephen 1806; Stephen 1809; Helena 1843; Timothy 1805; Tredesind, 1829; in Cork and Ross—James 1708; John 1717, Johanna 1738, Ann 1796, Catherine 1783, Edward 1779, John 1768, Joseph 1778, Mary 1826, Mary 1812, Mary 1829, Dr. Pat 1820, Redmond, 1829; in Cloyne:—Catherine 1783, Joseph 1764, Mary 1784; in Ossory:—Norah 1822; in Killaloe:—Bridget 1843, Bridget 1807; in Elphin:—Henry 1839; in Cashel:—Rev. Thomas 1837; in St. Georges Mayfair, John 1748, Jas. 1753; in the George's Hanover square, Jas. 1810, Daniel 1828. Moriarty names in University graduate lists include for Dublin T. C. D.:—Tim 1803, Mce. 1807, Thomas 1837, William 1838, Sylverius 1839, Edward 1839, Matthew 1840, Denis 1857, Thomas 1861, Matthew 1869, George 1884, Gerald 1885, Cecil 1898, Thomas 1900, R. U. I.:—Thomas 1858, Andrew 1898; Edin:—Mortogh 1804, Merion 1821; Aberdeen:—Stephen 1847; Rome:—Rev. Patrick 1839; Oxford:—Louis 1877, Arthur 1878, Gerald 1881, George of Harvard; Cambridge:—Gerald 1897, Gerald 1912. Gray's Inn admission:—Matthew 1837; Sylvanus 1838, James 1881; King's Inns Dublin:—Sylverius 1840, Matthew 1840, Edward 1836, John 1877, John 1907. The hearth money collectors in Kerry in 1663-7 included Donald, Edmond, Mortagh, Eugene, Maurice, Thomas, Tadg, Hugo, and Morriart. In the 1914-8 war:—killed: lieut-colonel Sylverius, R. Irish regt 1915; lieut. Jas. Hy. R.G.A. 1915; Corp Harry A. I. F. 1917; Private Mce A. I. F. 1917; Private Merion A. I. F. 1918; lieut Denis, Inniskillings, 1918; lieut D., N.Z. 1918; many were wounded, a large number served in the British, Dominions, and American forces, and received various decorations.

Morley, O'Murgaile; Dan of Lisnagrave, John of Doocarrigbeg, Pat of Tinnahally, John of Farrantooreen, Pat of Aghanboy, Catherine of Main street, John of Ballyhearney, Dan of Coomnakilla, Tom of Main street, Tim and Jas. of Pound lane.

Moroney, O'Maolruanaid chief of Crumthan in Killian barony in Galway; 20 families in Kerry, viz:—Matt of Dunmaniheen, Margt. of Listowel, John and Ml. of Ballylongford, Batt or Knockagurrane, John and Ml. of Cloonmore, Tim of Boherbee, Chas. of the Square, Johanna of Mill road, Dan and Ml. and Dan and Pat and Ml. and Tim of Cromane, Dan and Peter of Reen, Pat of Farrantooreen, Denis of Ballymacprior.

Morphy; John of Mount Prospect d. 1799; his will is in the Record office. John Stephen Morphy of Kerry was an Australian police magistrate; his daughter m. Ivo Bligh who in 1900 succeeded as Lord Darnley. Charles J. Morphy, Crown Solicitor for Kerry, d. 1913.

Morris; Jeffrey of Knockalibade. Jeffrey of Main street

Shea Households

Shanahan, O'Seanacain; 77 families in Kerry, viz.—Tom of Magh, Pat of Lackanooneen, Rd. of Tonebwee. Edw. of Lisheenbawn, Dan of Tullig, Tom of Castletown, Tom of Crotta, Con and Pat of Moyvane, Rd. of Kilbaha, Mary of Moher, James and Ml. of Kilcolgan, John of Knockmeal, Tim of Ballygrennan, Pat and Ml. of Knockalougha, Catherine of Carhoona, John and John of Coolatoosane, Michael of Dooncaha, John of Irrabeg, Mce. of Liscullane, Jerh. of Tullamore, Edm. of Candouglas, Ml. and Mce. of Glashananon, Dan and Dan of Beale, Edm. of Ballyline, Pat and Wm. of Dromlivaun, James of Dromin, Dan of Lissahane, Ml. of Knockbrane Pat of Ahanagran, John of Fahavane, Johanna of Listowel, Pat of Pallas, Michael of Knocknagun, Mary of Gullane, Jhlia of Glashnanoon, Thomas offf Glankeagh, Dan and Pat of Tubridbeg, John and Pat and Tim and John of Ballylahive, Denis of Tubridmore, Tom and Jas. of Ballysheen, Dan of Knocknacaska, Tom of Farran, Bridget and Margaret of Brogue lane, Hannah of James street, Tom and Dan of Bawnboy, Tom of Knocknahaha, Pat of Listanavally, Tom of Muing, John of Ballygarron, James of Shanakeal, John of Fybough, John and Pat and Dan and Michael and Eliza of Farranreagh, James of Doory, Tom of High street, Ml. and Edm. of Toomies. Ua Seanacain was chief of Tulla in Clare and Hy. Rongaile in Tipperary.

Shannon, O'Seanain; Bartley of Knockanarney.

Shantalliv, old land, in Killiney.

Sharkey, O'Searcaig; John of Spa road.

Shaughnessy, O'Seacnasaig; Edm. of Beeheenagh, John of Kilelton, Tom of Baltovin, Ml. of Lisardboola, Rd. of Listowel. Ua Seacnasaig was chief of cinel Ada, and Kinelea in Galway in 1224. Edward O'Shaughnessy of Caherciveen, d 1905, a. 38, journalist of Press Gallery in London, and "Irish Independent."

Shaw, Seadac; John of Inch, Chas. of Farranreagh.

Shea; O'Seagda, O'Seagha, Ua Seaghdha chief of Ui Raehach, in Corca Duibne, of the clan Conaire; 900 families in Kerry, viz:—Geo. and John of Gortdromerillagh, Jerh. of Rusheen, John of Longfield, Ml. of Curraghmore, Pat and James of High street Dan and Jerh. of Bohereencael Mort and John of Ballalley Lane, Con and James of New street, Dan of Knockreer, Pat and John of Inch, Con of Sunny hill, Pat of Mangerton view, Dan of Walsh's lane, James of Green lane, Dan of Ardshanavooly, Dan and John of Curragh, Julia of Bawnluskaha, Margaret of Glenlarehan, Denis of Killeen, Dan of Doonkinane, Con of Knocknagawna, Pat of Rossnacarteenbeg, Tim and Mary and John of Barraduff, Kate of Droumhumper, Matt and John of Kno,ckackullig, Pat of Glenlarehan, Mary of Bohereencael, Mary of Inch, Mary of Ardshanavooly, Edw. of Castleview, Con of Barleymount, Ml. of Faughbane, Pat of Ahane, John of Flemby, Jerh. of Coolnacalliagh, Ml. of Culleenymore, Dan of Kilmaniheen, Michael of Knocknagoshel, Tim of Pallis, John and Con of Gortnacollopa, Eugene of Gearha, Con of Rossmore, James of Killahane, Hanoria of Lyre, David of Dromin, James of Farranmanagh, James and Ml. and Martin of Gortahoonig, Tim of Killegy, Dan of Fieries, James and Con of Boolasallagh, Pat of Rockfield, Denis of Acres, Margaret of Broughane, Jerh, of Dromulton, Pat of Bally-

Shea Households

beg, John of Knockearagh, Dan of Knockaninane, John of Knockeenduff, Margaret of Ahaneboy, Pat of Baltovin, Ml. of Ballybroman, John of Ballinagare, Mary of Tullig, Kate of Knockunderval, Pat of Meenanare, Tim of Baltovin, John of Ballymacquin, Eliza of Clountubrid, John and John of Tullamore, Debora of Meenanare, Dan of Bedford, Pat of Scrahan, Bridget of Clahane, John of Fahavane, Ml. of Killeacle, Tom of Clountubrid, Pat of Ballinbrannig, Andrew and Wm. of Kildurrihy, Tom and Pat and John and Jas. of Cahertrant, Ml. of Fahan, Humphrey of Laharan, Jas. and Denis and Tim and Ml. and John of Cromane, Pat of Langford St., Dan of Garrahadoo, John and Slyv. of Mill road, Pat of Iveragh road, Denis of Tulligbeg, Dan of Lonart, Pat of Lahara, Tim and Ml. of Main St., Mce. of Rock St., Tim of Blennerville, Pat of Market place, Matt and John of Spa road, Jerh. and David and Jerh. and Thos. of Abbey street, John of Caheranne road, John and Denis and John of Francis street, Matt and John of Mary street, Jas. and Julia of Moyderwell, John and David and Denis of Connor's lane, Con and Ml. of Stephen's lane, Dan of Castlemaine St., Con of Bleach road, Jas. of old Chapel lane, Jerh. of Brackhill, Wm. of Milltown, Ml. of Cloonmore, Pat of Callinafercy, Pat of Boolteens, Dan and Pat of Farna, Mary of Fenit, Margt. of Abbey St., Kate of Ballymullen, Jerh. of Clahane, Thade of Caherslee, John of Leath, Jas. and Edm. and Pat and Jas. and Tim and Johanna of Tonevane, Ellen of Clashedmond, Mary of Derrymore, Pat of Knockenagh, Jane and Kate of Laharan, Dan of Gransha, Pat of Ballygarron, Dan and Dan of Lissavane, Jas. of Ballymacegogue, Mary of Kildurrihy, Kate of Kilvickadownig, Margt. of Tullig, Pat and Pat of Banogue, Mary of Lateevebeg, Ml. of Ballinclare, Pat of Gurteens, Eug. of Ardbeg, Bridget of Milltown, Mary of Myles lane, Tom and Jerh. of Ballyandreen, Tom and Tom of Ballintaggart, Jerh. of Ballycurrane, John of Moorestown, Ml. of Shanakyle, Pat of Ballybrack, John of Lisdorgan, Denis of Boherbrack, Pat of Emlagh, Ellen of Kilcooly, Mary of Slieve, Ellen of Ballintarmon, John of Camp, Margt. of Gurteens, Mce. of Gortadoo, Andrew of Smerwick, John of Lougher, Jas. of Tullig, Eug. of Emlagh, Edw. of Teer, Mary of the Mall, Jas. and Dan and Con of Lisardboola, John of Ballingowan, Jas. of Gortaleen, Tim and Jas. and Wm. and Edm. of Gortanedan, Tim of Shanahill, Ml. and John and Jas. of Ballyarkane, Tom of Aughills, Wm. of Caheracruttera, John of Killenagh, Pat and Mce. and John of Kildurrihy, John of Caheratrant, Jos. of Emlaghslat, Dan of Cantra, Dan of Ballylusky, John and Ml. of great Blasket island, Wm. of Ballyvickeen, John of Coumeenole, John and Edm. of Cloghaneanode, Ml. and Mce. of Coolroe, Ml. of Farrantane, Jos. of the Wood, Ml. of Spa road, Jerh. of Main St., John of Holyground, Ml. and Jas. and Ellen and Mary and Ellen of Aughacasla, Pat of Glenmane, John of Keelballylahive, Ml. of Lisnagree, Jas. of Kilcooly, Ml. of Caherscullibeen, Pat and John of Ballylusky, Tom of Carrig, Tom of Murreigh, Pat of Ballyameenbought, John of Cloghane, Tom and Jas. of Ballymore, Mce. of Caherboshina, John of Glens, Pat and Pat and Pat of Derrymore, Jerh. and Jerh. of Curraheen, Mary of Coomastour, Kate and John and Ml. of Kealafreaghane, Mary of Kilmackerrin, Pat and Tom of Loher, Jas. of Rineen, John of Canuig, Jas. of Islandboy, Ellen of Muingydowda, Bridget of Emlaghmore, Ellen of Doory, Jas. and Jerh. of Cloghanecanuig, John of Rathkieran, Mary of Drombohilly, Hanoria of Kilmackillogue, Mary of Glanmore, Margt. of Shronebrane, Hanoria of Fehanagh, Mary of Ankail, Mary of Driminamore, Mary of Gortamullin, Denis of Meanus, Jerh. of Gortaloughra, Sylv. of Groin, Jas. of Eightercua, John of Keelnabrack, Margt. of Clonee, Kate of Claddanure, Johanna of Derrynafeensha, Hanoria of Faha, Con and Denis of Claddanure, Julia of Letterdunane, Johanna of Earneen, Mary of Baurearagh, Jas. and Jas. and Mary of Clogheramore, Ml. of Treanmanagh, Owen of Tooreenasliggaun, Johanna and Margt. of Kilnabrack, Johanna of Coolroe, Batt and Con and John and Ml. of Droumalouhur, Catherine of Teeromoyle, Mary of Coomnakilla, Hannah of Killoughane, Kate of Churchtown, Bridget and Flor. and Ml. of Cloghanecarhan, Mary of Cloghaneleni-

Shea Households

ghan, Mary of Killurley, Julia and Pat of Coolmagort, Jerh. of Crossderry, Con of Aghatubrid, Hanoria of Tiernahilla, Ellen of Gurrane, Margt. of Knockaneden, Ellen of Fermoyle, Catherine of Sussa, Kate of Sallahig, Mary of Rath, Hanoria of Coad, Bridget of Feighmane, Ellen of Dohilla, Catherine and Mary of Tinnies, Denis of Gerhasillagh, Jas. and John of Greenane, John of Letter, Margt. of Callahaniska, Mary of Dooaghs, Mary of Muingaphuea, Julia of Commaun, Jas. and Chas. of Cappagh, Chas. of Kilgobnet, Catherine of Kill, Margt. of Keel, Johanna of Ballyledder, Lce. of Scariff, Con and Pat of Derrynanebeg, Ml. of Coomattoukane, Jas. of Coss, Peter and Peter of Shanacashel, Dan and Jas. of Glenmackee, Ellen and Gobnet of Dirrenedin, Mary of Octive, Johanna of Derreen, Mary and Bridget of Derriana, Norah of Cappanagroun, Deborah of Ballinakilla, Mary of Doughill, Ml. and Pat and Jas. of Emlaghnamuck, Tim and Denis of Cloon, Pat of Portmagee, John and Ml. and John and Denis and Ml. and John and Dan of Doory, Tim and John of Knockeenawaddra, Tim and John of Lateeve, Jas. of Bealdarrig, John of Gortbrack, John of Graignagreena, Tim of Gerah, John of Teoreenafersha, John of Scarteen, Pat and Tim and Ml. of Allagheemore, Con of Dungegan, John and Denis and John of Cools, Peter and Martin of Ballinskelligs, John of Cloghaneanad, Jas. of Cannug, Batt. and John of Curraghnanov, John of Creggeen, Denis and Ml. of Lounaghan, John of Slaghts, Crohan and Ml. and John and Pat of Loher, John of Derrenedin, Denis and Denis of Mahygrenane, John and Flor of Octive, Ml. of Derrenedin, John of Mastergeehy, Jas. and Ml. and Pat of Cappanagrown, Con of Dromnakilla, Denis and Jas. and Ml. of Ballinakilla, Dan and Ml. and Dan of Killeenleagh, Dan of Derriana, Jas. and Jas. of Lissantannig, Jerh. and Tim and Ml. and John of Canuig, Dan and John of Inchiboy, Tim of Bunaderreen, Jas. of Keelafreaghane, Pat of Inchbeg, Con and John of Kilmackerrin, Pat and Con of Ballyhearney, Pat and Con and Ml. of Coarhabeg, Jerh. and Tim of Bray, Con of Feighmane, Ml. of Farranreagh, Tom and Pat of Cool, Con and John of Dohilla, John of Kilbeg, John and Pat of Spunkane, John and Jerh. and Ml. and Jas. and Con and Pat of Tullig, John and Pat and John of Murreigh, John and Ml. of Garryglass, John of Farranahow, Dan and John and Dan and Ml. of Inchinaleega, Con of Drimnabeg, Ml. and Con. of Driminamore, Ml. and Pat of Bogare, Pat and Tim and Denis of Deerreenaclaurig, Hanoria of Cushcummeragh, Julia and Joan of Cannig, Catherine of Kilmackeriu, Ml. and Pat and Crohan of Ballard, John of Sussa, Johanna of Bunaderreen, Pat and Tim and Michael and John of Fermoyle, Pat of Ardcost, Dan of Aghagadda, John of Gurranes, Ml. and John and Tim of Dromlusk, John and Dan and Ml. and Tim of Russdohan, Jas. of Derreenamucklagh, John and Ml. of Brackloon, Ml. and John of Doon, John and Jerh. and Ml. and Pat of Rossmore, Denis of Creveen, Con and John of Lauragh, John and Denis of Clogherane, Jerh. of Shronebrane, Con. and Eug. of Cannagullen, Ml. of Fehanagh, Peter of Coolounig, Mort of Coolcreen, Mary of Killurley, Margt. of Ballinskelligs, Catherine of Cools, John of Coolcreen, Denis of Dromaclaurig, Denis of Deelis, John of Glanmore, John of Shronebirrane, Jerh. of Clogherane, Jas. of Creveen, Denis of Cunmeen, Jas. of Ballynagulla, Con. and Ml. of Maulagowna, Peter of Derreenknow, Tim and John of Coomnagillagh, Dan of Coornacaragh, Mort of Ballynafulla, Pat of Carks, Con of Gortalinny, Con and Pat of Lackaroe, Con of Doughill, Jerh. and Ml. of Dromatouk, Ml. of Lomanagh, Pat and John of Moneyflugh, Hanoria of Kenmare, Mary of Downing's-lane, Ellen of Williamstreet, Jerh. and John and Denis of Ardea, Jas. of Derryconnery, John of Kilmackillogue, Matt and John and Pat and John of Gurranes, John of Lehud, John and Con and Pat of Cummers, Dan and Jerh and John and Tim of Garrane, Denis of William Street, Dan of Kilcorrane, Denis of Carrignahihilan, Con of Droumcahan, Pat of Derrygarriv, James of Kilmurry, Mort of Shelbourne St., Ml. of Gortamullen, Ml. of Ken-

203

Shea Households

mare, Denis of Inchimore, Ml. of Sound, Con of Ballygriffin, Pat of Loughanacreen, Pat of Lehud, Pat and Ml. and Denis of Cummers, Tim of Drombohilly, Humphrey and Dan and Tim and Denis and Jerh. of Coomnakilla, Pat and Jerh. and John and Dan of Cappanacush, Jerh. of Capparoe, Tim and Ml. of Dreinagh, John and Matt and Pat and John of Bunglasha, Tim and Denis and Tim of Feorus, Jerh. of Drombane, Con of Coolnaroe, Denis of Dauros, Tim and Mort and Pat of Gearha, Mort of Esk, Pat and James and Pat and John and Pat of Earneen, John and Denis of Garryletter, Tim of Coorleagh, Dan of Crinagort, Pat and Ml. and Peter of Knockduff, Mort of Killabonane, Con of Dromagurteen, John and Pat and John of Barearagh, Denis of Letterdunane, Tim of Tullaha, John of Rath, Dan and Denis and Dan of Killeen, Pat of Derreensillagh, Denis and Dan of Liss, John and Denis and John and Pat and Batt and John of Reenanallagane, John and Pat and Ml. and Pat and Ml. and Thomas and Pat of Curraheen, Pat and John and Ml and Ml. of Kilnabrack, Ml. and Pat of Gowlane, Ml. and Pat of Ballinakilla, Dan and Pat and Batt of Droum, James and Ml. of Coolnaharrigill, John and Tim and John of Coolroe, Batt of Gortdirragh, Tim and Ballycarnahan, Denis and Denis of Brackaharagh, Pat and Denis and Pat and Dan and Tim of Rath, John and John of Beheghane, Crohan of Coomnahorna, Tom of Rathfield, Dan of Glanbeg, Ml. and Denis and Ml. and Jerh. of Cooleanig, Dan and Tim of Gortboy, Denis of Gearha, James and James and James of Ballyledder, Dan of Liss, Ml. and Ml. of Killeen, Denis of Skahanagh, Pat of Commaun, Matt and Pat and Matt of Treanmanagh, Tim and John and Tim of Treangarriv, Ml. of Callahaniske Ml. and Pat and Ml. of Glounagillaght Dan of Dooks, Pat and Tim and Denis of Ballintleave, James and Pat of Lauhir, Denis and Dan and James of Killoughane, Denis and John of Churchtown, John and Thade and John of Carhoonahone, Dan of Tullig, Dan of Teeramoyle, Ml. of Gortnagree, John of Toon, John and Batt of Gortaforia, Ml. and Tom of Gortnagree, John of Kells, Jerh and Batt of Gortnaforia, Dan of Gleensk, John and Ml. of Teeromoyle, Martin of Raecaslagh, Pat and Tom of Kimego, Pat of Inchintrea, John of Killurley, Don and Ml. and Dan and James and Dan of Cloghanelanaghan, Pat of Ballynahowmore, Con of Castlequin, Pat of Ballydarrig, Mary of Laharn, Margt and Ellen of High St., James and Tim of Killognaveen, Pat of Coars, Jerh. of Gurrane, Tim of Waterville, James and John ot Beenbane, John of Breaheg, Pat and Martin and Ml. of Caherbarnagh, John and Tim of Tarmons, Tim and Ml. of Lislonane, Tom of Derreen, Con and Jerh. and Tim and Pat of Lahara, Dan and Ml. and Ml. of Boola, Pat of High Street, John of Obermong, Pat of Reenard, John and Pat of Killognaveen, Pat of Gowlanes, Pat of Kilnaback, Pat of Letter, Frank of Quay St, Dan of Main St., Dan of Killoe, Tom of Lativemore, Batt and Tim and Ml. and Pat and Tim and John and John of High street, Con and John and Con of Killoe, John and James and John and Jerh. and Michael and John and Michael of Main st., Denis and Pat and Jerh. of Laharn, Pat of Valencia road, John of Derreen, Tim of Kilcoman, James of the Quay, Con and James and John and John of Church lane, Pat of Fair green, Dan of Moneyduff, Jas. and Denis of Inchiclough, Ml. and Mort and Con of Old road, Jerh of Rehill, Michael of Reenard, Denis of Pound lane. O'Shea is form used by—James of Ballyfinane, Dan of Cleeny, Arthur of Ballyvirrane, John of Bishop's lane, Dan of High St., Pat of Ardfert, Tim of Ballynamanagh, Tim of Gortahoonig, Mary of Listowel, Roger of Tullamore, T. of Bedford, Hy. of Dromkeen, Pat and Dan and James and Jerh and Eliza of Milltown, Catherine of Knockavota, John of Killorglin, Denis of Lisnakealwee, Julia of Oantra, John of Ballycurrane, Ml. and James and Ml. of Valencia road, Pat and Ellen of Main street, James and Ellen of William street, Dan of Gowlanes, Michael of Inchinaleega, Dan of Octive, James of Cahir, Ellen of Garranafulla, Denis of Droumaclaurig, Denis of Dauros.

O'Shea / Sheehan Households

O'Seagha was chief of Ui Rathach, in S. Corca Duibne, of the clann Conaire and tuath sen Eran. After 1261 the clan Cashel, Mac Carthys and O'Sullivans, driven out of Tipperary, settled in Desmond on the lands of the tuath sen Erann. The O'Shea sept of the clan Conaire remained in the old homesteads in Iveragh, and 900 families of the name, as given above, are now owners of a large part of the old land of Ui Duibna of good hosts. The O'Sheas should hold a gathering of the clan in Iveragh each year, and trace their cousinship back to the old times of 2,000 years ago when Staigue or caher Metuis was the headquarters of the clan. The Rev. Jeremiah O'Shea, 1858-1917, was P.P. of Kilgarvan, and brother of Rev. T. O'Shea, and John O'Shea of Knockearagh in Killarney parish. Rev. Thomas O'Shea, Archbishop of Wellington, N. Zealand, was born at Hawera, the son of Kerry emigrants, his mother being Johanna O'Sullivan of Lahern, who lived to the age of 85. P. J. O'Shea, a pioneer of the Irish language revival, has written several books in Gaelic.

Sheehan, O'Siodacain; 275 families in Kerry, viz:—Johanna of Knockadarrive, Mce. and Denis of Ahane, Mort of Tooreenmore, David and John of Meenbannivane, John of Knocknagoshel, Flor. of Ahaneboy, Edm. and Thos. of Brosna, Mort and Mort of Kilmaniheen, Jos. of Twohill's lane, Jerh. of Main street, Wm. of Moyeightragh, Pat of New St., Wm. of Annaghillymore, Jas. and Dan of Dromkerry, John of Lissyconnor, Con and Jerh. of Shinnagh, Pat of Gortnaprocess, Denis and Tim and Andrew and Dan and Pat of Tooreencahill, Ml. of Coom, Wm. of Tooreengarriv, Dan and Denis and Ml. of Knocknaboul, Ellen and Jas. of Clounmelane, Ellen of Shinnagh, Hanoria of Meentogues, Jerh. of Ballytrasna, Norah of Annaghbeg, Nora of Main street, Mary of old Market lane, Dan of Kilsarcon, Jas. of Knockadarrive, Jerh. and John and Pat of Maulykevane, Mary of Ards, Ellen of Derra, Mort of Crinny, Tom of Knockardtry, Martin of Meenleitrim, Jerh. and Pat of Knockanmirish, Johanna and Denis of Rahanane, Dan of Beheenagh, Tim of Ballincollig, Denis and Pat of Scart, Con of Knockeenalicka, Jas. of Knockatagglebeg, Jas. of Coolick, Bridget of Ballyaukeen, Dan of Shinnagh, Jerh. of Canguilla, John and Jas. of Acres, Tom of Kilbaha, Hy. and Jas. of Tarmons, Jas. of Doonard, Jane of Lixnaw, Dan of Irrabeg, Bridget of Cloonafineela, Mce. of Coilbwee, Maria of Commons, Mary and Pat of Ballynoneen, John of Carhooeragh, David of Lacka, John and John and Hanora of Finuge, Ellen of Beale, Julia of Listowel, Joh nof Tullahinnell, Sarah of Boheroe, Jerh and Tim of Knocknacaska, Pat of Dromcunnig, Wm. of Cappagh, Tom of Knoppogue, Johanna of Moybella, John of Ahabeg, Tim of Clahane, John of Ballylongane, Ml. and Jerh and Tom of Glenderry, Ml. of Maulin, Margt. of Barrow, Dan of Edward St., John and Anne of Market Place, Pat of Keelacloghane, Tim of Castledrum, Mce. of Farna, Tom of Liscahane, Tim of Knockanush, Deborah of Ballintobeenig, Dan of Quill street, Johanna of Ardcanaght, Ml. of Stealroe, John of Tinnahally, Denis of Knocknamon, Jas. of Ardrinane, Ml. of Gortanoorane, Rev. John of Main St., John of Gurrane, Tom or Douglas, Jas. of Shanahill, John and Tim and Jas. of Lassaboy, Tim of Corkaboy, Tim of Gortaleen, Chas. of Mill road, John of Market St., Dan of Ballymacprior, Pat and John and Julia and Pat and Ml. of Gurrane, John and Pat of Reen, Pat of Bansha, Pat of Killorglin, Eug. of Barrow, Tim and Edm. of Fenit, Ml. of Ballymacegogue, Pat of Twalaght, Edm. of Kilfenora, Mary and Julia of Main street, Tom and Pat and Ml. of Ardkearagh, Pat of Breahig, Pat of Beenbane, Dan of Knockroe, Julia of Baslickane, Pat of Emlaghdreenagh. Ml. of Portmagee, Bridget of Dromlusk, John of Curraghnanov, Mary of Ardea, Dan of Cummeen, Dan of Tragalee, Jas. of Kilmackillogue John of Confee, Pat of Raheens, John of Coars, Mary of Henry street, Margt. of Derryrina, Mary of Glanmore, Batt and Con of Ardacluckeen, Mary of Ballinakilla, Denis and Tim of Shronabirreenmore, Nora of Teeromoyle, Mary of Cloghanecarhan, Pat of Bunglasha, Denis of Boheeshil, Julia of Glencuttane, John of Cappagh, Mary of Meanus, Ellen of Feoramore, Bridget

Sheehan / Sheehy Households

of Derrynane, John of Cullinagh, Ml. of Coolmagort, Pat of Carhoonahone, John of Shannera, Andrew of Lyreboy, John and John of Cloghanecarhan, Denis and John and John of Teeromoyle, Tim of Glanbeg, Pat of Rath, Deborah of Ballycarnahan, John of Droumalouhart, Maria of Drimnabeg, John of Killowen, Jerh. of Pound lane, Dan of Derreensillagh, John of Needanone, Ml. of Glenlough, Jerh. and Con and Jerh. of Gortagown, Tom of Tahilla, Jas. and Ml. and Dan and John of Cahersavane, Ml. of Inchinatinny, Ml. and Jas. of Spunkane, Dan and Denis of Kilneigh, Pat of Murreagh, Ml. of Curravoola, Dan of Coomavoher, Denis of Toorsalleen, Jerh and Pat and Ml. and Pat of Coombaha, Ml. and David of Letterfinish, Dan of Maulagullane, Ml. and John and Ml. of Drimnabeg, David of Inchinaleega, John of Scrahanguare, John of Gortavallig, Jerh and Pat and Tim of Eskadower, Jas. and Ml. of Cannagullen, Pat of Glanmore, John of Clogherane, Tim of Reenakilla, John of Dromaclaurig, Pat and Crohan and Pat of Droumeragh, Pat and John of Dromirragh, Denis and Tim and Pat and Tim and Dan of Ballinakilla, Jas. of Curra, Dan and Bridget and Dan of High St., John and Flor of Old road, Jas. and Batt of Main St., Julia of Fair Green, Mary and Tom of Valencia road, Ml. of Boola, Ml. of Carhan.

Sheehy, Mac Sitig; 135 families in Kerry, viz:—Edm. and Thos. of Reenagown, Tom of Ardnamweely, Pat of Dunmaniheen, Margt. of Ballyfinane, Pat of Meenguee, Edm. of Gortinae, Jos. of Chapel St., Edm. of Islandboy, Pat of Lexnaw, Edm. of Ballinageragh, Jas. of Bealkilla, Ml. and Wm. of Finuge, John of Glenalappa, John of Meen, Pat of Tarmons, Ml. of Shanbally, John of Dromaddamore, Johanna of Dromartin, Denis of Ballinclemesig, John of Booleenshare, Jas. of Buncurrig, John of Cloonamon, Julia of Trieneragh, Pat of Knockane, Pat of Tullamore, John of Lahardane, John of Ahabeg, Tom of Kiltomey, John of Cloghanagleragh, Edw. of Banemore, Martin of Rathea, Ml. of Derryvrin, John of Lissaniska, Tom of Benmore, Pat of Leagh, Ml. of Knocknagree, Wm. of Ballinorig, Jas. of Rathela, Eug. of Dromartin, Edm. and John and Edm. of Ballykealy, Pat and Margt. and Catherine and Margt. and Ellen of Kilmoyley, Martin and John and Myles of Listowel, Mary of Dromurrin, John of Islandganniv, Wm. of Montanagay, Pat of Knocknacaska, Jas. of Meenanare, Pat and John and Edm. and Pat of Muingwee, Martin of Trieneragh Pat of Knockanoon, Johanna of Carrigcannon, John and Tom and Pat of Kilcaramore, John and Tom of Scrahan, Martin and Tom of Islandboy, John of Duagh, Pat of Knockundervaul, Ml. of Ballymacegogue, Eug. of Barrow, Johanna of Coumduff, Mary of Strand St., Mary of Rock St., John of Mullaghveal, John of Knockanush, Tom of Gallowsfields, John of Lisheenashingane, Tom of Ballykissane, John of Raheens, John of Caheratrant, Dan and Jas. of Caherpierse, Ml. of Banshagh, Ml. of Drom, Ellen of Kilderry, Ml. of Ballinacourty, Dan of Anagap, Mary of Lack, Lce. of Graffee, Edm. of Derrygorman, Kate of Ballinvounig, Pat of Foheraghmore, Pat of Ballyvickeen, Pat of Ballintemple, Edw. of Inchaloughra, Ellen of Ballyaglisheen, Mago of Ballintaggart, Pat and John of Ballyrishteen, Pat of Emlagh, Jas. and Jas. of Glin, Mary of Main St., Bridget of John St., Ml. of Dromthacker, Pat of Strand St., Ml. of Boherbee, Pat and Jerh. of Rock St., Edw. of Ruckett lane, Edw. of Dean's lane, Morgan of Dominick St., John of Dykegate lane, Tom and Pat and John of Strand road, Ml. of Green lane, Dan of Emlagh, Eliza of Bridge St. See Mac Sheehy.

Sheen valley, in Kenmare, is a terminal moraine.

Sheepwalk, baile in Rattoo parish.

Sheeres, Wm., vicar of Marhin and Minard, 1679.

Sheheree, baile in Killarney parish.

Shehy, hill, 1820 feet, in Knockane.

Sheldon, Wm., lieut, 1666, granted Cledereagh.

Shepherd, Walter of Cloghane.

Sheridan, O'Sirideain; Tom of Pound lane.

Sullivan Households

Stretton; Wm. of Knockroe, Mary of Francis St., John of Clahane, Mary of Feoramore, Tom of Cappagh, Jas. of Srugreana.
Stritch, Straoit; Edm. of Booleenshare.
Stromboili, in Dunquin parish.
Struicin beag in Ballyduff parish.
Struicin gualann in Kinard.
Struicin martain, in Marhin.
Stuart, Louisa of Lisardboola.
Studdert; Thos. of Strand Street; in 1821 Thos. of Banemore, Hugh of Listowel.
Stundon; Johanna and Catherine of Ballinglanna, Dan of Ballyheige, Tom of Mweevuck, John of Parknageragh, John of Dromkeen, John of Ballinascreena, Pat of Dromthacker, Mary of Muing.
Styles; Tom of Caherulla, John of Ballyronan, Simon of Tonreigh, Jas. of Balleightra. John of Tralee 1611. Simon of Drishane 1758.
Sugrue; O'Sullivan; O'Siocfrada; of clan Cashel and Knockgraffon in Tipperary; 160 families in Kerry, viz:—Pat and Tom and John of Gortatlea, Pat and Tim and Dan of Fleming's lane, John of Inch, Con of Knockanroor, Denis of Cordal, Jas. and John of Lahard, Dan of Knockasartnett, Mary of Fleming's lane, Margt. of New street, Tim of Knockariddera, Wm. of Glanbane, Ellen of Castleview, Phil of Cahercullenagh, Agnes of Broughane, John of Keam, John of Muingavrannig, John of Kilgulbin, Dan of Ardfert, Con of Commons, Ml. of Strand St., Jas. and Mce. of Balloonagh, Pat of Ballycarthy, Pat of Ballyvelly, John and Tim of Cromane, Ml. of Laharan, John and Catherine of Baltygarron, Ml. of Killacloghane, John of Lissavane, Mary of Caherleheen, Ml. of Ballyarkane, Pat of Burnham, Nano of Church St., Pat of Tullaree, Denis of Camp, Jerh of Dromavally, Ml. of Gortagown, Dan of Maulcalee, John o fBrackloon, Tim of Tullig, Tim and Pat of Moulnahone, Pat of Coomastour, Ml. of Kealafreaghane, Ml. of Doory, Dan of Scrahanguare, John of Eskine, Denis and Mary of Emlaghlea, Batt and Julia and Jas. of Emlaghnamuck, Johanna of Moyrisk, Denis of Lacka, Dan and Ml. of Beenbane, Joan of Maulcalle, Catherine of Fermoyle, Flor of Lehid, Bridget and Hanoria and Bridget of Coolnaharrigill, Pat of Commaun, Jas. of Cloghanecarnahan, Jas. of Droumdarragh, Jas. of Shronahirreebeg, Jas. and Ml. of Coomattoukane, Mary of Ohermong, Ellen of High St., Catherine of Spunkane, Tim of Cloghanelinaghan, Ml. of Coars, Johanna of Ardsheelane, Mary and Mary of Boolakeel, Dan and Jerh of Gortboy, Denis of Cooleanig, John and Pat of Ballymanagh, Ml. of Ballyhearney, Pat of Coarhabeg, Pat of Farranreagh, Pat of Mastergeehy, Ml. of Derrinedin, John of Cahersavane, Denis and Denis and John and Denis and John of Fermoyle, Denis and Con of Killoluaig, Ml of Ardcost Jas. of Caherciveen, Ml. and Pat of Ballinskellighs, Pat of Canuig, Pat of Bolus, Ml. and Jas. of Meelaguleen, Con and Batt and John of Cools, Jas. of Kinnard, John and Pat of Boolakeel, John of Canuig, Pat of Curraghnanav, Ml. and Ml. of Dungegan, Dan and Ml. and Pat of Killurley, Bridget and Deborah and Hanoria of Beenbane, Ml. and John and Pat and Ml. and Pat of Coolnaharrigill, John and Pat and Denis of Droum, Tom and John of Kilnabrack, Jerh and Tom of Brookhill, Tim of Whitefield, Jas. and Pat and Dan of Valencia road, Ml. and John and Jas. of Ohermong, Jas. of Letter, Batt and Jerh and John of Kilcolman. The Rev. Chas. Sughrue was bishop of Kerry, 1797 to 1824, and was buried in Killarney chapel.

Sullivan, O'Suileabain, of Clan Cashel; in 1193 the Anglo Normans drove the O'Sullivans out of their rath at Knockgraffon, and built a stone castle there; some of the O'Sullivans migrated, with the MacCarthys, into Desmond and settled on the lands of the tuath sen Eran in Corco Duibne, particularly in Iveragh and Beara, when the Eoghanacht Caisil return to Tipperary, the O'Sullivans to Knockgraffon, and Cashel, the clan Conaire and tuath sen Eran will restore the temair Eran, on Catair Conroi, for iar Muman. Of the 2,135 O'Sullivan families in Kerry, 1,150 are in South, 480 in East, 330 in West, and 175 in North of the county; the names of the householders and their location are as follows: Ellen of Glanlea, Mary of

Sullivan Households

Coolclogher, Jas. of Derryreag, Johanna of Coom, John and Jerh. of Gortacollopa, Kate of Cordal, Johanna of Shanavalla, Bridget of Gortaree, Mary of Dunmaniheen, Tim of Meenleitrim, Thade of Killeens, Pat of Urrohogal, blaha, Ellen of Toornanounagh, Mary of Lisbabe, Margt. of Annablaha, Ellen of Toornanounagh, Johanna of Awnaskirtaun, Bridget of Boherboy, Dan of Derrycarna, Hannah of Kilfallinga, Mary of Gurranedarragh, Mce. of Fahaduff, Nancy of Rahanane, Ml. of Ballymullen, Tom of Lissoleen, Ml. and Denis of Lyre, Nora of Liscarney, Ml. and Pat and Jas. of Ballincarrig, Jerh. of Shrone, Mary of Knocknaskeha, Mary of Knockanaroor, Dan of Racommane, Pat of Laccabawn, Dan of Portduff, Dan of Knockaruddera, John and Tom and Tim of Mullen, Tim and Pat of Gortnacoppul, Dan of Firies, Tim of Coolnageragh, Dan of Cloonydonegan, John of Caherdeane, Pat of Sheans, John of Ranaleen, Ml. of Dromulton, John of Ranalough, Pat and Eug. of Coolroe, John of Faha, Ml. of Knockearagh, Rev. Jas. of Fossa, Pat and Jerh. of Ballahacommane, Tom and Pat of Lissyvigeen, Ml. and Ml. of Clasheens, Pat of Coolgarrive, Dan of Knockeenduff, Tim of Knockanina, Ml. of Scart, John and Dan of Leamnaguilla, Julia of Gortnaglogh, Ellen and Ellen of Gurrane, Bridget and Catherine of Lacarhoo, Kate of Bishop's-lane, Deborah and Mary of old Market-lane, Johanna of Inch, Mary of Well-lane, Eliza of Green-lane, Ellen and Johanna of Banard, Hannah of Shinnagh, Con of Rossacroonaloo, Pat of Tullaha, Con and Dan of Shroneaboy, Pat of Rusheenbeg, Pat of Carrigeencullia, Jerh. and Dan of Knocknaskeha, Tim of Knockaninane, Tim and John of Knocknahoe, Ellen and Nora of Ahaneboy, Julia of Gortroe, Mary of Fevautia, Mary of Ballyduff, Jerh. of Lackbroder, Pat of Knockadurrive, Jerh. of Tooreenagoun, John of Knocknaboul, Pat and Con of Knockrour, Con and John of Ballinahulla, Jerh. of Cordal, Denis of Kilquane Mary and Catherine and Mary of Castleview, Eug. and Ter. and Tim of Gurranedarragh, Tim and John and Tim of Kilfallinga, John of Farrandoctor, Sylv. and Pat and John of 'Glanbane, Dan of Mweenalaa, Jas. of Nohoval, Pat of Scart, Denis of Ballyegan, Bridget and Andrew of Reenagown, Tim and John of Ballymalis, Jerh. of Listry, Tom and Tim of Slievegaura Andrew and Tim of Kilquane, Tim of Doocarrigbeg-Tim and John of Carran, Mary of Mullen, Johanna of Adraville Ml. and Con. and John of Ahaneboy, Ml. and John of Meenbannivane, Dan of Ahane, Lce. and Jas. of Gortroe, Pat and Tim of Fevautia, Pat of Ballyduff, Pat and John and Jerh. and John of Annaghbeg, Tim and Dan and Denis and Pat of Toornanounagh, John and Tom and Dan of Knockmanagh, Jas. of Mastergeeha, Ml. and John and Ml. of Maulykevane, Ml. of Maulyarkane, John of Toormore, Can and Ml. and Dan of Crinny, John of Ballyplimouth, Con of Kilcuspan, Sylv and John of Rusheen, Tim of Lacarhoo, John of Rathbeg, Tim of Kilnanare, Tim of Rathmore, Jerh of Gortdromerillagh, Ml. of Fieries, Jerh of Knockbrack, Wm. and Ml. of Curraghmore, Ml. and Pat of Gurrane, Dan of Tralia, John of Annabeg, Pat of Ranalough, Denis and Kerry and Pat of Ballybeg, David of Toornanoulagh, Pat and Denis of Beenateevaun, John of Cloonclogh, John of Dicksgrove, Johanna and Ellen of Killeagh, Hanoria of Corbally, Margt. of Ballinvarrig, Johanna of Knockaderry, Mary of Gearha, Mary of Dromore, Mary of Boolacullane, Tim of Faha, Jas. of Drombrick, Tom of Boulnamirisk, Ml. of Ahane, Denis of Lahard, Con and Jerh and John of Farranamanagh, Dan and Jerh and Keane of Corbally, Jerh of Ardmeelode, John of Coolbane, John and Pat and Mce. of Dromin, Tim of Knockreagh, Peter and Jas. of Anglont, John of Gortaree, John of Crohane, Tim and Tim of Shronedarragh, Pat of Knockysheehan, John of Barraduff, Pat of Headford, Dan of Cools, Andrew and John and Pat of Faughcullia, John of Reenasup, Pat of Scrahanaveal, Pat of Carhoonoe. Con and Jas. and Ml. of Coom, John and John and Ml. of Leamyglissane, Lce. of Gneeveguilla, Mary of Knocknaseed, Tim and Dan and Pat of Knocknageeha, John and

Sullivan Households

Dan and Con of Knockysheehan, John and Con of Barraduff, John and John of Raheen, John and Pat and Peter of Annaghillymore, Kate of Toornanoulagh, Jerh of Ardteegalcin, Ml. of Cloghane, Pat and Dan of Ballalley lane, Dan of Chapel lane, Dan of Avenue, Dan of Hogan's lane, Dan of Huggard's lane, Jerh of Bishop's lane, Dan and Hannah of Inch, John of Bohereencael, Deborah of Fleming's lane, Johanna of Dodd's lane, Hannah of Walsh's lane, Hannah of High street, Hanoria of Ballycasheen, Pat and Con of Bealegrellagh, Tom of Kylebeg, John of Tonreigh, Pat of Flemby, Matt of Ashill, Pat and John and Jas. and John of Ballahantouragh, Tim of Carker, Con of Glanlea, Jerh and Pat and Wm. and John and Thos. and John of Well lane, Pat of Moyeightragh, Jerh and Pat and John and Con and John of Brasby's lane, Pat and John of Twohill's lane, Jas. and John of Ballalley lane, Tom and Ml. of Bohereencael glebe, Ml. of old Market lane, Humphrey of High St., Ml. of Convent lane, Ml. of Mangerton view, Ml. of New St., Ml. of Inch, John of Fleming's lane, Denis and John of Hewson's lane, Pat of Chapel lane, Pat and Jerh of Ballalley lane, Dan and Pat of Ardshanavooly, Denis and Jerh and Pat of Fleming's lane, Con of College St., Tim of New St., Jas. of Well lane, Con of Bridewell lane, Pat and Dan and Edm. of Knockeen, Dan and Edm. of Bawnluskaha, Edm. of Killagorm, Tim and Robt. of Kilbannivane, John of Caheragh, Tom and Dan of Knockanatee, Jas. of Glenshearoon, John and Denis and Jerh of Castleview, Dan of Farran, John of Droumdeesart, John and Jas. and Pat and John of Knockalibade, John of Buddaghauns, Jerh and John of Rathanane, Tim of Knockancore, Ml. and Pat of Ballynamanagh, Edm. of Gortnatona, Con of Knockeenalicka, Mort of Coolbane, Pat of Cooliek, John of Inchicullane, Ml. and Edm. and John and Theo. and Ml. of Brosna, John of Knockbrack, Tom and Mce. and David of Kilmanihan, Con. of Bushmount, John and Jerh. and John and Jas. and Dan and Eug. of Dromore, Tim and Pat and Tim and Pat and Tim of Killeagh, Con and Ml. and Tim of Knockaderry, Tim of Boolacullane, Jas. and John of Gearha, Dan and Tim of Rossmore, Dan of Gortshanavough, Jerh. of Inchinveema, Con. and Ml. and Con of Lisheenacannina, Jas. of Graffeens, Pat and Eug. of Revaun, Jerh. and Ml. of Knockasartnett, Ml. of Knockmanagh, John and Tim of Bellahacommane, Dan and Dan of Minish, Peter and Ml. of Knockaninane, John and Pat of Knockearagh, Tim of Tullig, Dan and John of Tiernaboul, Pat of Clasheens, Pat of Dooneen, John of Coolgarrive, Flor, and Humphrey of Gortnaglogh, Tim of Keelties, John of Firies, Flor of Knockaneacoolteen, Pat of Gortdromerillagh, Jerh. and Con and Jerh. of Lecarhoo, John of Rathbeg, Eug. and Eug. of Ballyfinane, Ml. and Tim of Rusheen, John of Kilnanare, Jerh. and Ml. and Denis of Cloonts, Pat and John of Rathmore, Jerh. and Tim and John and Flor of Shinnagh, Denis of Islanderagh, Denis and Marcus of Banard, Ml. of Knockdooragh, Ml. of Gortnahaneboy, Jerh. of Glangristeen, Mort of Freemount, Wm. and Pat of Commons Jas. of Moyvane, Ml. of Kilbaha, Edw. of Clounbrane, Bridget of Tubridmore, Pat of Dineens, Ml. of Banna, John of Rahoneen, Jerh. and Ml. of Trieneragh, Deborah of Trien, Denis of Cappagh, Hannah of Banna, Nano of Sackville Jane of Brandonwell, Flor of Ballybroman, John of Knockadirreen, Mce. of Lisroe, Dane of Rathea, Ellen of Meen, Pat of Glashanoon, Con of Dromaddamore, Dan of Carrigcannon, Johanna of Finuge, Jas. of Cloghaneleaskirt, Hanora of Sleveen, Pat of Doonferris, Pat of Tullamore, Pat of Glouria, Pat of Knockaneacurraheen Garrett of Ballintogher, Pat of Corcass, Mce. and John of Beale Acres, Catherine of Ahabeg, Mce. and Jas. and John of Ballinclogher, Mary of Commons, Mary of Tullamore, Mary of Gullane, Dan of Dromurrin, John of Glenderry, Wm. of Droumatoor, Tom of Tiduff, Margt. of Ballinoe, John of Banemore, Ml. of Ahacrinna, John of Killahan, Catherine of Laccamore, Denis and Eng. of Ballydonoghue, Jas. of Moybella, John of Glenalappa, Ml. of Aughrim, Jas. of Doonard, John of

Sullivan Households

Tieraclea, Mary of Deerpark, Hanoria of Ballinageragh, John of Muckenagh, Ml. and Edm. of Ahanagran, Mary of Bromaddra, Mce. of Killocrim, Ellen of Asdee, Dan of Tullig, Jas. of Crotta, Roger of Lahardane, Eug. of Killehenny, Tim of Ballyeagh, Ml. of Doon, Mary and Johanna of Kilmore, Deborah of Heirhill, Bridget of Glanlea, Jas. of Ballinglanna, Pat of Ballinorig, Pat of Kilcooly, Flor of Kilfeighney, Kate of Ahanagran, Dan of Ahabeg, John of Sleveen, Tom of Addergown, Denis and Ml. of Bungarah, Dan of Trien, Pat of Pilgrim Hill, Dan of Ballynoneen, Con of Cloonamon, David of Larha, John of Glanawillan, John of Carrigane, John of Curraghdarrig, Pat and Dan of Farranwilliam, Jerh. of Skrillagh, John of Ardfert, Jas. of Commons, Pat of Gullane, Dan of Trippul, John of Derra, Ml. and John of Tullamore, Con of Meenagohane, Pat and Denis and Jas. of Ballinoe, Jas. of Castle Shannon, Martin of Dreemnacurra, Ml. and John and Jas. of Listowel, Tom of Ballygologue, Eug. of Laccabeg, Ter of Knockbrack, Tom and Jas. of Glenlea, Ml. of Doonmontane, Wm. and Ml. of Ballinclemesig, Tom of Heirhill. Ml. of Ballyheige, John and Pat and Dan of Kilmore, Ml. and Peter and John of Cloghane, Pat and Ml. of Ardagh, Pat and John of Ardoughter, Dan of Clahane, Denis of Ballinageragh, Wm. of Irrabeg, Ml. of Clogher, Tom and Dan of Cunnigar, Ml. and Wm. and Pat of Coilbwee, Tom and Tom of Derry, Pat of Meen, Edw. of Tubridbeg, Flor of Ballybroman, John and Pat and John of Lerrig, Jas. of Rareagh, Tim and Dan of Finuge, Wm. of Dromclough, Denis and John of Ennismore, Mce. and John of Killacrim, Jas. of Garrynaneskagh, Mce. and Jas. of Banemore, Ml. and Ml. of Kilmoyley, Pat of Dinneens, Pat of Ardcullen, Ml. and Pat and Jas. of Knoppogue, Pat of Knockananore. Ml. of Benmore, Ml. of Bedford, Mce. and Con of dromin, Jerh. and Wm. of Leanamore, John of Ballylongford, Tim of Ballymacassy, Jas. of Lislaughtin, Tim of Cloghane, Ml. of Ardoughter, Jerh. of Inch, Mary of Aunascaul, Ellen of Ballintarmon, Pat of Ardbeg, Denis of Ballyarkane, Mary of Acres, Kate of Gurrane, Jerh. of Listrim, Thade of Curravogh, John of Doon, Jas. of Ballygamboon, Dan of Gransha, Tim of Ballynamona, Ml. of Laharan, Pat of Caherfealane, Jerh. of Shanahill, Dan and Jerh. and Tom of Lissavane, Mary of Castlemaine, Ellen of Annagh, Kate of Ballyrameen, John of Fahan, John of Fahan, John of Ballyvickadownig, Ml. and Jas. of Emlagh, Jas. of Breenrannig, Bridget and Mary of Ballineanig, Jas. of Gurteens, Mary of Glenlough, Ellen of Illauncoum, Mary of Emlagh, Jerh. and Pat and Dan of Kilmore, Ellen and Mary of Minard, Johanna of Ballyheabought, Johanna of Clooshmore, Mary of Knockavrogeen, Mary or Ballinassig, Pat of Inch, Ml. and John and Eug. of great Blasket Island, John of Murrigane, Dan of Lisnakeelwee, Eug. of Camp, Pat of Ballinknockane, Margt. of Killeen, Bridget of Cloghanesheskeen, Pat of Knockanush, Tim and Pat and Denis and Tim and Philip of Callinafercy, Eug. of Brackhill, Tim of Rathpoge, Tim of Abbeylands, Jas. of Hogg's-lane, Matt of Dromtacker, Pat and John and Stephen of Leath, Pat of Cloghane, Ml. of Cappagh, Johanna of Coumeenole, Pat and Tom of Fahamore, Pat of Maherabeg, John of Matramane, John of Castle Gregory, Ml. and Pat of Graigue, Jas. of Ballyoughtra, John of Farranlateeve, John of Gortmore, John and Pat of Tonevane, John of Annagh, Ml. of Dykegate-lane, Pat and Eug. of Gortonora, Dan of Green-lane, Pat of the Mall, Jas. of Strand-road, John and Dan and Jerh. of Aughacasla, Dan of Carrigadav, Bridget of Baltygarron, Julia of Barrow, Mary of Fenit, Dan and Nich. of Castledrum, Mort and Pat of Boolteens, John and Dan and Jas. and Pat and Jas and Pat and Ewd. and John and Tom of Derrymore, Ml. and Denis of Curraheen, Denis of Cahervisheen, Jerh. of Gortbrack, John of Dromavally Timothy of Ballycarthy, John of Skahanagh, Andrew of Lisardboola, Pat of Ballintarmon, Jerh. of Ardrinane, Eug. of Aunascaul, Ellen of Reenboy, Bridget and Nora and Mary of Gowlane, John and Ml. and John of Glanminard, Jerh. of

Sullivan Households

Loughnagoppul, Con of Garrynadur-Jerh. of Minard, Ml. and John of Maumnagarrane, John and Jas. and Ml. of Callinafercy, Ml. of Kilburn, Tom and Denis of Myles lane, Dan of Ballynahow, Jas. and Ml. and Dan and Pat and Ml. of Feohanagh, Tom and John of Ballybrack, Tom and Dan of Ballinloghig, Pat of Ballydavid, Dan of Kilmalkedar, Tim and John and Dan of Kilcooly, Mce. of Coumgagh, John of Murreigh, Pat of Flemingstown, Ml and John of Caherboshina, John of Clooshmore, Ml. or Caherard, John of Beenbawn, Mce. and Pat and Mce. of Ballineesteenig, Tom and Martin of Cloghane, Ml. and John of Ballyameenbought, Tim of Ballymorreigh, Pat of Kinard, Tom of Lisdorgan, John of Deerpark, Pat and John of Tubbernamoodane, John and Dan and Pat and Ml. of Gowlane, John of Boherbrack, John and Con of Reenboy, Tom of Lissodigue, John of Ballygarron, Denis and Pat and John of Ballymacegogue, Pat and Jas. of Barrow, John of Tawlaght, Mary of Racket lane, Hanoria and Catherine of Dean's lane, Mary of Strand street, Hannah of Abbey street, Mary of Rock street, Mary of Boherbee, Kate of Dromavally, Anne of Bansha, Mary and Ellen and Kate of Lonart, Ellen and Margt. of Killorglin, Mary and Mary of Gurrane, Johanna and Catherine of Tullegbeg, Ml. or Clonmore, Dan and Pat of Muing, Tom of Quill street, Wm. and Jerh. of Clahane, Con and Tim and Con of Ballinahoulart, Jerh. of Ballydunlea, Dan of Lohercannon, Pat of Edward St., John and Denis of Rock street, Ml. of Boherbee, Stephen and Pat of Brogue lane, Dan of Cross lane, Pat of Blennerville, Mort and Jerh and Tim of Strand St,. Pat and John and Denis of Rae St., John of Castle Mac Ellistrum, Con and Jas. of James St., John and Jerh and John of Abbey St., Pat and Dan of Francis St., Tom of Ballymullen, Jerh. and John and Eug. and Denis of Boherbee, Pat of Pound lane, Pat of Brogue lane, Denis of Chute's lane, Ml. and Ml. of Caheranne road, Tim of Connor's lane, Jerh of Market place, Pat of Rock St., Rd. of Connor's lane, John and Jas. and John and Pat and John of Brogue lane, Tim of Dominick St., Roger of Rock St., Denis of Castle St., Dan of Cronin's lane, Pat of Strand St., Denis and Pat and Wm. and Flor of Abbey St., Pat of Green View tce., Eug. of Ballymullen, Dan and Dan of Dean's lane, John of Boherbee, Dan of Edward St., Ml. of Balloonagh rd., Pat of Mary St., Jas. of Courthouse lane, Tim of Moyderwell, John of Keane's lane, Matt of Russell St., Denis of John St., John of Douglas, Dan and Hy. and Jas. and Pat of Lonart, Denis of Main St., John and Tim of Ballykissane, Denis and Pat and John and Pat and John and Pat and Jas. of Tulligbeg, Ml. of Douglas, Ml. and David of Reen, John of Iveragh road, Ml. and John and Dan of Cromane, Dan and Pat of Laharan, Tim and John of Gurrane, Dan of Dromlusk, Lce. and Mary of Rossdohan, Pat and Con and Bridget and Kate of Tahilla, Julia of Letternadarrive, Mary of Inchynatinny, Julia of Maulagirkane, Johanna and Ellen of Bundarreen, Mary of Maulin, Ellen and Jerh of Ballyhearney, Catherine and Tom of Coarha, Mary and Johanna and John of Feaghmoan, Catherine and Denis of Farranreagh, Tim and Jerh of Tullig, John of Garranafulla, John of Kinneigh, Stephen and John of Sacriff, Mary of Ballybrack, Julia of Shanaknock, Mary and Barbara of Eightercua, Mary and Julia and Mary of Beenbane, Catherine of Keelagurteen, Mary of Commanes, Tim and Dan and Martin and Ml. of Dirreenedin, John and Ml. and Tim and Jas. and John of Dromod, Ml. of Doory, Hanoria of Kinneigh, Mary of Garranafulla, John of Ballyhearney, Pat of Farranreagh, John and Ml. of Cool, John of Tinnies, Mary of Baslickane, Margt. of Rineen, John of Inchinaleega, Denis of Fermoyle, Pat and John and Pat of Derryleagh, Ml. and John of Ardeen, John of Drimnamore, Jas. of Lettermoniel, John and John and John and Denis of Killagurteen, Ml. and Pat and Con and John of Beenbane, Pat and John and Ml. and Ml. of Tarmons, John of Sallaghig, Batt of Waterville, Austin of Breahig, Pat of Cahirbarnagh, Ml. of Commanes, Jas. and John of Cooryvanaheen, Martin and Pat and Tim and John and Tim and Denis of Caslagh, Dan of Knoppogue, Pat and Ml. of Cap-

Sullivan Households

panagrown, Mce. of Curravoola, Pat and Crohan and Ml. of Shanaknock, John and Jerh. of Ballybrack, John of Spunkane, Ml. and Ml. of Farranahow, Ml. of Moulnahone, Jas. and John and Dan of Murreagh, Tim of Garranafulla, Flor and Pat of Tullig, Ml. of Garryglass, Jas. and John and Ml. and Jerh of Rineen, Pat and John of Reenearagh, Ml. of Inchee, Ml. and Dan of Baslickane, Thos. and Ml. and Thos. of Ardkearagh, Pat of Toor, Dan and Tim of Loher, Tim of Reenearagh, John and Pat and John of Fermoyle, Ml. and Ml. of Ardcost, Pat of Emlaghpeastia, Ml. of Rathkerin, Mary of Inchinaleega, Ellen of Ardeen, Mary of Driminabeg, Catherine of Scrahanagower, Johanna of Kealaruddig, Wm. and Peter of Fermoyle, Pat of Maulagullane, John and Ml. and Pat and Jas. of Inchinaleega, Eug. and Dan of Ardsheelane, Con and Pat. and Ml. of Coomyanna, John and Dan and John of Drimnamore, Matt and Ml. and Pat and Denis of Derryleagh, Dan and Dan of Drimnabeg, John and John of Gearha, John and Pat and Ml. of Kealariddig, Bridget of Ballynahow, Mary of Aghort, Mary of Leahid, Ml. of Ballinskelligs, Tim of Loolakeel, Philip and Denis of Coom, Jonh of Curraghnanov, John and Pat of Dungegan, Jerh and Ml. of Kinnard, Eug. of Leabaleaha, Pat of Cloon, Pat of Emlaghdreenagh, Ml. and Martin of Emlaghmore, Pat and Ml. and Pat of Muingdowda, John of Reenroe, Jas. and John of Clonee, Eug. of Derrynabrack, Jas. of Ballinahow, Danl. and Ml. of Lehid, Bridget of Gearha, Pat of Tooreen, Pat of Ballynabloun, Ml. of Aghort, Ml. of Rathkieran, Martin and Ml. and Martin of Killurley, Dan and Roger and John and Pat of Ballinskelligs, John and Flor and Pat and Dan of Boolakeel, Ml. and Jas. and Ml. and Denis and Ml. and Pat of Kinnard, John of Canuig, Tim and Flor and Pat of Meelagullen, Ml. of Dunfeagan, Pat of Cools, Ml. of Leabaleaha, John of Kinnard, Jas. of Bolus, John of Ducalla, Flor. of Meelagullen, Helena of Muckera, Mary of Cummeen, Julia of Coornagillagh, Matilda of Lohart, Tim of Derry, John of Lomanagh, John C. Moneyflugh, Jerh of Slivenahaska, Jas. and John of Derryconnery, Dan of Drombohilly, Mary of Rosseightragh, Johanna of Lehud, Ellen of Ardea, Ellen of Canfee, Hanora of Cummers, Mary and Mary of Kilmackillogue, Bridget and Margt. of Leabaleaha, Mary and Johanna of Ballinskelligs, Ellen of Kinard, Julia of Cools, Hanoria and Julia of Kilkeaveragh, Mary and Kate and Mary of Knockeenawaddra, Lce. and John and Dan and Myles and Jerh of Derreenavarrig, John of Slievenasska, Pat and flLce. and Ml and James of Derreendrislagh, Pat and John of Derry, Ml. and Jas. and Ml. and John and Ml. and Pat and Ml and Pat of Derreenauliffe, John and James and Pat and John and Jas. and Pat of Moneyflugh, John and Ml of Maularostig, Ml of Lomanagh, Eug and Jerh and John of Collorus, Tim of Clogherane, Mortz of Eskadawer, Tim and Dan of Glanmore, John of Lauragh, Jas. of Shinnagh, Ml. of Emlaghpeastia, Pat and Dan and John of Fermoyle, John and John of Ballard, Dan and Matt and John of Ardcost, Martin of Sussa, Bridget of Slaheny, Margt of Ardtully, Mary of Caher, Ellen and Bessie and Bridget and Catherine and Susan and Margt. of Churchground, Jerh. of Clogherane, John of Shronebirrane, Dan and John and Denis and John of Collorus, James and Pat of Lehud, John of Garrane, Dan of Dromdirraowen, Tim of Ardea, James of Dereen, Wm. and Ml. of Derrynacolleha, Tim and Batt of Lohart, Flor of Coornagillagh, Dan of Muckera, Ml. of Derrynasallagh, Denis and Pat of Clonee, Eug. of Derrynid, Dan of Derreencolleha, Kate and Nora and Anne of Claddanure, Johanna of Dunkerron, Ellen of Reen, Ml. and Jerh and Ml of Fehanagh, Ml. and Eug and Dan and John of Clogherane, Jas. and Pat of Lauragh, Con and Stephen of Shinnagh, Flor of Cannagullen, Denis of Dromerkeen, John and John of Glantrasna, Eug of Eskadawer, Dan of Glanmore, Denis and Dan and James and Dan of Collorus, James and Pat of Cuhig, Denis of Glansrastel, John of Reenkilla, John of Castlekeelty, Flor of Coolcreen, Pat of Dromarkeen, Dan and John and Dan of Lehid, Pat and Tim and Pat of

Sullivan Households

Louyhaunacreen, Dan and Pat and Dan and Ml and Pat of Ardea, Dan of Derrylough, Jerh. and Dan and Ml and Jerh and Jerh of Kilmackillogue, John and Con and Sylv. of Garranes, Pat and John and Stephen and James and Ml. and John of Drombohilly, Flor and Jas. of Cummers, Dan of Derreen, Jerh and Flor of Caher, Denis of Cummeendurassig, Dan and John and Dan and Denis and Dan of Mangerton, Denis of Kilgarvan, Jerh. of Meelick, Flor and John of Churchground, John of Slaheny, Flor of Slaghts, Denis of Fussa, Dan of Coologues, Pat of Mangerton, Dan of Gortnaboul, Ml of Kilfadabeg, Flor and Pat and Jerh. of Rosseightra, Denis of Rusheens, Edw and John of Slaheny, Ml and Dan and Ml. and John and Ml. and Denis and Denis of Mangerton, John and Denis and Pat of Gortnaboul, John of Baurearagh, John of Coppanlivane, Ml. of Churchground, Pat of Caher, Denis of Lounaghan, Denis of Dromneycolman, Ml. and Dan of Knockanuha, John and John of Gortnaskeigh, Eugene and Peter of Gullaba, Hugh and Tom of Kilbonow, Con of Lomanagh, Denis of Cummeen, Con of Shandrum, Mort and Ml and Dan and Denis and Tim and James of Reen, Mort and Wm and Pat and Ml and Con of Claddanure, Catherine of Tubrid, Johanna of Gortamullen, Kate of Lissyclerig, Mary of Downing's Row, Margt. and Mary and Bridget of Pound lane, Ellen of Carhoomengar, Julia of Dromcahan, Margt. of Kenmare sound, Molly of William St., Catherine of Lackeen, Mary of Dromore, Ellen of Coomnakilla, Mary of Capparoe, Ml. of Gortaloughane, Denis of Lissaniska, Denis of Old Bridge St, Wm of Kenmare Old, Ml and Pat and John of Gortamullin, Pat of Lissyclarig, Pat of Killowen, John and Mort of Gortagass, Mort ond Denis of New St., Dan of Gortnadullagh, Dan of Gortrooskagh, John of Gortamullen, Batt of Rusheens, Pat and Denis and John and Dan and Ml. and Dan of Kenmare, Pat of Kilkeana, Stephen of Muckuna, Batt of Kilcurrane, Anne and Hanora of Glencuttane, Margaret of Coolnacappy, Johanna of Shannera, Tim of Gearhasillagh, Jerh and Denis of Letter, Jerh of Slieveaduff, Ml. of Maulnahorna, Dan and Pat and Dan and Tim of Greenane, Dan of Rossacosae, Pat of Derrygarriv, Eub and Pat of Derrynacoulobh, Peter of Rusheens, Denis and Dan of Henry St, Batt of Lissyclerig, John and John of Cappamore, Ml and Pat and Jerh.. of Gortagass, Denis of Killowen, Tim of Derrynacaheragh, Jerh of Carhoomeengar, Tim of Barraduff, Ml of Ballygriffin, John and John of Droumcahan, Dan of Droumanasig, James and Dan and Jerh and Dan and Con and Philip and Jerh and Ml and Thomas of Cappanacush, Ml of Gowlanes, Denis and Con of Lackeen, John and Humphrey and John and John of Capparoe, Denis and Dan of Coomnakilla, Denis of Derreendarragh, Eug of Reacaslagh, Edw and Dan of Rossboy, Dan of Cummeenboy, Jerh and John and Dan of Cahir, Dan of Cooraqueamish, John and Flor and Pat and James and Denis and James and Ml and Denis and Tim and Mary of Killah, Dan and Denis of Feoramore, Denis of Inchicloon, Dan and John and Eug of Dauros, Denis of Coolanaroo, John of Gortlecka, Ml of Derrygarranshagh, Dan of Bohacullia, Ml of Cappa, John of Derrylicka, Ml of Gortbrack, David of Inchinglanna, Dan and Ml of Graignagreena, Pat of Gortloughra, Denis and Pat of Gortaliny, Con and Ml and David of Gearhadiveen, Denis and Pat of Letter, Pat and Dan and Pat of Cappagh, Pat and Denis of Lackaroe, Pat of Gortalahard, James of Dromatouk, Barry of Doughill, Mary of Feorus, Mary of Coolanaroo, Catherine of Feoramore, Julia of Inchacloon, John and Catherine and Ellen of Shronahirree, John of Lettergarriv, Kate of Raleigh, Catherine of Coolnagoppogue, Flor of Cappantanavally, Ml of Gortnaganbeg, Dan of Lyranes, James and James of Dromleigh, Ml and John of Goulnacappy, John and James and Ml and Denis and James and John and Con and Tim and John and Denis and John and James and Dan of Glencuttane, John and Ml of Maghancoosane, Dan and James and Eug and Jerh and John of Shannera, Johanna of Churchtown, Johanna of

Sullivan Households

Coolcuminish, Ellen and Deborah of Kilcoolaght, Dan of Gortnagoppal, Dan of Baurearagh, Jerh of Coolnagoppogue, Mort of Rath, Jas of Cummeenshrule, Eug of Tullaha, Pat and John and Dan of Baurearagh, John of Killabonane, Denis and Tim and Ml and Tim and Dan of Esk, Eug and Pat and Eug of Milleens, Denis of Dromagorteen, John and Dan and Mort of Raleagh, Eug of Garryletter, Denis of Knockduff, Denis of Deelis, Julia and Mary of Dunloe, Kate of Ballagh, Julia of Derrygarriv, Ml and Jas. and Ml and John and Ml and Jerh of Gortloughra, Eug and Denis and John and John of Kilcoolaght, Jerh of Ownagarry, Pat and John of Cosha, Jerh and John of Dereenagh, Ml of Eunglasha, Pat and Pat of Neesha, Mary and Johanna of Letter, Andrew of Kilgobnet, Ellen of Curraheen, Tim of Ardsaw, Jas. of Brookhill, Ml of Ardlahas, John of Cappagh, Margaret of Gortnirragh, Mary of Coolnaharrigill, Jas. and Ml and John of Gortdirragh, Andrew and Ml and Pat and Pat and Pat of Kilnabrack, Thade and John and Tim and Ml and John of Letter, Tim and John and Jerh and Ml of Conearagh, Tim and Pat of Droum, Dan and Dan and John of Reenanallagane, Denis of Kilkeehagh, John and Ml of Balinakilla, John of Curraheen, John of Coolroe, Dan and Pat and Jas of Derrynanebeg, Jeremiah and John and Ml. of Coolroe, James and Tom and James and Denis and James and Tom and James of Ballyledder, Con and John of Gortboy, James and Denis and James of Kill, Jerh. and Philip and Denis and Tim of Shanacloon, John and Con and John of Cooleanig, Kate of Gurranearagh, Catherine of High St., Mary of Quay St., Dan of Curraghmore, John of Croughmore, Bridget of Killeen, Hanoria of Derreensillagh, Ellen of Skahanagh, Ellen of Bohocogram, Margaret of Gleesk, Bridget of Glenlough, Bridget of Gowlanes, Mary of Liss, John and Denis of Cahernageeha, Pat and James of Farranearagh, Tim of Derrynanebeg, James of Churchtown, Jerh. and Ml. and Matt and Flor and Con and Flor and Roger of Coolcummisk, Con of Cappaganeen, Tim of Alehart, David and Jerh. of Carhoonahone, Dan of Ballycarnahan, Eug. of Garrough, John of Brackeragh, Denis of Glounagillagh, Eug. and James and Tom and Pat of Tooreenasliggaun, Ml. of Commaun, Pat and Ml. and Pat of Callahaniska, Pat of Dooaghs, Jerh. and John and Tim and John of Ballintleave, Ml. and Ml. of Doolahig, Dan and Eug. of Illaunstookagh, John and John of Muningaphuca, John of Commaun, Mary of Ballycarnahan, Mary and Mary of Brackeragh, Kate and Mary of Behaghane, Julia of Rathfield, Jerh. and Pat and Ml. and Tim and John and Pat and Eug. and John of Gowlanes, Dan and John of Skahanagh, Tim and John and Tim of Derreensillagh, Denis and Ml. and John of Ardmore, Jerh. and Dan and Jerh. and James of Liss, Pat of Staigue, Ml. of Glenlough, John and Pat of Nedanone, Pat of Killeen, Tim of Bohccogram, Pat and Andrew and John of Scart, Jas. and John and oCn and Boetius of Coad, John of Garrough, Tim and Dan of Brackaharagh, Mce. and Jerh. of Coomnahorna, Jerh. of Behehane, Con of Caherdaniel, Humphrey and Crohan of Rath, James of Ballycarnahan, Hanora and Kate of Gortnagree, Mary of Teeramoyle, Mary of Knockanyouloo, Nora of Liss, Ellen of Maheramon, Ml. and Tom and Pat of Ohermong, Tim and Tim of Derreen, Ml. of Reenard, John and Dan and John and James and Jos. of Reenard, Dan and John and Pat and Pat and Pat and John and John of Caherciveen, Ml. and Denis and Tom of Ohermong, Tim of Inchlough, James and Ml. and John and Pat and Jerh. and Pat of Laharan, Dan and John and Ml. of Carhan, Ml. of Inchimateigue, Jerh. and Dan of Letter, Ml. of Gurranebane, Tim and Pat and Tim and Pat of Liss, John of Boulerdah, Dan and Matt of Cappamore, Dan and Tim of Gortnagree, Eug. and Jerh. of Garrydine, Pat and Dan and Pat of Knockaneyouloo, Ml. of Gortnagulla, Tim of Kells; Tim of Teermoyle, Pat and John and Ml. of Toon, Margaret of Garranebane, Kate of Church lane, Mary and Mary of Bridge street, Mary of Old road, Ellen and Bridget of High St., Mary of Main St.,

Sullivan Households

John and Eug. and Tom and Denis of Ohermong, Denis of Gurranebane, Pat and Nora of Main st, Ml. and Tim and Jerh. and Pat and John and Flor and Pat and Con and Tom and Pat and James and John and Kate and Mary and Kate of Cahereveen, Ml. and James and John and John of Carhan, Ml. and Eug. of Laharan, Dan and Con of Crosderry, Humphrey and Dan and Con of Derrycarna, Con and John and Con and Dan of Cullinagh, Pat and Jerh. and Pat and Pat of Coolmagort, John of Dunloe, John of Derryard, Ellen of Cuhig, Mary of Glantrasna, Nance of Lauragh, Tim and Ml. and Ellen and Ml. of Cloghanecarhan, Ellen and Bridget of Rhodes, Margaret of Brookhill, Bridget of Ballycarbery, Kate of Cappagh, Tim and Dan and Ml. and James and Dan and John of Cloghanelinaghan, Ml of Foilduff, Jerh. of Rhodes, Ml. and Tim of Killurley, Dan of Laharan, Eug. of Cloghane, Pat of Lisbane, Tim of Ballinahowmore, Pat of Roilduff, Dan and Tim and Denis and Eug. of Killognaveen, Pat and John of Derrymore, John and Tim and Deborah of Bahaghs, Ml. of Tiernahilla, Ml. of Madlagirkane, John of Maulin, John of Dromaragh, Kate of Gurrane, Denis and John and Tim and John and Pat and Con of Kilmackerrin, Tim of Kealafreaghane, John and Dan and Ml. and John and Tom and John of Coomastow, Ml. and Jerh. and Ml. of Dromaragh, Dan and Tom and Ml and Jerh. and Pat and John and Dan of Inchiboy, Tim and Ml. of Canuig, Con and James and Denis and John and John and Mort and Jerh. of Derreenafoyle, Denis and Pat and John and Syl. and John and Rd. and John of Tahilla, Pat and Dan and Tom of Gortagown, Jerh. and Jerh. of Derreenamucklagh, Flor and John of Rossdohan, Ml. of Doon, John and Denis of Letternadarrive, John of Ankail, Bridget and Johanna of Ballyledder, Mary and Mary of Shanacloon, Alice of Gortboy, Margaret of Derreendrislagh, Mary and Bridget of Derry, Mary of Derreenavourig, Pat of Tooreens, Dan of Toomies, John of Kilgobnet, Pat of Brookhill, Bridget of Tooreenyduneen, Pat of Pound, James and Owen of Knockeenawaddra, Tim and James of Doory, Jerh. of Coomanaspig, Pat of Reencaheragh, Ml. of Garrane. James of Keelkieveragh, Jas. and Tim and Pat of Portmagee, Pat of Cromane, Pat and Ml. of Killorglin, John and Tim and John and James of Tulligbeg, James and Ml. and Pat of Rangue, Stephen and John and Tim of Laharan, Tim and Jerh. and Ml. of Gurrane, Ml. and Pat of Lonart, Bridget and Norah of Emlaghmore, Johanna of Emlaghnamuck, Ellen of Gortalinny, Mary of Laskaroe, Margt. of Gullaba, Catherine of Callahaniska, Mary of Dooaghs, Johanna of Toorsaleen, Deborah of Knoppogue, Julia of Dromnakilla, Bridget of Maulnabrack. O'Sullivan is the form used by Ml. and John and Dr. Wm. (Senator) and Jerh and Ml. of New street, Dan and Pat and John and Kate of High street, Tim of Barry's lane, Tim of Main street, James and John and Kate of College street, Catherine and Wm. and Kate of Ardnamweely, Rev. Alex. and Jos. of Inch, Ellen of Sunny hill, Dan and Rev. Thomas and Dr. Dan of Rathmore, Pat and Dan of Rathbeg, Charles of Ballyfinane, Tim of Gurrawn, Eug. of Fieries, Mary of Coolick, Mary of Gortdromerillagh, Ellen of Gortnaglogh, Catherine of Ballyfinane, Tim and Mary of Killeen, Tim of Coolgreane, James of Ballinvarrig, Barbara of Dungeel, Barbara of Rathmore, Ml. of Dirreenacullig, Pat of Droumnavrauka, Mary of Knockanes, Flor of Farranamranagh, Jas. of Rockfield, Anne of Ballinvarrig, Bridget of Killeentierna, Pat of Knocknahoe, Tim of Greeveguilia, Tim and Edw. and Eug. and Pat and James and Julia and Annie and Mary of Listowel, John of Tieraclea, Gerald of Tarbert, Mce. of Kilcolgan, David of Ahanagran, Tim of Benmore, Wm. of Ballybunion, Annie of Doonard, Ml and Mce of Farrantorreen, Jas and Pat and Edw and Tom and Ml. and Con and James and Tim of Killorglin, Pat and Ml. and Tat and Tom and Mce. and Sam and John and Ellie and Eily of Dingle, Tim of Lissavane, Pat of Ballycacegogue, Ml. of Coillinafercy, Johanna of Fenit, Pat of Stealroe, Dan of Ardrinane, Eug. of Castlelrum, Nora of Gransha, Jerh. and Martin and Rev. Tim of Castle st; Maria of Clonee, John and John of

Sullivan Households

Inchie, Ml. of Toor, Pat of Loher, Tim and Denis of Coomnagillagh, Jerh. and James of Derryrid, Jerh. of Lohart, Eug. of Clonee, John of Dauros, Dan of Feoramore, Mary of Driminabeg, John of Ardmore, Deborah of Gortmore, Catherine of Lisbane, Ellen of Kilonecaha, John of Coolcreen, Matilda of Ardmore, Eliza of Lauragh, Dan of Behahane, Pat of Coolmagort, Bridget and Anna and Hanoria and Johanna and Mary and Hanoria and John and Dan and John and Eug. and Ml. and Eug. of Kenmare, Denis of Gortrooskagh, Denis of Lissyclerig, Con of Killowen, Con of Drominvane, Denis and John and Tim and John of Farranreagh, John of Ballyhearney, Dan and Jerh. of Tinnies, Eug. of Garrydine, Pat of Liss, John of Foilmore, Pat and John and Eug. of Teeragh, Flor. and Jas. and Eug. of Teeragh, Flor. and Jas. of Drimna, Eug. of Derryquin, John and Tim of Waterville, Mary and Hanoria and John and Dan and John and Pat and Denis and John of Caherciveen, Eliz. of Inchiclough, Eug. and Roger of Tahilla, Eug. of Derrylough, Jas. of Kilmackillogue, John and Flor. of Killabonane, Pat of Coolmagoppogue, Eug. of Gortabinny, Jerh. of Dromquinna.

Sullivan; see the history of the O'Sullivan family in the first edition of this work, at pages 394 to 440. Fingin, son of Aodh Dubh, about A.D. 628 was chief of the Eoghanacht Cashel in Tipperary, and was succeeded by his brother Failbhe Flan, the ancestor of the MacCarthys, who was unpopular apparently. "To be without Finghin, to be without Mor (his wife), to Cashel is cause of sorrow; it is the same as to be without anything if Failbhe Flann be the king." In 1193 the Anglo-Normans drove the O'Sullivans out of the rath of Knockgraffon in Tipperary, and the MacCarthys out of Rath MacCarthy; the Eoganacht Cashel then migrated into Desmond, and after 1261, when they defeated the Geraldines at Callan battle, they seized the Anglo-Norman castles, and held the country until they were confiscated in 1653. The farmer owners, the tuath sen Eran, remained as farmers, and the MacCarthys and O'Sullivans did likewise after 1653.

Gofraidh Fionn O'Dalaigh exhorted Donnell MacCarthy Mor, d. 1391, to lead the Eoghanacht of Caiseal back to their old homes, and to turn his back on Dairbre's shore and the bay of rough peaked Beirre and Corca Duibne and the ports of Uidhine and the fair-shored lake of Lein where he was born and reared. "For these lands thy folk left the hills around Caiseal; 'twas wrong to prefer wild glens, to exchange wine for small ale. Lead us back the same road O curly-haired, strong armed hero; too long our absence from our country, great our misery to miss it." O'Seagha, chief of Ui Rathach, and O'Conghaile, chief of the bushy-forted magh o g Coinchinn, in the old land of Ui Duibhna of good hosts, will be glad to see MacCarthy Mor leading back to the rock of Cashel all the MacCarthys and O'Sullivans and O'Denoghues to their old homes "on the place of Padraig's tent" in Tipperary. The pedigree of the O'Sullivans from Fingin, son of Aodh Dubh is given as:—Fingin, Seachnasagh, Fiachra, Flann, Dubhinracht, Moragh, Moghtigern, Maolura, Eochuid Suilebhan, of A.D. 950, Lorcan or Lawrence, Buadha or Victor O'Sullivan, Aodh or Hugh, Cathal or Charles, Buadha or Victor, MacCraith or Magrath, Donal Mor, Gilla Mochuda, Dunlang or Dunlaing, Murtogh, Bernard, Buochan or Buaidhigh, Dunlong, Ruadhri, Donal, Donal, Eoghan, Donal na Scraddy, Donal of Dunkerron d. 1580, Owen d. 1623, Donal d. 1633, Owen O'Sullivan Mor of Dunkerron forfeited in 1656, Donal 1699, Rory, Donal the last O'Sullivan Mor died, without issue, at Tomies in Aghadoe parish, in 1752. The O'Sullivan territory was subject to charges for MacCarthy Mor who paid some dues to the Earl of Desmond. The chief branches of the O'Sullivans in Kerry were Mac Gillicuddy, Cumurhagh, Glenbeigh, Caneah, Culemagort, Cappancuss, Capiganine, Fermoyle, and Ballyvicillaneulan. There are 43,000 O'Sullivans in Erin and many abroad also; the names and location of 2,135 O'Sullivan householders are given in this book.

Mac Sweeney Households

Mac Manus, Rev. Bro P. B. of Balloonagh.
Mac Maurice, see Fitz Maurice.
Mac Michael, Geo. of Ballinskelligs.
Mac Mullen, Mac Maolain; Frank of Spunkane.
Mac Namara; Julia of Craughdarrig, Ml. of Tieraclea, Tom of Kilomore, Mary of Inch, Mary of Dromclogh, John of Toor, Jas. of Doon, Poon, John of Beale, Jas. of Ahanagran, Ml. of Bromore, Ml. of Ballyhadigue, Margt. and Tom and John and John of Guhard, John of Daly's lane, Tom of Rae street. See story of the Mac Namara sept., by N. C. Mac Namara.
Mac Neill, Geo. of Canal new road.
Mac Pierce, Fitz Mauirce, see Pierse.
Mac Quaide, Mac Uaid; Pat of Burnham.
Mac Quinn, Mac Cuinn; Dan of Fiddane, Pat of Gurranedarragh, John of Ballyheige, Ml. of Ballinclemesig. John of Lackamoer, Mary and Martin and Dan of Banna, Mary of Ballinahoulart, Wm. of Listellick, Pat of Brogue Lane, John of Bridge street, Mrs. of Boherbee.
Mac Raith, Mac Rae; chief poet of Munster, d. 1098.
Mac Sheehy, Mac Sitig, see Sheehy, and Joy; Edmund was constable to Geraldines 1568.
Mac Sweeney, Mac Suibne; 143 families in Kerry, viz.:—Myles of Tiernaboul, Edm. of Ballydowney, John of Clash, John and Dan of Mastergeeha, Dan and Edm. of Toormore, Felix of Banard, of Annamore, Denis and Myles of Ranaleen, Hugh of Kilsarcon, Denis of Carker, Phillis of Sheheree, Julia of Maulyarkane, Ellen of Killeagh, Mary of Tooreenamult, Catherine of Barna, Nora of Coolegrean, Dr. Wm. of Killarney, David of Ardnamweely, Eugene of of Clashatlea, Eugene of Gortatlea, John of Killarney road, Edm. of Castleview, Ellen of Mounthawk, Dan of Ballymullen, Tom and Matt of Blennerville, Jerh. of Castle street, Edm. of Gerhadineen, Mary of Waterville; Sweeney is the form of name used by:—Denis of Lahard, Ml. of Aughacurreen, John of Gortnakilla, John of Carrigeencullia, Dan of Dromulton, Edw. of Scartaglin, Owen of Kilmaniheen, John of Tooreenmore, Edm. of Capelquarter, John of Rusheenmore, Denis of Inchincummer, John of Ballalley lane, Hannah of Barry's lane, John of Rusheen, Bryan of Freemount, Pat of Rathbeg, Ml. of Shinnagh, Bryan of Flemby, Edm. of Kilmeany, Pat of Carhooeragh, Tim of Sackville, John of Rylane, Dan of Ballyconry, Ml. of Tullaghna, Mce. of Farran, John of Ballyheigue, Denis of Clounmacon, Eug. and Pat of Killeacle, Stephen of Ballyoneen, Ml. of Ballyegan, Catherine of Tubridbeg, Johanna of Cloonafineela Con of Clieveragh, Dan of Listowel, John of Drimnacurra, Catherine of Cloghaneleesh, Tom of Brumaddra, Mary of Pallas, Hannah of the Rock, Catherine of Rock street, Ellen of Clounalour, Hannah and Dan of Brogue lane, Tom and Batt and Matt and Mrs. of Blennerville, Ellen of island of Geese, Tim of Mac Cowen's lane, Bryan of Curragh Mac Donagh, John of Laharan, Owen of Cromane, Bryan of Goat street, Rev. Pat of Gurteens, Dan of Muingaphuca, Jas. and Dan and Jas. of Glounagillagh, Tim and Ml. of Dooaghs, Tim and Jas. and Pat of Ballintleave, Roger of Letter, Wm. and John of Gortlahard, Pat of Lackaroe, John of Doughill, Pat of Gearha, Jas. and John and Batt. and Pat and Owen of Curraheen, John of Droum, John and Bridget of Kilnabrack, Dan and Pat of Carhoonahone, Ml. and Dan and John of Cappaganeen, Julia and Mary of Billinakilla, John and Edw. of Inchinanagh, Ml. of Grousemount, John of Ballagh, Ml. of Kilfadamore, Pat and Dan of Gullaba, Jerh. of Knockanuha, Dan of Gortloughera, Dan of Dromneycolman, John of Ballinlough, John of Coad, Ml. of mInchincoosh, Peter of Capparoe, Hannah of Kilbunnow, Eug. and Eug. of Gortrooskagh, Myles of Dreenagh, Ellen of Ballinlough, Tom of Shanacloon, Denis and Pat of Cullinagh, Johanna of Coolmagort, Annie of Carhoonahone, Julia of Grousemount, Mary of Valencia road. Owen Mac Sweeny, constable of Desmond, died 1582. The Marquis Mac Suibne Mag Seana Glais, b. 1871, son of Valentine, son of Dr. Valentine, is of Kerry origin; see the record of his services to the Papacy and to Ireland; he organised the Irish section of the Vatican Library

Index

Names arranged alphabetically, ignoring the Mac, Mc, or O' prefix, (i.e. for Mac Carthy see Carthy,.. O'Leary see Leary.). For a more complete listing of all family names in Ireland, see *The Master Book of Irish Surnames*, containing 60,000 listings, arranged in variant spelling groups, with source and/or location given for each name.

Be aware of variant spellings. Note that a person may be found with his name spelled in several different ways.

18th century *ix*
Acard *49*
Achard *49*
Mac Adaim *1*
Mac Adam *5*
Adames *xiv*
Adams *1, xiv, xvii*
Adams *xvii-B*
Mc Adams *159*
Agar *49*
Agard *49*
Agas *3*
Ager *49*
Ahern *1*
Oh Ailee *72*
Mac Ailin *1*
Mac Aindrui *2*
Oh Ainlige *74*
Ainsworth *1*
Ainsworth *xxiii*
Airachdan *52*
Ais *3*
Alcher *49*
Aldwell *1*
Aldwell, 161 Mary
Aldworth *1, 3*
Aldworth, sir *115*
Allan *1*
Allen *1*
Mac Allen *1*
Mac Allister *1*
Allman *1, 159*

Alltraighe *xvi*
ALMES *159*
Mac Alpin *73*
Alton *1*
Alton *xvii-C*
Altry, cantred *xvi*
Mac Alustruim *52*
Mac Amalgada *62*
Ambros *1*
Ambrose *1*
America *9*
America, to *xvii*
AMERY *159*
Ames *1, xvi*
Amory *2*
Amory *xvii-C*
Mac an Coilib *32*
Ancient *xvi* Peoples
Anderson *2*
Mac Andrew *159*
Andrews *2*
Anglesey *2, xvi*
Anglican *xxiv* church
Mac anGoill *63*
Angove *2*
(de) Angulo, *111* Gilbert
Mac anIascaire *56*
Oh Annain *74*
Annesley *2*
Oh Anracain *74*
Mac anScoloige *54*

Anthony *2*
Mac Aoda *32, 94*
Mac Aodagain *50*
ap Rees' *127*
Appleyard *2*
Archer *2*
ARCHER *159*
Ardea *142, 155* Castle
Ardfert *58, 155* Castle
Ardfert *xxiii* eccles.
Ardilaun, L. *150*
Armorica *151*
Armstrong *2*
ARNALDS *159*
Arnes *2*
Arnes *xvii-B*
Arnold *2*
Arnold *xvii-B*
Oh Arractain *75*
Oh Artagain *75*
Artagh, Co. *viii* Roscomm.
Oh Artgaile *75*
Arthur *2*
Mac Arthur *2*
Mac Artuir *20*
Ash *xiv*
Ashe *3, xiv*
ASHE *159*
ASHTON *159*
Ashwood *3*
Ashwood *xvii-B*

Asplen, G. *xxiii*
Mac assy *94*
Atasac *3*
Atkins *3, xvi*
Atkinson *xxiii*
Atkinson, J. *xxiii*
Aucher *49*
Auger *49*
Mac auley *115*
Mac Auliffe *3*
Austin *3, xvi*
Austin, Eliz. *99*
Australia, in *ix, xvii*
Austria, in *ix*
Austrian *14, 51, 119* Army
Averill *3*
Avery *3*
Aylward *3*
Aylworth *1*
B'hassett *34, 57, 94*
Babbage *3*
Babington *3*
Babington *xvii-C*
Baicer *4*
Bailey *3, 6*
Baille *3*
Baily *3*
Bainley *3*
Baireid *4*
Baker *4, xiv*
Baldwin *4*
Ball *4, xvi*
Ballard *4*

219 Names Arranged Alphabetically without the O' or Mac Prefix 219

Balluntyne *xxiii*	De Bartun *5*	O' Beoilain *10*	Blen'erhas'et *161* Sir Rowl.
Ballybeggan *107* Castle	Bass *5*	Bergin *7*	Blen'erhas'et *161* Thomas
Ballycarbery *165* Castle	De Bastabla *5*	Bernard *7, 8, 108*	Blen'erhas'ett *81*, Anne
Ballycarbery *71* Castle illus.	Bastable *5*	Bernard *xvii*-C	Blen'erhas'ett *6* arms hotel
Ballyheigue *166* Castle	Bastable *159*	Bernard *xvii*-B	Blen'erhas'ett *116*, Capt.
Ballykealy *58* Castle	Batchelor *5*	Bernard, *161* Edw. M.	Blen'erhas'ett *150*, Lucy
Ballymalis *50* Castle	Bateman *5, 131, 151, 159*	Berry *8*	Blen'erhas'ett *156*, married
Ballymalus *105* Castle	Bateman *xvii*-C	Berry *xvii*-B	Blen'erhas'ett *129*, Mary
Ballyneanig *105* Castle	Bateman, *161* John	Best *8*	Blen'erhas'ett *30*, R.
Bambury *4*	Bateman, *161* Row.	Best *xvii*-B	blen'erhaset' *159*
Bambury *159*	Bateman, *156* Rowland	Bibliogr'phy *ii, 157*	Blennerhas'et *9, 10, 76, 99*
Bannion *4*	Bayley *6*	Bigg *8, xvi*	Bloet, P. *138*
Barbodoes *148*	Bayley *xvii*-B	Binane *8*	Bloomer *10*
Barden *4*	O' Beacain *6*	Bingham *8*	Blount *10*
Barham *4*	Beale Castle *139*	Birmingham *8* as Ferris	Blundell *10*
Barham *xvii*-B	Beale, T. *161*	Mac Birney *8*	Blythe *10*
Bariod *4*	Beamish *159*	Black Irish *viii*	Boake *10*
Barkey *4*	Bean *6*	black & tans *193*	Boland *10*
Barnard *4, 7*	Bear *6*	Blacker *8*	Bolger *10*
Barnes *4*	Beaslai *6*	Blacker, St. *161* John T.	(de) Bolltun *10*
(de) Barra *4*	Beasley *6*	Blackwood *8*	Bolster *10*
Barrett *4, 51*	Beasly *6*	Blackwood, *161* Sir Henry	Bolton *10*
BARRETT *159*	Beckford *6*	(de) Blagd *10*	Bona *10*
Barrett *xvii*-B	Beckford *xvii*-B	Blake *8*	Bonguelimi *10*
Barretts *7*	Begley *6*	Bland *8, 159*	Bonham *10*
Barron *4*	O Begley *159*	Bland Arms *7*	Bonney *10*
Barrow *4*	Begly *6*	Bland, Eliz. *83*	Bordell *10*
Barrow *xvi*	Behan *159*	Bland, *161* Francis C.	Bordell *xvii*-B
Barry *4, 8*	Behan of *6* Leix	Bland, Mary *141*	Boreham *10*
Barry *xix*	O' Beirgin *7*	Bland, Ven. *161* Archdeacon	Boreham *xvii*-B
Barry, Col. J. *161*	Beirne *6*	Blen'erha'set *8* arms illus.	Boreman *10*
Barry, John *161*	O' Beirne *6*	Blen'erha'set *161* John	Boreman *xvii*-C
Bartholomew *5*	Bell *6*	Blen'erha'set' *xiv* xvi, xvii, xx	Boru, Brian *46*
Bartlett *5*	Benn *6*	Blen'erhas'et *161*, Arthur	Boston, MA. *7*
Bartley *5*	Benner *6*	Blen'erhas'et *161* Rowland	Boston. *106* Moriarty in
Barton *5, xiv*	Bennett *7*		
Barton *xvii*-B	Benson *7, 116*		
Barton, Rv. *xxiii*	Benson *xvii*-C		
	Benson *xvii*-B		
	Bently *7*		

Boston tobacconist *117*
Bothwick *10*
Bouldger *10*
Bounce *10*
Boundes *xiv*
Bourgh *15*
Bourke *15, 159*
Bourke, Maj. Gen. T. *161*
Boursin *10*
Bovenizer *10*
Bowen *10*
Bowen, Robt. *161*
Bower *10*
Bowler *11, 159*
Bowles *11*
Boy *xiv*
Boyd *11*
Boye *xiv*
Boylan *11*
Boyle *11*
Boyle *xvii-B*
Boyle, R. *14, 82*
Brackleyer *11*
De Brackleyer *11*
O' Bradain *56*
Bradbury, J. *xxiii*
Bradford *11*
Bradley *11*
Bradly *11*
Bradshaw *12*
Bradshaw *xvii-C*
Brady *12*
Brady, Wm. *xxiii*
Bramstone *xvii, 12*
Bramstone *xvii-B*
Brandon *12*
Mac Brandon *12*
Brandon, L. *12*
Brannagh *151*
Mac Braoin *12*
O' Braoin *12*
Brassel *12*

Brassill *12*
Mac Breandain *12*
O' Breasail *12*
Breen *12, 159*
O BREENE *159*
Bremmer *12*
BRENAGH *159*
Mc BRENAN *159*
O' BRENAN *159*
O BRENANE *159*
Brendan, St. *xxiii*
Brennan *12, xix*
O' Brennan *68, 159*
Brennan, Daniel *161*
Brett *12, xvi*
Brett, de Britt *xvii-C*
Brew *12*
Brewer *13*
Brewster *13, 55*
Brewster, Sir *8*
O' Briain *13*
O' Brian *13*
O' Bric *159*
Brick *13, 159*
Mac Bride *13*
Bridges *13*
Brien *13*
O' Brien *13, 90*
O' Brien, Donal Mor *27*
O' Brien, Donat *46*
O' Brien, Henry *xxiv*
O' Brien, J. *163*
O' Brien Thomand *vii, xii*
Bright *xiv*
BRINAGH *159*
(de) Briotun *14*
(de) Britt *12*
Broadhurst *13*
Broder *13, 159*
Broder Arms *12*
O Broder(ick) *159*

Broderick *13, 159*
O' Broin *16*
Broncar *14*
Brooke *13*
Brooke *xvii-B*
Brookes *13*
Brookes *xvii-B*
O' Brosnahan *159*
Brosnan *13, 159*
Brown *14, xiii*
Browne *14, vii, xvii*
Browne *159*
Browne, A. *138, xv*
Browne, J. P. *161*
Browne, John *161*
Browne, N. *33*
Browne, Rev. Geo. *161*
Browne, V. *43, 54*
Brownes *91*
O' Bruadair *13*
Bruce, *14*
Brunkar *14*
(de) Brus *14*
Bruton *14*
Bryan *13*
O' Bryan *13*
Bryant *14*
Mc BRYEN *159*
O BRYEN *159*
O' Buacalla *14*
Buckford *14*
Buckford *xvii-B*
Buckley *14, 82, 159*
Buey *14*
Buggy *14*
(de) Buitileir *16*
Bull *15*
Bunbury *15*
Bunce *15*
Bunnion *15*
Bunworth *15*
Bunyan *15*

(de) Burc *15*
Burchill *15*
Burden *4*
Burghleys *xviii*
(De) Burgos *73*
Burke *15*
Burke, Fitzwilliam *15*
Burke, Sir *65*
Burke's Armory *xix*
Burkett *15*
Burnham *15*
Burns *16, 159*
Burren barony *viii*
Burscough *16*
Bustead *16*
Busteed, Isabella *161*
Busteed, Mary *161*
Butcher *16*
Butcher Arms *15*
Butler *16*
Butler, Arabella *161*
Butler family *xii*
Butler, James *161*
Butterly *16*
Butterly, Lau. *161*
Bynane *16*
Byrne *16, xix*
Byrne, M.J. *xxiv*
Caball *16*
Mac Cabe *16*
Cade *17*
Cade *xvii-B*
Cades *23*
Cadgan *17*
O' Cadla *87*
Cadogan *17*
Mac Cafferty *17*
Cagney *17*
Cahalane *159*

Cahan 85	(De) Cantlon's Castle 17	Mc Carthy 20-23	Mac Carty of T'hilken.. 15
CAHANE 159	Cantwell 18	Mc Carthy 159	Cary 22
O CAHANE 159	Canty 18, 32	Mc Carthy, Alex. 163	Cary xvii-C
CAHASSY 159	O' Caoimh 86	Mc Carthy 20 Arms	Casey 22, 159
O CAHESEY 159	O' Caomain 87		O' CASEY 159
Cahill xix, 159	Cap'an'cushy Castle 143	Mac Carthy vii banished	Castle 94 Connell
O' Cahill vii, xxii			
O' Cain 85	Cap'anacos' Castle 142	Mac Carthy 34 branch	Castle Cor 64
Cairach 19			Castle Drum 105
Callaghan 159	(de) Capella 144	Mac Carthy, Capt. 115	Castle Forbes 117
O' Callaghan, G. 163	Carew 18, 19, 83, 138	Mc Carthy, Dan. 163	Castle Gregory 82, 135
O' Callaghan, John 89			
	(de) Carew, Wm. 18	Mc Carthy, Dermoid xii	Castle Lyons 91
O' Callanain 17	Carews 7, 113		Castle Mac-Ellistrum 151
Callen Glen viii battle of,	Carey 19, 159	Mac Carthy, Dermot xi	
	Carhoo 19		Castle Magne xvii-b illustrated
Callinane 17	Carish 19	Mac Carthy xvi Eoganacht	
Callues 17	Carmody 19, 159		Castle Maine 115
Callues xvii-B	Carney 19, 85	Mac Carthy & F'maurice 58	Castle Mayne 129
Calverly 17	Carney xix		Castlequin 96
Cambrensis xii	Carpenter 19	Mac Carthy, 21, 54 Flor.	O' Catain 85
Cambridge 17	Carpenter xvii-B	Mc Carthy 173 hous'holds	O' Catasaig 22
Cambridge xvii-B	Carr 19		Mac Cauley 23
Cameron 17	O' Carra 19	Mac Carthy, Jane 154	Cavan 23
Cameron xvii-C	Carrick 19, 153, 159		Cavanagh 23, 85
Camp xiv		Mac Carthy, 78, 82 Justin	Caxon 23
Campbell 17	Carrig 19		O' Ceadagain 17
Campe xiv	Carrig-A-Phuca castle 90	Mac Carthy & M'Sw'eney 144	O' Cearnaig 19, 85
Canada police xxiv		Mac Carthy 18,104, Mor 143	Cecil 23, 24
Canlon 17	Carrigan 87		Ceileachair 86
Mac Cann 17	Carrique xvi, 19, 120	Mac Carthy xiii, ix Mor	Ceilor 23
Mac Canna 95			O' Cein 85
Cannell 17	O' Carroll 19, vii, 159	Mc Carthy Mor xxiii Drama	O' Ceirise 87
(de) Canntual 18	O' Carroll xxii Loch Lein	Mac Carthy xxiii Reagh	O' Ceitearnaig 85
(de) Cantelowe 17			Chambers 23, 159
(de) Cantelupe 17	(de) Carrun 18	Mac Carthy 20 septs	Champ 23
Cantillon 17, 18, 32, 159	Carson 19		Champion xiii, 23, 82
	Carter 20	Mac Carthy xxiv tomb	Chandley 23
(de) Cantillon 17	Carterett 20, xvi		Chant 23
Cantillon 166 Castle	CARTHER 159	Mac Carthys xxiii petition	Chapman xiii, xvii, 23
	Carthy xvi	Mac Cartie xvii, 9 Mor	
Cantillon, 28 Mary	Mac Carthy 134, .xvii		Chapman xvii-B
Cantillons 91		Mac Cartie of 136 Dungeele	CHAPPELL 159
Cantlon 17	Mac Carthy xx		Cheke xvii
	Mac Carthy 159	Mac Carties xi	

222   Names Arranged Alphabetically without the O' or Mac Prefix   222

Chesterfield, *1* Lord	cinel Eoghain *93*	O' Cobhthaigh *25*	Collum *26*
Chesters *23*	Civerac, *70* countess	Cock *25*	Colmain *25*
Chestnut *23*	clan Cashel *134*	Mac Coclain *25*	Colman *25*
Cheston *23*	Clan Conaire *28, 87*	Coffe *xix*	Colohan *26*
Chetwood *xx*	Clan Fergail *73* arms	Coffey *25, 159*	Colthurst *159*
Chicago, IL. *6*	Clan- *xi* Maurice	Coffey, *98* Bishop	Colthursts *30*
Chrisholm *23*	Clancy *24*	Coffie *25*	Coltsman, *161* Daniel
Christian *xiv, 23, 141*	Mac Clancy *24*	de Cogan *67, viii, xi*	Coltsmann *26, 33*
Christison *23*	Clandeboys *90* transplanted	Cogan, *xii* Miles	Coltsmann, *161* Catherine
Church *23, 119, 159*	Clandenan *24*	Coghlan *25*	Mac Coluim *26, 35*
Church *xvii-C*	Clangibbon *xii*	Cohey *25*	Mac Coluim, F. *175*
Church *xvii-B*	Clanmaurice *xvi, 58, 141*	Coilens *25*	Columb *26*
Church Rep. *161* Body	Clapman *24*	O' Coinin *30, 31*	Colvin *26*
Church *161* Temp Body	Claridge *24*	COINYN *159*	O' Comain *27*
Chuse *24*	Clarke *24*	Coke *25*	Mac Comdain *32*
Chuse *xvii-C*	Clayton *24*	O Colahan *159*	Comerford *27*
CHUTE *159*	Cleary *24*	Colclough *25, 35*	Commane *27*
Chute *xvii-C*	(de) Cleatun *24*	Coleman *25*	Commyns *27*
Chute *xvii-B*	Clegg *24*	O' Colgan *25*	Compton *27, xvi*
Chute, *161* Algernon	O' Cleirig *24*	Coll *25*	Comyn *27*
Chute, *161* Capt.R.	Clenesha *24*	O' Colla *35*	Comyn *xvii-C*
Chute, Capt. *161* Thos.	Clifford *24, 159*	O Collaghane *159*	O' Conaing *31*
Chute, *161* Charles	Clifton *24*	Collier *25*	Mac Conarchy *27*
Chute, Dan'l *51, 135*	Mac Clintock *24*	Collier *xvii-B*	M'c Conarchy *175* ho'sehldrs
Chute, *161* Francis B.	M'c Clintock *175* householdr	Colligan *25*	Conary, race *87*
Chute, Mgt. *122*	(de) Clohuile *38*	Collingwood *25*	Condon *27, 159*
Chute of *24, 52* Chute Hall	Clohulle *24*	Collins *25*	Mac Conduib *52*
Chute, Rev. G. *161*	(de) Clohulle *24*	Collins *xvii-C*	Condun *27*
Chute, Rich. *161*	Clontarf, *43, 104,* Battle of *132*	Collins *25* Castle	Confiscated *136* lands
Chute, Wm. *153*	Clotherty *24*	Collins of *vii* Connelo	O' Conghaile *53*
O' Ciarda *19*	O' Clumain *24*	Collins, *122* Rev.	O' Connaghain *31*
Ciarraige, the *xxi*	Mac Clure *25*	Collis *26, 144, 159*	Conneff *27*
Cicill *24*	M'c Clure house *175* holders	Collis *xvii-B*	Connell *xix, 159*
Cicill *xvii-B*	Mac Cluskey *25*	Collis of *100* Monaree	Mac Connell *27*
Cicill, John *xviii*	M'c Cluskey *175* ho'sehldrs	Collis of *26* Tieraclea	O' Connell *xx, 27-8, 92, 159*
Mac Cineait *65*	Mc Cnocgor *159*	Collis, S. E. *161*	O' Connell *xxii*
	Coakley *25*	Collis-Sandes *25* arms illus.	O' Connell, *133* Alice
			O' Connell *20* arms illus
			O' Connell, C. *163*

O' Connell, *xxiii* Col.
O' Connell, D. *163*
O' Connell, *163* Dan.
O' Connell, *28, 90* Daniel
O' Connell, *91* E. Dhuv
Mac Connell *175* ho'sehldrs
Connell *182* households
O' Connell, J. *107*
O' Connell, M. *163*
O' Connell, *xxiii* Mce.
O' Connell, *20* Morgan
O' Connell of *27* Derrynane
O' Connell *xxiv* records
O' Connell, Sir *163* M. J.
O' Connell, *163* Thos.
O' Connells *vii*
O' Connells of *46* Limerick
Connelly *28*
Connelly *176* householdrs
Conner *28*
O' Conner *xvii* soldiers
Connolly *28*
Connor *28, 159*
O' Connor *28-9, 159*
O' Connor arms *19*
O' Connor, *91* Baron
O' Connor *vii* Ciarraighe
O' Connor *131* confiscated
O' Connor, Ellen *51*
O' Connor, *163* Francis

O' Connor, *163* Gerard
O' Connor *176* househldrs
O' Connor *176* households
O' Connor, J. *111*
O' Connor, *163* John, M. D.
O' Connor *28, 104,*.. Kerry *xvi*
O' Connor *xxiii* Kerry
O' Connor, King *104* of Connaught
Connor lands *131*
O' Connor, M. *xxiii*
O' Connor, *163* Mrs. H.
Connor of *xvi* Dublin
Connor, Rev *116*
O' Connor, *163* Rev. M.
O' Connor *58* territory
O' Connor, *163* Thos.
O' Connors *xi*
O' Connyn *30*
O' Conor, C. *xxiii*
O' Conor *xxii* Kings
Conroi *29*
Mac Conroi *87*
Mac Conroi *131* confiscat'd
Mac Conroi *175* ho'sehldrs
Conroy *29*
Contents, *v* table of
Conway *29, 30, 104*
Conway *xiii, xvii,* *159*
Conway *xvii-B*
Conway, *47* Avice

Conway, 9, 57 Capt.
Conway, *27* Eliz.
Conway *xiv* History
Conway, *128* James
Conway of *29* Bodrythan
Conway of *30* Killorglin
CONY *159*
Conyers *30, 159*
Conyn *30, 31*
O' Conyns *30*
Cooke *30*
Cooke *xvii-B*
Cooke, *118* Maude
Cooke of *140* Skehenerin
Cooney *30*
Cooper *30, xix*
Coote *31, xvi*
Copley, *117* portrait
Corbet *31*
Corbet *xvii-C*
Corca *53, 82, 142* Duibne
O' Corcain *31*
Corcoran *31, 159*
O' Corcra *31*
Corcu *vii, viii* Duibne
Corcu *xvi* Duibne
Cork, Earl of *161*
Corkerry *31*
Corkery *159*
Corkery, D. *161* O'B.
Mac Cormac(k) *31*
Mc Cormack *159*
Mac Cormack *175* ho'sehldrs
Mac Cormacke *15*

Mc Cormacke *21*
Mac Cormaic *31*
Mac Cormaic *175* ho'sehldrs
Mc Cormick *31*
Cornwall *31*
O' Corra *35*
Corradain *31*
O' Corragain *31*
O' Corrain *35*
Corridan *31*
Corridon *159*
Corrigan *31*
Corrodan *159*
Cosgrave *xvi*
Cosgrove *31*
Costelloe *31*
Costigan *31*
Cotter. *31*
Coulthurst *31*
Counihan *30, 31,* *35, 36*
(O) Counihan *159*
County *32*
Cournane *32*
(O) Cournane *159*
Coursey *38*
Courtney *32, 159*
Cousins *32*
Covert *32, xvi*
Covert *xvii-C*
Mac Cowen *32, 116*
Mac Cowen *175* ho'sehldrs
Mac Cowen's *156* Lane
Cox *32*
Coxon *32*
Mac Coy *32*
Mac Coy *175* ho'sehldrs
Coyle *32*
Craddock *159*
Mac Crah *32, 142*
Crane, C.P. *xxiv*

224   Names Arranged Alphabetically without the O' or Mac Prefix   224

Cranfield *32*	O Cronin *159*	Culhane *35*	Cusack, M. *xxiii*
Cranfield *xvii-C*	Cronnelly, R. *xxiii*	Mac Cullagh *10*	Mac Cushion *36*
Cranitch *32*	Crosberry *33*	Cullen *35*	Cussen *36*
Craobac *32*	Crosbie *xv, 34, 90*	Mac Cullen *35*	Cussen, E. *51*
Crassus *xi*	Crosbie *37* arms illus.	Cullinane *35, 122*	Mac Cutcheon *36*
Mac Crath *143*	Crosbie, B. *xxiv*	Culloty *35, 159*	Cuthbert, *161* Thos.
Crawford *32*	Crosbie, *51* Bishop	Cullum *35*	Cuthbertson *36*
Creagh *32, 140*	Crosbie, *129* Catherine	Cully *35*	D'Alton *xxiii*
Mc CREAGH *159*	Crosbie, *130* Col. D.	Cummane *35*	Mac Daboe *30*
O' CREAGH *159*	Crosbie *xiv* family	Cummins *27*	Dackham *36*
Creagh, *161* Fr. & John	Crosbie, *161* Maj. James	Cun'ingham *31, 35*	Dagg *36*
Creagh, *161* William	Crosbie *165* Mansion	Cuninghame, *150* R. Gun	Mac Daibid *37*
O' Creain *33*	Crosbie, *161* Margaret	Cunningham *159*	Daibis *37*
Crean *33, 159*	Crosbie, W. *161*	CURAN *159*	Daily *36*
Creed *33*	Crosbies *9, 17*	O' Curathain *36*	Dairsig *37*
Creegan *33*	Crosby *34, 159*	Curbstone *35*	O' Dalaig *36*
Cregan *33*	Crossan *34*	Curbstone *xvii-B*	Daley *36*
Crehan *33, xi*	Crowe *34*	Curinys *35*	DALLY *159*
Mac Crehan *33*	Crowley *34*	Curlestone *xvii, 35*	Dalton *36*
Mac Crehans *143* descent	Cruden *xix*	Curlew *35*	Daltons of *95* N. Kerry
Cremin *33, 159*	O' Cruitin *36*	Curlew *xvii-B*	Daly *xix, 36, . . 159*
Cremins *33*	Crumpe, *161* F., M. D.	O' Curnain *32*	O' DALY *159*
Crewly, J. *xx*	Crumpe of *34* Barleymount	O CURNANE *159*	O' Daly, A. *xxiii*
O' Criagain *33*	O' Cuanacain *31*	Curran *35, 159*	O' Daly, Rev. *xxiii*
Crimmins *33*	O' Cuarthain *36*	O' CURRAN *159*	Daly's lane *88*
Critchley *33*	O' Cuil *122*	Currane *35, 159*	Dalziel *36*
Mac Crohan *33, xx*	O' Cuileannain *122*	O Currane *159*	Damer *36*
Mc CROHAN *159*	Mac Cuill *35, 122*	Currans *35* Castle	Damer *xvii-C*
Mac Crohan *175* ho'sehldrs	Mac Cuinn *123*	Currens *35*	Danaher *37*
O' Croidain *33*	O' Cuinn *123*	Curry *35*	Danesfort, L. *16*
O' Croideain *33*	Cuinneagain *31*	Mc Curtaine *159*	Daniel *37*
O' Croinin *33*	O' Cuirc *123*	O Curtaine *159*	Daniel *xvii-C*
Croke of *33* Tralee	(de) Cuirteis *36*	Curtais *xix*	Mc DANIEL *159*
Croker *33*	Mac Cuirtin *36*	Curtayne *xix, 31, 36*	Mc DANIELL *159*
Croker, T. *xxiii*	Cuisin *32, 36*	Curtayne, J. *161*	Daniels *23*
Cromwell *xv, 159*	(de) Cuitleir *123*	Curtesse *xiv*	Danville, IL. *100*
O' Cronain *33*	Culclough *35*	Curtin *36, 159*	Mac Darac *37*
O CRONEENE *159*		Curtin, J. *xxiv*	Darby *37*
Cronin *33, x ix, . . 159*		Curtin, John *161*	Darby *xvii-C*
		Curtis *36*	Darcy *37*
		Cusack *36*	Darcys *7*

Darley 37	de Canntual 18	de Stacabul 139	Denny, 5 Letitia
Darley, Henry 161	de Cantelowe 17	de Stack 138	Denny, Maynard 161
Darrack 37	de Cantelupe 17	de Stokke 140	Denny of Tralee 40
Darrynane, poems xxiii	de Cantillon 17	De Thick 41	Denny xix records
Dashwood 37	De Cantlon's Castle 17	de Wilton xvii	Denny, Rev. xxiv
Dashwood xvii-B	de Capella 144	de Wyk 156	Denny, Sir E. xxiii
Datun 37	de Carew 18	Dea 38	Denny, Sir Edward xiv
Daughton 37	de Carrun 18	O' Dea 38, 39, 159	Denny, Sir Edward, 161
Mc DAUID 159	De Clahull 38	O' Deadig 39	Denny, Ven. Archd. 161
Davidson 37	de Cleatun 24	Deady 39, 159	Denny's tutor 137
Davies 37	de Clohuile 38	O' Deagaid 39	Dennys 9
Davies, Eliz. 67	de Clohulle 24	O' Deagain 39	O' Deorain 46
Davis 37	de Cogan 67, viii, xi, xii	Deane 39	dePrendeville 121
Davis xvii-B	De Courcey, Wm. 161	Deane, Jas. 161	dePri'ndargas 121
Mc DAVITT 159	De Courcy 38	Dease 39	Mc DERMOD 159
Dawson 37	de Cuirteis 36	DEATICK 159	Mac Dermott 40
Dawton 37	de Cuitleir 123	Dee 39	Derrick, S. xxiii
Day 38, 39, 124	De Dannan 122	Deegan 39	Derriquin Castle 152
Day, Catherine 161	de Freins 60	Deegin 39	Desmond 41
Day, Francis 161	de Gaillide 62	Deen 39	Desmond, King of vii
Day, Isabella 100	De Grandison 92	Deenihan 39	Desmond xi lands of
O' Day, O'Dea 159	de Hal 72	Deering 141	Desmonds viii Sovereign
Day, Rev. xxiii	de Hore 17	Del 39	Dethick 41, xvii
Day, Rev. John F. 161	de Keting 85	O' Del 39	Dethick xvii-B
Day, Robt. xxiii	De La Cousa 82	Delaney 39	Dettrick 41
Day, Very Rev. Dean 161	De la Huse 82	DeLap 39	Devane 41, 159
Day-Stokes 38	de la Roche 128	Delmege 6	Devaney 41
O DAYLY 159	de Lacy 88	Deloughry 39	Devereaux 41
de Angulo 111	De Laundre 89	Dempsey 39	Devine 41
de Barra 4	de Marascal 98	Dennehy 39, 159	Devlin 41
de Blagd 10	de Marisco viii, 54,. 149	Dennehy, Mary 161	O' Devoy 159
de Bolltun 10	De Moleyns 38	Dennis 39	Dew 41
De Brackleyer 11	De Moleyns, Wm. 161	Dennis, M. 161	Dew xvii-B
de Briotun 14	de Nais 111	Denny 65, xiii, xvi, xvii	Mac Diarmada 40
de Britt 12	de Nogla 111	Denny xviii, 159	Digby 41
de Brus 14	de Pierce 119	Denny, Arthur 18, 52	Diggin 41, 159
de Buitileir 16	de Pionbroc 117	Denny, 52 Arthur dies	
de Burc 15	de Poer 121	Denny, Col. xxiii	
De Burgos 73	de Portuil 122	Denny, Collingwood 161	
	de Ruthyen 9	Denny, E. 9, 139	

Dignan *41*
Dillane *41, 159*
O Dillane *159*
Dillon *41*
(le) Dillon *41*
Dillon of *41* Queens Co.
O' Dinan *47*
Dineen *41*
Dinnahane *159*
Dinneen, Rev. *xxiv*
O' Diomasaig *39*
O' Dobailein *41*
Dobbs, Dob *41*
Docartaig *42*
Doda *41*
Dodd *41*
Dodd, W. H. *161*
O' Dogair *46, 47*
Dogherty *42*
Doherty *42*
Dolin *41*
Domnaill *42*
Mac Domnaill *42*
O' Domnaill *42*
Mac Donagh *xx, 42*
O' Donaghoe *159*
Donaghue *45*
O' Donaghue *ix* Glenflesk
Donahoo *45*
Donahue *45*
Mac Donald *42*
Donegan *42*
Donegan *186* households
O' Donnabain *46*
O' Donnagain *42*
Mac Donnell *42*
O' Donnell *xxii, 42*
O' Donnell *176* househldrs
Donnell *186* households

O' Donnell, *86* Red Hugh
O' Donnells of *27* Donegal
Donnelly *42*
Donnelly *186* househldrs
Donnelly *186* households
O' Donngaile *42*
Mc Donnogh *159*
O' Donnoghue, *15* Glinfleiske
Mc DONOGH *159*
Mac Donogh of *42* Duhallow
O' Donoghoe *xi* Glenflesk
O' Donoghoe *xi* Mor, Ross
Donoghue *43-5, 159*
O' Donoghue *xxii, 159*
O' Donoghue *42* arms
O' Donoghue *vii* arrives
O' Donoghue *xxiii* Denis
O' Donoghue *27* Dhuv
O' Donoghue *xvi* Eoganacht
O' Donoghue *xvii* forces
Donoghue *186* households
O' Donoghue *43, 104* Mor
O' Donoghue *xxiii* of Ross
O' Donoghue of *43* the glen
O' Donoghue, *163* The
O' Donoghue *xxiv* tomb
Mac Donough *159*
Donovan *46*
O' Donovan clan *27*

O' Donovan, J. *xxiii*
Donovan, *161* Nicholas
O' Donovan of *46* Cashel
Donovan, *161* Patrick
Doody *46*
Doohig *46*
Doolan *46*
O' DOOLAN *159*
Dooley *46*
Dooling *46*
Doona *46*
Door *46*
Doran *46*
Doran arms *46*
Doran *46, 90* transpl'nt'd
O' Dorcain *46*
Dore *46*
Dorgan *46*
O' Dorney *xvi*
O' Dorney *47* Parish
Dorohy *47*
O' Dorohy *159*
Doughertie *42*
Douglas *47*
DOWD *159*
O' Dowd *47*
Dowdal *xiv*
Dowdales *30*
Dowdall *47*
Dowdall *82* lands
Dowdall, Pat *118*
Dowdall, Sir *118*
Dower *47*
O' Dowlin *41*
Dowlin of *46* Queens Co.
Dowling *46, 47*
Dowling of *47* Canada

Dowlins *90* transplanted
Dowman *47*
Downes *47*
Downey *47*
O' Downey *159*
Downing *47, 159*
Downing, F. *161*
Downing, M. *xxiii*
Downing, *161* McCarthy
Doyle *47, 159*
O' Doyle *47*
Drake *47*
O' Drea *159*
Drew *47*
Drew, Rev. B. *161*
Drew, Sarah *162*
Drew, Sarah *162*
Driscoll *48*
O' Driscoll *48, 159*
Driscoll, J. *xx*
Driscoll, *162* John
O' Droma *48*
O' Druaid *48*
Drum, *48*
Drummond *48*
Drummond, *162* Robt.
Drury *48*
O' DUANE *159*
O' Dubagain *48*
O' Dubain *41, 47*
O' Dubda *41, 46*
O' Duben *41*
O' Dubhghuill *47*
O' Dublainn *46, 47*
O' Dublavic *46*
O' Dubtaig *46, 48*
O' Dubuidir *49*
Ducey *48*
Duckett *48*
Duckett, *162* Thomas M.

Dudgeon *48*
Dudley *48*
Duffesy *48*
Duffield *48*
Duggan *48, xix*
Duhig *48, 159*
O' Duibginn *39, 41*
O' Duibluacra *39*
O' Duilleain *41*
O' Duineacair *37*
O' Duineacda *39*
O' Duinin *41, 47*
O' Duinn *49*
Duke *48*
O DULINGE *159*
Dumas *48*
O' Dunadaig *47*
O' Dunady *159*
Dunahoo *45*
Dunford *48*
Dunkerron *143* Castle
Dunlea *48*
Dunleavy *48*
Dunlevy *48*
Dunloe *96, viii* Castle
Dunlop *48*
O' DUNNADY *159*
Dunne *49*
Dunraven, *162* Earl of
Dutchman *49*
Dutchman *xvii-B*
DWANE *159*
Dwyer *49, 159*
O' Dwyer, Rev. *35*
Dyche *49*
Dyer *49*
Dyer *xvii-B*
Eachard *49*
Eadie *49*
Eagar, Agar *49-50,*
Eagar, Alex. *13, 55*

Eagar *50* armorial
Eagar, E. *162* M'G.
Eagar, F. J. *162*
Eagar, J. H. *162*
Eagar, Oliver *162*
Eagar, Rev. *162*
Eager *49, 156*
Eager *159*
Ealcher *49*
Oh Eamtaig *76*
Oh Eanna *76*
Earl of *155* Listowel
Earls of *50, 155* Kerry
Eaton *50*
Eber *49*
Echard *49*
Edalicke *50*
Edalicke *xvii-B*
Edgeworth *50*
EDMOND *159*
Mc EDMOND *159*
Edwards *50*
Egan *50*
Mac Egan *xx, 50*
Egar *49*
Egelton *50*
Egyr *49*
Oh Eilide *76*
Einey *xix*
M'c El'istum *52, 131*
Mc ELIGOD *159*
Eligot *51*
Mac Elligots & *24* Chute
Mac Elligott *51-2,* . *159*
Mac Elligott *xxiii*
Mac Elligott, M. *xxiii*
Mc Elligott, *163* Wm.
Elliott *52*
Elliott, Alex. *162*

Elliott, Mary *162*
Ellis, Maj. *16, 52*
Mac Ellistrum *151* Castle
Mc Ellygott *159*
ELLYOTT *159*
Elrington *52*
Emigrants *ix*
Emmet *52*
Emmett *99*
Endean *52*
Mac Endoo *52*
Mac Enery *52*
Mac Enerys ln. *155*
English *52*
English   *xi* invasion
English   *xii* settlement
Mac Ennery *52*
Enright *52, 159*
Entivistle *52*
Eoganacht *vii*
Eoganacht *96* Cashel
Eoganacht *xvi* Loch Lein
Mac Eotac *67*
Erraught *52*
Eugenian *xvi*
Evans *52, 121*
Eve, Dorothy *118*
Eveleigh *53*
Everatt *53*
Mac Evoy *53*
Exham *53, 107*
Exham *xvii-B*
Eyles *53*
Fagan *53*
Fagan, Capt. *162* W. A.
Fahy *53*
O' Failbe *53*
O' Failbhe *53*
Fairfield *53*

Falhan *53*
O' FALLON *159*
FALUEY *159*
FALUY *159*
Falvey *53-4*
Falvey *ix,xix, . . 159*
O' Falvey *xvi,xxii, 159*
O' Falvey   *vii* banished
O' Falveys *134*
famine, the *ix*
O' Faolain *118*
Farding *54*
Farding *xvii-B*
Mac Farland *54*
FARLEY *159*
Farmer *54*
Farrell *54*
Farressy *54*
Farris *55*
Farthing *xiv*
Fay, O'Feic *54*
Fealy *54*
O' Feargail *54*
O' Fearguis *54*
Fearris-Beal *136* -ahamalis
Mac Fearriss *55*
Feeney *54*
O' Feibeannaig *63*
O' Feic *54*
Fell *54*
Fell *xvii-B*
Fenaghty *54*
Fenix *54*
Fennell *54*
Fenton *54,98,159*
Mc FERGUS *159*
Ferguson *65*
Ferguson's *6* Brewery
FERIS *159*
Ferreter *55*

Ferris 8, 55, 104	FITZEDMD. 159	Fitzimmons 57	Flahavin 58
Ferriter 11,55, xv,159	FitzEdmund 121	FitzJames xvi	Flaherty 59, 159
Mac Fheorais 55	Fitzell 56, 116	FitzJohn 18,57, 135, 153	Flahive 59
O' Fiaca 62	Fitzelle 159	FitzJohn xiv	O' Flaiteamain 58
O' Fiaie 60	FitzErin 56	Fitzmaurice 2,17,11, 51,58.	Flaitim 59
Mac Fiarais 87	FitzErin xxiii	FitzMaurice xi,xii, xvi,119	Flanagan, 59
O' Fidgeallaig 54	Fitzgerald 18-9,56-7, 135,153	Fitzmaurice 155	O' Flannabra 59
Field 55	Fitzgerald 159	Fitzmaurice 159	O' Flannagain 59
Figgis 55	Fitzgerald 56 arms illus.	Fitzmaurice, 162	Flannery 59
Finaghty 54, 55	Fitzgerald, E. 122	FitzMaurice 30 -Ballykealy	O' Flanngaile 59
Finch 55, 159	Fitzgerald, J. 164	Fitzmaurice, xxiv Baron	O' Flavey 14
Mac Fineen 55, 139	Fitzgerald, 162 Jas.	Fitzmaurice, 34 Col.	Flavin 58-9
Finn 55	Fitzgerald, 162 John	Fitzmaurice, 159 Francis	Fleete xiv, 59
Mac Finn 95	Fitzgerald, 138 Julia	Fitzmaurice 58 L'ndsd'wne	Fleete xvii-B
O' Finn 55	Fitzgerald, 162 Knight of	FitzMaurice xxiii Lord	Fleetwoods 152 & Watkins
Mac Finneen 56,159	Fitzgerald, 117 Lady E.	Fitzmorrice 159	Fleming 59
Mc FINNEEN 159	Fitzgerald, 31 Lord T.	Fitzmorrish 159	(le) Fleming 59
Mac Finneen xvii forces	Fitzgerald, 38 Lucy	Fitzmorriss 159	Flemyng 59
Finnegan, 56	Fitzgerald, 26, 98 Mary	FitzNicholas 11	Fletcher 59
Finnerty 56	Fitzgerald, 35 Maurice	FitzOtho 58	Fletcher xvii-B
O' FINNERTY 159	Fitzgerald of 146 Meenascarty	FitzPatrick 58	Fletcher 121 /Preste
Mac Finnin of 136 Artulihie	Fitzgerald, 151 Thomas	Fitzpatrick, xxiii D.E.	Flinn 59
Finnucane 56	Fitzgerald, 162 W. N. F.	FitzPierce 119	O' Floin 59
Mac Finnucane 159	Fitzgeralds 91, 104	FitzRhys 127	Mag Floinn 67
Fintan 54	Fitzgeralds - xii McCarthys	Fitzsimmons 57	Florette 59
Finucane 56	FitzGibbon 56,159	FitzSimon 56	Flower 59
O' Fionnacta 54-6	FitzGriffin 58	Fitzsimon xxiii	Floyd 159
O' Fionnagain 56	Fitzharris 159	FitzStephen xi,xii,... viii	Flyming 59
Fiontain 54	FitzHenry 17, 104, 159	FitzSymon 56	O FLYNE 159
Fisher 56	FitzHenry, viii Meiler	FitzSymons 56	Flynn 59
Fisher, Fanny xxiii	Fitzherbert 159	Fitzthomas 56-8,	O' Flynn, Fr. xxiv
Fisher, xxiii Lydia		Fitzwalter 159	Flynn of 116 Ballyvelly
O' Fitceallaig 55		FitzWilliam 58	O' Fogartaig 59
Fitgerald, J. 162		Fitzwilliams xiv	Fogarty 59
Fitz xxiii Maurice		FIZZELL 159	O' Foillide 67
FitzAnthony viii, 56, 57			Foley 59, 159
FitzAucher 49			O' Foley 159
FitzAuger 49			Foley, E. H. 162
FitzAunger 49			Foley family 112 at Anglont
			Foley, Jas., 162
			Foran 59

Forbes Castle *117*
Forde *59*
Forest *60*
Forest *xvii-B*
Forest, Sir *xiii* Anthony
Fornan *60*
Fort Wayne *47*
Fosberry *60*
Fosbery, Mr. *162*
Foulkes *60*
Foulkes *xvii-B*
Foundes *xiv, 60*
O FOWLUE *159*
Fox *60*
Foy, O'Fiaie *60*
France, to *ix*
Francis *60*
Franciscan *xxiii* annals
Franks of *38* Dublin
Fraser, J. *xxiii*
Fraser, S. *140*
Frasier *60*
Frawlcy *60*
Frazer *60*
O' Freagaile *60*
Freeman *60*
(de) Freins *60*
French *60*
French Army *96*
Frewan *60*
Friend *60*
Friseal *60*
Friuin *60*
Frizelle *60*
Froude, J. A. *xxiii*
Fry *60*
O' Fuartain *59*
Fuedal *ix* System
Fuller *11, 61, 117*
Fuller *159*
Fuller *xvii-B*

Fuller Arms *60*
Fullerton *61*
Fyfe *62*
Gabriel *62*
Gabriel *xvii-B*
O' Gadra *63*
Gaffney *62*
Gage *62*
Mac Gailey *62*
(de) Gaillide *62*
Gaine *62*
Gainor *63*
O' Gairbit *62*
O' Galain *62*
Gallagher *62*
O' Gallcobair *62*
Galleghor *159*
Gallen *62*
Gallerus *151* Castle
Gallivan *62, 159*
Gallway *xix, 99*
GALLWAY *159*
Gallwey *62*
Gallwey, *162* Edw.
Gallwey, T. *xxiii*
Galvin *62, 159*
O' Galvin *159*
Galway *53*
Galwey *xix*
Galwey, M. *162*
O' Gamna *62*
Gander *2*
Gandsey *62*
Gannon *62*
Gannon, N. *xxiii*
O' Gaoitin *63, 71*
O' Garbain *66*
Garrett, T. *119*
O Garvan *159*
Garvey *62, 159*
Mac Garvey *159*
Gavan *62*

Gavey *63*
Gaynor *63*
Geahan *63*
O' Gealbain *62*
Geaney *159*
Geany *63, 71*
O' Gearain *63, 71*
Geary *63*
Mac Gee *63*
Geehan *63*
O' Geibinn *62*
Genney *66*
Gennis *65*
Gennys *65*
Gentleman *65* Arms
Gentleman *63, 159* Bal'yhorg'n
Gentleman, *162* G.
Mac Geoghegan *138*
Geraldine *63*
Geraldines *57*
Geraldines *xxiii*
Geraldino *57*
Geran *63*
GERRALD *159*
Mac Gib *63*
Mac Gibbon *63*
O' Gibealla *63*
Gibson *63*
Gibson *xvii-B*
Mc Gil'ycud'y *xxiv*
Mac Gil'ycud'y *xxiii* papers
Gilbeart *63*
Gilbert *63*
Giles *63*
Mac Gilgoddy *xvii* forces
Gill *63*
Mac Gill *63*
Gillacoddy *64*
Mac Gillacoddy *64*

Mac Gillicd'y *xvii* forces
Mac Gillicuddy *91,.. 143*
Mac Gillicuddy *159*
Mc Gillicuddy *ix, 159*
Mac Gillicutty *51*
Gilliesaght *93*
Mac Gillycuddy *64, 159*
Mac Gillycuddy *65* arms.
M' Gillycuddy, *163* The
Mac Gillycuddy's *64* Castle
Mac Gillycuddy's *64* Reeks
Gilmour *64*
Mc Gilsacoddys *64*
Giney *66*
Mac Ginley *65*
Mac Ginn *65*
Ginnaw *65*
Ginney *66*
Ginnis *65-6*
Ginnis *xvii-C*
Ginnis's *119*
Mac Giobuin *87*
Mac Giolla *63*
Mac Giolla Eain *90*
Mac Giolla *64* Mocuda
Mac Giolla *64* Muire
Mac Giolla *69* Riabaig
Mac Giolladuinn *72*
O' Gionnain *62*
Girvan *66*
Giunings *66*
Giunings *xvii-B*
O' Glaimin *66*
O' Glaisne *63*
Glanbehy *156* Castle

Glandore, 66 Earl of	Goodlake 68	O' Greefa 70	Gul 68
GLANVILL 159	Goodman 68	Green xvi, 69	Gun 72
O' Glasain 66	Goodwin 68	green & tans 193	Gun Family xv
Glavin 66, 159	Goold 68	Mac Gregor 69	Gun of 155 Ploverhill
O' Glavin 66	Gordon 68	Mac Gregor xxiii	
Glazier 66	Gorges, Mary xxiv	Gregory 69, 159	Gun, T. G. 162
O' Gleasain 66	Gorham 68, 99	Gregory 82, 135 Castle	Gun, Town. 155
Gleason 66	Gorham xvii-C		Gun, W. 162
O' GLEASON 159	Gorham xvii-B	Greville xvii	Gunn 72, 159
Gleasur 66	Gorings 23, 32	Mac Grevy 70	Gunning 72
Gleasure 66	Gorman 68	Grey xviii	Guppy's xix
Gleeson 66	Goss 68	Grey xvii-B	Gurnett 72
Glissane 66	Mac Gotraid 67	Grey(s) 9, 70	Gynes 65
Gloster 66, 159	Mac Gough 68	Grice 70, 120	O h Uaitne 69
Glover 66	Gough, Jos. 162	O GRIFFEN 159	Habbart 72
Glynn 67	Gould 68	Griffin xix, 70, 159	Habbert 72
Mac Glynn 67	Gould xvii-B	O' Griffin 70	Hackett 72
Goddard 67	Goulding 67-8	Griffiths 70	O' HAGARTY 159
Godding 67	Gouran 68	Grinson 70	Mac Haiceid 72
Godfrey 67, 98, 159	Mac Govern 69	O' Griobta 70	(de) Hal 72
	Mac Gowen 136	O' Griobtain 69	Hale 72
Godfrey 137, 162	Grace, Gras 69	O' Griobtha 70	Hale xvii-B
Godfrey xvii-C	O' Grada 69	Grogan 70	Hall, de Hal 72
Godfrey xvi family	Grady 69, 159	Gromail 71	Hall, S.C. xxiii
	O' GRADY 159	Groome 70	Hallaran 73
Godfrey of 117 Kenmare	Graham 69	Groome xvii-B	O' Hallaran 73
	O' Grainne 69	(le) gros, R. 18, 58	Hallett 72
Godley 67	Grainseir 69	(Le) Grosse xi	Halley 72
Godolphin 67	(De) Grandison 92	Grover 70	Hallidan 72
Godolphin xvii-B	Granfield 69	Groves 71, 159	Halliden 72
Godson 67	Granger 69	O' Gruagain 70	Hallinan 72
Goff 67	Grant 69	Grummell 71	Hallisey 73
Goff, Jos. 162	Granville 52, 69	Guaine 71	Hallissey 73
Gofton 67	Gras 69	Guare 71	Hallissey 159
Goggin 67, 116, 159	Mac Grath 69	Guerin 71	Hallissy 73
	Graves 69	Guihan 71	HALLISSY 159
O' Goidin 68	Graves, A.P. xxiv	Guiheen 71	O' Halloran 73
O' Goillide 68	Graves, Dr. 79	Guinaw 71	Halloron 73
Gold 159	Gray 69	Guinell 71	Halluran 73
Golden 67, 159	Gray, Dan. 40, 139	O' Guinide 71	Halpin 73
Mac Goldrick 67	O' Greacain 69	Guinies 65	Halsey xiv
Goode 68	Greaney 159	Guinis 65	O' Hamailltin 73
Gooding 68	Greany 69	Guinness 65	HAMBERY 159
Gooding xvii-B	GREANY 159	Mac Guire 71	Hamilton 73

Hammond 73	Harran 75	Healy 76, 87, 160	HERLIHY 160
Hampton 74, 81	Harrington 75, 160	O HEALY 160	O' Herlihy 78
Hampton xvii-B	Harrington 27 clan	Heanne 76	O' Hery 73
Hamptson 74		Heaphy 76	Hetreed 78
O HANAFANE 159	Harris 75	Heard 76	Hewson 78
Hanafin 74, 159	Harrison 75	Heardinman 76	Hewson, G. 162
Hancock 74	Harrison xvii-B	Hearnden 76	Hewson, Geo. 162
Hand 74	Harrowe xiv, 75	HEERD 160	Hewson, J.F. 74
HANIFIN 159	Harrowe xvii-B	O' Heerin 19, 53, xxii, 134	Hewson, 162 Miss
Haniford 74	Hart(e) 2, 75		
Hanley 74	Hart families 96	Heffernan 76	Hewson, 162 Rev. F.
HANLON 159	Hart Harte xvii-B	Hegarty 76	Hewson, 162 Rev. R.
Hannafin 74	Harte, L. 79	Hehir 76	
Hannon 74	Harte, Mahoney 162	Heily xix	Hewsons 99
Mac Hannraoi 75	Hartigan 75	Helliwell 76, 146	Hickey 78
Hanover 74	Hartley 75	Hempenstall 77	Hickie 78
Hanrahan 74	Hartnett 75, 117, 160	Henchy 77	Hickie, Wm. 162
Hansard 74		Hendericken 77	Hickman 78
Hanswell 74	O Hartnett 160	Henderson 77	Hicks 78
Hara 74	Hartnett, Wm. 162	Henigan 77	Hicks xvii-B
O' Hara, Cath. 99		Hennessy 77	Hickson 16, 38, 79, 160
Harbord 77-8,	Hartney 75	Hennigan 77	
Harbourne 74	Hartop 75	Henry 77	Hickson Arms 77
Hardier xvi, 74	Hartopp, e. B. 162	Henry II xii, 58	Hickson, 162 Capt. R. M.
Hardiman 76	Harty 75	Heraghty 77	
Harding 74, 160	Harty 160	Herald's xix Visitation	Hickson, M. xxiii
Harding, Rd. 133 granted land	Harvey 76		Hickson, R. 162
	Hassett 76, 160	Herbert 77-8,	Hickson, R. A. 162
Hardy 74	Hassett, Col. xvi	Herbert 29, 35, 82	Hickson, R. C 162
Hare 74	Hastings 76	Herbert xiii, xiv, xvii, 160	Hickson, Rev. 122
Harenc(?), 162 H. B.	Hatheron 76		Hickson, Rg. 162
	Hattery 76	Herbert, A. 162	Hickson, Wm. 162
Hargrave 74	Hawkin 76	Herbert Arms 77	O' Hicky 78
Harley 74	Hawney 76	Herbert, xii Edward	Hifle 79
Harman 75	Hayden 76		Higgins 79
Harman, 144 John	Hayes 76	Herbert, 162 Henry	Hill 79
Harman, T. 162	Hayslip 76	Herbert, Lord 142	Hillee 79
Harms 75	Haywood 76	Herbert, 162 Rev. E.	Hilliard 79
Harnett 75, 160	O' Hea 160		Hilliard 160
Harnett of 132 Sandville	Headley 76	Herberts 5	Hilliard, B. 162
	Headley xxiii estate	Herberts of 29 Muckross	Hilliard, Eliz. 103
Harnett, Wm. 162		HERBERTT 160	Hilliard, G. 162
Harold 75, 160	Headley, 156, 162 Lord	Hercules xiv	Hilliard, H. 162
Harraghton 75			Hilliard, J. 162

Hilliard of *132* Listrum	Hourighan *80*	Hussey *x v* family	Jakeman *84*
Hilliards *99*	Housaye *82*	Hussey, Joan *119*	James *84*
HILLY *160*	Howard *80, 84, 160*	Hussey of *38* Edenburn	James I I *130*
Hinchy *77*	Howatson *80*		James I I, *148* to France
Hingey *79*	Howe *80*	Hussey, Sam *123*	Jameson *84*
Hipwell *79*	O HOWRANE *160*	Hussey, Sam *162*	Jarlath, Fr. *xxiii*
Histon *79*	Hoyle, C. *xxiii*	Hussey, W., *107* estate of	Jeffcott *8, 84*
Hitchcock *79*	Hubbort *80*		Jeffcott *xvii-C*
Hoar *80*	Huddlestone *81*	Husseys' land *118*	Jeffcott *xvii-B*
Hoar Hoare *xvii-B*	Huddlestone *xvii-B*	HUSTON *160*	Jeffers *84*
HOARD *160*	Hudleston, I. *90*	Hutchinson *83*	Jeffreys *84*
Hoare *xix, 80*	Hudson *81, 160*	Hyde *83*	Jennings *66, 84*
Hobbins *80*	Hudson, E. *162*	Hyde, in *83* America	Jenynges *66*
Hodgins, *119* Mary	Huggard *81*		Jerm *84*
	Huggard, *154* Eliz.	Hynes *83*	Jess *84*
Hodson, *98* Meriel		Hynton *83*	Johnson *84*
	Huggard, *162* Stephen	Hynton *xvii-B*	Johnston *84*
Hoffman *80*		IL. Auto. *6* Company	Jones *xvi, 85, .. . 116*
Hogan *80*	Mac Hugh *81*		
Hoibeard *72*	Hughes *xvi, 81*	Mac Ilhaney *102*	
Holbrow *80*	Huihir *81*	Inchiquin, *viii* Co. Clare	Jones *xvii-B*
Holland *80, 160*	Humphreys *81*		Jones of *38* Moneyglass
Holley *160*	Humpton *xvii, 81*	Mac Inerney *83*	
Holloran *73*	Hunt *81*	Ingoldsby's *156*	Jordan *85*
Holly *xiii, xvii, .. 80*	(Le) hunt *90*	Innisfallen *26*	Joy *85, 135*
	(le) Hunt, Col. *82*	Mac Intosh *83*	Joy *xvii-B*
Holly *160*	(Le) Hunte *40*	Mac Intosh *xxiii*	Joyce *85*
HOLMES *160*	Hunter *81*	Mac Ionnractaig *52*	Julian *85*
Holt *80*	Huolahan *xix*	Ireland, to *xvii*	Julian, Sam *162*
Holyoake *80*	HURD *160*	Ireton *83*	Justice *160*
Hooks *80*	Hurley *27, 81, 116*	Irish Brigade *51, 96, 138*	Kanturk *166* Castle
Hooper *80*	Hurley, *162* Conway		
Hooper *xvii-B*		Irish Forces *xvii*	Kavanagh *85*
Hopgood *80*	Hurley, John *162*	Irish in *viii* battle	Kavanaugh *85*
Horan *80, 160*	Hurley of *9* Fenit		Kay *86*
HORD *160*		Irish *124* Monthly	Mac Kay *85*
(de) Hore *17*	O' Hurley, T. *81*		Kealiher *45, 86*
(le) Hore *80*	Hurly *70, 81*	Irwin *84*	Mc KEANAN *160*
Horgan *80, 160*	Hurly, Alice *14*	Isham *51, 84*	Keane *85*
Horwick *80*	Hurly arms *83*	Isham *xvii-B*	KEANE *160*
O' Hosey *82*	Hurrell *81*	Ivers *80, 84*	Kearney *85*
HOSKINS *160*	Hussey *78, 82-3, 160*	Jackson *84*	Kearny *85*
Houlihan *80*		Jackson *xvii-B*	Keasit *85*
HOULIHAN *160*	Hussey, Edw. *162*	Jacobite *xxiii* list	Keating *85, 160*
			Keay *86*

Kedihan 86
Mac Kee 86
O' Keefe 86, 160
Keeffe, 86, 160
Keely 86
O' KEESHAN 160
KEITH 160
Keliher 86
KELLEHER 160
O' Kelleher 160
Kelliher 45, 86, 160
Kelly xiv, 86
Kelly, Dan. 139 killed by
Kelly, H. xxiii
O' Kelly, P. xxiii
Kellys 90 transplanted
Kelter 86
Mac Kemmie 86
O' Kenealy 86
Kenmare, 162 Earl of
Kenmare, 86 Lady
Kenmare, 114 Protestant
Kenna 86
Mac Kenna 86, 160
Mc KENNA 160
Kennedy 86
O' KENNEDY 160
Kennedy, 123 Sarah
Kennelly 86
Kenney 86
Kennington 86
Kenny 86
Keogh 87
Keough 87
Kerin 87, 160
O Kerins 160
Kerrigan 87
Kerrisk 87, 160
Kerry Castle 155

Kerry Eagle xxiii Ballad
Kerry 79, 125 Magazine
Kerry People, 131 editor of
Kerrys Army xvii
Mac Kessy 87
(de) Keting 85
Kevane 87, 160
Kiarraide xxii
Mac Kibbon 87
Kidd 87
Kiely 87
Kifee xix
Killaha 44 Castle
Killaha 42 Castle, illus
Killarney xxiii sources
Killian 87
O' Killian 87
Killorglin 57 Castle
King xiv, 87
King from 29 MacConroi
King, Giles xvii
King, Henry xx
King Henry xi II
King Henry xiv VIII
King, J. xviii
King John viii
King, 162 Nicholas, M.
Kingston 87
Kinnealy 86
Mac kintosh 83
KINVETON 160
Kirby 87, 160
Kirwan 87
Kissane 88, 160
Kitchener 88
Kitson, G. L. 162

Klincke 88
Knight 88, 160
Knight xvii-B
Knight of 88 Kerry
Knightley 88
Knightly 88
Knights of xxiv Kerry
Knights 57 Templars
KYERY 160
(De) La Cousa 82
(De) la Huse 82
(de) la Roche 128
Lacey 88
O' Lactnain 93
Lacy 88
(de) Lacy 88
Lacy, T.H. xxiii
Ladden 88
Laid 88
Laide 88
O' Laidig 91
O' Laidin 88
O' Laigin 94
Lake 88
Lally 88, 108
O' Lalor xv, 160
Lalours 90
Lamb 88
Lambert 88
Lander 89
Landers 89, 160
Landers of 29 Keel
Landon 89
Landsdown xxiii Bibliothec
Lane xxii, 89, 91
Langan 89
Langford 89
Langford, 124 Ann
Langford of 100 Keel

Lansdowne, 162 Marquess of.
O' Laoghain 91
(De) Lap 39
O' Lapain 39
Larcom, T. xxiii
Larkin 89
Larmer 89
Latchford 89, 116
Latimer 89, 160
Lauder 89
Laulors 90 transplanted
(De) Laundre 89
Lavery 89
O' Lavery, Capt. 125
Lavin 89
Laweless 89
Lawlee 89
Lawler xx
Lawless 89
Lawlor 90
Lawlor, D. 162 Shine
Lawlor in 48 Duel
Lawlor, 162 Martin
O' Layne 92
le Dillon 41
le Fleming 59
le Gros, 18, 58 Raym.
Le Grosse xi, xii
le Hore 80
Le hunt 90
le Hunt, Col. 82
Le Hunte 40
le Marshall 98
le Palmer, Sir 115 Ralph
Leade 88, 90
Leader 90
LEAGHY 160
Leahy 90, 160
O' LEAHY 160

Leahy Arms 90	Leslie, R. 163	Lombard, 33 Mary	O LYNE 160
Leahy, Col. 162 Arthur	Lett, Anne 100	Long 93	Lynne 94
Leahy, John 162 White	Letters 92	Long, J. xxiii	Lynne xvii-C
	Leventhal 92	O' Longaig 93	Lynne xvii-B
Leahy, Mary 16	Levison 92	O' Longain 89	Lynnes of 153 Essex
Leahy- 154 White fam.	Lewin xiv	Looney 93	Lyons 94, 160
	Lewis 92	Lord 93	Lyons Castle 91
Leake 90	Leyne 160	O' Lordain 93	Macassy 94
Mac Lean 90	O' Leyne 91-2, xxii	Lordan 93	Macauley 115
Leane 91, 160		LOUE 160	Macintosh 94
O' Leannain 92	Leyne, Jerh. 163	Loughlin 93	Mack 4
Leary xx, 91, 160	O' Liatain 91	Mac Loughlin 93	Mackassy 94
O' Leary xx, 160	O' Liathan 94	O' Loughlin 93	Mackessy 94
O' Leary, A., 91 dirge	Lick Castle 92	Mac Loughlin, 99 Avis	Mackey 94
	Liddane 92		Mackintosh 83
O' Leary, 119 Phyllis	Limerick, viii from	Loughnane 93	Macrehan xi
Ledman 91	Limerick, 89 John	Lover, S. xxiii	O' Madagain 95
Ledmon 91		Lovett 93, 160	Madden 95
Lee xx, 91	LINANE 160	Lowden 93	Madden 191 househldrs
Leech 91	O' Linchy 94	Lowe 93	Madget 95
Leehey 160	Lindesay 92	O' Luain 88	Madgett xx, 95
Leen 91	Lindon 92	O' Luasaig 93	
Leeser 91	Lindsay 92	O' Lubaig 93	Madgett, N. 191
Leeser, J. xvii	LINNANE 160	Luby 93	Madigan 95
Leeson 91	Linnegar xx	Luby, Cath. xxiii	Madigan 191
Lehane 91, 160	Lisack 93	Lucey 93, 160	Mag Guyn xvii forces
Mac Leish 91	Liscahane 69, 138 Castle	Lucid 93	
LENCY 160		Lucy 93	Magane 95
O LENCY 160	Listowel 58, 155 Castle	Ludlow 40	Magane 191
Lenihan 92		Mac Lugada 93	Magarthy, D. 138
Lennane 92	Listowel, 163 Earl of	Luiseid 93	Magee 63, 95
O' Lennon 160	Lloyd 93	Lumsden 93	Magee 191
Lentall 92	Lock 93	Lunham 94	Magill, 163 Capt. James
Lentall xvii-B	Locke 93	Lunney 94	
Mac Leod 92	Mac Loclainn 93	Lunny 94	Maginn 95
Mc Leod of 51 Galway	O' Loclainn 93	Lupton 94	Maginn 191
	Lodge xii peerage	Lyden 94	Magrath 69
Mac Leoid 92		Lyn 94	Maher 95
Leonard 92, 160	Loftie, Rev. xxiii	Lynch 94	Maher 191 househldrs
Leonard, Dan 162	Logue 93	Lynch 189 households	
Leonard, 163 Rev. S. B.	O' Loideain 92		Mahon 191
	O' Loinn 94	Lyndon 94	Mac Mahon 95
Leslie 3, 92, 160	Lombard 93	Lyne 94, 160	Mahoney xx
Leslie, J. xxiii	Lombard, D. 163		O' Mahoney 96-7,

235 Names Arranged Alphabetically without the O' or Mac Prefix 235

Mahoney, *xxiii* Agnes
Mahoney, D. *57, 83*
Mahoney *ix, 21,* Dromore *38, 63*
Mahoney *191* households
Mahoney of *150* Kilmorna
O' Mahoney of *43* Munster
O' Mahoney's *46*
Mahoneys *xi*
Mahony *96, 160*
Mc MAHONY *160*
O' MAHONY *160*
Mahony, *163* David
Mahony, *163* Edw.
Mahony, *163* Eliza
Mahony, *163* Geo. P. Gun
Mahony, *163* John
mahony, *163* John H.
Mahony, *163* Kean
Mahony, *163* Kean
Mahony of *97* Brosna
Mahony of *97* Kilmorna
Mahony, P. *xxiii*
Mahony, *163* Richard
Mahony, T. *163* McD.
MAHOWNY *160*
Mac Maige *100*
O' Maille *97*
Main *97*
Mac Maine *97*
Mac Maine *193*
Maine River *viii*
O' Mainin *98*

O' Mainnin *98*
Mair *97*
Malachy *97*
Malachy *193*
Malley *97*
Malley *193* househldrs
Malone *97*
Malone *193* househldrs
Maloney *102*
Malvey *97*
Malvey *193*
Manaanan *193*
O' Manacain *102*
Manaher *97*
Manaher *193*
Mangan *98*
MANGAN *160*
Mangan *193*
O' Mangan *160*
Mannering *98*
Mannering *xvii-B*
Manning *98*
Mannion *98*
Mannix *98, 160*
Mansell *98*
Mansfield *98, 160*
Mac Manus *98*
O' Maolalaid *88*
O' Mara of *29* Milltown
Mareschall *98*
Marisco *98*
Maroney *106*
Marshall *xvi, 91, 98, 160*
(le) Marshall *98*
Marshall, R. *163*
O' Martain *99*
Martel *99*
Martelli *99*
Martin *99*
Martin *xvii-B*
Mason *99-100,*

Mason *xvii-B*
Mason, J. *163*
Mason, James *99*
Mason, *163* Susan
Mason, W. *163*
Massereene *xxiii*
MASSY *160*
Mathews *100*
Matson *100*
Matthews *160*
Maunsell *100*
Mac Maurice *100*
Mac Maurice *217*
Mawe *100*
Mawe, Dr. *100*
Maxwell *100*
May *100*
Maybury *100, 160*
Maybury, *163* Geo., M. D.
Maybury, J. *164*
Maybury, *163* Thos.
Maybury, *163* Wm.
Maynard *100*
O' Meacair *95*
Meade *100*
O' Meadra *101*
Meagher *95, 101*
Meahan *101*
Meara *101*
O' Meara *95*
Meehan *101*
Meehan, C.P. *xxiii*
Meek *101*
Mehigan *101*
Melbourne, *124* city of
Melville *101*
Mercer *xvi, 101*
Meredith *3, 101*
Meredith *xvii-C*
Meredith *xvii-B*

Meredith, H. *149*
Meredith, *97* Margt.
Meredith of *52* Dicksgrove
Meredith, R. *163*
Mernagh *101*
Meskill *101*
Meyer, K. *xxiii*
Mac Michael *101*
Mac Michael *217*
O' Midir *97*
O' Midir *193*
Midleton, *13* Visc.
Mihigan *101*
Mildmays *7*
Miles *102*
Mac Miles *110*
Milner *102*
Milward *102*
Minard *90, 131* Castle
Minchin *102*
Mingane *102*
Minogue *102*
Mitchell *102*
Mochlehayn *102*
Molahiffe *57* Castle
Moleyns *109*
(De) Moleyns *38*
Molloy *102*
Moloney *102*
Molony *102*
Molyneaux *102*
Monahan *102*
O' Mongain *98*
Monighan *108*
Monson *102*
Monteagle *16*
Monteagle, *163* Lord
Montgomery *102*
Montgomery *xiii* Castle

Mooney 102	Morley 200 househldrs	Mullally 108	Mac Namara 111
Moor 103		Mullane 109	Mac Namara 217 ho'sehldrs
Moore 103	Morly 106	Mac Mullen 109	
O' Moore 34, 160	Moroney 106	Mullens 109	Nammock 111
Moore 194 househldrs	Moroney 200 househldrs	Mullens xvi family	Nangle 111
			Nash 111
Moores 90 transplant'd	Morony 106	Mullens of 14 Burnham	Nash, C. F. 163
	Morphy 106		Nash, Sarah 153
Moorhead 103	Morphy, 163 Edw.	Mulligan 109	Natt 111
O' Moors xv		Mullineux 160	Natt xvii-B
Morahain 103	Morphy 200 househldrs	Mullins 9, 57, 109	Naughton 111
Morahain 194		Mullins of 38, 127 Burnham	Naylor 111
Moran 103	Morrice xv, 107		
Moran xxiii	Mac MORRICE 160	Mullis 109	O' Neal 112
O' MORAN 160	Mc MORRICE 160	Mulquinn 110	O' Neale 112
Moran 194 househldrs	Morris 107, 160	Mulvehill 45, 110	Neales views 26
	Morris xvii-B	Mulvihill 110	Nealon 111
O' Morda 103	Mac Morris 103	MULVIHILL 160	O' Nedi 160
More 103	Mc MORRISH 160	O' Mulvihill 160	Neenan 111
O' MORE 160	Morrison 108	Munchas 110	O' Neigill 113
Morgan 103	Morrissey 108	Mundy, Maj. 163 Gen.	O' Neil family 112 at Anglont
Morgan 194 househldrs	Morrogh xx, 7, 8, . . 108		
		Munro 110	O' Neil rebells xii
Morgell 103	Morrogh, W. 163	O' Murcada 110	Neilan 111
Morgell 194 househldrs	Morrogh-Bernard of Faha 53	Murdoch 110	Neill 112, 160
		Murdock 110	Mac Neill 112
Moriarty 104-6, 160	Moryson xiii	Murhill 110	O' Neill 32, 112, 116
O' Moriarty 160	Mosley 108	O' Murnain as Warren 152	
Moriarty, 163 Anne,	Moylan xx, 108		O' Neills defeat 93 McLoughlin
	Moynihan xx, 108, . . 160	Murnane 110	
Moriarty 104 arms		Murphy xx, 110, 160	Neilson 112
	Muckross 26		Neligan 112
Moriarty, 95, 98, 121 Bishop	Muckross xxiv Abbey	O MURPHY 160	O' Neligan 160
		Murray 110	Neligan, J. 163
Moriarty xxiv Bishop	Mucross xxiii Abbey	Murrie, 105 (English)	Neligan, W. 163
Moriarty, 105 branches	Mug xvi descendants		Nelligan 112
		Muschamp 110	Nellson 112
Moriarty 194 households	O' Muiray 54	Musgrave 110	Nelson 112
	Muirlihy 108	Muster Roll xiv	Neville 112
Mac Moriarty 104 Kerry	Mulally 108	Myaghe 110	Nevin 112
	Mulcahy 108	Myers 110	New Haven 47
Moriarty vii LochLein	Mulcare 108	Myles 110	New York 9, 108
Moriartys 105 Hotel	Mulchinock 108, 160	Nagle 111-12.	New York, 126 Reilly of
	Mulchinock xxiii	(de) Nais 111	
Morley 106	Mulchinock, 163 Edw.	Nally 111	New Zealand ix, 6
		Mac Nally 111	NEWLIN 160

237 Names Arranged Alphabetically without the O' or Mac Prefix 237

Newspapers *xix* listed
Newton *38, 112*
O' Niallain *111*
Nicholas *112*
Nicholls, M, *149* baptised
Nichols *112*
Nihell *32*
Nihill *112-13.*
Nihill *xvii-B*
Nihilly *112*
O' Nihilly, Rory *151*
Mac Niocoil *112*
Nixon *112*
Noble *112*
(de) Nogla *111*
Nolan *113*
Nolan of London *113*
Noonan *113*
Norman knights *xi*
Norreys *113*
Norris *113*
Norris *xvii-B*
Northcott *xvi, 113*
Norton *113*
Norval *113*
Nott *113*
Noughane *113*
Noughton *113*
O' Nuallain *113*
Nugent *113*
Nurse *113*
Nye *113*
Nyle *113*
Oaks *113*
Oatts *113*
Offerba *xvi*
ogam *xvi*
Ogg *113*
Mac Oisin *36*
Mac Oitir *31*
Oliver *113*

Oliver, Maj. *163*
Oliver, R. S. *163*
Oloynsig *94*
Onaght *14*
O'Donoghue
Orange Party *114*
Orkney, Earl of *163*
Orm'thwaite Lord *163*
Ormsby *113*
ORMSBY *160*
Ormsby, A., heir *149*
Orpen *114, 160*
Orpen, R. H. *163*
Orpen, Sir Rd. *163*
Ortelius Map *147*
Ortelius Map illus. *iv*
Osbaldiston *114*
Mac Osticin *31*
Otnonia *114*
Otway, C. *xxiii*
Ovens *114*
Mc OWEN *160*
Owens *xvi, 114*
Ozzard *114*
Page *xiv, 114*
Page *xvii-B*
Pails *114*
Paine *117*
Palatine families *xvi*
Palmer *115, 160*
Palmer *xvii-B*
Palmer arms *115*
Palmer, Caleb *163*
Palmer, E. Orpen *163*
Palmer, John *163*
Palmer, L. *110*
Palmer, M. *75*
Palmer of Ashgrove *114*

Palmer, R. *163*
(le) Palmer, Sir Ralph *115*
Panorma *115*
Papists list *xix*
Paradine *116*
Paris, France *15, 52*
Park *116*
Parker *116*
Parkes *116*
Parkinson *116*
Parr *116*
Parsons *116*
Partridge *116*
Patt *116*
Patterson *116*
Pattison *116*
Patwell *116*
Paul, Sir R. *163*
Paulin *116*
Payne *xvii-B*
Payne Paine *117*
Payne Paine *xvii-C*
Peacock *117*
Peacocke *117*
Pearson *117*
Pedestrian *xxiii*
Peet *117*
PEET *160*
Peet, Francis *163*
Peevers *117*
Pegum *117*
Pelham *117*
Pelham, Peter *117*
Pelican *117*
Pellican *117*
Pembroke *117*
penal laws *ix*
Pendergast *121*
Pendeville *121*
Pendred *118*
Pendred *xvii-B*
Peppard *118, 139*

Peppards at Cappa *118*
Pepys *118*
Pepys *xvii-B*
Pepys lands *82*
Periman *118*
Periman *xvii-B*
Perry *118*
Perryman *118*
Pery *118*
Petty *58, 118, 160*
Petty, Sir W. *xvi*
Petty, Sir W. *xxiv*
Petty, Wm. *xxiii*
Phaire *57, 118*
Phelan *118*
Phelips *118*
Philip *118*
Philips *118*
Philips *xvii-B*
Phillips *xiv*
Pickford *118*
Pierce *119*
(de) Pierce *119*
Mac Pierce 2 *17*
Piers *119, 160*
Pierse *119*
Pierse 2 *17*
Piersey, Miss *83*
Pierson *117*
Piggott *119*
Pigott *119*
Pilcher *119*
Pinchin *119*
(de) Pionbroc *117*
Plowman *119*
Pluinceid *120*
Plummer *33, 119*
Plunkett *xx, 120*
(de) Poer *121*
Poff *120*
Polard *120*
Pollard *116, 120*

Ponsonby *xv,xvi,9, 19,120*
PONSONBY *160*
Ponsonby *xvii-C*
Ponsonby, H. granted *138*
Ponsonby, T.; Thos. *70, 156*
Pope, W. *163*
Port *120*
(de) Portuil *122*
Potar *121*
Potter *121,160*
Pottinger *121*
Powell *121*
Power *xvi,98, 99, 121*
Power, H. *2*
Prendergast *121*
Prendeville *121*
(de) Prendeville *121*
Preste *xvii-B*
Preste, or Fletcher *121*
Price *xiv, 121*
Price, Dr. *66, 127*
Prince *xiv*
de Priondargas *121*
Prionnbiol *121*
Pris *121*
Prise *xiv*
Procter *121*
Proctor *121*
Proinseis *60*
Prosser *121*
Prossor *121*
Protestant Religion *ix*
Public Record Off. *xix*
Purcell *xx, 122*
Purcell, expelled by *92*
Purdon *122*
Purdon, Symon *29*

Pursell *122*
Purtill *122*
Mac Quade *122*
Mac Quaide *122*
Quane *122*
Queen Anne *xvi*
Queen Eliz. *xii,xiii xiv*
Quill *35, 122*
O' Quill *160*
Quill, Eliz. *163*
Quillinan *122*
Quilter *123*
Quin *123*
Quinlan *123*
QUINLAN *160*
O' QUINLAN *160*
Quinliven *123*
Quinn *123*
Mac Quinn *123*
Mc QUINN *160*
Quinnell *123*
Quinty *123*
Quirk *123,160*
Quirke *123*
QUIRKE *160*
Quit rent *xxiii*
Rae *124*
Mac Rae *32, 124*
Rae, Edw. *163*
Rae, Langford *163*
Rae, Wm. L. *163*
Rael *124*
Mac Ragnaill *125-6*
Rahilly *126,160*
O' Rahilly *44, 124*
O' Rahilly dies in Dublin *110*
O' Rahilly, E. *91*
O' Rahilly, E. *xxiv*
O' Rahilly of Slieve *124*
O' Raigue *126*

Railway, G. S. and W. *163*
Mac Rait *124-5*
Mac Raith *124*
Raleigh *xvii, 125*
Raleigh *xvii-B*
Ramage *125*
Randal *125*
Randal *xvii-B*
Randall *xiv, 125*
Randle *125*
Randles *125*
Ratoo Castle *155*
Rattray *125*
Rawleigh *125*
Rawlins *125*
Ray, *125*
Mac ray *32*
Raycroft *125*
Raymond *xvi, 125,160*
Raymond *xvii-C*
Raymond, Anne *52*
Raymond, Anne *163*
Raymond, Frances. *153*
Raymond, Geo. *163*
Raymond, James *163*
Read *126*
Reading *xvi, 125*
Ready *126*
Reagan *126*
Reany *126*
Reardon *128*
Reaves *126*
Records on Co. Kerry *xviii*
Reddin *126*
Redin *126*
Redmon *126*
Redmond *126*
Reed *126*

Reen *126,160*
(ap) Rees' *127*
Reeves, *126, 130*
Regan, *126*
Mac rehan *xi*
Reid *126*
Reidy *126,160*
Reilly, *126*
O' Reilly *124*
O' Reilly's poem *70*
Relf *126*
Relihan *126*
RELIHAN *160*
Research sources *xviii*
Restrick *126*
Revington *6, 126*
Reynolds, *126*
Rezin *126*
Rhys *121, 127*
Mac Riabaig *70*
O' Riabaig *124*
O' Riagan *126*
Rice *xvi, 121, 127,160*
Rice, Edw. *135*
Rice family *xv*
Rice, J. *164*
Rice, Justice *164*
Rice of Paris *152*
Rice, Steph. *61*
Mc RICHARD *160*
Richards *127*
Richardson *xvi, 127*
O RIEDY *160*
O' Rielly *126*
RIERDANE *160*
Riley *126*
Riney *127*
Ring *127*
Rinn *127*
O' Rinn *126-7,156*
Rinuccini *128*

Riordan *xx, 128,.. 160*
O' Riordan *160*
Ritzgerald, Rev. *162*
River Maine *viii*
Rly., G.S.W. *xxiv*
Roachford *128*
Mac Robert *151*
Roberts *128*
Robinson *128*
Robinson *xxiii*
ROCH *160*
Roche, *128*
Roche, Catherine *164*
Roche *131* confiscated
Roche, Fr. *35*
Roche, Redmond *164*
Roche, Redmond *164*
Roche, Stephen *164*
Rochfort, C. *124*
Rodd *128*
RODGERS *160*
Rodk. Dan. *xxiii*
Roe *xvii, 128*
Roe *xvii-B*
Roe, Miss. *29*
Rogers *128*
Rohan *128, 160*
Rokes, Simon *xiv*
Ronan *129*
O' Ronan, Wm. *51*
Ronayne *124, 129*
Rook *129*
Rooke *129*
Rookes *129*
Rookes *xvii-B*
Roome *129*
Rooney *129*
Roper *129*

O' Rorke, C. D. *163*
Rose *129*
Rosney *129*
Ross *129*
Ross Castle *43*
Round Towers *xxiv*
Rourke *129, 160*
O' Rourke *xx*
Rowan *129*
Rowan *xxiv*
O' Rowan *129*
Rowan, A.B. *xxiii*
Rowan, Archdeacon *125*
Rowan, Cherry *122*
Rowan, Dr. *79*
Rowan, Maj. *164*
Rowe *130*
Rowland *130*
ROYDY *160*
Roynane's Island *129*
Ruachtain *130*
Ruairc *129*
Rubin *130*
Rudd *130*
Ruddle *130*
Rumney *130*
RUMNY *160*
Rumsby *130*
Rusk *130*
Russell *xiv, 130*
Russia *14*
(de) Ruthyen *9*
Ruttle *130*
Rvoes, K. *29*
Ryan *130*
Ryan, Jas., M. D. *164*
Rycroft *130*
Rycroft *xvii-B*
Ryder *xiv, 130*
Ryder *xvii-B*

Ryeeves *130*
RYERDANE *160*
Ryeves *130*
Ryeves *xvii-B*
Ryeves, W. *52*
Ryle *131, 160*
Ryle, M.P. *xxiv*
Rynd, W. R. *164*
Sadler *131*
Sadler, Col. *82*
Sadlier *40*
Sampson, *131*
Samson *131*
Samsun *131*
San Francisco *47*
Sanders *131*
Sanders, Dr. *110*
Sandes *xxiv*
Sandes arms illus. *133*
Sandes, C. *5, 164*
Sandes, Geo. *164*
Sandes, L. *xvi*
Sandes, M. *164*
Sandes of Sallow Glen *131*
Sandes, Thos. *164*
Sandes, W. *164*
SANDFORD *160*
Sands *xvi, 160*
Sandys, D. *xv*
SANFORD *160*
Sankey *xvi, 131*
Sankey, Col. *151*
O' Saoraide *60*
Saunders *131*
Saunders, A. *164*
Saunders, Marshall *110*
Saunders, Rev. W. H. *164*
Savadge *131*
Savage *131*

Savin *131*
Sawers *131*
Sawyer *131*
Sawyer *xvii-B*
Sayers *131, 160*
Scaife *131*
Scanlan *132, 160*
O' Scanlan *xx, 160*
Scanlan, Maria *164*
O' Scanlan of Fusan *132*
SCANLON *160*
O' Scanlon *160*
O' Scannail *132*
Scannell *132, 160*
Scannlain *132*
O' Scannlain *132*
Scargill *132*
Scollard *132*
Scott *132*
Scott of Cahircon *3*
Sculles *132*
Scully *132*
O' Seadha *134*
Mac Seafraid *84*
Seaganstown *132*
Mac Seain *84*
Sealy *3, 132*
Sealy, Deborah *164*
Seambar *23*
Sears *132*
Seary *133*
Seaward *133*
Sedgewick *133*
Seekins *133*
Seever *133*
Segerson *xx, 133*
Segerson, Alice *27*
Seghrue *xiv, xx*
Segrue *xiv*
Selick *133*

Sellers *133*
Selles *134*
Mac Seoin *85*
Settlers *xiii, xvii*
Sewell *134*
O' SEXON *160*
Sexton *134*
Shade *134*
SHAGROE *160*
Shakelton *160*
Shanaghan *xx*
Shanahan *134, 160*
O' Shanahan *134*
Shanahan *201* househldrs
Shannon *134*
Shannon, B. *201*
Sharkey *134*
Sharkey *201*
Shaughnessy *134*
O' Shaughnessy *134*
Shaughnessy *201* househldrs
Shaw *134*
Shaw *201*
SHEA *160*
O' Shea *53-4, 134, 160, xvi*
O' Shea *206*
O' Shea *vii* banished
O' Shea, chief *xxii*
Shea, D. *116* schoolmast'r
Shea house- *201* holds
O' Shea, poem *133*
SHEAHAN *160*
Sheapallh *144*
Sheehan *134, 160*
O' Sheehan *160*
Sheehan *206* households
Sheehy *135, 160*
Mac Sheehy *xx, 85, 135, 160*

Sheehy 205 househldrs
Sheeres *135*
Sheeres, Wm. *205*
Sheldon *135*
Sheldon *205*
Shepherd *205*
Sheridan *135*
Sheridan *205*
SHEWELL *160*
Shiell *135*
Shiercliffe *135*
Shine *xx, 135, . . 160*
O' SHINE *160*
Shirley *135*
Short Castle *121*
Shortal *135*
Shortall *135*
Shortcliffe *135*
Shortcliffe *xvii-B*
Shortcliffe, *153* Anthony
Shortis *135*
Shorttliffe *160* (Shortcliffe?)
Shuel *135*
Shuell *135*
Shute *135*
Shyne, Denis *90*
Sigerson *133, 160*
Sigerson, G. *xxiv*
Sigurd *133*
Silies *135*
Silles *135*
Simms *136*
Simon *136*
Simons *xiv*
Simpson, R. *164*
Simpson, S. *164*
Sincox *136*
Singleton *136*
Sinnette *136*
O' Sionan *145*
O' Sionnaig *60*

Skiddy *xvi*
Skinger *136*
Skinner *136*
Skipworth *136*
Skipworth *xvii-B*
Slattery *136*
SLATTERY *160*
Sleath *136*
Sleator *136*
Sloan, Slone *136*
Smith *xi, 136*
Smith, alias *xiv* Warren
Smith, C. *xxiii*
Smith, Ed., *149* baptised
Smith, G.N. *xxiii*
Smith, *xiv* Richard
Smithworthe *136*
Smyth *136*
Somers *136*
Sources *xxiii*
Sources for *xviii* records
Southwell, *164* Visc.
Southworth *55* granted land
Spain, to *ix*
Spanish *viii* Armada
Sparks *136*
Speart *136*
O' Spellan *136*
Spencer *xiv*
Spenser *xvii*
Spicer *136*
Spillane *160*
O SPILLANE *160*
Spillane, D. *45, 136*
Spotswood *137*
Spotswood, *164* Mce, M. D.
Spratt *137*
Spratt *xvii-B*

Spratt, H. D. *xxiii*
Spread, C. *117*
Spring *xv, 137-8, 160*
Spring *xvii-C*
Spring *xvii-B*
Spring, A. *52, 130*
Spring, Edw. *164*
Spring, F. *99*
Spring, T. *67*
O ssulluayn *114*
St. Leger *117*
(de) Stacabul *139*
Stack *xx, 40, 69, 138-9, 160*
(de) Stack *138*
Stack, Maj. *164* Gen. N. M.
Stackpoole *139*
Stackstown *xv, 138*
Staigue Fort *78*
Stainstreet *139*
Stak *138*
Stake *138*
Stanley *xiv, 139*
Staughton *xiv, 116*
Steele *139*
Steere *139*
Stephens *139*
Stephens, *6* Ann
Stephenson *139*
Sterne *xvi, 139*
Stevenson *139*
Stewart *139*
Stewart, Rev. *89*
Stiles *140*
Stiles *xvii-C*
Stiles *xvii-B*
Stiles, J. *xvii*
Stock *140*
Stokes *5, 140, 160*
Stokes, *164* Capt. O. D.

Stokes, Capt. O. R. *164*	Sugrue *57, 83, 142, 160*	O' Sullivan Mor, dau. *115*	Talbot-Crosbie *xxiv*
Stokes, Col. *55*	Sugrue, Chas. *164*	O' Sullivan, Owen Rua *70*	Tangney *145, 160*
Stokes, E. *11*			Tansley *145*
Stokes, E. D. *164*	Sugrue householdrs *207*	Sullivan, T. *164*	Tapper *145*
Stokes, Frances *70*	Sugrue, Jas. *164*	O' Sullivan, the great *64*	Tara, Four Tribes of. *126*
Stokes, G. *164*	Suipeil *144*	O' Sullivan Tomies *136*	Tarrant *145*
Stokes home *60*	SULLEUAN *160*	SULLIVANE *160*	Taylor *xiv, 145, 160*
Stokes, J. D. *164*	SULLIUAN *160*	O' Sullivans *18, 134*	Taylor, Eliza *141*
Stokes, John *139*	Sullivan *xx, 160*	O' Sullivans Country *xi*	Teahan *145, 160*
Stokes, Oliver *30*	O' Sullivan *xiv, xx, 142-43*	Sunderland *143*	Tedmarsh *145*
Stokes, R. B. *164*	O' Sullivan *160*	Supple *3, 144*	Teer *145*
Stokes, W. *xxiii*	O' Sullivan, Ardea *xxiii*	Supple, E. K. *164*	Mc TEIGE *160*
Stokes, Wm. *164*	Sullivan Arms *143*	Surname origins *xix*	test oath *xx*
Stokesfield *140*	O' Sullivan arrives *vii*	Sutcliffe *135*	(De) Thick *41*
(de) Stokke *140*	Sullivan, baptised *149*	Sutton *144*	Thistall *145*
Stokys *140*	O' Sullivan Beare *ix*	SUVANE *160*	Thomas *145*
Stone *xiii, 140*		Swanzy *144*	Mc THOMAS *160*
Stoughton *141, 160*	O' Sullivan Beare *xxiv*	Swayne *144*	Mac Thomas, John *51*
Stoughton *xvii-C*	Sullivan, Bishop *95*	Sweaney *144*	Thompson *146*
Stoughton *xvii-B*	O' Sullivan branches *142*	Sweatman *144*	Thomson *146*
Stoughton Arms *140*		Sweeney *xx, 160*	Thornhill *146*
Stoughton, C. *164*		Mac Sweeney *xx, 144*	Thornton *146*
Stoughton, T. *164*	O' Sullivan Cashel *142*	Mc SWEENEY *160*	Thurston *xvii-B*
Strange *141*	Sullivan Castles *142*	Mc Sweeney hous'holds *217*	Thwantes *146*
Strange, Miss B. *164*	O' Sullivan, Dan'l. *163*	SWEENY *160*	Tidings *146*
Street *141*	O' Sullivan Eoganacht *xvi*	Sweetman *xvi, 144*	O' Tiegrnach *146*
Street *xvii-B*		Swift *144*	Tierney *146*
Stretton *141*	O' Sullivan forces *xvii*	Swift *xvii-B*	Timmins *146*
Stringer *xiv*	Sullivan households *207*	Swindel *144*	Timony *146*
Stritch *141*		Mac Swiney *xx*	Tisdall *146*
Strongbow *147*		Switzer *144*	Tobin *146*
Stuart *141*	Sullivan, John *164*	Swords *145*	Tobyn *146*
Studdert *141, 160*	O' Sullivan, John *2*	Symons *xiv*	Togher Castle *165*
Studdert, T. *164*	O' Sullivan Lahern *134*	Synan *145*	Tong *146*
Stundon *142*		Synge *145*	Tooher *146*
Styles *140, 160*	Sullivan, M.J. *xxiii*	Syvrac *145*	Topham *146*
SUGHERNE *160*	O Sullivan *ix, 57,* Mor *83, 150*	Taaffe *38, 107*	Topping *146*
Sugrena sept -MacCarthy *22*		Tackaberry *145*	Tough *146*
		Taite *145*	Towell *147*
		Talbot *145*	Towell *xvii-B*

Names Arranged Alphabetically without the O' or Mac Prefix

Townes *147*	Turner *149*	Vauckler *150*	Warren *xvii-B*
Townsend *147*	Turner *xvii-B*	Vaucleere *xvii, 150*	Warwick *152*
Tracey *147*	Twiss *5, 11, 35*	Vauclier *150*	Waterson *152*
Tralee *xvii,* ... families *xviii*	Twiss, E. *164*	Vauclier *xvii-C*	Watkins *152*
	Twiss, Ed. *112*	Vauclier *xvii-B*	Watkins *xvii-B*
Tralee *xix* Library	Twiss, *164* Francis	Vaughan *150*	Watson *152*
Tralee source *xxiii*	Twiss, J. R. *164*	Ventry, Lord *14, 164*	Watters *152*
Tranfield *147*	Twiss of *26* CastleIsland	Vesey *150*	Watts *153*
Trant *xv, xvi,*		Vicars *150*	Watts *xvii-B*
147-8.	Twiss of *149* Kileentierna	Vickery *150*	Weatherup *153*
TRANT *160*		Vigors *66*	Webb *153*
Trant arms *147*	Twiss of *154* Steelroe	Vincent *150*	Weekes *153*
Trant Castle *147*		Vine *150*	Weeks *153*
Trant of *148* Fenit	Twiss, R., *164* M. D.	Virginia *xvii* refuge	Weir *153*
			Weldon *153*
Trante *148*	Twiss, Wm. *122, 164*	Virginia, to *89*	Weldon, Rose *120*
Trassy *148*	Twohig *149*	Voakley *150*	Welland *153*
Trassy *xvii-B*	TWOMEY *160*	Vynes *xvii-B*	Wellings *153*
Traunte *148*	O' Twomey *160*	Vynes, Vine *150*	Welshmen *151*
Trawdsome *148*	Tyler *149*	Wade *150*	Welstead *xvi, 135, 153*
Trawdsome *xvii-B*	Tyndall *149*	Walker *150, 160*	
Treawant *147*	Tyter *149*	Wall *150*	WELSTED *160*
Treddle *148*	U. S. A., to *ix*	Wallace *151*	Welton *153*
Treddle *xvii-B*	U. S. civil *100* war	Waller *40, 151*	West *153*
Trench *148*		Waller, Sir *118*	West Indies *148*
Tretton *148*	Ua Ciardha *19*	Walpole *151*	Westbrook *153*
Trimlet *148*	Mac Uaid *150*	Walsche *151*	Westcombe *153*
Tristam *148*	Ufford *54, 149*	Walsh con-*131, 151* fiscated	Westcombe *xvii-B*
Tristam *xvii-B*	ui dTorna *xvi*		Wharton *116, 154*
Trodden *148*	ui Fearba *xvi*	Walsh, Edw. *xxiii*	Whelan *154*
Trowent *147*	Ui Ferba *xxii*	Walsh of *151* Sneem	WHELTON *160*
Truman *149*	Oh Uiginn *79*		Whiston *154*
Truman *xvii-B*	Undertaker *xviii* or yeoman	Walter, *xii* Theobald	White *154*
tuath sen *142* Eran		Warburton *151*	White *xvii-B*
	undertakers *xiii* for land	Ward *151*	White, Geo. *164*
Tubriddy *149*	Underwood *149*	Wardell *151*	Whitson *154*
Tucker *149*	Uppington *128*	Warden *152*	Whittaker *154*
Tuff *149*	Usburne, T. *164*	Warden, Col. *8*	Wholly *154*
Tuite *149*	Usher *149*	Ware *152*	wild geese *ix*
Tuohill *149*	Usher, Henry *29*	Ware *xvii-B*	Wilde *154*
Tuohill, R., *164* M. D.	Vale *150*	Warham *152*	Wilkie *154*
	Valle *150*	Warham *xvii-B*	William I I I *122*
Tuohy *149*	Vancouver, *102* Ottawa	Warner *152*	Williams *116, 154*
Tuomey *149*		Warren *152, 160*	Williams, F. *164*

Willis *154*
Willmore *154*
Willoe *154*
Willove *154*
Wilmot *9, 155*
Wilmot, Sir *18, 58*
Wilson *155*
(de) Wilton *xvii*
Wimpris *155*
Windele *155*
Windele, J. *xxiii*
Windele, J. *xxiii*
Windle *155*
Winn *76, 156*
Winn, Hon. Roland *164*
Winters *155*
Winters, Samuel *149*
Wise *155*
Wise, Francis *164*
Witherall *155*
Woodhouse *155*
Woods *155*
Woolf, B.S. *xxiv*
Worthington *155*
Woulfe *155*
Wreil *156*
Wren *156*
Wren family *xv*
Wren, Leslie *164*
Wright *156*
Wright, G. *xxiii*
Wrixon *156*
Wyk *156*
(de) Wyk *156*
Wykehamist *xxiii*
Wyllie *156*
Wynne *156*
Yeeden *xvi, 156*
Yielding *5, 156*
Yielding, Samuel *164*
Ykeleachair *86*

Young *156*
Zouche *xvii, 156*